Jewish Frontier Anthology
1934-1944

Jewish

FRONTIER

Anthology

1934-1944

Essay Index Reprint Series

BOOKS FOR LIBRARIES PRESS

FREEPORT, NEW YORK

Library of Congress Cataloging in Publication Data
Main entry under title:

Jewish frontier anthology, 1934-1944.
    (Essay index reprint series)
    Verse and prose.
    1. Zionism--Addresses, essays, lectures. 2. Jews--
Addresses, essays, lectures. 3. Jewish literature.
I. Jewish frontier.
DS149.J43 1971   910'.03'924   76-167370
ISBN 0-8369-2459-2

PRINTED IN THE UNITED STATES OF AMERICA
BY
NEW WORLD BOOK MANUFACTURING CO., INC.
HALLANDALE, FLORIDA 33009

CONTENTS

CONTENTS (*Cont.*)

PALESTINE

EUROPE

OTHER SUBJECTS

Editors' Foreword

The first issue of the JEWISH FRONTIER appeared in December, 1934. In our first editorial we defined our main objectives: As a Labor-Zionist publication our chief purpose was to delineate the creation of a *Jewish* homeland in Palestine built on *cooperative* principles. We wished to interpret this twin struggle, organically allied in method and purpose. We sought to reflect the pioneering will of the Jewish worker, determined from the first to integrate the reconstruction of the land with the construction of a progressive society, knowing that neither could be effectively achieved without the other.

At the same time we were fully conscious that no divorce could exist between the problems of Palestine and those of the rest of the world. Being American Jews, we were particularly concerned with the American scene, in all its aspects. Nor could we fail to react to developments throughout the Diaspora. As Americans, as Jews, as believers in a liberal social order everywhere, it was our function to participate actively in the manifold issues of our period. This was the task we set ourselves.

Although when we began publication, the Hitler decade was already one year advanced, we could not foretell what a large order we had assumed. In our first issue, we spoke of the "catastrophic events in Germany," but, like the rest of the world, we had no inkling of how catastrophic these events were to be. We spoke of concentrating Jewish energy upon the speedier development of Palestine as a home for millions of uprooted Jews. We could not know then how complete that deracination was to be. We could not know of the millions to be murdered because there was no country to bid them live; nor could we anticipate the anguished need of the shattered remnant for Palestine. And though we were aware that World War II was in the process of being brewed in the fascist caldron, no one could imagine the measure of its extent, nor the ferocity of its nature.

The ten years that have elapsed since our first issue, proved to be the most tragic in Jewish history, and the most evil in that of mankind. As we glance over the back numbers of our publication, one cannot help being struck by the simplicity, the innocence, with which we advanced towards the precipice—how unprepared we were for the cataclysm in which we were to be involved. Now, in grim retrospect, despite the ebb and flow of contemporary incident from which false fears as well as hopes sometimes emerged, the main current is plain. Whatever the occasional shifts of emphasis, an inexorable pattern emerges: the destruction of European Jewry; the intensification of reactionary and anti-Semitic trends in the United States; the growing realization of the role which Palestine must play in the physical and psychic healing of the Jewish people.

The purpose of this anthology is not merely one of historic record. The articles that we have selected not only reflect successive stages in the development of the major issues that we have faced between 1934 and 1944. They have also a present relevance, and can serve to illuminate the urgent questions before us. As the table of contents indicates, we have sought to review the chief problems in our several spheres of interest. Two notable omissions will be observed. In the section under "Palestine," we have left out all articles dealing with the White Paper. This has been done because our special issue on the White Paper was widely reprinted in pamphlet form. Similarly, since we devoted a special issue to the extermination of European Jewry, which was also reprinted in pamphlet form, we felt it would be an unwarranted duplication of our material, were we to republish any of those articles. The pamphlets in question may be viewed as complementary to the anthology.

We have chosen no articles, no matter how excellent in themselves, which were mainly of topical significance. In this way we have sought to achieve a unity of purpose, and to increase the usefulness of this anthology as record and commentary. We have tried to present a picture of events as they happened, and to interpret the totality of which these events are a part.

February, 1945

ZIONISM

Norman Angell

David Ben Gurion

Norman Bentwich

Kurt Blumenfeld

Carl J. Friedrich

Hayim Greenberg

Moshe Shertok

Marie Syrkin

Dorothy Thompson

What We Stand For

EDITORIAL

T HE THOUGHTFUL Jew can no longer escape the conviction that he must take a definite stand in regard to the pressing Jewish problems of our time. Assimilation as a deliberate policy has long become an anachronism; indifference has replaced the assimilationist viewpoint among fairly large Jewish circles. This indifference, essentially a masked form of assimilation, though still widespread, has lately begun to yield to an increasing sense of unease. Recent economic and political developments, together with the social neuroses that followed in their wake, have brought the Jew again sharply face to face with the eternal Jewish question. He has to realize that the business of being a Jew may be either a blessing or a curse, but that apathy is impossible.

The catastrophic events in Germany have profoundly agitated every Jew. Unless one adopts Germanophobia as a doctrine and believes in the inherent barbarism and wickedness of the German soul, one must ask whether such paroxysms are not possible in other civilized countries under given conditions of national stress. Those who are not in the habit of thinking in terms of "saintly-nations" and "sinner-nations" see in the German upheaval manifestations of subconscious forces which lead an independent life under a thin layer of rationality, and break out into the open at the first favorable opportunity. Such a realization causes a sharpened sense of personal insecurity and isolation in whatever environment the Jewish minority finds itself.

Naturally enough, many modern Jews find themselves turning hopefully to Soviet Communism. Even non-communists have ample reason for considering the eventful October revolution of 1917 as the most significant milestone in the history of a new world. The modern Jew feels a specific sympathy towards a country where radical change in social-economic conditions goes hand-in-hand with a vigorous fight for racial and national equality

3

and where every vestige of anti-Semitism is staunchly repressed. However, a closer examination of the formulated and unformulated problems of Soviet Jewry leads one to the melancholy discovery that there is no *ipso facto* solution of the Jewish question even in the land of social revolution.

It is true that Jews are becoming an organic part of the Soviet economic structure in increasing degree. A considerable number of Jews have been settled on the land. An even larger number have been absorbed by industry and by many branches of government service. Insofar as the concrete economic problems of Soviet Russia are being solved in general, they are also being solved for Russian Jewry. Provided there are no unexpected upheavals one may hope that in time there will remain no "declassed" Jews, but that all will be "re-classed" into the economic structure of that huge workers' country. This process of economic integration, however, is accompanied by group disintegration. Ethnic individuality, the cultural profile of a group which draws its vital sap from its own sources, is lost. For this no one is to blame. Within the limitations of the Soviet regime (because of which Zionism is persecuted, Hebrew is taboo, and the religious expressions of Jewish life are barely tolerated) the Jewish population enjoys all legal rights for the development of its individuality. Theoretically, Jews enjoy a wide cultural autonomy: Jewish courts, a Yiddish language State School, Jewish theatres subsidized by the State, and Jewish publishing houses which are maintained by govment funds. But legal rights are merely a fig-leaf to cover the collective impotence of a group which seeks to retain its own culture without a distinct economic basis. The Jewish courts do not function; a steadily decreasing minority of Jewish children study in the Jewish schools; Yiddish is being increasingly supplanted not only by Russian but by Ukrainian and White Russian. It is an open secret that an intensive process of "Red assimilation" is going on in Russia. From the standpoint of the national will to live, it makes little difference to the Jew whether he is molten in the liberal or in the socialist melting-pot.

A new "galut" feeling is developing among Soviet Jews which explains the awakened interest in Biro-Bidjan as a Jewish national territory. The very existence of the Biro-Bidjan experiment supports our thesis that social revolution as such is incapable of solving the Jewish problem in its full scope. Biro-Bidjan is a Soviet edition of Zionism, Russian Jewry's confession of homelessness. It is a new expression of the old idea that no general social changes can automatically solve the Jewish problem.

In the light of these new experiences—the nightmare of the German calamity, and the danger of the Russian "idyll"—"The Jewish Frontier" will fight for the concentration of Jewish energy on Palestine so as to create a home for those millions of Jews who feel themselves economically, politically or spiritually homeless in various countries of the world.

We give preference to Palestine as a potential Jewish territory, first of all because of its rich historic and traditional associations—imponderabilia which furnish immense treasuries of creative energy. Besides this sentimental motive, which even the most realistic calculations cannot ignore as a source of national inspiration, we insist on the primacy of Palestine on more tangible grounds. The pioneering of Jewish workers has already created the foundation for agricultural and industrial mass colonization. More Jews are entering Palestine today than any other country in the world. An annual immigration of forty or fifty thousand Jews is no longer Utopian. It is fast becoming an established fact. The results already achieved in Palestine are in themselves sufficient grounds for considering Palestine the chief channel for the flow of Jewish energy.

At the same time we must give ourselves a strict accounting of the dangers which threaten the reconstruction-work in Palestine. We are considering now not so much the outer, purely political, dangers as the inner ones. It would be the greatest calamity, (as well as folly) if Palestine were transformed merely into a refuge for Jewish capital without Jewish labor; if the Jews of Palestine were to figure primarily as employers while labor would be recruited from among the Arabs. Such a Jewish society would have neither a firm moral nor material base. It would become a national shame. A country belongs to those who labor on it and not to those who hold the "title". We will therefore fight with all our might against the narrow selfishness of those Jewish elements, in and out of Palestine, who would deny employment to organized Jewish workers. These groups are hindering Jewish labor in its effort to become an organic part of the economic structure of the country and are undermining the foundations of the national renaissance. Therefore in all fundamental reconstruction problems we will support the "Histadrut Haovdim" —the organization of Palestine Jewish workers whose aim is to create a homeland based on cooperative principles and founded on social justice. We see in the Histadrut not a party organization, not a sect with canonized dogmas, but the most vital instrument of national responsibility. This body of Jewish labor will keep the Jewish homeland from being transformed into a new Congo or a new Liberia. The struggle of the Histadrut for Jewish labor, for the dignity of labor in general and for the dignity of Jewish labor on Jewish soil in particular; its formation of independent economic cells in agriculture and industry which will serve as the beginnings of a future cooperative society in Palestine—will receive our active assistance.

We consider the creation of a Jewish labor society in Palestine as the chief task of our generation. This does not mean, however, that we will disregard the tormenting problems of Jews in the Diaspora countries. We consider it our function to mirror the Jewish struggle for existence in the difficult transition period which whole countries and continents are now experiencing. Because we are "Palestinocentric", we cannot ignore the Diaspora. We cannot be indifferent to the problems of world Jewry in general or American Jewry in particular because the Diaspora is the reservoir from which the Jewish homeland must be fed, and because we feel that the anguished problems of Jews the world over must be examined in the light of our analysis. Heartened by the social and cultural rejuvenation of the Jewish worker in Palestine, we will conscientiously seek means of reconstructing our American Jewish life on the basis of productive labor and of cultural self-expression.

We believe that the new values created in Palestine—the rapture of pioneering, the ennobling of human labor, the heroic attempt to elevate social relationships—are beginning to stimulate Jewish life everywhere. We seek to strengthen the dynamic influence of Palestine Labor on Jewish life in America by means of an informed, alert public opinion. Particularly today, when reaction and suicidal cupidity threaten to invalidate all that has been achieved in Palestine, we feel that there must be a publication which will interpret contemporary events in Palestine and take its stand on the frontiers of Jewish life throughout the world. We represent that synthesis in Jewish thought, which is nationalist without being chauvinist, and which stands for fundamental economic reconstruction without being communist. Only such a synthesis can answer the need of the disoriented modern Jew.

December, 1934

A Liberal Interprets Zionism

by NORMAN ANGELL

WHAT ARE the reasons which prompt a non-Jew, especially one of my particular predilections, to support the Zionist cause, and the continuance of the present Palestine Mandate—a non-Jew with no Jewish affiliations of any kind, and with sympathy for Arab causes in various parts of the world; an anti-Imperialist pacifist who has at times been extremely hostile to some manifestitations of British Imperialism, who believes in democracy, and accepts the principle of the rule of majorities. How are these predilections reconciled with warm support of the Zionist cause as against many British Imperialists who desire to see Britain surrender her Mandate and leave Jews and Arabs to fight it out between themselves as best they can?

Perhaps that can best be answered by answering a question which English friends often put to me: How do you reconcile anti-Imperialism with your support of the presence of British bayonets in Palestine; self-determination with the defiance of the will of the immense majority of the people of Palestine?

In replying, I am sometimes tempted to remark that I would like to see the definition or interpretation of sweeping slogans like "self-determination," "independence," "majority rule" applied as an intelligent test to those who profess to deal with social and political affairs. Majority of what? The world, the nation, the state, the city, the religious community, the race, the industrial groups? What makes the unit within which the rule shall operate? Similarly—as to "self-determination." Does it mean that Moslems may claim to be ruled by Moslems, Jews by Jews, Protestants by Protestants? Then why not Baptists by Baptists, blondes by blondes, brunettes by brunettes? That may seem a silly retort. But for centuries it was deemed far more important to apply self-determination to the religious than to the national or geographical

8

groups (as indeed it is deemed more important in parts of India today) and for centuries men fought over just such problems. And as to self-determination based on color, we shall hear a very great deal about it when the colored races begin to assert themselves more effectively, whether in Asia or in Alabama.

"Majority" and "self-determination" have no meaning until we have agreed upon what the unit to which they are to be applied shall be. Southern Irishmen invoke both principles as the basis of the right to include Ulster in their State. Just as passionately Ulstermen invoke both principles as the basis of the right to remain outside. However useful as briefly descriptive terms of certain general principles or methods, to be applied to social or political units whose extent and nature we have broadly agreed upon, such words as "independence" and "self-determination" as abstractions or absolutes are meaningless.

It is plain why I indulge in these reflections. The Arabs of Palestine, in their objections to the creation of a Jewish home in that country, invoke these principles of "independence" and "self-determination" which are in part a legacy of not very sincere wartime slogans and which threaten to shatter European unity everywhere. The Arab thesis is a simple one. Arabs are in a majority. The country is "theirs." They are entitled to be ruled by their own people. The making of their country a national Jewish home is, therefore, a violation of democracy, independence, nationalism, self-determination, as well, they allege—here wrongly—as of promises made to them by the British Government.

In our modern world, which has managed to annihilate space, absolute independence has become as impossible for groups and peoples as for individuals, and as anti-social a claim. Absolute independence implies that you have no obligations to the rest of the world at all, that you are entitled to do as you please, however much it may damage the other inhabitants of this planet. But there are many problems now in which, when we speak of "majority right," the unit which we must postulate is the world itself. If some tribe in Arabia should establish a historical and ancestral claim to a portion of the desert through which flows, say, the Suez Canal, would they have the right, as against the needs of the whole world, to forbid the passage of the world's ships because the Canal was in "their" territory? When, within a State, a single individual's private property stands in the way of some great public utility like a water-works or railway, he is not permitted to hold up the public interest indefinitely by invoking for all time the "inviolable rights of private property." The public as a whole invokes a counter-principle; and there is a "right of eminent domain" as applicable to groups of individuals as to single persons. Would the Red Indians of North America, because they were the aboriginal population, have the right to demand the evacuation of New York or Boston or Chicago by the Palefaces? These absolutes can easily become fantastic, and it is not in terms of any such absolutes that we non-Jews of the West must approach the Zionist experiment.

The Jewish question was, and is, a world question which has arisen largely because of gross offenses committed by non-Jews against the Jewish race. Anti-Semitism is a moral attitude of that xenophobist nationalism, which we have all alike nursed. Anti-Semitism is indeed at once the assertion of the worst side of nationalism and the denial of its best.

The homelessness of the Jewish people made the problem a more difficult one, and the upheaval of the Great War and the settlement of the world seemed to furnish an opportunity for the non-Jewish peoples to make some sort of contribution in cooperating to create a Jewish home—a homecoming which has been an age-old and indestructible tradition of that race, woven into its spiritual bone and sinew.

The Turkish Empire of which Palestine had been a part was in dissolution. Its liquidation was indeed long overdue and would have been achieved generations before if there had been such a thing as European or Christian unity. Of the three religious groups —Jewish, Christian and Moslem—attached to Palestine by their religious traditions, the two most deeply concerned, the Jewish and Christian, were in agreement in the sense that the representatives of Christendom were prepared to agree to Zionism as a contribution towards the settlement of the age-long conflicts between them. The traditional and religious ties of the dissenting Moslem minority centered elsewhere than in Palestine. Jerusalem is not the religious capital of Mohammedanism. It is the Mecca of the Jews.

Conceived as a general problem concerning civilized mankind as a whole, to be solved only by some measure of give-and-take, the case was plainly one in which the lesser consideration—certain prejudices of a small proportion of the Arab world—had to give way to the larger consideration, aspirations common to nearly the whole of the Jewish world and to the easing, at least, of the problem which the presence of the Jews in non-Jewish States has constituted in the past. To give those wanderers at last a visible abiding-place and spiritual home, a refuge for thwarted creative will, a place where the shattered altars of tradition could once more be erected, was small enough restitution for the non-Jewish world to make.

The Jews had no right to ask, and did not ask, material sacrifice on the part of the Arabs. The economic position of the population as a whole has not been worsened by the coming of the Zionists, it has been enormously improved. It cannot even indeed be said that the Arab has been asked to surrender his agelong habit of nomadic half-civilized life. For the portion of the desert which the Jew asks leave to reclaim for his home is but a tiny portion of that vast sandy ocean in which the Arab who may be so inclined may wander at will. The Jews do not demand "independence" for the Jewish home, the right, that is, to live under a Government of their own people. They demand an impartial government in which their community and special cultural traditions and qualities can be freely developed side by side with those of other elements in the population. The government of Palestine is not, as I have said elsewhere, a British Government, nor a Jewish Government, nor an Arab Government; it is a government—"international" government, if one must give it an adjective—though "impartial" should be the description towards which it should strive.

Not the least service that the Palestine Mandate may perform is that, if successful, it may be a forerunner of a type of government which, as populations, by reason of the annihilation of space, become more heterogeneous, will be more and more necessary, in some form or other, in various parts of the world. That British Imperialists should be among those who disparage this effort, and who in some cases at least plainly do not desire it to succeed, is proof of how little any worthy idealism inspires some of the noisier kinds of imperialism. We have talked in the past of world responsibility, burdens thrust upon us and much else of the same kind. But never surely was greater honor conferred upon a State than when it was chosen to be the Mandatory of mankind to act as umpire and arbiter between three great religions of the world, in carrying out an act of restitution on that soil whose story during forty centuries makes the sacred literature of every home where the Old or the New Testament finds a place. If ever a task should appeal to the imagination of a great people it is this. If that people is to be worthy at all of what it has so often declared to be its chief contribution to the problems of the world's government, this task must be carried through.

March, 1939

To the Communist International

by HAYIM GREENBERG

I BELIEVE that this is the first time that a man of my political persuasion is addressing you directly in an open letter. I know that I have no grounds for optimism in regard to the probable effect of my communication on your views and position. Nevertheless I cannot free myself from the faith which has been mine all my life, that no outcry in the universe is wholly lost, that though apparently unheeded it registers somewhere, somehow. And I write to you now in this belief that no protest against injustice is ever senseless.

I shall deal with the grave accusation that thousands, perhaps millions, of Jews have made against you because of your attitude towards the drama, one act of which is now unfolding in Palestine. I have received no mandate from these masses but I am certain that I express a widespread sense of pain and astonishment.

What is the accusation?

No one can accuse you of enmity or indifference towards the national liberation movements of our time. You have never suffered from the superstition of "cosmopolitanism," and you have more than once stated your conviction that the satisfaction of legitimate national aspirations is the prerequisite of a true internationalism. You oppose the crushing of any national group by a stronger one, even though the group in question be without a "history" in the accepted sense, or even the rudiments of a national character. Tchukches and Mordvines, peoples whose names are unknown in the Western Hemisphere save to students, have been accorded the status of recognized nations by Soviet Russia. I do not believe that Stalin's formula "socialist in content and national in form" bears logical dissection, because form and content are as indissoluble in national culture as they are in painting or music. However, an unsuccessful formula may sometimes make possible the successful pursuit of a wise policy.

Speaking more specifically of the Jewish question, no one can accuse you of anti-Semitism. It would be better perhaps if you did not occasionally betray the bad taste of boasting that under the Soviet regime no pogroms occur and that anti-Semitism is energetically fought. The fact that an anti-Semitic government cannot be classed among civilized nations does not mean that a "philo-Semitic" one should claim an order of special merit. Nevertheless, leaving aside fine points of taste, no one can charge you, either, with that peculiar form of ultra-friendliness which holds that the Jews are fine fellows and should therefore lose their identity in a general amalgam. The Soviet regime has limitations which I do not propose to discuss now, but within the confines of the measure of liberty possible in Russia, Jews have received the maximum opportunities for development as a distinct community. You have gone even further. You are giving symbolic demonstration of the fact that the Jews are a nation and have a right to national existence by your attempted creation of a Jewish republic in Biro-Bidjan. By this alone you have subscribed to our old Zionist contention that the *national* problems of Jews cannot be solved without a Jewish territory. Obviously you recognize the right of the Jewish people to a territorial center. But you have announced more than once (through President Kalinin and the declarations of the Komzet) that the colonization of Biro-Bidjan must not be considered as a "new Zionism" and that the autonomous region in Biro-Bidjan must not be viewed as a "new Zion" for world Jewry. Through these warnings you have left unsolved the question of a more extensive territorial center, suitable for the six-sevenths of the Jewish people who live outside the Soviet Union. Russia does not propose to fling open her doors to mass immigration. As far as Biro-Bidjan is concerned, the Russian official press has made it clear that only small numbers of foreign Jews would be permitted to enter, chiefly in cases of a shortage of given categories of skilled workers among Soviet Jews. By this I wish to state that neither you nor the Soviet Government (I hope you will not take amiss my identification of you with the Soviet Government without further diplomatic hocus-pocus) have set up Biro-Bidjan as a rival to Palestine. You have not declared that a Jewish territorial center should be created not in Palestine, but in Biro-Bidjan; you have not said that the millions of Jews from various countries who need a national home should go to Biro-Bidjan rather than Palestine. Up to date you have offered to develop Jewish colonization in Biro-Bidjan till it can be proclaimed a Jewish republic. I do not recall off-hand how large the population of a region must be before, according to the Soviet Constitution, it can be recognized as a republic. I do remember, however, that the Soviet Union contains many republics whose population is negligible: the Abkhazian Republic, proclaimed in 1921, had at the time, no more than 200,000 inhabitants; the Adzharian Republic, established in the same year, had no more than 131,000; the Nakhichevan Republic established in 1923, had a population of only 104,000. I am pointing out that you can fulfill your promise to create a Jewish Republic merely by bringing a trifling number of the sixteen million Jews in the world, into Biro-Bidjan. This of course would still leave the Jewish territorial problem unsolved. Millions of Jews have directly or indirectly shown their Zionist will by their participation in various Palestinian activities. However, instead of welcoming the revival of creative energy in an ancient, martyred people, you are doing all in your power, morally and politically, to discredit and injure the liberation movement of the Jewish people. Far though you be from anti-Semitism, you actually serve an anti-Semitic purpose by hindering the reconstruction of our people.

I know how you answer accusations of this kind: the national emancipation of one people must not be achieved at the expense of another people. Zionism, you claim, builds Jewish weal on Arab woe. Were that really so, were Zionism to be achieved through the destruction and exploitation of the Arabs, not only every communist and socialist, but every decent man would be obliged to fight it as an unforgivable form of national egoism. But the time has come for you to revise your conception of Zionism as well as

to analyze critically some of the deductions you have drawn from
principles correct in themselves.

One people may exploit another economically, culturally and
politically. The most vicious form of exploitation is the economic
because both the cultural and political status of a people depend
in a large measure on its economic condition. The first question in
our controversy therefore, is whether the Arabs of Palestine are
being exploited economically by the Jewish settlers and the Zionist movement.

I have good reason to be weary of this particular theme. One
grows tired of endlessly answering a libel which some spread
through malice and others believe through ignorance and intellectual apathy. Possibly you will never free yourselves of your
misconception of the economic role of the Jews in Palestine until
you send a delegation (consisting not of party politicians but of
experts in economics, your experienced "sovnarkhos" men) to
study the situation on the spot. I propose this plan in all seriousness, and I should like to take the liberty of making two concrete
suggestions: first, acquaint yourselves with the data of the Mandates Commission of the League of Nations in regard to the
mythical "displaced Arabs" (if you consider the available information at Geneva insufficient, Russia's representative at the League
of Nations will easily be able to secure a new investigation);
secondly, send a delegation to Palestine. I have reason to believe
that both the government and the Jewish Agency would assist the
delegation in its investigation, though I cannot guarantee the attitude of the Arab leaders towards a Bolshevist Commission despite
your pro-Arab policies. In the meantime, I think it will be enough
for me to mention a few of the grosser fabrications about the
Jew's economic exploitation of the Arab.

First of all, let me remind you that the overwhelming majority
of the Jewish population of Palestine consists of laboring elements.
Zionism liberates the modern Jew from the curse which has pursued him for centuries in the Diaspora—the curse of unproductive
occupations. You know what difficulties the Soviets encountered

because of the peculiar, one-sided economic life of the Russian Jew, a life ill-suited to a workers' society. In most European countries with a large Jewish population the Jews have a very limited scope of functions in the economic structure of the country. In Poland, for instance, 65% of all the tradesmen are Jews; in Lithuania, 77%; in Hungary where Jews are only 5% of the population, they form 50% of the merchants. This situation is the inevitable result of the restrictions and quotas placed on Jews in practically every form of employment and profession. Outside of Soviet Russia where, thanks to the revolution, Jews have become economically restratified, Palestine is the only place where, *due to an inner revolution,* Jews are developing without those social-economic anomalies to which history has doomed them. The Jewish population of Palestine is proportionately larger than that of any other country, but only 33% of the traders are Jews, whereas the majority of the Jewish population is engaged in agriculture, handicrafts, industry and the professions. Jewish immigration of the last fifteen years consisted chiefly of workers; it had none of the earmarks characteristic of imperialist invasion of colonial lands. The occupational distribution of the Jewish settlers in itself makes the charge of exploitation absurd. Furthermore, if one compares conditions in Palestine with those in Syria, one realizes what the economic influence of Jewish immigration has been. Thanks to the Histadrut, the eight hour day has been introduced in numerous enterprises in Palestine, whereas in Syria the twelve hour day is still in force. If one compares conditions in industries that exist in both neighboring countries, one is startled by the difference in wages. In the Syrian shoe industry the unskilled worker gets 50 to 90 mils and the skilled worker from 100 to 150 mils per day, whereas in Palestine the unskilled worker gets 100 to 150 mils and the skilled worker 300 to 400 mils per day. In the silk industry a Syrian worker gets 60 to 80 mils per day, a Palestinian 400 to 500 mils. In the macaroni factories a Syrian male worker gets 80 to 100 mils a day, and a woman as little as 30 to 40 mils whereas in Palestine men get 300 mils per day and women 200 to

250 mils. These figures, only a small part of similar statistical data which I could furnish you, speak for themselves; such victories for the working class would be impossible if Jews came to Palestine as exploiters, or if Jewish workers strove to "capture" work from the Arab or to "underlive" him. It is true that the average Jew in Palestine lives better than the average Arab, but is a higher degree of economic well-being always a sign of exploitation? You have now in Soviet Russia some workers barely able to get necessities, while others ride around in their own automobiles. Are you prepared to admit that one group of workers exploits another in the socialist fatherland? Your explanation is that one group is more capable, more energetic and more productive than the other. It is not our fault that a Jewish hen lays an average of 150 eggs, annually, whereas an Arab one lays no more than 80; nor are we to blame because a Jewish cow gives an average of 4000 litres of milk annually, while an Arab cow produces not more than 700. The Jewish pioneers responsible for these economic "crimes" deserve awards rather than abuse. Jonathan Swift must have had such pioneers in mind when he wrote: "Whoever could make two ears of corn or two blades of grass grow upon a spot where only one grew before, would deserve better of mankind and do more essential service to his country than the whole race of politicians put together."

Since the Jews do not keep their knowledge secret—an esoteric mystery to be shared with none—Arab farmers are gradually learning modern methods. Judging from their present rate of adaptation they may attain a high degree of economic development within our generation.

The growth of population is a significant index to economic conditions. Before the war there were not more than 600,000 Arabs in Palestine. This number remained static for the fifty years preceding the World War. Today, there are about 900,000 Arabs. This means that the Arab population increased by 50% in the very years of intensive Jewish immigration. True, the addition of 300,-000 was not due solely to the rate of natural increase (excess of births over deaths) but also to Arab immigration from adjacent countries, but the very fact that Arab emigration from Palestine has decreased while Arab immigration into Palestine has greatly increased—it would perhaps be truer to say has begun—demonstrates the economic value of Zionist colonization to the country in general and the Arabs in particular. It is no accident that in the very midst of the present tragic occurrences in Palestine the Grand Mufti's party has come out for a mass immigration of Arabs from other Arab countries which are much larger in circumference and much more thinly populated. This proposal is being made at a time when the cry is raised that Jewish immigration be stopped, a cry in which your press joins presumably on the grounds that Palestine is "overpopulated." It is a little hard to reconcile these circumstances. Apparently "overpopulation" is a relative term depending on who is to do the populating. In antiquity nearly five million people lived in Palestine on both sides of the Jordan. Today there is still room for millions of new immigrants. The demand to stop Jewish immigration and prohibit the sale of land to Jews (a "reform" reminiscent of the policy of Russian Czars) is motivated not by economic, but by purely political considerations.

I shall be able to pass quickly to the political phase of the question, because, fortunately, no one charges us with cultural exploitation. No one dares to accuse Zionism of degrading the cultural standard of the Arab population. Everyone recognizes that the immigration of elements with a higher cultural level stimulates the original creative energy of the Arab. No Arab will claim that there were better Arab schools, or a more highly developed Arab press before the "Zionist invasion." Our bitterest enemy will not accuse us of attempting to Hebraize the Arabs, or of interfering in any way with their cultural development. On the contrary, if there is any academic institution seriously devoted to the study of Arab history and philology, it is the Hebrew University of Jerusalem, which receives assistance neither from the Arabs, nor from the government, but is open to Arabs, Christians, and foreigners from all lands. I shall dwell no longer on the question of cultural exploitation because in this respect, at least, no one has as yet accused us of "poisoning the wells."

The only charge which has some shadow of justification—true, of a purely outward and superficial character—is the political one. Honest Arab leaders are prepared to admit that Zionism constitutes no cultural or economic danger for Arabs. However, they claim that we represent a serious political menace, because unless Jewish immigration is stopped we will soon become a majority in the country, and the land will lose its "Arab" character. One must agree that there is considerable truth in this argument. We are convinced that Palestine, if properly developed through intensive agriculture and industry, has room for many more millions, and that these millions, unless artificially checked, will be Jews. No other people has the devotion or the will for the reconstruction of the country to make mass-immigration possible. This means that in the course of time the Jews will become a majority, even though the number of Arabs will not decrease, but will increase much more rapidly than before Zionism. Nationalist Arabs and international communists believe that this means "seizing a country" from its rightful owners, that this is imperialism.

Yet this charge of Zionist imperialism, which you advance so often, is in its essence a discrimination against Jews. You do not realize how anti-Semitic it is objectively, though not subjectively or consciously. Assuming the status of a national minority to be less than ideal, you are prepared to let the Jews be a minority in every country, but the Arabs not in a single land. Remember that you yourselves do not consider the Palestinian Arabs as a separate national entity; you view them as a part of a large nation. Therefore your proclamations demand the union of all Arab countries into a larger national federation. You know very well that the Arab nation branches out over a large area. Even if we exclude the Arab-speaking lands of North Africa—Syria, Mesopotamia and Saudi Arabia still occupy approximately 615,000 square miles (that is somewhat more than France, Germany, Italy, Belgium, Czechoslovakia, Denmark and Holland put together). Palestine, on the other hand, together with Transjordania, is only 26,000 square miles in area—less than 1/23 of all the land under Arab rule. You know this geographical fact as well as we do, but the deductions that you make resemble Hottentot rather than socialist morality: your conclusion seems to be that 22/23 are not enough for 10 to 12 million Arabs, but 1/23 is too much for 16 million Jews, and, finally, that Arabs must not be a minority anywhere, the Jews everywhere.

I don't know what will happen in the distant future. Possibly the dream of a central European reformer (Bluntschli) will come true, and the world's population will be so regrouped that there will no longer be national minorities. For the present, national minorities cannot be avoided. Millions of Russians live outside of Russia—they live in the Ukraine, in White Russia, in Turkestan and outside the Soviet Union as national minorities. Millions of Germans live in Czechoslovakia, in Hungary, in Rumania, in Russia and in the United States. Millions of Italians, Magyars and other peoples have been incorporated as minorities in larger national organisms. But when the Arabs are involved you consider it an imperialistic crime to place a small number of them in the position of a national minority in a comparatively small area of land—even though this should be done in the interests of the most completely homeless and landless people in the world. Unless my information is wrong, the recently deceased Henry Barbusse put the same question to you in a letter which he sent you in the last months of his illness. His death freed you from the necessity of answering his charge that your attitude towards Zionism was the contrary of communist principles and of true internationalism, that it was motivated by a dubious political opportunism, rather than by socialist ideology. But has not the time come for you to give yourselves a conscientious answer?

And may I ask, whether within the Soviet Union you have always practiced the theory which you wish to apply to Arab-Jewish relations? Because of weighty political considerations which I need not discuss now, I know that in 1924 you founded a Moldavian Republic in South Ukraine with Balta as capital. The Moldavians happen to be a minority in that region, and the Ukrainians the majority. Where was your adherence to the principle of majorities in this case, and why did you give preference to the minority? Was it not because Ukrainian nationalism could find free scope in a comparatively large territory, while Moldavian nationalism had only this small corner of Ukrainia in which to express itself? May I point out still another fact? Several years before the Biro Bidjan project hove into view, you planned to transform Crimea into a Soviet Jewish territory. (Our Jewish communists in America once nurtured the same tender sentiments towards Crimea they now do towards Biro Bidjan.) The Soviet government even negotiated with American Jewish philanthropists in regard to financing the Crimean project. Was Crimea uninhabited at that time? Did not a non-Jewish majority of several hundred thousand live there? Were not the Tartars the most considerable ethnic group in that region? In other words, did not Crimea have its Arabs? Nevertheless President Kalinin permitted himself the optimistic prophecy that should Jewish colonization develop at a sufficiently rapid tempo, the time would come when the Sea of Azof would be called the "Jewish Sea."

There even appeared Russian historians who unearthed the fact that blooming Jewish communities had existed in the Crimea in ancient times. They were delighted to recall that in the early centuries of the Christian Era, Hellenized Jews had come together with Greeks on the shores of the Black Sea and the Sea of Azof, and that as late as the eighth century, the city of Phanagoria on the peninsula of Taman was practically a Jewish city. These excursions into history were to demonstrate the Jewish "historic right" to the region of Crimea. I do not quite understand why the Soviet government gave up the Crimea project so quickly. However, its place was eventually taken by Biro Bidjan. Yet Biro Bidjan, after a number of years of Jewish colonization still has its non-Jewish majority. Have you ever inquired whether this majority is willing to become a minority? Did you hold a referendum in regard to the right of the Jews to colonize there? Did the Jews receive an invitation from the non-Jews of Biro Bidjan?

I ask these questions because I wish you to consider a geographic fact with which we Jews must reckon and which you cannot possibly ignore. On the whole globe there is no corner which is wholly uninhabited, which has not its "majority," its "Arabs." Wherever Jews may now go to build a national center, no matter how large or uncultivated the land may be, they will always find inhabitants with no enthusiasm for being transformed into a minority. Even Greenland has a population of 16,000 with "historic rights." Should a hundred Jewish immigrants arrive there with the intention of bringing over thousands of others—assuming that the absorptive capacity of the country permitted—the Greenlanders would probably soon raise the cry of "Zionist imperialist invasion." True, there is a difference between the population in Biro Bidjan, or Greenland, and the Arabs. Arabs are a *historic* people, whereas the others are not. But I should not care to hear such an answer from you, because that would mean that you give premiums for *historicity* and penalties for *non-historicity,* that you make distinctions between higher races whose rights must be respected and lower races which may be injured. No, such an explanation would be motivated not by ethics, but by convenience It is not more just, but simply easier to exploit an "unhistoric people." It is the exploiter's line of least resistance.

The situation is such that you can approach the Jewish national problem in only one of two ways. You can tell us—if you have the temerity: "You have come too late. The world has already been parcelled out. Every people has its place and every place its people. Do what you will—go under, commit national suicide, jump into the sea—there is no share for you."

If you do not say this, if you dare not say it, if you recognize our right to a national life and the importance of a territorial center for the normalization of our existence, then you must come to another conclusion. You must admit that a people which owns a number of large territories and does not cultivate all of the soil at its disposal, is duty-bound to permit Jewish national colonization even though that might mean a Jewish majority. You must realize that the principle of national equality demands that Jews be not hindered in their attempt to reconstruct a national center in a land which represents 1/23 of the total area which Arabs hold, as national territory. I need not point out to you which of these two conclusions is truer to the spirit of socialism and internationalism. Until you change your fundamentally false attitude towards Zionism, I shall charge you with supporting a narrow, greedy Arab nationalism at the expense of the most elementary rights of the Jewish people.

I have grave and difficult differences with communism. But no matter how deep the division between us—in regard to your means, not to your goal—I should not want the objective historian of the future to write: "Jews finally rebuilt their national center in Palestine, despite the enmity of Arab chauvinists, despite the propaganda of Hitler and Italian fascism, despite the duplicity of British imperialism, and despite the criminal heedlessness with which the Communist International supported these reactionary forces."

Marx has a great utterance familiar to everyone: "From each according to his means, to each according to his need." These words represent the new ethical concept which socialism offers the world. This principle guides your reorganization of economic order, and your view of the relations between individuals. It is no less valid for determining the rights of nations. You, as socialists, should be the last to claim that formal or physical possession whether for use or abuse, constitutes a moral title of ownership. You do not recognize the rights of an idle heiress to squander a fortune which she has not earned. Such social outrage seems to you the dark remnant of a barbaric economic order. Similarly no nation has the right to place "no-trespassing" signs around lands which it does not use, around soil which goes to waste. The draining of a marsh by a Jewish pioneer makes more room for Arabs as well as Jews. There is no question of dispossessing the Palestinian

Arab. His numbers will continue to grow as they have grown, thanks to the economic expansion of the country resulting from Jewish colonization. Nor are his interests in any way injured by the still greater increase of the Jewish population in accordance with the absorptive capacity of the country. Or do you really believe that the perpetuation of barren Arab marsh and desert represents a higher social equity than the transformation of this waste into fields cultivated by Arabs and Jews according to their means, and used according to their needs?

August, 1936

Why Not Biro-Bidjan?

by HAYIM GREENBERG

TWO YEARS ago the Russian government seemed about to take steps calculated to make a Jewish republic in Biro-Bidjan a reality. At that time the Soviet government promised to permit the entrance of 1,000 foreign Jewish families into the Siberian territory destined for Jewish settlement. On the strength of this promise, various Jewish philanthropic societies became interested in the Biro-Bidjan project primarily for the purpose of making possible an appreciable immigration of Polish Jews into Biro-Bidjan. Now, however, the American Jewish Joint Distribution Committee is liquidating all its affairs in Russia. Dr. Rosen, the representative of the Agro-Joint in Russia for the last ten years, has recently returned to America with the statement that the Soviet government will not permit the immigration of foreign Jews. Dr. Rosen makes definite what had long been obvious— that Biro-Bidjan cannot be viewed as a haven for the persecuted Jews of Europe. Its significance as a land for Jewish immigration must be limited to the Jews in Russia. So far the fact that less than 20,000 Russian Jews have settled there gives little immediate promise of a vigorous Jewish center. What about the future?

If the question whether Biro-Bidjan *can* be built up were a purely technical matter, I should agree that it is possible to develop agricultural mass colonization in Biro-Bidjan, to introduce industry, to establish trade connections with the whole of Soviet Russia and, through the Central Government, with foreign lands.

The area of Biro-Bidjan is not small. Its climate has a rather bad reputation, but one cannot expect the whole world to be made up of Monte Carlos and Nices. History tells us that men have adapted themselves to widely varying climates and have even used their science and technology to improve the climate. It is said that there are too many insects in Biro-Bidjan. But the more people

26

settle in a place the less room is left for these parasitical creatures; the more centers of civilization, the less chance for the reproduction of insects. It is said that the soil has its faults. It may be. But science in our day has more than once forced the earth to change its ways and experts say that the quality of soil is often very relative: if it is useless for one purpose, it may be suitable for another. In Petakh Tikvah an attempt was made to grow wheat fifty years ago and it failed: the soil was unsuitable. In later years, however, it was discovered that the capacity of this soil to produce first-class oranges and grapefruit had been overlooked. Soviet experts who studied the region of Biro-Bidjan reported that the soil was not of bad quality. If oats and barley cannot be grown in all parts of the area, why are not rice and soya beans equally desirable and useful products? American experts studied the region, and their reports, too, were far from despondent. There is no reason to suspect the experts and scientists of dishonesty or ulterior motives.

I assume, therefore, that from a purely geographic point-of-view it is possible to build up a significant Jewish center in Biro-Bidjan. How large can the Jewish population there become in the course of time? This can never be known in advance. Some say a million, others two million, and a practical colonizer, who accompanied the American Commission of Experts to Biro-Bidjan, once proved to me, pencil in hand, that all of three million Jews could be settled there. It may be that even this figure is not Utopian. A reliable conclusion can be reached only by experiment: somebody must undertake to make the attempt.

But the fact that Biro-Bidjan is large enough and its climate and soil are suitable, or can be made suitable, for large-scale Jewish colonization, is far from sufficient evidence to allow us to expect the establishment of a Jewish Republic with a large Jewish population in a short time. For the accomplishment of this there is required an additional element, *will*. Two sides must will it, and will it strongly and earnestly: the Soviet government and the Russian Jewish community. It is not something which can happen by chance. Republics and territorial centers are not the sort of things that spring up spontaneously on unplowed and unsown land. Just as the building up of any land, so does the development of Biro-Bidjan demand a relatively long period of pioneering labor and pioneer life.

Does present-day Russia have the prerequisites for this? The Soviet government says that it would like to have a Jewish Republic in Biro-Bidjan. The plan was officially proclaimed nine years ago; it has never been reported that the government retracted its original promise. Why Moscow needs its own "Zionism" has, I admit, rather puzzled me all this time. Detractors have told us that the Soviet plans in Biro-Bidjan are somehow concerned with strategic considerations, that the government must build up a population there which will have the strength to resist a possible or, as others believe, an inevitable attack by Japan. Such an explanation does not sound very plausible; and with the greatest respect for Jewish military prowess I should say that for such a purpose it would be better to settle Russian Cossacks in Biro-Bidjan. We have never had any unofficial "rationale" of the Biro-Bidjan plan from Soviet sources. The President of the Soviet Union, Kalinin, did have something to say on a few occasions, I believe, regarding the "ideological" side of the matter: and his words were reminiscent of Ahad-Haamism. He spoke of the danger of assimilation, of the uncertain prospects of Jewish culture in the Soviet Union, and from his words it appears that a sort of *Mercaz Rukhani* (a Spiritual Center) for Soviet Jewry must be created in Biro-Bidjan. Jewish Communists were probably shocked by such a "petty bourgeois-nationalistic" theory and ignored it almost entirely. I do not, therefore, undertake at present to explain why the Soviet government "would like" to have a Jewish Republic in far-off Siberia. I have twice intentionally used the expression "would like to have," for a strong *will* has never been manifested in the matter. Everyone has a right to his own opinion regarding the Soviet rulers, but one thing cannot be denied them: their *will* is always positive and dynamic. In the Biro-Bidjan plan, however, this dynamism of the Soviet will has been lacking for all those years. Moscow has not made the matter a test of its prestige. It was precisely for this reason that Moscow allowed the project to be discredited in foreign countries by the petty cash collections of Icor, by the pious contributions of Friends of Russia towards a romantic *Khovevei Biro-Bidjan* movement. The Moscow government would never have permitted American Communists to pass the hat at weddings and Bar-Mitzvahs for Dnieprostroy, for Magnitogorsk, for plans in which Soviet ambitions are really involved.

We have never had a clear definition of the scope or the intended size of the Biro-Bidjan enterprise from authoritative Soviet quarters. For many years now Moscow has been accustomed to think and speak in terms of long-range plans; in the next five years Russia must produce so many and many pairs of shoes, tons of of coal; there must be born so and so many sheep or hogs; there must even be "educated" such and such a number of atheists. All is planned and calculated, and all with the desire to surpass past achievements. The results are sometimes good, sometimes bad, sometimes brilliant, sometimes miserable. But the ambition, the resolute will is there. Yet concerning the final magnitude of the Biro-Bidjan project we have heard practically nothing. It is not, apparently, a problem in which the Soviet government is seriously determined to achieve success. We did occasionally hear figures quoted by high sources; they have never been greater than a hundred thousand (in a period when Palestine, under highly unfavorable conditions and with a government which is continually obstructing Jewish work, absorbed many more than 100,000 persons in two relatively good years!)

Without government ambition, in a country where there is practically no place for private initiative and free play of energy. nothing great can come of Biro-Bidjan. I do not mean that, because of the semi-apathetic conception of the plan in high Soviet quarters, a Jewish *Republic* cannot be created in Biro-Bidjan. In present-day Russia a region does not need a large population in order to acquire the status of an autonomous republic. The Kalmuk Republic has no more than 185,000 inhabitants, the

Ajarian Republic with Batum as its capital has even less (154,-000), the Nakhichevan only 117,000. If about 100,000 Jews should somehow gather in Biro-Bidjan (and at the present rate even this would take a goodly number of years) the region can very well be given the title of a "Jewish Autonomous Republic." This too may have some value, for even such Lilliputian Republics do not grow on bushes among Jews; but there would certainly be no cause to blow the trumpet of the Messiah if it should come to pass.

And there is a strong impression, that, in fact, Moscow has no greater aims for a Jewish Republic than just this.

The question now arises as to the energy which the Jewish community in Soviet Russia could call forth for the upbuilding of a territorial center. As far as I can judge from a distance, it amounts to very little. For whence could the community draw this special energy? Without good reason great numbers of people do not abandon the places where they have established themselves and traverse a distance of thousands of miles in order to build up a new settlement there. Something must urge them or drive them out of their present homes, or something must draw them to the new place.

There is no such force which urges the Jews to move. Their economic life in Russia has become normalized to a great extent in past years. This does not mean that Russian Jews are living in an economic Paradise. Their condition is however, in general, not worse than that of the majority people—the Russians (large numbers of Jews in Ukraine, Crimea, and White Russia have gone into agriculture, even larger numbers into the expanding industry and the far-flung administrative service). There were years when the tendency was for Jews to emigrate from the small town to rural areas, at a time when industry was still weak and could not absorb them. In recent years, characteristically, the process has been reversed: a flight from the Jewish farms is beginning; not to the small town, indeed, but to the industrialized large city with its attractions and opportunities. In 1926, 226,000 Jews still lived in villages; in 1935, after the success of industrialization, about 194,000; and now, by all indications, many fewer. On the other hand, the number of industrial workers has more than doubled; in 1926 there were 241,000, and in 1935 there were 558,000. The number of Jews in "civil service" had already reached the imposing figure of 560,000 in 1935. The majority of Russian Jews now have more or less steady occupations and incomes; in agriculture, industry, administration, state-commerce, and in the liberal professions. To be sure, the livings they earn are only "Soviet livings," but non-Jews, too, have no other. In 1928 the Soviet Union still counted nearly a million *declassed Jews* (according to Larin's official statistics). This category is no longer to be found in the statistics of the Jews. How did they disappear? The older and weaker ones died of want and hunger, undernourishment, physical ailments, and misery; the younger and stronger ones adapted themselves to the new conditions of life and vigorously dug their way tooth and nail into the various Soviet occupations. There is consequently no economic force which might motivate large numbers of Jews to leave Ukraine, White Russia, or Central Russia and set out for Biro-Bidjan where living conditions cannot be any better, where because of the pioneer character of the project, they must perhaps be worse for a long time to come. So long, therefore, as the economic situation of the Russian Jews does not become worse, so long as they are not pushed out of industrial enterprises because they are Jews, and are allowed to retain the numerous government positions which they now occupy; so long as no storm of open, aggressive anti-Semitism arises, all of which are phenomena which most of us believe to be impossible under present Soviet conditions—the Jews *are not driven* to go to Biro-Bidjan.

And if nothing drives them, then something must draw them. If not economic interests, there must be spiritual, national, social, cultural sentiments to motivate a young and active Jew to go to a distant place and there by arduous pioneering labor and endurance to build up a Jewish national *milieu*.

But the whole education which the younger Jew has received

and is still getting in Soviet Russia has not only failed to cultivate such constructive motives but has strangled them. The mere fact that Yiddish has been granted official status and that large numbers of Jews have graduated from "Jewish Schools" (Jewish schools, which failed to teach such insignificant subjects as Jewish history) means nothing. Jewish self-hatred can be taught in Yiddish, too. It is possible, if one cares to do so and has control of the school system, to teach even anti-Semitism in Yiddish. That very many of the Jewish parents in Russia have stopped sending their children to the so-called Jewish schools, with their lifeless Soviet-Yiddish jargon as the language of instruction, and prefer to have them in Russian or even in Ukrainian or White Russian schools, is in a very great measure a result of Soviet "careerism" which has taken possession of such large sections of the people. (In spite of all the "privileges" which Yiddish has received, Russian and Ukrainian are still, naturally, better grind-stones upon which to grind an ax.) One can imagine however, that Jewish traditionalists, too, have concluded in their desperation that rather than such a "Jewish education" with its grossly cynical attitude towards Jewish tradition, towards basic folkways and historical values, they would prefer a school which is "Goyish" entirely. The result is a decline in the number of Yiddish readers, a scene of desertion in many Jewish libraries—"red assimilation."

Whence shall come the spirit of Jewish pioneering for Jewish ideals? And if there are still great numbers of young Jews who speak a colorless, stilted Yiddish, what of it? Their mentality is already un-Jewish, reduced to the Soviet common denominator, emotionally dulled. What have they to do with quasi-Zionist romanticism, with the upbuilding of a Jewish land?

They know as their unofficial motto Stalin's already canonized formula, "Culture must be socialist in *content, national* in form." Interpreted this means one and the same life-interests for all the nations and tribes of the Soviet Union; *translated,* however, into the various Soviet languages. But if form is merely translation, and if national culture is simply a linguistic variation of some-

thing which is called "general Soviet culture" then why does one
have to have it ? The young Jew is well able to learn Russian, as
experience has shown us.

When cultural life is regimented, when self-expression is subject to an imposed discipline, when individuality cowers under the
threatening regulative eye of the censor, why should anyone want
Biro-Bidjan, a Jewish *milieu* of one's own and a Jewish Republic?
What specifically Jewish can be expressed in Biro-Bidjan, for
which it is worth while to offer sacrifices?

As a rule great mass migrations, when not caused by hunger
and need, have proceeded in a definite direction: from less freedom to more freedom. But under a centralized, totalitarian regime,
like the present regime in Russia, nobody can expect to feel more
free as a citizen and more free in the manifestations of Jewish life
in Biro-Bidjan than in other parts of the Union. The national republics in the Soviet Union are free in only one respect: in language. But those republics did not have to be built up; they were
territories with populations of long standing. The Jewish Republic,
if it is seriously intended and if it is to be thought of in terms of
a large Jewish mass population, must still be built up. For such
a task *khalutzim* are needed. Where can they be gotten in Russia?
How can one imagine a *khalutz* in chains?

Sholem Asch, I believe, told us, years ago, about a Jew who
had "a talent for Eretz Israel." In order to build up a large Jewish
center in Biro-Bidjan, one must have a sort of "talent" for Biro-
Bidjan, a "talent" for being Jewish and for Jewish life. Such talents
are not to be found among Jews in Russia. They are simply not
being cultivated.

March, 1938

Supplementary Homelands

EDITORIAL

O NCE AGAIN suggestions of a territorialist solution for the Jewish problem have cropped up in the press. Jews, we are told for the n-th time, need a land, any land, wherever it may be found, or wherever there are people kind enough to let them in. Palestine must not be the only place for Jewish settlement. The authors of this shopworn suggestion hint very broadly of a large country with a sparse and civilized population where free land is available aplenty. We are further informed that there exist souls in that country who would be broad-minded enough to welcome Jewish immigration in order to help develop their hitherto uncultivated lands. That country is Australia. In recent years its name has been linked a number of times with plans for Jewish colonization. The chief advocate of Australia for Jewish settlement, Dr. I. N. Steinberg, now visiting in America, has spent four years on that continent and established certain contacts.

Glad tidings of countries with a surplus of available land, with favorable climate, and other geographic appurtenances suitable for Jewish settlement are no longer a novelty. Ever since 1903, when a plan for an autonomous Jewish territory outside of Palestine was brought up for the first time, some version of this idea has been advanced every two or three years. In succession there were trotted out before us Uganda (which we now know possessed many more favorable features to recommend it than we suspected forty years ago), Angola, Cyrenaica, Texas, Abyssinia, the Crimea, Biro-Bidjan, Alaska, Lower California, Ecuador, British Guiana, and San Domingo. The results of all the various schemes and plans are familiar, and the fact that so many projects ended with naught should scarcely encourage any new venture of this sort. Will the Australia plan meet with better fortune? Is the Kimberley region more suitable and easier to colonize than the above enumerated territories? Are political conditions in this region more favorable?

It would be difficult to formulate a clear-cut answer to these questions. Special knowledge and long, laborious investigation would be required. We are convinced that Dr. Steinberg, the author of the plan, is sincere and that during the time of his sojourn in Australia he made a conscientious effort to familiarize himself with its potentialities for Jewish colonization. Nonetheless we feel fully justified in declaring outright that his project does not merit serious attention. The reason is that Kimberley is in Australia and not in Palestine.

We can easily visualize the reaction of non-Zionists or anti-Zionists who will read such a statement: These people are obsessed with a fixation; they are dominated by a kind of fetishism which blinds them to realities; they cherish romantic aspirations at the expense of real needs. Disparaging remarks of this sort have long become familiar to Zionists. Nearly forty years ago Eliezer Ben-Yehudah, the father of modern spoken Hebrew, from his home in Palestine seized upon the plan for colonizing Uganda as the final and ultimate salvation. At that time, too, colonists in Petakh-Tikvah and Rekhovot viewed the first groups of *khalutzim* who reached Palestine from Russia as incorrigible day-dreamers who had bypassed Uganda, a land flowing with milk and honey, and come instead to a land without a future, Palestine. Looking back at these advocates of Uganda, we do not feel that we have a right to condemn any of them today. From a purely rationalistic standpoint they were probably right. But at this late date we also know that certain logical conclusions and rational deductions are not respected by history; while other ideas, which may at some time be characterized as fantastic, are smiled upon by history and are borne onward to fruition. Something of this nature has occurred to territorialism on the one hand, and to Zionism on the other.

Forty years ago those Zionist leaders who favored Uganda lacked the courage to say: Uganda *instead* of Palestine. Herzl

and Nordau as well as Zangwill then evolved the formula that
Uganda was to serve as a temporary asylum—a *Nachtasyl*—on the
road which led ultimately to Palestine. The territorialists were
more candid in this respect. Uganda, they said, or some other suitable territory, should be an end in itself and not merely a way
station on the road to permanent settlement in Palestine. Dr.
Steinberg and his *Freeland* group avoid the mistaken idea advanced by Herzl and Nordau, the idea of building up a country,
and then leaving all that had been created with much labor to
begin all over again in Palestine. Nor do they offer their plan as
a substitute for the settlement of Palestine. The present Jewish
community in Palestine is too significant a factor, Jewish achievements in Palestine are on too broad a scale, and the potentialities
of the community are too great to be ignored by any sensible person. But is it true that there is no contradiction between the continued upbuilding of Palestine as a Jewish Commonwealth and
large-scale colonization in Australia? On the surface, this view
may appear to be correct. But unfortunately, contemporary political realities are full of "illogical" factors that compel us to say that
there is a sharp contradiction between the two.

In so far as Jews are at present interested in colonization,
it must be in a compact settlement capable of embracing large
numbers. Settling even a few thousand Jews on good land in
a neighborhood of decent people is a worthwhile accomplishment, but one of little significance from a broad, historical viewpoint. What, we may ask, is the potential contribution of settling
fifty or even a hundred thousand Jews toward solving the problems of the Jewish people as a whole? Can a community of such
size become autonomous, not only in the technical administrative
sense of exercising such self-government as does any county or
township in a civilized country, but in the sense of helping to
create a national mode of life and fostering its own civilization?
There is no scientific yardstick for determining the exact number
of people required in order that a community may retain and develop its individuality as a group and not be engulfed by the sur-

sounding overwhelming mass. But there are grounds for doubting whether in our day a small group can hope to survive. To preserve its identity, an ethnic group in the twentieth century must consist at least of hundreds of thousands, if not of millions. Our problem today consists not merely in colonization as such, but in *large-scale* colonization. Our task is to concentrate a maximum number of Jews in compact settlements in one area. Is this possible in Australia? From a purely geographic standpoint it is not impossible. The Kimberley region is approximately the size of Belgium. Natural conditions do not present unsurmountable obstacles, and it is conceivable that a community of millions should be settled on Kimberley's seven million acres. But would Australia tolerate the establishment within its borders of such a large community aiming to develop autonomously along Jewish lines? Australia needs a rapid increase in its population, and many farseeing Australians had adopted the slogan, "Populate or Perish!" just before the outbreak of the present war. But is Australia willing to permit its Kimberley district to be developed into an enclave resembling the French province of Quebec in Canada? Is ethnically homogeneous Australia willing to transform itself into a binational state like Canada, or like South Africa, with its English and Boers? These questions would not be of such great importance if we were discussing a mere welfare project for a number of homeless Jews; but what we are considering is a territorial plan for the Jewish people. On this aspect of the problem, Dr. Steinberg, its author, has said nothing. If this plan envisages only a small scale settlement in Australia, then the entire project becomes of such minor importance, when compared with the scope and significance of our enterprise in Palestine, that one may justly doubt whether we can afford to divide our energies for its sake. The coming years will be difficult ones and all our forces will have to be mobilized for the huge principal task ahead of us.

* * *

It is our misfortune that in the coming post-war years the "emigration pressure" of the Jewish people will be far less than it was only a short time ago. When Dr. Steinberg went to Australia four years ago to study its potentialities for colonization, Jews were a relatively large people. During the time he spent there we became a much smaller people. Hitler has reduced to a considerable extent the Jewish need for emigration; and it would be senseless to ignore the fact that in Poland, the greatest reservoir of Jewish emigration, there may remain only about a million Jews, according to reports reaching us. Poland is still in the Nazi grip. How many of those still alive today will survive to see the end of the war? And how many of them will remain physically capable of pioneering colonization tasks after their ordeals? Now, at the end of 1943, we can no longer think in terms of 1939 figures, nor even of the number of Jews alive at the beginning of 1942, before the Nazis undertook the total physical annihilation of the Jews.

The emigration of great masses of Jews from Europe is no longer possible. The number of potential emigrants we must provide for at the end of this war will be less than at the end of the first World War. Concretely we will have to consider the needs of the surviving Jews in Rumania and Hungary; the tragically reduced remnant in Poland; the few Jews of Turkey, for whom life becomes ever less tolerable under an extremely nationalistic regime; and the few hundred thousands living in Arabic-speaking lands—North Africa, Iraq, Yemen—where hopes for peaceful coexistence of Jew and Arab are dim indeed. Our "emigration potential"—omitting the Soviet Union and the American countries—is therefore no more than about two million. And this number can be settled in Palestine, without resorting to additional territories, even according to conservative estimates of Palestine's "absorptive capacity."

A non-Jewish legislator in Canada hinted some months ago that the United Nations are purposely abstaining from an attempt to save the Jews of Europe, because they would prefer not to be burdened with a large Jewish problem after the war. Whether this hint has any basis in fact or not, it is true that Hitler has already "eased" the headaches awaiting the post-war democratic world when it attempts to cope with Jewish emigration, or with the problem of reintegrating uprooted Jews into the economic life of their erstwhile homelands. We have become a smaller people; and unless we should plan an exodus not only from occupied Europe but also from Russia, England, and America (an idea not in conflict with the Zionist view, but hardly one now on the order of the day) we must realize that Jewish population pressure is much weaker today then it was a short time ago. It is therefore impractical and senseless to indulge in speculations concerning territories to supplement Palestine. It should also be remarked here that two million Jews concentrated in a single country, whether in Palestine or some district of Australia, would be a much more potent and dynamic force, politically and economically as well as culturally, than two groups, one million in Palestine and one million in Australia. Everyday arithmetic does not apply to such problems.

But how can one be sure that Palestine will be open to emigrating Jews after the war? Granted that geographically and economically there are no obstacles, is that sufficient to assure that they will be colonized there? It is not enough that a country contains free land, opportunities for irrigation and industrial development, and favorable commercial relations with the outside world. To put into effect such a large-scale program of colonization, favorable political conditions are required. And what if England, or other forces in conjunction with England, should not permit the realization of this plan? Can anyone guarantee that we will be permitted to utilize Palestine's absorptive capacity to the full for those Jews who are so much in need of a home?

No one can *guarantee* such an eventuality. (Even less can one guarantee that Australia will allow a Jewish community of two million or even of one million to be settled in Kimberley.) But it is precisely because no one can offer such a guarantee that we believe it is harmful to advance new territorial projects at this time. The political situation of Zionism is far from secure today. Many dangers and pitfalls beset Jewish hopes and Jewish efforts

in Palestine. It should not be hard to grasp that the more concentrated our political effort as a people, the more it is fixed on
one spot, the better are our chances of succeeding. On the other
hand, the more parallel demands we make and the more diverse
plans we advance, the more alibis will be forthcoming from our
opponents in their effort to evade our basic demand. In the fall of
1938 certain groups in England tried to undermine political Zionism in a gentle and "painless" manner. Let the Jews "have" British
Guiana instead of Palestine, they said, and cease clamoring that
England had deceived them. In Washington certain official circles
feel that quarrels with the Arabs should be avoided and that Jews
should be compensated for their disappointment in Palestine by
being granted opportunities for colonization in Angola,—the same
Angola which once before, in pre-World War I days, was touted
as a suitable area for Jewish colonization. One of the serious dangers confronting the upbuilding of a Jewish Palestine, and one
which we must recognize at all times, is the plan, ever-present in
the background, to "compensate" Jews elsewhere, in some place
where the political complications are less serious, or where it can
be alleged that this is the case.

It is true that latter-day territorialists are no longer opposed
to settlement in Palestine; and when Dr. Steinberg advances his
plan for colonization in Australia, he adds at the very beginning
that his plan is auxiliary to Palestine and not in competition with
it.

Yet, a Jewish colonization plan in Australia, no matter how
far it is practicable, plays directly into the hands of those who are
interested in scrapping Jewish claims on Palestine, and destroying
the moral force behind those demands. From this standpoint, Dr.
Steinberg's plan for colonization in Australia falls in effect into
the category of anti-Zionist plans, no matter how much its pro-
ponents reiterate that they do not intend to enter into competition
with Zionism, and that personally they are even pro-Zionist.

December, 1943

Zionism and Dual Loyalties

by NORMAN BENTWICH

I T IS singular that, twenty-five years after the issue of the
Balfour Declaration, the hoary objection to Zionism has been
raised again, that it involves a dual loyalty on the part of those
Jews at any rate who are not British subjects. Loyalty to Palestine,
it is suggested, might be in conflict with loyalty to the country in
which they are citizens. The objection was current in the early
days of the Zionist movement, before the British Government had
pledged itself to facilitate the establishment of the Jewish National
Home, and the Allied Powers and, later, the League of Nations
adopted that purpose as a part of the international order. As that
view is still held—often by persons of good will—both in non-
Jewish and Jewish circles, it may be worth while to examine the
questions afresh.

One of the primary causes of the difficulty is the ambiguous
use of the word "nationality." The same term is used to denote
membership of a State which is more properly called citizenship,
and membership of an ethnic group which is bound together by
language, religion, history and common aspirations. In English,
sometimes "nation" is used for the political unit and the word
"nationality" for the cultural unit. The two things are fundamentally different because the modern nation-State is regularly
composed of a number of ethnic nationalities. So at the time of
the movement for Italian unity, one of the writers of the Risorgi-
mento distinguished between *"nationalita naturale,"* which signifies the cultural association, and *"nationalita politica,"* which
signifies the tie with the State. Normal nationalities, indeed,
inhabit a geographic unit, which is the national home. It is the
essential aim of Zionism to make the Jews again a normal nationality in this sense. The Jews have been outstanding in world
history for two thousand years as a people who have the strongest

41

sense of nationality and have preserved with unparalleled devotion their national culture, but have lacked a national home.

The French Revolution introduced the idea of the nation-State, the political unit, in which all the inhabitants should share a common culture and feel themselves part of a single nationality. Under the influence of that conception a sacrifice was asked of the Jews as a condition of their political emancipation. They should renounce their belief that they were a nationality, and in place of it regard themselves as members of a special religious community. Israelites by religion, Frenchmen, Dutchmen, etc., by nationality was the principle of liberalism for a time. But in other countries that idea did not take hold. In the United Kingdom and the British Empire there has always been an unquestioned recognition of many nationalities within the single citizenship and State— Welsh, Scotch, Irish are obvious national groups; and in the course of the nineteenth century, Canadians, Australians and South Africans also developed a strong sense of separate nationality. So the English retained an understanding and respect for Jewish nationality. Such movement as there was for its renunciation came from within the Jewish community; and the non-Jewish Englishman has tended to have greater respect for the Jew who holds to his separate culture and consciously recognizes his distinctiveness than for the Jew who claims that he is differentiated only in religion. In Central Europe, also, before the hideous relapse into Nazism, the State recognized the existence of a number of nationalities, enjoying equal civil and political rights, but preserving their language, culture and ideals. At the end of the last war the Jew in Central Europe secured recognition through the Minority Treaties that he was a member of a nationality.

Historical philosophers of our time have emphasized the value to the State of preserving and fostering these national differences. Thus, Lord Acton, the champion of the Liberal tradition, wrote: "The presence of different nations under the same sovereignty is similar in its effect to the independence of Church and State. It provides against the servility which flourishes under the shadow of a single authority by balancing the interests, multiplying associations, and giving to the subject the restraint and support of outward opinion." And Lord Bryce, another great champion of Liberalism, stressed the benefit of differentiation of cultures within the States. That idea was expressed by an English man-of-letters of the last generation: "Let us hang on to our sacred differences." And one of the big minds in American Jewry, the late Justice Brandeis, wrote with special reference to the Zionist outlook: "Each race and people, like each individual, has a right and duty to develop, and only through such differentiated development will a high civilization be attained." Recently another leading thinker in America, a Christian professor at the Union Theological Seminary, has said: "The philosophy of Jewish nationalism is an expression of a national will to live which transcends traditional orthodox religion. Collective survival impulse is as legitimate as an individual one. Justice in history is concerned with collective, as well as with individual, rights." He deduces that the Gentile world must on the one hand preserve and extend the democratic standard of tolerance and of cultural pluralism to allow the Jews a place as a nation among nations; and must, on the other hand, support more generously the legitimate aspirations of Jews for a homeland. Jewish dissimilation is as important for the well-being of the community as Jewish assimilation.

So much for the question of Jewish nationality. But what of the dual loyalty of the Zionist who works for the restoration of the Jewish National Home in Palestine and is a citizen of a State which is not the sovereign of Palestine? For British Jews the difficulty does not arise because Great Britain, as the mandatory for Palestine, exercises sovereign rights. But for Zionists who are not British subjects, it is said, the conflict of loyalties may occur. The objection is based on that false conception of the nation-State which denies the right of the group to foster its own tradition and culture. The Jew, Zionist or non-Zionist, recognizes and, indeed, cherishes his duty to carry out fully the obligations of citizenship in the country of which he is a member. In times of peace that does not prevent him from taking a deep interest and exercising his talents in the cause of the home where his people are re-establishing their national center. His loyalty to their culture and tradition does not only not reduce his loyalty to his country of birth—or adoption—but may strengthen it. For loyalty, like charity, is not a fund which is exhausted by expenditure on an object, but is nourished by exercise. And just as Scots and Irish abroad who are devoted to the country of their ancestors are frequently outstanding citizens of other countries, so Jews who are enthusiastic for the revival of Jewish life in Palestine are often leaders and contributors to the cultural wealth of the countries of which they are citizens. To take a ready example from another democratic country: the late Justice Brandeis and Justice Frankfurter would be accepted as outstanding Americans of their generation. And they were Zionist leaders.

We may compare with that liberal conception in the democratic countries the bitter lot in the totalitarian States. Tragic expression is given to the failure of the Jew seeking to be completely assimilated in Germany, in a poem written a few years before the outbreak of this war by the Jew Lissauer, who won notoriety in the last war as the composer of the German Hymn of Hate:

"I carry the burden of two nations:
To the German I am a Jew masked as a German,
To the Jew I am a German faithless to Israel."

But in time of war, it may be urged, the loyalty of the Zionist is imperilled. He will be unwilling to take up arms or, if compelled by law to do that, to merge himself in the struggle to destroy the State which is responsible for the Government of the National Home. The objection is rather a logical than a human dilemma. It has been the fate of the emancipated Jew during the last 150 years to take his part in the armed forces of his country, knowing that he may have to fight Jews in the forces of the enemy country. That hardship is not exclusive to the Jew. In a world which has been becoming steadily internationalized through movement of masses of people from one country to another, war has meant for hundreds of thousands of non-Jews likewise the same harsh prospect. But the supreme claim of the State in time of war is accepted by all, except conscientious objectors; and no case, I believe, is known where a Jew has put forward conscientious objections on the ground that he might be called upon to shoot another Jew.

Looking, as we must, for a better order after the war, in which peace between nations will be assured by the instruments of world community, we may feel that the Jew in his loyalty to the Land of Israel may render a genuine service to the country of which he remains a citizen. It is obvious that vast numbers who survive the war will continue to be citizens of European and American States. The Jews have been for centuries an international people in the special sense of being distributed among many nations, and yet retained consciously everywhere a special outlook and hope. Through the building up of Palestine in the last generation the Jews have become international in a fuller sense, because they have now a greater self-respect and pride through the existence of their National Home and the contribution which the people in that land are making to their country and the larger world. They should be able to help, therefore, wherever they live, to bring about understanding between nations, peoples and races, and to interpret one to the other. An Englishwoman of vision wrote a few years ago on this service which they might render through their double loyalty: "It might be that they are the founders and pioneers of that true internationalism for lack of which the world perishes. We seek to make links between nations, classes or interests. Scientists come together; women come together; workers come together, in their congresses. But, when the strain comes, the links break and nationalism remains. The Jews' loyalty to the country in which he lives and to his Jewish descent, these are two things which have never broken yet. Is there not here a natural priesthood, an order of service to the world?"

The Land of Israel is uniquely a country which belongs to humanity because from it there has gone out the message of human brotherhood and of justice and peace between nations. In his endeavor to rebuild the life of that country and to become again an active conscious force of civilization, the Jew, wherever he lives, is loyal to the service of humanity which, in a better world, should be combined with loyalty to the State. For it is an essential ideal of a peaceful international order that every person shall feel himself a citizen of the world community, as well as a citizen of the multi-national State, and a member of a cultural nationality which he inherits from his ancestors.

January, 1943

To Young India: An Open Letter to Gandhi

by HAYIM GREENBERG

I DON'T know how to address you. Some years ago, I might have called you "Mahatma" (great soul)—the name with which millions of your people have crowned you. But I know that you have forbidden its use, that in a moment of spiritual protest you declared yourself to be no more than a "scavenger." Nor do I dare call you teacher. I know of you since the time I first read Tolstoy's "Letter To A Hindu," to you; I have followed your work since 1914; I carry sharp-engraven in my memory each step of your martyr's path—each arrest and trial, each vow, each fast, each triumph and each passing defeat which never shook your faith. I have read, in the languages familiar to me, all that you have written and there has been no social-religious thinker who has exerted so fruitful an influence on me. If, despite the fact that in various periods I have been stirred to the depths of my soul by your teaching and your life, I am far from being your disciple or follower, the fault is not yours. You know how hard it is to follow you sincerely and completely in India itself, a land where both race and cultural heritage have created conditions favorable to the growth of your teachings; still harder is it in the lands of the West, particularly for a man of my generation, who grew up in the heroic period of the Russian revolution—an epoch seething with moral conflicts. But it is easy for me to call you "brother," if only because I belong to a people, from whose prophets thousands of years ago there flashed the conception of God's universal fatherhood, as well as of the brotherhood of all whom He created "in His image." Therefore, permit me to use the name of "brother" together with the two names you heard in childhood—Mohandas Karamchand.

But before I take up the purpose of my letter, before I state the request which will perhaps sound like a challenge, allow me to

47

congratulate you on the recent great victory in your struggle for human equality. I have in mind the proclamation of the young Maharajah of Travancore which ended the religious and political disabilities of the great number of untouchables in that region. Without questioning the noble intentions of the progressive ruler of Travancore, and believing that his revolutionary reform sprang from the vigor of his awakened conscience, we know that the Maharajah would have been unable to immortalize his name through that greatest reform in the history of new India, if you had not for years prepared the soil, if you had not, on the one hand, aroused the untouchables themselves to struggle for their human dignity, and on the other, stirred the conscience of the thousands of members of the privileged castes. I remember well that throughout these years you were not the only champion of the millions of "unclean." Possibly, Rabindranath Tagore gave more forceful literary expression to the moral revolt against the ancient wall standing in India between man and man; I know of a number of significant figures in your country—men and women—who have gone farther and more directly toward the goal of equality. But we may justly ascribe the great reform which sheds luster on Travancore, primarily, to you. All the purely intellectual arguments for the equalization of the untouchables, all the theological proofs and textual criticism which many progressive Hindus have proffered, pale before your brief words: "I should not like to be born again, but if I am fated to enter the world once more, let it be among the untouchables." Even more influential was the courage you displayed through "direct action," when you adopted a child from among the untouchables and made it a member of your family. This practical example in the breaking down of canonized historical walls proved contagious. Hundreds of others of the highest castes were stirred to a noble defiance which led them to engage publicly in the "base" work to which pariahs were doomed, in order to expunge the stain of "baseness" through their participation. Your example gave the untouchables self-respect and moral courage; it made them braver and more capable of the bloodless uprisings with which they have several times distinguished themselves. If any concrete proofs were needed to show that not only exceptional heroic spirits, but masses of plain, uneducated people are capable, under certain circumstances, of being aggressive without resort to violence, and that a system of passive resistance may be victorious, the passive fight of the untouchables must be reckoned as among the most persuasive. Of great historic significance is also the fact that if the two million former untouchables of Travancore may now enter the temples and pray together with members of the higher castes, if they may use the public wells and highways, and send their children to the general schools, the outcome is due to an inner revolution, a spiritual renewal in India itself, rather than to the pressure of European "civilizers." I remember that for years you were unwilling to use English dominion for reforming the inner life of India. You would not have been content with a reform that came from above or from outside. You waited for a welling up of fighting energy in the degraded masses themselves and for a growing sense of repentance among the higher castes. I rejoice that you have lived to see the first green sprouting on the hard soil you ploughed and sowed. Without English intervention, without outside pressure, Travancore made its revolutionary beginning. I am sure that the example of Travancore will affect all of India, and that the natural rights of the sixty million untouchables will be restored within our generation.

Those of us in Europe and America who were deeply affected by the intolerable plight of the untouchables, have long been troubled by the peculiar theological aspects of the problem. We know that the orthodox Hindus, among them many who are not motivated by selfish caste considerations, opposed emancipation because of a dogma of the Hindu religion. According to this dogma, the members of the lower castes are being penalized for past sins, "judged by God." If I am not mistaken, orthodox Hindus have attempted through this specific interpretation of the caste-system, to solve the problem of *theodicy*—the same problem of vindicating the way of God to man which agitated the unknown author of Job. According to this interpretation, the oppressed castes suffer for sins committed in past incarnations. They have returned to the world to expiate a former sin, to purify themselves and perform their period of *Karma*. In a later incarnation they may be reborn into a higher caste if their virtues warrant this promotion. To emancipate an untouchable therefore prevents the full cycle of expiation and meddles with the plans of divine Providence. I am in no position to judge to what extent this dogma or traditional concept is an organic part of Hinduism. I cannot tell in what measure those untouchables, who some years ago began to consider turning to Christianity or Islam in order to be free of a religion which discriminated not only socially but metaphysically against a large number of its adherents, were justified in their purpose. I am, therefore, not quite clear as to how orthodox Hindus will reconcile their religious integrity with the emancipation of the untouchables. However, I was happy to chance on a publication of the Central Hindu College of Benares ("An advanced textbook of Hindu religion and ethics") which contained a significant new interpretation of the doctrine of *Karma*. According to this viewpoint it is a serious error to explain suffering in terms of "Karma," and to abstain from aiding a sufferer so as not to interfere with the process of his *Karma*. Our moral ability to help a man is in itself evidence that the Karma under which he suffers is fulfilled. Furthermore, by refusing to help a fellow-being we commit a sin, and so prepare an evil future *Karma* for ourselves. It is not the task of a stranger to solve the problems of an ancient, complex religious system belonging to another people, but I think there are trends in modern India which indicate that the complete emancipation of the untouchables will be achieved without a destruction of the Hindu religious system and without artificial reforms of Hindu doctrine. Jews once believed literally in the Biblical "an eye for an eye, a tooth for a tooth." The later Talmudical interpretation that the formula meant material compensation for an eye, or a tooth, in no wise weakened religious Judaism; on the contrary, it strengthened it. I imagine that similar organic developments will take place in the religious life of India.

And now to turn to the specific purpose of my letter. May I remind you that untouchables exist not only in India? Not everywhere in the same numbers, nor of precisely the same status, but nevertheless "untouchables," human beings who are persecuted, insulted, starved and frequently slain only because they belong to a different ethnic group, or serve God in their own fashion. There are still millions of such untouchables in the country from which I write you. You know that though many years have passed since slavery was abolished, the practical emancipation of Negroes in the U. S. is far from complete. And there are still other millions of "untouchables" scattered over all parts of the globe, in dozens of countries: these are the millions of my tormented fellow Jews. To uncover one's wounds and seek sympathy is neither pleasant, nor perhaps even dignified. But no doubt word has reached you of the torment of my people in countries where they have lived hundreds of years, where the first Jews settled long before their present oppressors, and which they enriched with their toil and sweat. After a thousand years of existence in Germany the remaining 400,000 German Jews find themselves outcast and tormented; their state is made more tragic by the knowledge of the great contribution, both material and spiritual, which they and their ancestors had made to the progress of Germany. Approximately the same thing is happening in Poland and Rumania, and (for the time being) to a less catastrophic degree, in a number of other countries. Disfranchisement, defenselessness, *numerus clausus* and *numerus nullus* in the universities, separate benches and an inferior status for Jewish children in the public schools, economic and social boycott, murders which are not only tolerated but often encouraged, lynchings which anti-Semitic governments do not even trouble to combat, closed doors facing Jews who wish to immigrate into new countries—this is our lot in many parts of the world at the present time. India is remote from Jewish wretchedness. She is taken up with her own great cares and unsolved problems—the destiny of a fifth of the human race—but I am sure that you have heard of what has happened to millions of my fellow Jews in Europe, North Africa and parts of Asia.

We Jews now strive to redeem ourselves from our state of "untouchability." We seek bread, work, freedom, and human dignity. These we wish to secure by emerging from that anomalous state to which history has doomed us—the state of homelessness and landlessness. For over fifty years, the best of our youth have been devoting the fullness of their energy toward the re-creation of our former national center in Palestine. We need a country for the millions of persecuted Jews, and this country must be the land which cradled the civilization we once created there. This need is more than economic or political in its origin. Among those who are returning to their ancient fatherland are not only refugees driven by alien might but pilgrims inspired by historic forces— human beings who seek integrity and harmony in a new life of their own. Judaism is not only a religion, a system of abstract thought, or a series of tenets and rules. It is also, perhaps primarily, a particular way of life, action and self-expression. Our particular genius, our capacity for self-expression is throttled in us because we live in alien environments and cultures. We are always adapting ourselves to our stronger neighbors, existing in a state of perpetual mimicry dangerous to our spirit. Zionism is not only a movement for the hungry and persecuted. It draws to itself increasing numbers of courageous Jews even in those countries which are free from brutal anti-Semitism and where Jews are not stigmatized as "unclean." These Jews know—as your great patriot Lajpat Rai once put it—that chains are chains no matter how gilded. You yourself once lived in a strange land, in the small Indian community of South Africa, and you know how the spiritual energy of a national or racial group which lives as a minority in an alien environment becomes choked. May I, in this connection, quote the lines of the great modern Hebrew poet, Bialik—lines which I believe you will not misinterpret as evidence of a materialistic attitude: "Each people has as much heaven over its head as it has soil under its feet."

Landless and heavenless, many thousands of my brothers have in recent years returned to the soil of their fathers, laid waste through the neglect of centuries. You in India understand how a land may degènerate and grow barren. One does not have to be an expert in Indian history to know that your country was once richer, more fertile and more civilized than it is today. The excavations in Mohandja Dara have clearly demonstrated that a highly developed civilization with large cities, varied industries and comfortable homes existed in your country 3,500 years B.C. According to the historian Megasthenes, when the armies of Alexander the Great invaded parts of India over 2,200 years ago, they found a people no less civilized and artistic than the Greeks of that time. In Palestine, too, there once existed a higher state of civilization than we found when our generation began to return. The remnants of terraces on the mountains, the magnificent synagogues excavated in Capernaum and Beth Alfa, the signs of a former irrigation system, all bear witness to this. During the centuries of our absence, war and oppression raging for generations, reduced our land to a state of barrenness and decay. This did not dishearten our pioneers. In every spot where they were given the chance, they built again prospering villages and towns. Where the earth was swampy they drained it; where it was barren and parched, they made water spring from hidden depths. They drove out the curse of malaria. The mountains of Judea and Galilee had been denuded as far back as the Roman wars, but this desolation has been lifted by our youth. In many places which recently were but sand and rock, the green woods of ancient Palestine bloom resurrected. Within a comparatively short space of time we have developed Jewish agriculture and industry, making possible a still larger mass immigration of Jews. At the start of our reconstruction work we had psychological as well as physical difficulties. We had the problems resulting from a false conception of manual labor. Once a people of shepherds and farmers and artisans, in the course of our wanderings we had been transformed into a people of tradesmen primarily. We lost contact with nature, lost the habit of healthful and cleansing physical labor, and began to look with unjustified, well nigh sinful contempt upon so-called "lower" social functions. Our religious cult of learning unfortunately changed into the cult of a pseudo-aristocracy. Many of us ceased to understand the moral and aesthetic worth of simple labor. You are familiar with the paradoxical ways by which a people arrives at so corrupt a scale of values. You in India will also have to wage a bitter struggle against the social implications of this pseudo-aristocratic scholasticism. We understand the challenge in the title "scavenger" which you assumed. In Palestine and through Palestine we are freeing ourselves from the moral hump which rose on our backs during centuries of unsound development. We have given back to physical labor its dignity and sanctity. We have returned to the truly Jewish, profoundly human concept of our Talmudists who taught that "he who does not teach his son a manual trade is like one who teaches his son robbery." Through our renewed understanding of the dignity of labor many of us came to understand that all kinds of labor are of equal social worth and are to be equally rewarded. In the same places where the pre-evangelical communities of the Essenes, dedicated to the principle of "mine is thine, and thine is mine," once existed, large villages built on the basis of voluntary communism have arisen. I have been told on several occasions that some groups in India have gathered the impression that our communes are breeding-places of vulgar materialism and atheism. It would take me far beyond the confines of my letter were I to explain why I regard their irreligion as true religion. Let me say but one word. Remember the utterances of your great mystic Ramakrishna who declared that "religion is not for empty stomachs," and of his flaming disciple, Vivekananda, who said that "as long as a single hungry man remains in my land, my sole religion will be to feed him!" Such is the motivation of the "materialism" of our communist experiment in Palestine.

Arab enemies of my people, and, I am convinced, of their own people, have lately mobilized ignorant and fanatical elements against this Jewish renascence. All impartial observers who have visited Palestine, all honest students of the question, have come to the conclusion that our movement has in no way injured the Arab people, that, on the contrary, the mass of the Arab population has profited socially, economically and culturally from Jewish immigration. If you would care to acquaint yourself with the available data, you would see for yourself that the Arab standard of living has risen significantly due to the peaceful, progressive methods of Jewish reconstruction. In recent history, Zionism is the first instance of colonization free from imperialist ambition or the desire to exploit any part of the population. The present Arab rulers know very well that Zionism spells no threat of colonial oppression for the Arab people. However, they do fear that the influence of Zionism on the Arab masses will hasten the process of economic and social emancipation in Palestine, and will endanger their selfish caste interests. For this reason, they kindle the savage passions of national hate and religious fanaticism. They have sent poor, ignorant wretches to destroy Jewish property, to uproot trees planted by Jews, to set fire to Jewish houses, to murder old and young—men, women and children—to throw bombs into schools and kindergartens, and to shoot down Jewish nurses who tended Jewish and Arab patients alike. I am sure that you have heard of the anti-Jewish terror let loose in Palestine for over half a year, and no doubt information has reached you of the Arab leaders' intention to renew this terror and increase its scope so as to attain their goal—the stoppage of further Jewish immigration and the liquidation of Zionism. Why then, I dare ask you, have you been silent all this while? Why are you still silent?

I know how small a place the Jewish question must take in the consciousness of people in India. I know how enormous are your own problems and cares. But the drama now being enacted in Palestine has its direct and indirect repercussions in India. A harmful and thoroughly false propaganda against Jews and

Zionism is now being conducted in your Mohammedan communities. The none too fastidious agents of the present Arab leaders
are spreading malicious lies to the effect that Jews are a menace to
Mohammedanism, that they propose to destroy or tamper with
Mohammedan mosques and holy places. An intense hatred of
Jews is being fanned among the millions of Mohammedans in
India. Please believe me that I think not only of my own people,
when I feel duty bound to warn you against the effects of this
incendiary propaganda. Jew hatred is a poison, dangerous both
to the hated and the haters. For the sake of your country and
your people as well as my own, I would not wish the bacilli now
undermining the moral foundations of so many European countries, to befoul the air of India. I do not understand why you
have taken no note of this kindling of religious fanaticism and
blind hate among your Mohammedan fellow Indians, why you
have ignored the effects of Arab incitement which became apparent even in the ranks of the Indian National Congress. You
are silent. Your friend and desciple, Nehru, is silent. And
unless I am mistaken, only your poet and noble champion of
human rights, Madam Naidu, has raised her voice in behalf of my
people.

Let your clear and courageous voice be heard—for our sake,
for your sake, for the sake of the awakening East to which we return. Do that which is in your power to end the venomous anti-
Jewish propaganda amid the millions of Mohammedans in India.
When Hindu and Mohammedans made murderous attacks upon
each other, you declared a fast in protest against fratricide and
false piety. I remember the strict solemnity of your three weeks'
fast. I remember also the effect of this particular "dictatorial"
measure: the two religious communities made peace under the
pressure of your prayer and fast. I am not so naive and egocentric
as to assume that you could protest with an equal passion against
the onslaught on Jewish work and a Jewish future in Palestine. It
is not my place to suggest how you should influence Moslem public
opinion and particularly the leaders of your national congress. Do

what you can to stop the anti-Jewish agitation for which Islam is being exploited cynically and destructively. I know how greatly you honor Islam and its followers. But all your life you have shown the daring and ability to fight against religious hypocrisy in political life. As the proven friend of the Moslems, you have a particular right to protest against the exploitation of Islam and its institutions for unworthy political ends.

May I remind you how a European observer characterized the reaction of a Hindu to the usual sermon of a Christian missionary? His first response was "Christianity is not true"; his second, "Christianity is not new," and his third rejoinder was "Christianity is not you." He perceived the truth in Christianity, while realizing the untruth in the Christian. The same may be said in varying measure of all religions and their representatives. It may also be said of Islam and of those who seek to transform a noble creed into an instrument for anti-social and anti-religious purposes. You are the man in India who can challenge the unscrupulous Arab agitators with the cry "Islam is not you."

Will we hear your voice, the voice of Young India?

April, 1937

Einstein on Zionism

by KURT BLUMENFELD

IN 1922, when it became known that Einstein had become interested in the Zionist movement, and the Jewish press even called him a Zionist, he was asked how he, who had always pointed to the danger of nationalism, could suddenly declare himself a Jewish nationalist. His answer was: "If someone who has two arms insists on saying 'I have a right arm,' he is a chauvinist. But a person who has lost his right arm, must try unrelentingly to compensate his loss. That is why I am a Jewish nationalist. The Jewish people lacks the most primitive conditions of life; it has a right to create for itself in Palestine the conditions for its free development."

How deeply Einstein understood the Jewish question is indicated in an appeal that he issued to the Jews in Hungary in which he says: "The greatest enemy of Jewish national consciousness and Jewish dignity is well fed degeneration, that is, indifference resulting from wealth and luxurious living, as well as a kind of inner dependence on the non-Jewish world which grows out of a laziness in the Jewish community. The best in man can flourish only when he grows up in a community. Then how great must be the moral danger to a Jewish person who has severed his ties with his own people and is regarded an alien by his master people! Enough of contemptible, unhappy egotism has grown out of such a situation.

"The external pressure that is now being exerted against the Jewish people is particularly great. Yet this very suffering has been a boon to us. We have witnessed a revival of Jewish communal life that the past generation did not even dream about. Devoted and far-sighted leaders, who have been influenced by the awakened spirit of Jewish solidarity, have promoted the colonization work in Palestine under seemingly insurmountable difficulties, yet with such remarkable success that I have no doubt of its permanent results. This work is of supreme value to the Jews of the world as a whole. Palestine will become the cultural center of all the Jews, and it will be a haven of refuge for the most oppressed, a field of activity for the best among us, a unifying ideal and a source of inner wholesomeness to the Jews the world over.

"Jews of Hungary, show that you do not stand aloof from your brethren in the rest of the world!"

In a letter to Pinchas Ruttenberg, Einstein expresses his attitude toward Jewish youth, the pioneers and the revival of the Jewish people through labor. This letter is particularly interesting as it is a message to Ruttenberg in connection with his planned visit to the United States. Einstein writes:

"I have seen our youth in Palestine engaged in hard, persevering labor which could be made easier and more productive through better equipment and preparation. I have seen how the small but most valiant group of pioneers in Dagania had to carry a burden of debts which could be easily removed by their inspired brethren abroad. Their struggle, as well as the struggle of the others, must be alleviated. Above all, their bodies must be protected for they are sacrificing themselves for the spirit and honor of the entire Jewish people.

"We must show that we are a people which still possesses enough power and will to live to create a great work that will become the unifying center and mainstay of our future generations. The land shall be for us and our progeny what the Temple was for our ancestors.

"I have often seen that when a Jew has felt this deeply, he joyfully offered his energy in service to the cause. May you succeed in awakening the dormant and in kindling the spirit of those who are awake."

Einstein took a stand on most questions pertaining to Zionism and Jewish life. He has known of Herzl's work which he characterized in a letter addressed to the Zionist magazine *Selbstwehr* in Prague, on the occasion of its jubilee, as follows: "Herzl recognized with the vision of a genius that the Palestine enterprise would give the Jewish people a new feeling of belonging together, a new content and new self-esteem. It is up to us not only to participate in this enterprise, but to adhere to the noble sentiment that inspired its founder." He understood that Herzl introduced into the Jewish world the idea that Zionism is in the first instance a matter of human character.

Einstein did not know much of Jewish tradition, but he appreciated what the Jewish past might offer to the Jewish present. He therefore sought eagerly to obtain knowledge and information from scholars in the Hebrew language and in Jewish literature. A friend of mine, who is religious, once said that Einstein had no sense for religious problems. I asked Einstein what was his attitude toward religion, and he formulated it in his simple creative manner, as follows: "Certainly, I am religious, for I am always conscious of an absolute dependence and yet I am comfortable in that feeling."

In a preface which he wrote to a Hebrew translation of the theory of relativity, Einstein revealed how much he appreciated the Hebrew language. In that preface he said: "The appearance of my booklet in the language of our fathers fills me with particular joy. It indicates the transformation that this language has undergone. It is no longer limited to expressing matters pertaining to our nation for the use of our people, but is capable of embracing everything that is of interest to mankind. It constitutes an important factor in our striving toward independence."

Toward the end of World War I, I had the pleasure of speaking with Einstein about Zionism and of gaining his support for Zionist activity. At that time only the specialists among his colleagues knew of his scientific accomplishments, but the great mass of laymen knew nothing of his unique importance. A certain incident brought me to Einstein who was at the time warming up to the Zionist idea only gradually and after long deliberation. He joined the movement when he felt that it was actually a matter of a struggle for spiritual freedom, for human rejuvenation, and when he became convinced that the conquest of Eretz Israel for the

Jewish people was a conquest through labor and that the movement was free from tendencies of profiteering and exploitation.
Later he learned of the Arab problem. When opponents of Zionism urged him to investigate whether the Jewish "invasion" did
not harm the Arabs who lived in Palestine, he retorted, alluding
to a saying of Goethe's, as follows: "The Jewish people must live,
and no one can prevent it from exercising its right to live. To live
is to do injustice. We shall see to it that we do as little injustice
as possible, but nobody can expect us to pursue this endeavor to
the point of self-annihilation."

An experience I had with Einstein is revealing of his attitude
toward the Zionist Organization. I received a lengthy telegram
from Dr. Weizmann in which he requested that I induce Einstein
to go to the United States in the interests of the Keren Hayesod
and the Hebrew University. Einstein declined the invitation. He
was then not yet connected with Palestine so closely that he should,
for example, fully appreciate the importance of the University.
He preferred to work in the interest of educational possibilities for
Jewish youth in Eastern European countries. I did not succeed in
refuting his arguments and I already thought that I would have
to send to Weizmann Einstein's negative reply. Before parting, I
said: "I do not believe that we can weigh arguments against each
other in this case. Our work can succeed when all of us are moved
by a new spirit of national discipline. I too know only part of
Dr. Weizmann's reasons. I do not know what he would say to
you in my place. But I know that he has been entrusted by the
Jewish people with the responsibility of realizing the Zionist program. Not Dr. Weizmann, as an individual, but the president of
the Zionist Organization has ordered me to persuade you to go to
America, and I have the right to expect that you subordinate your
considerations to Dr. Weizmann's decision." Einstein replied:
"You are right. If it were left to every one to behave according
to his own desires, it would be impossible to accomplish any united
enterprise. Tell Dr. Weizmann that I accept the invitation."

June, 1939

Chaim Weizmann

by DOROTHY THOMPSON

IT IS A GREAT personal pleasure to me to welcome Chaim Weizmann here, in America. He is known to the world as a great Zionist leader, but for many people he is still another personality. He is a great chemist, a great scientist. We know him as the brilliant director of the British Admiralty Laboratories in the last war, when his scientific contributions to the Allied Victory were enormous. About the origin of these contributions we can learn from an interesting passage in the memoirs of David Lloyd George: "As Chairman of the Munitions of War Committee I took this matter greatly to heart. (The matter of acetone for cordite for munitions.) While I was casting about for some solution of the difficulty, I ran against the late C. P. Scott, Editor of the Manchester Guardian. He was a friend in whose wisdom I had implicit faith. I told him of my problem and that I was on the look-out for a resourceful chemist who would help me to solve it. He said: 'There is a remarkable professor of chemistry in the University of Manchester willing to place his services at the disposal of the State. I must tell you, however, that he was born somewhere near the Vistula, and I am not sure on which side. His name is Weizmann.' Scott could guarantee that whatever the country of origin, Weizmann was thoroughly devoted to the cause of the Allies, that the one thing he really cared about was Zionism, and that he was convinced that in the victory of the Allies alone was there any hope for his people. I knew Mr. Scott to be one of the shrewdest judges of men I had ever met. The world renown of his great paper had been built up on the soundness of his judgment—of men as well as of affairs. But I also trusted his patriotism implicitly. Pacifist as he was, he believed in the essential jus-

Address delivered at a dinner in honor of Dr. Chaim Weizmann in New York on June 10th, 1942.

tice of our intervention in this war. I took his word about Professor Weizmann and invited him to London to see me. I took to him at once. He is now a man of international fame. He was then quite unknown to the general public, but as soon as I met him I realized that he was a very remarkable personality. His brow gave assurance of a fine intellect and his open countenance gave confidence in his complete sincerity. I told him that we were in a chemical dilemma and asked him to assist us. I explained the shortage in wood alcohol and what it meant in munitionment. Could he help? Dr. Weizmann said he did not know, but he would try. He could produce acetone by a fermentation process on a laboratory scale, but it would require some time before he could guarantee successful production on a manufacturing plane.

" 'How long can you give me?' he asked. I said: 'Cannot give you very long. It is pressing.' Weizmann replied: 'I will go at it night and day.'

"In a few weeks' time he came to me and said: 'The problem is solved.' "

Now it is very rare that a man at the same time should be a distinguished scientist and a great political leader. But as I see it, the two activities have very much in common. Ordinary people think that wheat is wheat and rubber is rubber. But a great scientist thinks: Wheat is rubber and rubber is wheat — we can change things. In other words he asks himself: What are the basic chemical ingredients of everything; how can this or that be broken down to its basic chemical ingredients and then reassembled, in in another form. He disintegrates in order to re-integrate.

Now that is exactly what a great politican has to do. Conventional political leaders believe they have to take a nation or a society as it exists. Germans are Germans and Jews are Jews, for instance. But a scientific mind will ask: What are Germans and what are Jews? Are Jews a race doomed to wander the earth? That is a mystic view. Are Jews a semi-religious, semi-racial society of

merchants, bankers, lawyers, doctors and peddlers, whose fate it
is to continue such a weighted life forever?

Are Jews a race, a religion, or a destiny? And, if their fate up
to now is unhappy, how can the elements in Jewry be reassembled
to a happier destiny—and in what does a happy destiny lie?

And as a chemist goes back to the atom, to the smallest element
in any composition, such a scientifically minded political leader
goes back to the human entities in his society and asks: What can
I do with them? How can I re-group them?

Now it is also characteristic of the scientific mind that it deals,
not with what ought to be, but with what is. He does not ask
himself should there be Jews—he knows there are Jews. He does
not say, "Let us settle them where they are," when he knows that
where they are may be in a very precarious ghetto, living as a
strictly segregated minority, or floating around. Observing the
status of millions of Jews in the world, the rhyme of Gelett Burgess
comes to mind:

"I wish that my room had a floor,
    I don't so much care for a door,
    But this floating around without touching the ground.
    Is getting to be quite a bore."

So Weizmann, as a scientist, studied the elements of the Jewish
people or Jewish society. He had plenty of chance to study it.
For he was born in the Russia of the Tsars—that is to say in a
ghetto—he studied in the free Swiss Republic, and then came
the whole world.

So he knows all types and situations of this species of human
being called the Jew. He knows the specific and the generic
features.

But in studying the Jews all around the world, he had to study
something else: he had to study the surrounding world. Again
he was using the scientific approach. A scientist in his laboratory
makes experiments in a test tube. But when he starts to build an
industry around his inventions he has to study outside conditions of

the world in which he places it. And even in the test tube the reactions are different in one solution and in another.

If you ask me why the Zionist politics that started as a Utopian dream became realistic in the last twenty years, one must answer: Because they have had such realistic leadership. Realism is not the stupidity of that conservative attitude that cannot envisage change. It is action based upon a correct analysis of factors. Weizmann's correct analysis in the last war was that only the British Empire could give a chance to Zionism. His correct analysis in this war is that only democracy and political freedom can give a chance to Zionism. So he forgives and forgets the nuisances and setbacks that the Palestine Jews have had in the last twenty years. Rome was not built in a day, and neither is a Jewish state.

And, as a chemist knows that there are processes that can only be achieved step by step, one process after the other, so a good politican knows that history is a logical process taken step by step.

When Weizmann came over this time, and talked with many important Americans, he did not speak of Zionism. He spoke of ways of winning the war. Now we are in this process, at this step. Even when he was asked: Why don't you speak about Palestine, he said, with a smile, "I'll come back." Se he announced that there is another step to be taken.

Now, the scientist is also skeptical regarding over-all solutions of problems. Dr. Weizmann, for instance, knows that there is more than one way to make synthetic rubber—and that there is more than one way of using corn; for instance, you can eat it. You can also drink it; and you can also make tires out of it. Strange as that may seem that is also true of the Jews. The quarrel between Zionists and assimilationists has always seemed to me to be quite unscientific quarrel. The scientist, for instance, finds the transmutation of corn into rubber more exciting and interesting than its transformation into blood and muscle by way of the digestive tract.

But, that doesn't mean that he wants to starve men and nations of corn, or that ordinary corn is something inferior. The whole world today consists of nations and assimilationists. Every country has assimilated vast numbers of individuals from other nations, and yet the nations have remained.

From an American viewpoint, it is a good idea to have an asylum, and more than an asylum, a homeland for the Jews in this world. But it is not the whole thing: it does not suggest that we want to send all Jews to Palestine, any more than we wish to send all Europeans back to Europe—for if we did we would have nothing left by Americans.

But for assimilationists, there is a certain necessity: the assumption that those people to be assimilated are equal. Critics of the Jewish race have often said: the Jews are not constructive; they have no nation-building qualities. And for them the construction of Palestine is proof of equality. It is a proof that the Jews, given soil of their own, held by them as a nation, possess the same characteristic as other civilian-building peoples who have the same opportunity.

I do not assume that all these characteristics are good. The concept of nationality has been both creative and destructive, and rabid nationalism is the curse of the world. But here again, I have confidence in Dr. Weizmann, and in his illuminated and scientific mind. For if a community is reborn it has the chance to avoid many mistakes that have become historical in other nations. The Palestinian state has not been created by conquest, which is expropriation of the soil of others. It has been created by purchase and political agreement. The political agreement rose out of an attempt to make good some of the wrongs that had been inflicted and to reward benefits that had accrued from the last war.

And as this was the situation in the last war, it is much greater in this one; for the evils inflicted on the Jews and the benefits received from them to the democratic world are both incomparably greater.

So, Dr. Weizmann is in a happy position. For the unrolling of the Jewish question on a gigantic scale demands a logical solution to it. That solution must be either extermination, assimilation, or nationhood—or a combination of the last two.

Now, in considering Palestine, and looking at it as a Gentile, there is a definite Palestinian contribution, not only to the Jews but to the Gentile world. It concerns the question of *Lebensraum*. The antiquated ideas of the aggressor nations are that the areas of the earth must be redistributed on a sort of quota system in order to assure everybody equal prosperity. But the scientist sees that prosperity does not depend upon how much each person has, but how that soil is used. The Jews, in building up Palestine, have actually created more *Lebensraum* for the Arabs and not less. For they have taken parched, eroded, and exhausted soil, and by scientific methods of soil rebuilding and soil conservation have *created* the land on which they live. And that is a real contribution to the solving of even larger problems than the Jewish problem. It means for us, that the earth as a whole is not over-populated but under-populated and that every nation can get its vital space without exterminating or enslaving other nations. Dr. Weizmann's chemistry goes into his politics as well. Palestine was a land flowing with milk and honey, centuries ago, in the annals of the Old Testament. For epochs it lay waste. And it is again a land flowing with milk and honey in the hands of the Jewish colonists. If the Arabs, instead of fighting the Jews in Palestine, would emulate their soil conservation methods, they would have more land than they know what to do with, and could create a blooming Arab civilization.

And it has not only been science, but the historical social sense of the Jews that has recreated Palestine. The experiment has proved what every religious society, such as the Catholic monastic system or the Mormons, learned long ago in the field of economics, namely that cooperative organization is the creator of individual prosperity. They have also proved that there is no logical cleavage between town and country. The agricultural economy of Palestine is created by urban-minded people and is the better for it.

July, 1942

Essence of Revisionism

by MARIE SYRKIN

THE GREATER interest in Revisionism in the United States is not due solely to the recent arrival of Jabotinsky. Naturally the brilliance and great personal charm of the *Fuehrer* are compelling factors but there are profounder causes at work which should be faced openly. Psychologically, the moment is a propitious one for the man on a white horse. Precisely because Jews have never felt so desperate, so helpless, so terrified as today, the sound of sabre-rattling and trumpet-blasts is welcome. The sabre may not cut; the blast may frighten nothing more deadly than sheep, but the gesture is an emotional release and a defiance. We remember how in November, 1936 a few hundred Polish Jews, without passports, visas or money, began to march on foot from Warsaw to Palestine. Their sole equipment for the proposed pilgrimage through the lands of Europe and the Orient was a commander-in-chief, uniforms, flags, and a rallying-cry, "Awaken Israel." The would-be redeemers of Zion were dispersed by the Polish police a few miles outside of Warsaw and no more has been heard of them or their enterprise. But who does not understand the anguish from which this fantastic "redemption-march" sprang? Who does not understand their ultimate readiness to cease reckoning with reality entirely when its pressure became too intolerable? The over-burdened spirit takes refuge in illusion, a world of dreams which gives a kind of logic to the unbearable confusion of existence.

In a sense, it is a similar mood that Revisionism can now capitalize. In a world-crisis which has engulfed not only the Jewish people but nation after small nation, when Zionism like every other liberal movement is fighting for its life, Jabotinsky appears in the gloom and brightens the air with slogans: A Jewish State on both sides of the Jordan; Jews to be shipped into Palestine at once not by the thousands, but by the millions; a Jewish army; and a few other trifles! Naturally there is no Zionist anywhere who does not desire the largest possible immigration into the largest possible area of the Jewish homeland. But those who have actually assumed the day-by-day struggle for the economic and political entrenchment of Zionism cannot afford the luxury of tumultuous and provocative battle-cries. Those who are engaged in the disheartening inch-by-inch labor of realizing the maximum attainable within given conditions, cannot indulge in sonorous maximalist demands. However, it is obvious that shouting for the immediate admission of a "million" Jews has a greater romantic appeal than bleak negotiations about actual immigration certificates. The gentleman on the platform who bravely proclaims, "Let them all in," is bound to strike a sympathetic chord in even the most sober. The simulation even of non-existent might may be a comfort when the sense of impotence grows too oppressive.

In the March issue of *Hadar* (Revisionist Youth monthly) are some verses which the Editors characterize as "a consummate expression of the spirit of *Betar*" (Revisionist Youth Organization.) This apparently definitive formulation of the Betar creed urges: "To your tents, oh Jews! To your guns, tanks, bombers." It also advises "Spit back with machine-guns, and they will respect you; Spit back with air-bombs and they will admire you." It closes with the exhortation, "Answer them with steel, answer them with fire, answer them with death—that is the language they understand."

Disregarding for the moment the ethical level of this utterance, one can readily see that in certain moods of despair and rebellion against repeated outrage, youth and perhaps its elders can be won by the counsel of despair to mythical "tanks" and "bombers." And it is not hard to understand the impulse which made the brown-shirted members of Betar stand in military formation before "Commander-in-chief" Jabotinsky, when he recently "inspected" his "troops" with all due soldierly precision

in the Capitol Hotel in New York City. Not that the martial fanfare of Brith Trumpeldor is a novelty. In Poland, "dress reviews,"
"militia manoeuvers," uniforms complete in every detail from
spurs to epaulettes, had long been the order of the day. There
used to be only one hitch in the pomp and circumstance of
Jabotinsky's "dress parades." The Polish government would permit the Revisionists to dress up in fancy uniforms, but it forbade
the use of arms, so that even the redoubtable *Kazin* (Colonel)
boasted neither sword nor pistol.

Of course, there is nothing humorous about Jewish weakness.
The Revisionist mimicry of a force which it does not possess is
tragic rather than funny. One might even go so far as to say that
if the aping of military attitudes were eventually to lead to
greater strength, Jews could well afford to appear temporarily
ridiculous. Furthermore, one may grant that the instinctive liberal
repugnance to everything that savors of militarism can in the
present hour no longer be considered as an absolute criterion. If
its magniloquent phrases contained either a record of achievement,
or a promise of success, Revisionism would have the right to say
to Zionism, to Jewry, that the era of Hitler is no time for a stubborn adherence to noble ideologies.

On the basis of the record, has Revisionism this right? What
is the truth?

Revisionism began as an opposition group within the Zionist
movement, being founded by Jabotinsky in 1923. In 1935, the
Revisionists left the Zionist Organization and formed what they
call the New Zionist Organization. Their program has varied little
in these years. They started *crescendo* and have maintained their
vocal pitch consistently. However, these years have provided an
opportunity for discovering just what Revisionism means when it
proceeds to activities other than flag-waving.

First of all, what are Revisionist political achievements? What
have these clamorers for a "Jewish State on both sides of the
Jordan," these fiery denouncers of Great Britain, done to advance Jewish independence in Palestine? It is hardly necessary to

dwell on the obvious fact that only a politically irresponsible group could permit itself the pleasure of 100% slogans, happen what may. The "maximalism" of the Revisionists has not brought the Jewish State any nearer; it has, however, provided ample ammunition to the Arabs and opponents of Zionism in Great Britain. There has been more than one time in the tragic tension of the past decade, when political Zionism was seriously jeopardized by the uncontrolled vaporings of the Revisionists.

At this point, it may be well again to remember that even Herzl—to whose Zionist will there were certainly no bounds—substituted the tamer "publicly and legally assured home in Palestine" for "Jewish State," when he became a responsible political leader. And it might also be salutary to recall that a signature affixed to the Churchill White Paper of 1922, which separated Transjordania from Palestine, is that of Vladimir Jabotinsky.

Yet it would be a mistake to assume that Revisionist contributions to the political front have been solely an excess of zeal and lung-power. They have more substantial achievements to their credit.

In 1934, against the expressed will of the Jewish Agency, the Revisionists circulated a world petition on the question of Zionism.

This petition was presented to the Mandates Commission of the League of Nations. As at that time the Revisionists were still theoretically within the Zionist Organization, they committed a flagrant breach of Zionist discipline by this act; but far worse was the "political" result that they achieved with their bold stroke. The Mandates Commission ruled that the Revisionist petition "does not fulfill the conditions of admissibility since it raises claims which are incompatible with the Mandate for Palestine." In other words, thanks to the Revisionists, the world was explicitly informed that a Jewish State was incompatible with the terms of the Mandate. This damaging interpretation had not been volunteered by the Commission. Responsible Zionist leaders had always cautiously refrained from any step likely to precipitate such a pronouncement. The Revisionists, however, managed to secure this signal political defeat by their passion for meaningless gestures.

Time and again, we have been treated to the extraordinary spectacle of these "uncompromising" opponents of the Mandatory Power running to the British Government with requests that Jewish self-government be diminished. In 1937, when Jabotinsky appeared at the session of the Royal Commission held in London, he did not hesitate to request the British Government to liquidate the Jewish Agency, which is the accredited representative of the Jewish people before Great Britain and the world. That is to say, in a crucial moment for Zionism, Jabotinsky's contribution to the Zionist case, carefully constructed and presented by the Jewish Agency, was to question the Agency's competence as a representative body.

Nor is this the only evidence of Revisionist super-patriotism in action. As recently as a month ago (February 1940) the Revisionists in Palestine presented a memorandum to the Government requesting the British to assume the task of regulating employment, and thus deprive the Jewish labor bureaus of this power. In the same memorandum they asked the Government to outlaw strikes. The question of the Revisionist attitude toward organized labor will be considered separately. In this connection, it is important to observe the readiness of the Revisionists to hand over basic Jewish rights, fundamental signs of Jewish autonomy, to the British Administration.

The *Kofer Ha Yishuv* (Self-Defense Fund), the tax assumed by the Jewish community of Palestine and one of the symbols of Jewish self-government in Palestine, has been savagely fought by the Revisionists—again a paradoxical act for these perpetual praters about Jewish "independence."

Another plank in the Revisionists platform is a "Jewish army." Do they not strike heroic poses, and shout *Tel Hai?* Again, what is the actual record? Unfortunately, the three years of disturbances in Palestine have provided us with sufficient samples not only of Revisionist statesmanship but of Revisionist valor.

The extraordinary courage of the *Yishuv* during these years, the evolution of the concept of *Havlaga*—self-restraint—which imposed on the population a policy of active defense against attack but forbade blind retaliation, has by now become legendary. It forms one of the great chapters in human, as well as Jewish history. What was the Revisionist offering to this period? They did not participate in the general self-defense. But when the endurance of the population was strained, Revisionists proceeded to commit a number of wanton terrorist acts. We need not dwell on the immorality of the indiscriminate slaughter of possibly guiltless Arabs. What the Revisionists should have been able to realize, even if they were insensitive to the ethical considerations involved, was that the sole practical result of a Jewish counter-terror would be to inflame all sectors of the Arab population to active hostility and provide the British with legitimate excuses for suppressing the Jewish population as a lawless element. The consistent purity of the Jewish position, as well as its energetic self-defense under every onslaught, was the strongest weapon which the *Yishuv* could forge. It is this weapon which the revisionists attempted to destroy. *"Break Havlaga"* became their slogan. They canonized Shlomo Ben Yossef, the young Revisionist who was executed in 1938 for shooting at some passing Arabs from ambush. This same Ben Yossef was held up by Jabotinsky as a model of Jewish heroism to the youth of Brith Trumpeldor, when he "reviewed" them recently in New York. In a sense, the young terrorist is a more suitable saint for Revisionist veneration than the socialist Trumpeldor whom they adopted, because the epic defense of Tel Hai by Trumpeldor was *opposed* by Jabotinsky. This apostle of action declared to the *Vaad Leumi* (1920), "if we shall, ourselves, rise to defend our settlements, we shall certainly fail!" But now characteristically enough, the Revisionist war-cry is *Tel-Hai*.

To every critical period in Palestine, the Revisionist contribution has been merely provocative demonstration. From 1929, when they precipitated Arab riots by their senseless March to the Wailing Wall, till 1939 when they imperilled *Havlaga*, their acts have consistently jeopardized the safety of the country. Yet who can compare the personal heroism or the national vision of the workers who built Hanita in the midst of the disturbances with that of the irresponsible element which shot at an Arab bus, or planted a bomb in an Arab market-place?

What else have the Revisionists done to further the actual progress of Zionism? They roar for mass-immigration; their deeds, however, are of a character best calculated to render a large influx of Jews into Palestine impossible. It is a truism by now to point out that the absorptive capacity of Palestine depends on the continuing entrenchment of the population in the economic life of the country. If unemployed Jewish workers wander through the colonies, it is obvious that there will be less opportunity for other Jewish workers to enter. It is equally obvious that the most persuasive argument for maximal political elements is the solidity and extent of Jewish constructive achievement in Palestine. The 57 new settlements founded by Jewish workers in the past three terrible years have an infinitely greater political significance than a swash-buckling parade. Yet the Revisionists have done their utmost to undermine the position of the Jewish worker in Palestine. "Breaking" organized labor has been as holy a Revisionist purpose as breaking the *Havlaga*. Jabotinsky's notorious "Yes, destroy" has provided Revisionism with one slogan by which it punctiliously abides. The Revisionist explanation of their typically fascist attacks on organized labor is that as devoted nationalists they oppose the "class struggle." The miracles of national reconstruction wrought by the "class struggling" *khalutz* require no elaboration. It would be an impertinence to rehearse the *khalutz* history of sacrifice and martyrdom for the national ideal. But Revisionist strike-breaking, Revisionist alliances with the most reactionary elements among Jewish employers, bear examination. What happened in 1934 in Kfar Saba is an excellent illustration of the brilliance of Revisionist tactics. Kfar Saba belonged to a group of colonists from whom the Histadrut had secured the employment of Jewish workers. Even though 18% of the workers of the colony were not members of the Histadrut, they abided by its decisions. Then there appeared on the scene the "super-nationalist" members of Brith Trumpeldor and concluded separate agreements with the employers. The first result of this strategy was the immediate "liberation" of the colony from "Marxian" workers. But this bit of social progress was followed by another act of liberation. It dawned on the colonists that Arabs were even cheaper than strike-breaking Revisionists. Kfar Saba became free of Jewish workers till the riots. When their groves began to burn, the colonists re-discovered the merits of Jewish labor.

Despite such demonstrations of the net "national" gains achieved through strike-breaking, the Revisionists continue cheerfully in their attack on the Jewish worker. At present we have the example of *Gan Litvinsky,* one of the largest orange groves in Palestine. Till 1936, the Brothers Litvinsky had employed only Arabs. After the outbreaks, when work became dangerous, contracts were given to the agricultural department of the Histadrut. Recently, the Histadrut brought evidence showing that it was losing one cent on every box of oranges. During the negotiations with the Brothers Litvinsky, Revisionist strike-breakers stepped in and underbid the Histadrut by a considerable sum. Perhaps after a while the Brothers Litvinsky, with the able help of the Revisionists, will be able to return to the idyllic, pre-1936 era, when the still more economical Arabs were at their disposal. Do the Revisionists really believe that by lowering the standard of living, by destroying the cardinal principle of Jewish labor without which Zionism is doomed, they are creating conditions conducive to "mass-immigration"?

The Revisionists have always clamored for "arbitration" of labor disputes, yet when Rutenberg, as President of the Vaad Leumi, ruled in favor of the Histadrut workers in the *Gan Litvinsky* conflict, they refused to abide by his decision. This, despite their previously professed admiration for the "strong" figure of Rutenberg.

Since the war, a General Labor Bureau has been established in which all Zionist workers' groups are represented (Histadrut, Hapoel Hamizrachi, Poale Agudath Israel, General Zionist). The function of this Labor Bureau is to apportion work to applicants. The Revisionists have refused to participate in the Bureau, but they clamor endlessly that they are wronged in the apportionment of working days.

The Revisionist record is uniformly one of sabotage and destruction. These devotees of "unity" and "discipline" have repeatedly broken the discipline of the Zionist Organization and the Jewish Agency by irresponsible, unauthorized action with invariably disastrous results. These would-be builders of Zion have carried on active propaganda against the national funds; they have interfered with collections; they have broken Jewish National Fund boxes on the grounds that these were "socialist" because the land purchased belonged in perpetuity to the Jewish people. They have set up rival funds of their own, and then have had the consummate effrontery to complain that *Keren Kayemeth* and *Keren Hayesod* were not supplying them with enough cash. Their culpable mismanagement and shameful exploitation of *Aliya Bet* (the smuggling of refugees into Palestine) has become notorious.

"Breaking" Jewish labor; breaking Havlaga; breaking the Zionist Organization; breaking the National Funds; breaking "unity"—that is the sum total of the Revisionist achievement. Even some Revisionists have begun to rebel against this eternal chaos. The "National Federation of Workers," the Organization of Revisionist workers in Palestine has issued a bulletin in which it accuses the Revisionist officials of deliberately fostering labor disputes: "All their (Revisionist leaders') struggle has been limited to fostering competition and strife with regard to the working day."

However, in order to savor the full fragrance of Revisionism one has to go to its chief spokesman. Did not Jabotinsky himself proclaim that a state must be built "on slavery, filth, and blood?" Did not Abba Achimair, hailed by Jabotinsky as "friend and teacher" urge: "We must create groups for action; to exterminate the Histadrut physically; they are worse than Arabs," and still better: "It is by the amount of bloodshed that you can evaluate a revolution, and not by the beautiful ideas for which it is shed." And finally, did not Uri Zwi Greenberg, writing in the Revisionist paper *Hazit Haam*, give as his journalistic *credo*: "holy falsehood"; "smear it on thick"; "exaggerate as much as possible"; "Start scandals. Say they are thieves. This will reverberate both in Palestine and in the Diaspora."

With two editions of "Mein Kampf" in circulation it is hardly necessary to point out what spirit these quotations breathe. In method and ideology Revisionism is viciously fascist lacking the sole asset of fascism—might. A movement which is both provocative and impotent is dangerous only to the cause it advocates. Despite its ambitious profession, there is only one field in which Revisionism has made an effective display of strength. It has shown a suicidal energy in attempting to destroy hard-won achievements of Zionism. This spirit must not be allowed to infect American Jewry. As long as actual work may be done in and for Palestine, spectacular or unspectacular, we must not retire to that asylum of illusion where spurious Napoleons brawl with each other.

April, 1940

Partition—Again?

by HAYIM GREENBERG

THE RUMOR mills of Cairo grind ceaselessly and turn out a continuous stream of reports concerning vital military and political questions. By this time, however, world opinion has taken the measure of the information from the Egyptian capital and regards it with well merited skepticism. Nevertheless, this does not mean that political gossip datelined Cairo is always entirely without foundation. Some reports, at least, must be regarded as reflecting proposals and plans concerning which official circles desire to obtain a preliminary reaction of public opinion. It is possible, therefore, that the Cairo reports of the past several months concerning a British plan for a new partition scheme in Palestine constitute trial balloons released for some such purpose.

The burden of these rumors is that Britain has reached a final, "definitive" decision to grant the Jews a State or Commonwealth in a part of Palestine, and either establish an independent Arab State in the remainder or annex it to a neighboring Arab State. One cannot say with certainty, of course, whether such a plan exists or, if it exists, how "definitive" a stage it has reached. It is significant, however, that an important non-Anglo-Saxon government has become aware, through its own channels, of the possibility of such a decision. It would be foolhardy on our part to ignore such a report, coming from several quarters.

At the present time, no serious discussions are being held with Jews concerning Palestine's future: we are told that there is no time, for "more important and greater matters" are at stake; but when the time comes we shall be treated "with full justice." As a result, it is by no means impossible that one fine morning we shall be faced, if not with a *fait accompli,* then with the following quasi-ultimatum: either the Jews accept a promise of national self-government in a part of Palestine designated in advance—or the whole question will have to come up for reconsideration, with unpredictable consequences. If the "partition" question is being discussed so widely and so passionately in Palestine today, it is undoubtedly because certain groups in the Jewish community have a "premonition"—based quite probably on better information than we have here—that a new partition plan is more than a mere possibility. Under the circumstances, it would surely be bad policy to remain unprepared for a new partition proposal, or, on the other hand, to allow those who are to decide the issue to remain without any indication of Jewish attitudes on so vital a matter.

When the partition plan was first broached in 1937 there were some among us who hailed it enthusiastically, but even they demanded more generous frontiers and better conditions for the envisioned Jewish state. On the other hand there were categorical opponents. A third group was bitterly opposed to the plan, but felt compelled to accept it because they saw no better prospect under the political circumstances of those times. The Peel Plan, as it was then known, was viewed by this group as an integral part of a general scheme to protect the world from the danger of impending war by a series of appeasement maneuvers at the expense of the weaker and smaller nations. In a sense, the Partition Plan was a precursor of Munich. Whatever one felt about the appeasement policy, it was plain that, at that time, it was the dominant political factor. Jews knew very well that their opinion could have no effect as against it. But today the circumstances are entirely different. Appeasement has long been discredited, and motives which compelled a number of us in 1937 and in 1938 to acquiesce against their will in the project to partition Palestine no longer have any foundation. Today it is reasonable to assume that, after Victory, such Great Powers as the United States, Soviet Russia, and Great Britain will not need to yield to blackmail threats on the part of their enemies or certain of their questionable allies. From this point of view, the political situation should not lead Jews to resign the full measure of their just political and territorial demands in Palestine, as might have been the case before the war.

On the other hand, a mere dogmatic insistence on abstractly formulated demands on the part of Jews would be totally ineffective as a policy. We cannot come to the Powers and say simply: Give us what is ours by historic right. One need not deny the significance of what we call "historic rights" to understand that, even when recognized, they have only a conditional value. The traditions of the Jewish religion may obligate the orthodox to believe that Jews should have much more than Palestine in its present limits, or even with Trans-Jordan added. When God made his pact with Abraham, he specifically promised him the whole land between the Nile and the Euphrates. But such Divine credentials are obviously something apart from the criteria which must govern political decisions in the present epoch. Pious Jews will readily make peace with the idea that there are promises which only the Almighty can fulfill, in ways which no man can presume to dictate. And if our historic rights are to be considered from a non-theological viewpoint, then one faces immediately a series of embarrassing questions concerning the delimitation of the area which we are historically entitled to regard as Jewish. What, historically, is "the whole of Palestine"? Is "Galilee of the Gentiles" really part of it or not? Is Akaba (Ezion-Gever) an organic part of the historic Jewish State or not? To what extent is Trans-Jordan historically Jewish? How long must a region have been part of the Kingdom of the Jews, or been populated predominantly by Jews, to be considered a part of Palestine, within its historic frontiers? Another question, also, must be faced. What would be our position today if there had remained no more than 100,000 or 150,000 Jews in the world? Would we then also have the right to the whole of Palestine within its historic boundaries, or would we have to lower our demands? This hypothetical figure is not chosen completely at random, for this is approximately the number of Icelanders, for whom an independent state has recently been set up. Nor is it an altogether inconceivable assumption. The kind of world we live in has been such that it is far from impossible that we should have been reduced to such a number. Of what value would our historic rights have been in such a case?

I have raised such questions in order to emphasize the principle that we cannot base demands upon abstractions, upon dogmatic claims of justice; nor can we make a fetish of boundaries extending to every section of the Palestine area to which, on certain hypotheses, we can claim historic rights. Our claims must be based chiefly upon our need, upon the actual and the potential migratory pressure of large numbers of Jews, desiring to build a home in that country which we began to resettle two generations ago. The area to which we are "entitled" in Palestine must be measured primarily by the extent of Jewish needs, both those which are apparent today and those which may become apparent tomorrow. It is with regard to these needs that we must be prepared to discuss proposals of partition in Palestine.

*   *   *

From one point of view, the end of the war will find us much weaker politically than we would have been, let us say, in 1941, before the mass slaughter of the largest Jewish communities in Europe. Millions of Jews have been slain—and one of the results of that holocaust is that former sources of Jewish immigration to Palestine have been drastically drained. There is no longer the same population pressure, the same search for emigration outlets as existed a few years ago. The political consequences of this loss may be grave. In regard to Palestine, the millions of Polish, Lithuanian, and Rumanian Jews, with their dynamic urge towards Palestine, were a greater political force, despite their impoverishment and oppression at home, than the five million comparatively wealthy and influential American Jews, without such a mass movement towards rehabilitation in Palestine.

It should surprise no one therefore if we hear officially the argument which has already been voiced privately both by Englishmen and Americans that, unhappily, there is no longer the same necessity for a large area to absorb homeless or impoverished Jews as existed several years ago. It will be suggested that considering the numbers of immigrants who may have to be provided for, it will not be necessary to have the whole of Palestine. We must be prepared to answer, therefore, "for how many Jews" do we wish to have Palestine.

If we may judge by reports of the number of Jews found in cities liberated by the Red Army, there have remained, literally speaking, only one in a city and two in a clan. Of course, one need not be a convinced and thoroughgoing Zionist to favor the speedy, systematic resettlement in Palestine of the great majority of Jews who will have survived the Nazi occupation. The reconstruction of Jewish communities in Eastern and Southern Europe and even in certain parts of Central and Western Europe will be so difficult and complex an undertaking that, for nine out of ten Jews in Europe, immigration to Palestine would be the most rational and constructive solution. Psychologically too, there will be the unwillingness to remain in places where such indescribable horrors and such deep humiliation have been experienced. And yet even if the bulk of all Jewish survivors in those parts of Europe are resettled in Palestine, it would be unwarranted optimism to assume that large numbers will be involved. We shall be fortunate if, including the Jews of Hungary and Roumania, there will be one million to admit to Palestine. If this is what we mean by the need of Jews for Palestine, we cannot argue the existence of a very great population pressure—a fact which may very easily play into the hands of groups interested, for one reason or another, in partitioning Palestine.

*   *   *

But Zionism can never accept this criterion of our need for Palestine. Zionism was not created as a result of the Nazi invasion of Europe, and it will not have fulfilled its mission by providing a new home for the Nazi victims. The unique Jewish problem, which Zionism analyzes, whose potentialities it prognosticates, and for which it offers a practical solution, is not restricted to any land or to specific social conditions. Zionism offers a general analysis and prognosis which, in principle, may be applied to all countries where Jews live as small and easily distinguishable minorities—in short to the whole "exile." However bitter our feelings towards Germany, it would be a great error on our part to regard the cruel devastation wreaked upon us in the past few years as a specifically German phenomenon. The slaughter of several million Jews by Germany is not merely an incident in the criminal history of the Germans, or a result of a unique tension between Jews and Germans. It could never have happened if the seeds of the same complex had not been widespread outside German frontiers as well, and if there had not been some specific tension between Jews and non-Jews everywhere in the world.

This does not mean that we may look for massacres and violent persecution in the future in every land where we live. It does mean that latent anti-Semitism is far greater than its manifestations, and that, under conditions over which Jews have very little control, the chronic disorder is liable to break out in the acute form. Nobody can predict the next outbreak of this perennial disease, but the long, tragic story of "Israel among the Nations" gives us every right to a high degree of skepticism about the future. No reasonable man believes that the Allied victory will solve all the world's problems; and so long as major problems remain unsolved, occasions may arise when we shall again be first among those who suffer. Not England, nor the United States, nor Russia can guarantee that in fifteen or twenty years, certain parts of the Jewish people may not find themselves in such a position that the opportunity to be received in a Jewish State would be highly welcome.

When we speak of conditions capable of causing a need for Palestine, we cannot think only in terms of such a position as the Nazis created for the Jews in Europe. In fact, Zionism, in its gloomiest prognoses, did not conceive of the possibility of so inhuman a fate. Now, however, the Hitler treatment of the Jews has begun to make people feel that there can be no greater prospect of happiness for a Jew than merely to be let live. But the bulk of Jewish emigration for the past century was not a flight from Hitler slaughter; yet it was caused by real needs and objective compulsions. The same sort of need may very well appear in other parts of the Diaspora. In fact, it already exists in certain countries outside Europe.

Turkey was not occupied by the Nazis, but in recent times it has become practically impossible for the Turkish Jews to remain there. There have been no important changes in Turkish law, which formally still guarantees equal rights for all citizens of the country; but it is perfectly clear that Turkey is determined to get rid of the remainder of its ethnic and religious minorities. Let no one console himself with the thought that the Jewish situation is no worse than that of the Greeks or Armenians: they, too, by all the signs, will have to find some place to emigrate after the war —the Greeks probably to liberated Greece, and the Armenians to Soviet Armenia.

It is quite apparent that the situation of substantial Jewish communities in Arabic-speaking North Africa, in Iraq, and particularly in Yemen, as well as in the non-Arab Moslem country of Iran, has also been deteriorating. It is true, of course, that these are countries where outside Powers can easily be called upon to see to it that Jews are treated "equitably." But the social tension between Jew and non-Jew in such places is so acute that, regardless of governmental assurances given under international pressure, the Jewish situation will long be unbalanced. Nationalism is on the increase in those countries and is taking an ever more chauvinistic turn. As a result, the Jews, with their distinctive mode of living, their special economic functions, and their "affinity" for western culture and civilization, are more and more regarded as a foreign element.

Thus, even today, the number of probable candidates for resettlement in Palestine is much greater than the number of Jews who will survive in Europe. Only a prophet, capable of foreseeing whether or not other countries will be visited by social catastrophes for generations to come, could possibly give us assurance that Jews elsewhere may not find themselves in a similar situation in the course of time.

From its very beginning Zionism never concerned itself solely with providing a place to receive Jews emigrating under the pressure of acute anti-Semitism. From the days of Herzl its aim was formulated as "A Jewish State for those Jews in various countries who *cannot* or *do not wish to be assimilated."* This formulation underscored a dynamic process in Jewish life, arising not only from the need of a refuge for the persecuted and impoverished but also from the need for a congenial environment in which Jews would find it possible to express themselves more spontaneously and more creatively. It is as valid today as it was in 1896; in fact it is probably more appropriate to our situation than ever before.

Our times have not only experienced crueler persecution than the earlier generation, but, in addition, for those Jews who "do not wish to be assimilated," the feeling of frustration grows ever sharper. The forces making for assimilation are much stronger and the power of the Jewish community to resist much weaker than a generation ago. It is obvious that nationalist sentiment and values of culture are much less powerful drives to emigration than economic necessity, or political or social pressure. Yet these are real motives and not mere abstractions, as is attested by the thousands of Jews who came to Palestine from various lands, including America, driven much more by inner than by outer compulsions.

One cannot estimate how many Jews will wish to go to Palestine for "idealistic" reasons of this sort. It depends on how widespread and how strong is the will for national survival among Jews—a factor which can hardly be measured. It will depend also on general conditions in Palestine, as well as in other countries. If living conditions and economic opportunities should substantially improve in Palestine, it may become easier for many, who would like to go to Palestine, to live there undeterred by the "hardships" of a pioneer community. It is by no means impossible, on the other hand, that in the United States, for example, a certain section of our community of five million Jews will find itself disappointed in the economic prospects that it had hoped to enjoy. Many may conceivably be forced to take up a "lower" range of occupations than that they were previously engaged in, or hoped to be engaged in. If, also, the political status of Jewish Palestine should be stabilized, it might encourage many of those who "do not wish to be assimilated" to migrate to Palestine. It is possible therefore to conceive of a situation in which the number of those desiring to immigrate to Palestine for "idealistic" reasons would attain significant proportions.

We come therefore to this conclusion: There is no reason to consider our potential immigrants, particularly with respect to Palestine, as consisting solely of the economically uprooted from war-ravaged Europe. The Palestine problem must be considered not from the point of view of a definite number of Jewish war victims, but from the point of view of a whole people, possessing the will to establish a National Home for itself. Thinking in these terms, it is quite impossible to define today how many individuals will, in the future, find themselves in need of Palestine, whether for economic, political, or "psychological" reasons.

Thus, those who ask us for which Jews we need Palestine, must expect to be informed that we need it for an untold number of anonymous Jews located in places not all of which are presently identifiable. Such a reply would be far from an evasion or a paradox; it is the natural, inevitable expression of the unique problem of the Jews, as we have come to know it over the past two thousand years. We are under no obligation to state categorically "how many Jews" we wish to settle in Palestine, nor whether we can colonize its whole area in a short time with the number of settlers who will have to be cared for on the morrow of victory. It may be that half of Palestine would be sufficient for the European Jews who, at that moment, will be prepared to embark at once for Palestine; but for the whole Jewish people, thinking not in terms of a few years but of a substantial period, the whole of Palestine is not so large that we may light-heartedly contemplate partition. Nobody would be justified in regarding it as "baseless maximalism" or nationalistic caprice, if we demand a *reserve zone* for Jewish colonization in Palestine which we may not be able to settle in the few years immediately following the end of the war.

* * *

This is not a question of ideological stubbornness or of a fetishism of principles. It may be that our views will be very little regarded in the final decision on Palestine's political destiny, that we shall not be consulted, or that we shall be consulted merely for form's sake, so that certain promises made to us by high authority may be technically fulfilled. We may be faced with a situation in which opposition on our part to proposed "solutions" will have no significance, and "obduracy" may ever. become a danger. "All or nothing" may sometimes be a highly successful policy, but may also become an empty gesture leading to fatal results. Thus, a political situation may conceivably arise in which to accept a part of Palestine, with smaller possibilities than we need or think we need, will be the only rational policy for Zionists. But, we must never deceive ourselves about what would be involved in such a decision and never forget what we would sacrifice if we should find ourselves forced to submit to the partition of Palestine.

At the time of the Peel Commission there were some who optimistically calculated that even the restricted area offered us then, if intensively developed, could support millions of Jews. To be sure, this viewpoint could easily be maintained by logic, by selected facts, and particularly by comparisons with highly industrialized and densely populated countries. It would be pointless to argue whether these calculations meant anything or not. These are matters which are proved not by reasoning but by action. *Technologically,* of course, it is quite conceivable that Haifa should become a second Liverpool or New York. Whether it is *historically* possible depends not only upon Jewish skill and energy and industrial ability, but on finding foreign markets for the planned industries. It is within the realm of possibility, to be sure, that, in the course of events, such markets will be found. But to build our political decisions upon this possibility would be exceptionally naive.

It is impossible, therefore, for any Jews to accept with equanimity a proposal whereby enough of Palestine will be cut off to form an Arab State there. If it were merely a question of certain boundary adjustments, of ceding small sections of Palestine to a neighboring Arab State rather than carving out a complete Arab State within Palestine, this might become a basis for negotiations with responsible Jewish bodies in which, under certain circumstances, we should not show ourselves too stubborn. It is not the wholeness of Palestine as a matter of principle in which we are interested. We are concerned rather that in any territorial changes made in Palestine, the section which is set aside for a Jewish State shall be large enough and supplied with sufficient natural resources to satisfy the Jewish need for immigration and colonization, in so far as we can foresee its extent in the near and in the more distant future.

September, 1944

The "Peace" of Judah Magnes

EDITORIAL

IN HIS article entitled *Toward Peace in Palestine* in the January issue of *Foreign Affairs*, Dr. Judah L. Magnes reiterates for the benefit of the educated American his views on the Arab-Jewish question. Engaged in his peace-making mission he would have it known that in this world of fanatics and chauvinists there are still individuals in Palestine who have a sense of political fairness. Both the demand for a Jewish state, he maintains, and the demand for an Arab state in Palestine are wrong: Arabs do not want to be ruled by Jews, and the Jews have rights, too, including the right to come and settle in their National Homeland. What Palestine needs is an Arab-Jewish state, but the Jews must be in the minority.

Dr. Magnes approaches the problem in a peculiar spirit of compromise, arising not out of moral considerations, but out of sheer expediency—as he sees it. This is hardly in keeping with the spirit of the Prophets which Dr. Magnes never tires of invoking. Rather is it a kind of *Realpolitik* garnished with idealistic rhetoric.

The solution propounded by Dr. Magnes seems to be based on the implicit assumption that the Arab people are endowed by the Creator with the inalienable right never to be a minority in any country in which they live, but that, conversely, the Jewish people were destined by God always to be in a minority everywhere. Dr. Magnes does not think it desirable for Palestine to form a separate state, but rather a constituent part of a federation which should include Palestine, Transjordan, Syria and the Lebanon. Within the framework of this federation, Jews may be suffered by the Arabs to settle in Palestine in large enough numbers to form up to fifty percent of the Palestine population—but still constituting a minority in the state as a whole. If, however, the proposed federation does not materialize, the number of Jews permitted to enter Palestine must be limited so as not to encroach on the sacred rights of the Arabs to be in the majority. This has nothing to do with the economic absorptive capacity of Palestine which, Dr. Magnes admits, is larger than is generally supposed and may be large enough to support a population of four million. It is simply that the Jews must never be allowed to become the "dominant" people, but must always remain dependent on the good will of the Arab majority. Such is Dr. Magnes' unique conception of international justice and equality of rights for Jews and Arabs.

Dr. Magnes advocates a bi-national state, but since he does not trouble to explain the meaning of the term, it is to be assumed that he implies a recognized pattern for such a state. But so far there are only three bi-national states in the world: Belgium, Canada and the Union of South Africa (The Swiss confederation is not a tri-national state, but rather a union of twenty-two cantons). None of these countries can serve as a model for Palestine mainly for two reasons: First, they contain distinct territories in which the respective constitutent nationalities are in the majority (as the Flemings in Flanders and the French-Canadians in Quebec); secondly, the question of immigration does not arise in determining the rights of the respective nationalities, as it does in Palestine. In the case of South Africa where the English and the Boers have equal rights, we find a situation none of us would like to see duplicated in Palestine: three quarters of the population, officially designated as "other than white," do not enjoy full civic rights and are *subjects* rather than *citizens.* Thus there is no "classical" pattern for a bi-national state.

But this is not the only point. Dr. Magnes fails to elucidate, how and by whom Jewish immigration—even if it is to be limited with a view to safeguarding the majority status of the Arabs—is to be regulated in the proposed bi-national state. Nor does he make it clear whether the Federal government or the local Palestine government in the proposed Federation is to have jurisdiction over Jewish immigration into Palestine. These are important questions, and, as the solution of the Palestine problem affects the very existence of the Jews as a people, we cannot be content with the vague generalities Dr. Magnes offers.

The most important question, however, is how Dr. Magnes visualizes the realization of his plan. Has he any grounds for believing that this modest Zionist program with its very moderate demands can be put into effect without opposition on the part of the Arabs? Does the safeguarding of the majority status for the Arabs make for peace and do away with the danger of civic strife in Palestine? Nothing of the sort. Even in Dr. Magnes' view there is no chance of a voluntary consent on the part of the Arabs to this scheme, and only the pressure of the "moral and political authority" possessed by England and particularly America can put his peace scheme into practice.

It is to be fervently hoped that the victorious United Nations will be in a position to impose certain "adjustments" in Palestine, as well as in other countries in which old nationality feuds and boundary disputes will have to be settled. But what makes Dr. Magnes think that America and England will be just strong enough to impose his minimum plan and not one which is in harmony with plain justice? Why not assume that the Allies will be in a position to grant all legitimate Arab demands for full sovereignty—subject to the general limitations on sovereignty to be imposed as a guarantee of universal peace and co-operation—in every country with an Arab majority outside of Palestine, but at the same time granting sovereignty to the Jews in Palestine?

Dr. Magnes does not seem to doubt the power of America and England to impose a just settlement. What he does doubt, perhaps subconsciously, is the right of Jews to demand full-fledged nationhood. Such doubt, due to a sense of inferiority with which some Jews are afflicted, may perhaps explain the so-called moderate nature of Dr. Magnes' Zionism. Akhad Ha-am, in whose writings Dr. Magnes is well versed, has a name for it: "Slavery in the guise of Freedom."

February, 1943

The United States and Palestine

by CARL J. FRIEDRICH

F RIENDS OF mind have often asked, "Why are you interested in Palestine?" This is asked of me by non-Jews as well as by Jews. Quite frankly, for a long time I was not interested in Palestine. I am a strong adherent of internationalism; and it seemed to me that Zionism was a form of nationalism, an idea to which my general outlook is opposed, and that I had no particular reason to adopt a different attitude toward Zionism. But things changed, and they changed my own views.

After 1933 I became increasingly concerned in a very personal and direct way with the problem of the Jewish people. It was forced upon my attention day in, day out, week in, week out, in the very real form of persons coming to my office, wanting help in getting settled; letters from the other side of the ocean asking for help in getting to one place of refuge or another. It suddenly began to dawn upon me that the term "home" had a very real, concrete and human significance; that it was not, in other words, the same thing as nationalism in the sense I had thought of it hitherto. It had a markedly different connotation. Then came those exhausting and exasperating conferences of Evian, and those committees and commissions and investigations, all of which ended in complete failure. There came long sessions in the Consulates and Vice-Consulates of Switzerland, France, and England, when one tried to persuade an American consular office once more to grant a visa, and again and again this fact was borne in upon me: that there was no place that one could expect a Jew to go to if he could no longer be in Germany; that there was literally no place for him to go.

That is how I became genuinely concerned with Palestine and

Address delivered at annual JEWISH FRONTIER *dinner, New York, May 10, 1944*

with the work of the Zionist movement. As a result, I devoted
myself for a very considerable period to studying the policy toward
the Jewish National Home in Palestine and toward Zionism. I
have come away with certain definite conclusions, conclusions
which will be presently published as a small book under the title
of "Palestine and Peace: American Policy Toward the Jewish
National Home in Palestine."

* * *

The first of these conclusions is that the American policy
toward the National Home has been essentially a phantom policy.
It has consisted of words unaccompanied by deeds, of verbal sops
thrown to the Jewish electorate in the United States. It started
with the Balfour Declaration and it went on through the years
with Congressional resolutions and Presidential declarations of
sympathy, always worded in the vaguest of terms which could be
cited by anybody for any purpose. That tradition, which dominated the entire period from 1922 to the present, is blamable,
in my opinion, to some extent at least, on the Zionists themselves.

There was too much willingness to let words suffice. I have
been through a great deal of the literature of the various Zionist
organizations and I have got a little bit allergic, to be quite frank,
toward the ever-present inclination to place the most favorable
interpretation upon Presidential declarations and suchlike generalities. It was very natural, to be sure, for the Zionist organizations to be preoccupied with building up the National Home in
Palestine within the existing framework. It is a magnificent
achievement, as Lowdermilk has shown recently and as can be
seen in many other documents, such as the Royal Commission
reports of the British government. Yet in doing so they succumbed to an error very characteristic of people with practical,
craftsmanlike attitudes toward life; they neglected the over-all
political considerations. Although I am still confident that disaster will be averted, the whole activity and effort that the Jewish
people have put into the upbuilding of Palestine is now endan-

gered, and it may all have been for nothing, owing to the fact that political fences were not being mended while the resettlement activity went forward.

The vagueness of United States policy on the Palestine question started with President Wilson's share in the Balfour Declaration. His participation was, in a personal sense, quite real; and yet when one consults the historical record to find out specifically just what was done, he discovers a rather tenuous link. A memorandum was evidently handed to President Wilson by Colonel House together with a mass of other business, which Wilson carried around in his pocket for weeks. Eventually House inquired, "Have you made up your mind regarding what answer you will make?" Wilson replied a month later, "I find in my pocket the memorandum you gave me about the Zionist movement. I am afraid I did not say to you that I concurred in the formula suggested by the other side. I do, and would be obliged if you would let them know it." Such, more or less, was the approach to that unquestionably historic occasion. Yet on March 3, 1919, some months after the issuance of the Declaration, Wilson stated that "the Allied Nations, with the fullest concurrence of our own government and people, are agreed that in Palestine shall be laid the foundations of a Jewish Commonwealth." Where was the evidence for this concurrence of our own government and people? I should think that realistic friends of such a Commonwealth would have wanted to make more certain of their ground. Wilson here, as in the other issues of the peace settlement, fell prey to his inclination to identify his personal views with those of the government and the nation. Besides, what is the constitutional significance of such an informal Presidential participation in establishing the Jewish claim to Palestine? If Zionists had asked themselves that question, they would have been forced to conclude that it does not mean very much; it binds nobody to anything.

Later an attempt was made to remedy that situation. A Joint Congressional resolution was adopted which at least formally put the Congress and the President of the United States on record as approving the Balfour Declaration. But in the Congressional discussions on the 1922 resolution a number of leading Congressmen, including the chairmen of the Congressional committees, stated that this resolution did not bind or commit the United States government to any specific action and that therefore it was an entirely innocuous step to take. If I had been a Zionist at the time, I should have said: "I want this aspect brought out. I want to have our people told that the Congress before adopting the resolution told themselves, 'This does not mean a thing.' It is just a 'sop' thrown to us, and therefore we have to follow it up immediately." In that case, the Anglo-American convention might have become the basis for genuine collaboration with Britain in making the Mandate work.

The resolution presented to Congress this past spring is better, of course, than the 1922 resolution, because at least this resolution says that the government of the United States "shall take appropriate measures," which is far more than the 1922 resolution said. I testified before the House Foreign Affairs Committee in favor of that resolution, but I told the Congressmen that while I was altogether for the resolution and felt they must adopt it, nevertheless I did not think there was much to it unless they faced the policies that that resolution involved. I then proceeded to read six points of policy that it seemed to me were involved in the resolution. Then, because I saw that certain faces were falling around that table, I turned to the chairman, the Honorable Sol Bloom, and said, "Mr. Chairman, I am afraid I am stepping on some people's toes here." He replied, "Professor, you are not stepping on their toes; you are stepping on their necks."

There is no doubt that that was probably the truth; but I am convinced that the United States government and the people of the United States have a real interest in this problem of Palestine and the Jewish National Home in Palestine. And hence we must adopt concrete and practical policies to make it work.

Related to this issue is the second point which I want to make tonight. I feel that Zionists have not brought home to the American public why they should have an interest in Palestine, in the Jewish National Home. Your arguments have tended to be moralizing, not, "You *have* an interest in Palestine," but "You *ought* to have an interest in Palestine." Yet the American people have a clear interest in the matter, and it is up to those of us who see it to show them what it consists of.

What, then, is the interest of American people who are not Jews in the Jewish National Home? I think it is essentially linked to what I consider the key interest of the American people in foreign policy—peace. American foreign policy has always been dominated by the interest in peace, and if you ask the common man, "What do you think American policy should be directed toward?" the answer will be, in nine cases out of ten, "It should be directed toward peace." It is true that Walter Lippmann wants us to have an American policy directed toward survival. Thinking in terms of Old World diplomacy, he looks upon foreign policy as a shield. The American people have never looked upon foreign policy as a shield, but as an arrow to their bows, as a medium for projecting outward the American conception concerning the world.

One of the great things about Wilson was that, for the first time, he projected the underlying conception of American life into the world at large. The depressing thing about the situation today is that somehow that same thing has not as yet happened. Maybe it will not happen. But I for one should be tremendously downcast if the American people should turn from its own conception of foreign policy to the Old World conception of survival. To me, the great thing about the American people has always been that survival was taken for granted. A foreign policy was not necessary to guarantee survival. Such a view was right for Switzerland or Italy, but the United States would survive of itself. But a foreign policy is needed for the building of a democratic world, because that is what peace calls for.

When people talk stuff about peace nowadays they should ask themselves a very simple question: Has there ever been peace without government? Of course, the answer is that there never has been peace without government, and the American people want peace, so they must necessarily seek to establish international government.

Nobody knows better than the Zionists do that peace is impossible without government, because anyone who has studied the history of Palestine under the Mandate must realize that we had civil war in Palestine because we had no government there. The Mandatory government was a patent failure; for whenever civil war breaks out it means that a government has failed.

Very clearly, Zionists are not interested in seeing Palestine independent immediately. I do not see any answer to the problem except for Palestine to become an internationally administered territory; there will be others of that kind in the world. But the tremendous danger is that if we do not get strong international authority, we shall get weak government, and you have seen in the last twenty years what happens when there is weak government: terror and civil war and the breakdown of authority. Therefore, I contend that it is in consonance with American policy toward Palestine, as well as the proper policy for all those who favor the upbuilding of a Jewish Commonwealth in Palestine, that there should be a strong international government. Any other position is self-contradictory.

Thus it seems to me that the relation of Zionism and internationalism is very different from that of nationalism in the usual sense. There is, in any case, a profound difference between the nationalism of small nations and the nationalism of big and imperial nations. Jewish nationalism is like the nationalism of the Swedes, the Swiss, the Danes, none of whom, because they cannot aspire to domination, ever can be truly hostile to international organization; or rather, in this day and age they must be *for* international organization. The small nations of Europe today have become the protagonists of international government. There is no thoughtful Swede or Swiss today who is willing to defend the idea of sovereignty, and nobody should ever use the phrase of "a sovereign Jewish state," because that harks back to a conception of government and of relations between nations which is outmoded. If Zionists continue to think in these terms, they will deprive themselves of the support of the one key group in America and England that are destined to be their friends, the people who are convinced of the importance of international organization and international government.

There is one more point that must be made to round out this picture. It is the relation between democracy and the Jewish National Home in Palestine. I have already alluded to the fact that, in my opinion, American foreign policy is vitally linked to the promotion of democracy throughout the world. When I say "promotion," I do not mean that we should go forth and force democracy upon other people. I could not mean that, because democracy cannot be forced upon any people. But forcing something and not doing anything about it are very far apart, and there are a great many things between that can and should be done.

I find that Gentiles have no conception of two vital points about Zionism. One is the fact that the Jewish National Home in Palestine is not something financed by the rich Jews, but something financed by the poor Jews; that it is not something wanted by a few men, but that it is wanted by the masses of the Jewish people. I find, time and again, in talking with Gentiles, that nobody has the vaguest idea that Palestine has been built up by contributions of $1.00, $3.00, $5.00, year in, year out, by piling one brick on top of another. Connected with this fact is the supremely important point that the Jewish National Home in Palestine is the spearhead of democracy in the Near East. It must be driven home to the non-Jew in this country, to the average American citizen, that the problem in Palestine is not a case between the Jew and the Arab. From the standpoint of American policy, which is foreign policy in terms of democracy, the Arabs as a people have never been a factor in this situation. It has only been a group similar to the Prussian Junker class that has been in the picture.

I have not said anything so far about oil, but it seems to me quite characteristic for the pattern we have lately been reverting to in our foreign policy. There always has been in American foreign policy the conflict between the specific interest of a particular business group wanting to utilize the government for the purpose of securing a particular concession or something else of that kind and the over-all interest of the American people in peace and the advance of democracy. Think of China, think of India, think of various parts of Europe. It is always the same story.

I may appear to you visionary, but personally I believe that the sound position to take is that we do not want the oil pipeline in Arabia. We do not want to be mixed up in imperialistic ventures overseas. The Germans have demonstrated in this war that one can make all the gasoline we need here in the United States, and if such gasoline costs a penny or two more by that process, it will be worthwhile.

In conclusion, let me say this. I should like to see the issue portrayed to the American people under three headings: First, the Jewish National Home is of profound interest to Americans who are not Jewish because it is vitally related to the pacification of the world. It is vitally related to the establishment of a lasting peace because we must solve the problems that the Nazi scourge has raised.

The second point is that the upbuilding of the National Home has been one of the most striking manifestations of democratic forces in our generation. It has been the result of a mass effort by the Jewish people.

And third, that if we are ever to have democracy in the Near East, we have no better chance of securing it than to back the efforts the Jews are making to build a Jewish Commonwealth.

June, 1944

Test of Fulfillment

by DAVID BEN GURION

W E ARE here to take the measure of the ability of Zionism to achieve its purpose. The war, and this is a civil war involving the whole human race, confronts all peoples, civilizations, political institutions and aspirations with the ruthless test of survival. Our own people were singled out by the Nazi enemy for complete physical extermination. We believe we will emerge victorious from this war and that our people as a whole will survive. Zionism will then be faced with the hardest and severest of all tests: the test of fulfillment.

In two vital aspects the position of Zionism after this war will be quite different from what it was after the last war. The situation of both the Jewish people and the Jewish homeland has changed. After the last war when England, America, and the two other free western democracies—as they then were—France and Italy—resolved to undo the historic wrong of the Jewish people and recognize its right to restoration in its ancient homeland, the position of the Jews, even in the countries where they had suffered most, was not yet as desperate and hopeless as it will be at the end of this war. It seemed then that our task of rebuilding Palestine to absorb new settlers could proceed at a leisurely pace.

After this war we will be faced with quite a different situation. The size and urgency of Jewish migration will be unparalleled even in Jewish history. The old debate, whether Zionism is spiritual or political, is obsolete. Either Zionism will provide a substantial and speedy solution of the burning need of large numbers of uprooted Jews and through a mass immigration and colonization will lay the sure foundations of a free self-governing Palestine, or it is meaningless.

Address delivered at Extraordinary Zionist Conference, New York, May 12, 1942

In the last war Palestine as a unit did not exist, nor did Syria and Iraq. They, as well as most of Arabia, were all parts of the Ottoman Empire. Under Turkish rule for 400 years, Palestine had no Turkish population or Turkish culture. It was practically an unclaimed country except by the Jewish people who never, for all these many centuries, ceased to regard it as the Land of Israel.

We are now facing a different situation. Some of the neighboring countries became independent Arab kingdoms and Palestine is claimed as part of an Arab Empire. The post-war settlement will have to include a decision about Palestine one way or the other.

The achievement of Zionism raises two major problems, one economic, the other political. I will begin with the economic: the so-called problem of absorptive capacity.

Since the last war Palestine has taken in more Jewish refugees than any other country, and, in certain periods when artificial limitations of immigration were relaxed, more than all other countries combined. But in view of the magnitude of the Jewish refugee problem after this war, the question legitimately arises: how many more Jews can settle in Palestine on a sound economic basis.

No one can seriously pretend to give a clear-cut arithmetical answer. Science has not yet discovered, nor do I know whether it will ever discover, a safe method for predicting how many people can be settled on a given area in any country. The whole speculation of absorptive capacity is a peculiarly Zionist, or perhaps an anti-Zionist invention.

What is usually called absorptive capacity is not a fixed and static measure, but a fluctuating, dynamic quantity, which depends as much, if not more, on the human factor, as on the nature and area of the country. Among the human factors nothing is more decisive than need and our desperate need is a powerful element for the creation of absorptive capacity. A second element is our creative ability, our enterprise and our pioneering courage. Important, too, is our deep love and devotion to our historic homeland. A paramount factor is the regime of the country: the political, legal and administrative conditions affecting Jewish immigration and colonization. The purely economic aspect can be discussed under three headings: agriculture, industry, the sea.

Agriculture

Potential agricultural development is certainly determined largely by the size of the country and the amount of land available for additional settlers. But even land is not a static, fixed quantity, from the point of view of colonization. For although it has two dimensions which cannot be increased—length and breadth—it also has a third dimension—fertility or productivity—which can be intensified, as was demonstrated in Palestine.

At the London Palestine Conference in 1939, the Arab delegation made public a statement that in the whole of western Palestine, there are only seven million dunams of cultivable land. The whole area of the country is twenty-six and a half million dunams, so that, according to the Arabs, some nineteen million dunams are uncultivable and are certainly not cultivated by the Arabs. Practice has shown that what is uncultivated and considered uncultivable by the Arabs is cultivable and has been cultivated by Jews. In fact a large part of the area settled by Jews is on land up to now considered uncultivable: the sands of Rishon le Zion, the swamps of Hedera, the rocks of Motza, the stony hills of Hanita, and—the most conspicuous example—the largest malarial area in Palestine, the Huleh Basin, which had been classified not only by the Arabs but also by the Government as uncultivable land, is now being turned by our khalutzim into the most prosperous and productive land of Palestine.

Jews had not merely to acquire land but to reclaim, drain, reforest, fertilize, and, wherever water could be discovered, irrigate it. In this way, and by the introduction of modern and intensive methods of cultivation, modern machinery, new breeds of cattle and poultry, new plants and seeds, rotation of crops, and by utilizing surface and sub-soil water to the best advantage, they made new land available for settlement and increased the yield to such a degree that they were able steadily to raise the standard of living, while gradually reducing the subsistence area from the 250 dunams per family necessary in the earlier stages of colonization, to 100 dunams in irrigated plain land, 50 dunams in the mountains where fruit trees were planted, and 20-25 dunams in irrigated land.

In purely Arab districts, the Arab population remained almost stationary, whereas in areas of Jewish settlement it increased considerably. The economic standard of the Arabs was raised and they made use of the improved methods of cultivation of their Jewish neighbors.

For the purpose of agricultural settlement western Palestine can conveniently be divided into four areas: plains, comprising 4,602,900 dunams; the hill country, 8,088,000 dunams; the Negev (southern Palestine) 12,577,000 dunams; the wilderness of Judaea, 1,050,900 dunams.

In the plains some 3,500,000 dunams are irrigable; at present only 350,000 are irrigated. One irrigated dunam yields at least as much as ten unirrigated dunams. The three million dunams, when fully irrigated, make room for from twenty-five to thirty thousand new settlers, leaving sufficient land for former occupants, whether Jews or Arabs.

In the hill country some 4,500,000 dunams are at present uncultivated, and officially considered uncultivable. So far Jews have acquired some 350,000 dunams of such "uncultivable" land and established flourishing villages in the hills of Jerusalem, Samaria and Galilee. At least another 2,500,000 dunams of waste hill country can be brought under cultivation by Jews, making room for another 50,000 families.

With regard to the Negev, Sir John Hope Simpson, sent by the British Government in 1930 to make a survey of the agricultural possibilities of Palestine, reported: "Given the possibility of irrigation there is practically an inexhaustible supply of cultivable land in the Beersheba area. . . . Up to the present time there has been no organized attempt to ascertain whether there is or is not an artesian supply of water." The Peel Royal Commission in 1937 pointed out that "since the date of this Report, it appears that very little has been done by Government to discover water in Palestine." But water was discovered by Jews in many parts of Palestine where it had not been believed to exist, and it is the view of Jewish colonization experts that water for the Negev can be made available either by (1) boring artesian wells; (2) building dams; (3) bringing water from the rivers of the north (Yarkon, Jordan, Yarmouk, Litani). Given the necessary authority and means to provide the Negev with water, it will be possible for hundreds of thousands of new immigrants to settle on the land in that section alone. At present the Negev, half of western Palestine, is wholly unoccupied except for a few roving Bedouins.

The experience of Jewish settlement in Palestine has been that for each family in agriculture at least another three families can be settled in industry, trade and liberal professions.

Industrial Development

Though Palestine is deficient in some important raw materials, it has the advantage of a favorable geographic position as the bridge between three continents of the Old World, Asia, Europe and Africa. It has an easy access to the sea in two directions: through the Mediterranean and the Red Sea; it has the inexhaustible mineral riches of the Dead Sea and it possesses its own electric power. It also has a large hinterland, the whole of the Near and Middle East as far as India as a market for its products. And with the proved ability of the Jews to develop industry in many countries there is no reason why Palestine should not become the industrial center of the Middle East.

In 1937 the Peel Royal Commission stated: "Twelve years ago the national home was an experiment, today it is a going concern. The number of inhabitants has increased fourfold. . . . The process of agricultural colonization has steadily continued . . . yet more impressive has been the urban development. Tel Aviv, still a wholly Jewish town, has leaped to the first place among the

towns of Palestine. Its population now probably exceeds 150,000
. . . rising so quickly from a barren strip of sand it is quite startling.
. . . There is the same effect at Jerusalem. The population of Jerusalem has grown to 125,000 and of that some 75,000 are Jews.
The growth of Haifa, too, which now has a population of over
100,000, is only less remarkable than that of Tel Aviv . . . about
one-half of its inhabitants are now Jews and much of the business
of its port is Jewish business. . . . Broadly speaking the remarkable urban development in Palestine has been Jewish. The relation between rural and urban areas, between industrialists and
agriculturalists has remained fairly constant from the start. . . .
From 1918 to the present day over £14 million has been invested
in Palestine through 'national funds' and roughly £63 million by
private industrialists. The total investment therefore amounts to
£77 million and of this at least one-fifth has been contributed by
the Jews in the United States. Lastly the amount of Jewish deposits in Palestine banks amounted to £16½ million. These are
all startling figures. They bear witness to quite an extraordinary
measure of economic expansion."

Since then there has been further expansion. New industries
have been started—textile, chemical, wood, metal, electrical, food,
building, clothing, which supply the home market and the Near
East as far as India. In 1941 alone over 200 new Jewish industrial
undertakings were established.

The Sea

The youngest Jewish adventure in Palestine is the sea. Jews
as a seafaring people may seem fantastic to those who know the
Jews in Europe and America. Forty years ago the idea of Jews
becoming tillers of the soil also seemed fantastic. But it happened. Six years ago there was not a single Jewish sailor on the
seas of Palestine, although the main sea trade and transport were
Jewish. On May 15, 1936 the High Commissioner of Palestine
personally telephoned the Jewish Agency to tell us that he recognized the justice of our claim that, since the Mufti had closed the

port of Jaffa, we should be allowed to unload in Tel Aviv. And, literally almost overnight the beginning of a Jewish port was established. Thousands of Jews became sea workers in Haifa and Tel Aviv. And Jewish boats manned by Jewish captains and sailors traversed the seven seas.

It was a Hebrew-speaking tribe who gave to the world maritime trade and navigation: the people of Tyre and Sidon, who founded the great empire of Carthage. It was destroyed by the Romans. There were also Jewish pirates who fought the Romans in a bloody sea-battle in Jaffa before the fall of Jerusalem. The maritime people of Tyre and Sidon perished and disappeared. But the descendants of the Jews who fought the Romans are very much alive. Many of them are back in Palestine and more are to come. They went back to the soil. They are going back to the sea. There is no reason why the Italians should preserve their monopoly in maritime, passenger and sea traffic on the Mediterranean as it is now. There is no reason why Palestine merchandise and passenger traffic to Palestine should not be carried in Jewish ships. Palestine is a small country. But the two seas of Palestine, the Mediterranean and the Red Sea are big, and Jewish sailors and fishermen will add the large seas to Palestine and the Jewish people will take its place among the maritime nations of the world.

I want also to mention that Jews in Palestine have begun to engage in civil aviation and, recently, in military aviation.

The Arab Problem

I will come now to the political aspect: first of all, what is usually called the Arab problem.

In few of the complicated problems of Zionism, and there are many, is there so much confusion and misunderstanding as in what is usually called the Arab problem. The first thing to make clear is that there is no Arab problem in the sense that there is a Jewish problem. There is no homeless Arab people; no problem of Arab migration. Just the contrary. The Arabs are of the very few races who are almost entirely, with insignificant exceptions, concentrated in their own territories. They are in possession of vast land and if they suffer from anything it is from a paucity, rather than a surplus, of population.

In a paper prepared in 1926 for the Royal Central Asian Society, Ja'far Pasha al Askari, the then Prime Minister of Iraq, stated:

"The size of the country is 150 thousand square miles, about three times that of England and Wales, while the population is only three million . . . what Iraq wants above everything else is more population."

The same thing applies to Syria. All Syrian economists are agreed that the small numbers and inadequate means of the present Syrian population prevented the development of the country's productive assets to the full. Transjordan, almost four times as large as western Palestine, has only one-fifth of its population. The sparseness of the population in the Arab countries constitutes not only an economic impediment, but a grave political danger, as the case of Alexandretta proves.

A second point must be made clear: the immigration and settlement of Jews in Palestine has not been at Arab expense. In the industrial and sea development, this is self-evident, as there is practically no Arab industry and the sea is entirely unoccupied. But even in agriculture, either we occupied so-called uncultivable land, or, in cases of cultivated land, we increased the yield to such an extent that the same area does not merely provide for additional settlers, but makes it possible for the old settlers to enjoy a higher standard of living. A mass immigration and colonization on the largest possible scale, such as we must expect after this war, can be effected without the slightest need for displacing the present population.

In several quarters the idea of transfer is advanced as the most ideal settlement of the Palestine problem. Let us once and for all understand that to enable Palestine to absorb all the Jews who may be expected to need a new home in the post-war period, there is no economic need for any transfer whatsoever. In post-war

Europe, a re-settlement of population may become necessary and inevitable. In the period between the last war and this, we had one conspicuous example of transfer of population as between Greece and Turkey. It was in fact a transfer of all Asia Minor Greeks to European Greece. Syria and Iraq may also have an interest, economically as well as politically, in strengthening their position vis-a-vis their Turkish and Persian neighbors by transferring new Arab settlers to their country and the only source of such settlers is Palestine. But this is a purely internal Arab problem, in which we may help if asked by the Arabs, but in which we neither can, nor ought to take any initiative. It is not a prerequisite condition for a large-scale Jewish settlement, and it is necessary and wise that we should make all our future plans for the rebuilding of Palestine on the assumption that we have to reckon with the presence of something like a million Arabs, their rights and needs.

There is no conflict of economic interests between Jews and Arabs in Palestine. There is no conflict between the economic interests of the present population of the country and the new arrivals. The very fact that the Mufti and his friends and the Chamberlain-MacDonald government, which tried to appease them, insisted on abolishing the principle of economic absorptive capacity as the only measure of Jewish immigration implies that the Arabs as well as the authors of the White Paper, clearly realized that on purely economic grounds there is room for a very large Jewish immigration, which may turn Palestine into a Jewish country.

What is usually called the "Arab problem" means in reality the political opposition of the Arabs to Jewish immigration into Palestine. Many people, ignoring this simple, although disagreeable truth, attempt to solve the "Arab problem" where it does not exist. One solution offered is a bi-national state. If bi-national state means simply that all the inhabitants of Palestine—Jews and Arabs alike—must enjoy complete equality of rights not merely as individuals, but also as national entities, which means the right of free development of their language, culture, religion, etc., then certainly no Jew, much less a Zionist, can fail to advocate such a regime, although I am not quite convinced that the Arabs will agree to such equality, if they have the power to determine the constitution. When the Mufti was asked by the Royal Commission on January 12, 1937 how they would treat the Jews already in the country, if they had control of Palestine, he said: "That will be left to the discretion of the Government which will be set up under the treaty and will be decided by that Government on the considerations most equitable and most beneficial to the country."

When asked whether the country could assimilate and digest the 400,000 Jews now in the country, he replied: "No."

The chairman then remarked: "Some of them would have to be removed by a process kindly or painful as the case may be?"

The Mufti answered: "We must leave all this to the future."

Thus far no other Arab leader has publicly differed from the Mufti. We must also remember the bitter experience of the Assyrians in Iraq to whom protection was guaranteed under the Anglo-Iraq treaty as well as by the League of Nations. The Anglo-Iraq treaty is still in existence and, at that time, the League of Nations was still alive. But the Assyrians were massacred.

Other people offer parity as a solution, or interpret a bi-national state to mean parity, so that irrespective of numerical strength of Jews and Arabs these two peoples should, in all main departments of government, legislative and executive, be represented on a fifty-fifty basis. I was one of those who strongly advocated parity between Jews and Arabs under the British Mandate. But I doubt whether a regime of parity without a mandatory is practicable, whether a self-governing state can operate at all under such a system, which may mean a permanent deadlock. So far not a single Arab leader has been found to agree to the principle of parity, with or without the Mandate.

But assuming that parity and a bi-national state are workable, assuming that not only Jews but Arabs also will agree to it, it does not in the remotest way solve the only problem that really matters: that of Jewish immigration. The example of Switzerland, where

the difficulty between several nationalities was satisfactorily resolved, is not applicable to Palestine, because the crucial problem
and the root of all friction between Jews and Arabs is not so much
the problem of the Jews and Arabs who are in Palestine, but, almost exclusively, the problem of further Jewish immigration.

Crucial Problem: Immigration

Should there be or should there not be Jewish immigration?
That is the question. No solution, real or imaginary, for all other
Palestine problems, real or imaginary, means anything at all, if it
does not give a clear and simple answer to this simple but all-
important question.

Can the Arabs be expected to agree to Jewish immigration
and under what conditions? There is no deception worse than self-
deception. We must face facts: If Jewish immigration into Palestine depends on Arab consent, there will hardly be any Jewish
immigration at all. It is vitally important, politically as well as
morally that our position on this crucial question should be made
unequivocal. Jewish immigration to Palestine needs no consent.
We are returning as of right. History, international law and the
irresistible vital need of an indestructible people—these three have
ordained Palestine as the rightful home of the Jewish people.

A Jew is no stranger, no intruder, no immigrant in Palestine.
He is at home. History, historical connection, an unbroken attachment for thousands of years, despite all vicissitudes, despite repeated expulsions, made Palestine the inalienable home of the
Jewish people. Just as it is a historical fact that there are a million
Arabs in Palestine, who legitimately regard themselves as children
of that country, whether we like it or not, so it is an historical fact,
however disagreeable it may be to the Arabs, that Palestine was
and has remained for more than 3,000 years, Eretz Israel, for
the Jewish people. This was explicitly confirmed by international
law.

The Mandate for Palestine explicitly states that recognition
was given to the historical connection of the Jewish people with

Palestine and to the grounds for reconstituting there their national home. But there is something even stronger than international law, and that is the living, desperate need of a people for whom a return to Palestine is the only means of salvation and survival, both individually for all those who want to settle in Palestine and, collectively, for the Jewish people as a whole.

No political opposition or obstruction on the part of the Arabs, no terrorist intimidation, no restrictions of a morally and legally invalid White Paper will prevent Jews from getting back to the Land of Israel. And if there is still anyone who doubts this, the story of the *Patria,* the *Struma,* and many other vessels of that kind, provide the proof. Their plain meaning was—Palestine or death. As soon as this war is over, hundreds of such vessels will sail to Palestine.

Ours is a realistic generation. After the many disappointments of the last war and peace, people are afraid of idealistic illusions and want to be sober and practical. And he must really be a visionary dreamer who overlooks the grim, bitter reality of Jewish migration after this war, the Jewish urge for Palestine. No other reality of Palestine can exceed in vehemence and urgency the irresistible Jewish surge toward Palestine where the deepest biological and psychological roots of our very existence combine together.

The Arabs will acquiesce in Jewish immigration and will accommodate themselves to the new reality when it becomes an established fact.

When after the last war, England, America and other democracies decreed the reconstitution of the Jewish National Home in Palestine, the representatives of the Arabs who pleaded the Arab case at the Peace Conference, agreed and accepted that decision. They made Jewish Palestine part of their scheme for the future of the Arab countries. There was Feisal (later King Feisal) son and representative of King Husein with whom England negotiated during the war. He signed an agreement with Dr. Weizmann (January 3, 1919) where it is laid down that:

"In the establishment of the Constitution and Administration of Palestine all such measures shall be adopted as will afford the fullest guarantees for carrying into effect the British Government's Declaration of the 2nd of November, 1917.

"All necessary measures shall be taken to encourage and stimulate immigration of Jews into Palestine on a large scale, and as quickly as possible to settle Jewish immigration upon the land through closer settlement and intensive cultivation of the soil."

In a letter written on March 3, 1919 to Felix Frankfurter on behalf of the Hedjaz Delegation, he states:

"We Arabs, especially the educated among us, look with the deepest sympathy on the Zionist movement. Our deputation here in Paris is fully acquainted with the proposals submitted yesterday by the Zionist Organization to the Peace Conference, and we regard them as moderate and proper. We will do our best, in so far as we are concerned, to help them through; we will wish the Jews a hearty welcome home. . . . The Jewish movement is national and not imperialist. Our movement is national and not imperialist, and there is room in Syria for us both. Indeed I think that neither can be a real success without the other."

There was also a delegation of Syrian Arabs, representing all communities; Moslems, Christians, Jews, among them was Jamil Mardan, later Prime Minister of Syria.

In the concluding part of his statement before the Supreme Council of the Allies, on February 13, 1919, M. Chekri Ganem, the Chief Representative of the Central Syrian Committee, said:

"May we say one word as regards Palestine, although the subject is said to be a thorny one. Palestine is incontestably the Southern portion of our country. The Zionists claim it. We have suffered from too much suffering resembling theirs not to throw open wide to them the doors of Palestine. All those among them who are oppressed in certain retrograde countries are welcome. Let them settle in Palestine, but in an autonomous Palestine, connected with Syria by the sole bond of federation. Will not a Palestine enjoying wide internal autonomy be for them a sufficient guarantee? If they form a majority there, they will be the rulers."

It is then a historical fact that when the decision was taken there was no Arab opposition. Indeed, there was even explicit consent. When and why did this opposition arise? When the implementation of the decision was handed over to people who cared very little for its success. The Mandatory Administration in Palestine had neither the understanding, the vision and the sympathy, nor the ability to carry out what is admittedly a complex and difficult task, that of bringing back the scattered and dispersed Jews from different countries and developing Palestine for their resettlement. And some of the Arab leaders in Palestine were not slow to perceive the rather reluctant way—to put it mildly—in which that decision was being implemented by the Colonial Office and Colonial officials. They immediately, of course, took advantage of this hesitancy and half-heartedness—believing that after all that decision was, perhaps, not very seriously meant and could be easily reversed.

The Mandatory Failed—
The Jews Succeeded

It was the British Royal Commission which condemned the instrument designed to carry out the international pledge for a Jewish National Home in Palestine and coined the phrase the "unworkability of the Mandate." Whether or not we agree with all the reasoning of that Commission, one thing can hardly be disputed—the administration set up to work the Mandate proved to be unworkable.

Though we had, and still have, many and frequent differences with the Mandatory Power, some of them very bitter and tragic, especially since the inauguration of the White Paper policy, culminating in the controversy over the Jewish Army in Palestine and the *Struma,* we cannot say that the failure to implement the Mandate by the British Administration for the last twenty years is due to the fact that they are British.

What the Peel Royal Commission called the unworkability of the Mandate was inherent in the unique situation which had been created in Palestine: the incongruity between the nature of the task and the nature of the instrument. The Administration of Palestine was composed of a colonial bureaucracy trained in the administration of backward countries, used to dealing with primitive peoples, where their task was mainly the preservation of the existing order as far as possible.

In Palestine they were faced with an advanced and progressive community, as far as the Jews were concerned, a dynamic situation requiring constant initiative, unrelenting effort and creative energy, and it was merely human nature that these officials should feel themselves much more at ease in dealing with Arabs and administering to their needs, where they could indulge their colonial habits of maintaining their status quo.

A mass colonization on a large scale will be necessary to meet the needs of Jewish migration after this war. This will obviously require a large outlay of capital to be obtained from inter-governmental sources. The main readjustment, however, indispensable for a task of such magnitude, is a new regime—political, legal and administrative—especially designed for the maximum development of the resources of the country and the absorption of the maximum number of immigrants in the shortest possible time. The fundamental laws of the country, land and water regulations, labor legislation, fiscal regulations, trade regulations, must be entirely changed to suit the requirements of intensive colonization, the speedy building up of industries, the growth of cities and villages. And not only the laws, but their daily administration must be guided and inspired by the steadfast and unwavering purpose of building the country and absorbing new immigrants on a large scale. Only a Jewish Administration can be equal to that task—an administration completely identified with the needs and aims of the Jewish settlers and whole-heartedly devoted to the upbuilding of the country. Jewish immigration on a large scale is bound to result in the not distant future in a growing Jewish majority in Palestine and in the establishment of a self-governing Jewish Commonwealth.

Reviewing the history of the past twenty years, and taking into account the needs facing us in the immediate future after this war, our first conclusion is that the Mandate must be entrusted to the Jewish people themselves.

I do not mean the formal Mandate as of twenty years ago. The whole Mandate system may go. But the responsibility and necessary governmental authority to rebuild the country and secure the return of the Jews to their own homeland, should now be handed over to the Jewish people themselves. First of all immigration and colonization should be entrusted to the Agency of the whole Jewish people, which will act on behalf of prospective immigrants and settlers.

Three Principles

It is premature to lay down a detailed plan for the constitution of Palestine after the war and to attempt a reply to all questions which may arise. It is, however, possible and necessary to lay down the most essential principles for our own guidance and for the immediate political job facing Zionism in educating Jewish and general public opinion, in America, England, Russia and other countries, toward a Zionist solution of the Jewish problem and toward a Zionist solution of the problem of Palestine.

These principles are three:

1. A clear and unequivocal reaffirmation of the original intention of the Balfour Declaration and the Mandate to re-establish Palestine as a Jewish Commonwealth, as made clear by the President of the United States on March 3, 1919.

2. The Jewish Agency for Palestine, as the trustee for the prospective immigrants and settlers, should have full control over Jewish immigration and be vested with all necessary authority for the development and upbuilding of the country, including the development of its unoccupied and uncultivated lands.

3. Complete equality to all inhabitants of Palestine, civil, political and religious; self-government in all municipal affairs;

autonomy for the different communities—Jewish and Arab—in the management of all internal affairs—education, religion, etc.

Whether Palestine should remain a separate unit or be associated with a larger and more comprehensive political entity—a Near Eastern Federation, British Commonwealth of Nations, Anglo-American union or some other larger association, will depend on circumstances and developments which can neither be determined by us nor at present be foreseen, and it does not constitute a special Jewish or Palestinian problem. We will be part of the new world and the new pattern, which, we believe, will come out of this war, with victory on our side. But whatever will be the constitutional relation of Jewish Palestine to other countries, there must be continued willingness and readiness for close cooperation with the Arabs in Palestine as well as the neighboring countries. Once the bone of contention of Jewish immigration is removed by clear-cut international decision on the one hand, and assuring Jewish control over their own immigration on the other, there is no serious reason to give up the hope for Jewish-Arab cooperation.

Zionism in action means nation-building, state-building. There were many who admitted the justice and beauty of the Zionist ideal and the right of the Jewish people to its own free national existence as an equal to all other nations. But they seriously questioned the ability of the Jews to become a nation again and to re-establish an independent state. They could not believe that Jews who for many centuries had become more and more denationalized, divorced from their original soil, segregated in cities, confined to a very limited number of occupations and trades, who had forgotten their national language and loosened their national ties, who remained Jews largely because they could not become something else—could again become a nation, rebuild a country and re-create an independent economy and culture.

It cannot be said that this was an idle argument. There was much more in it than those who advanced it realized. While the idea and vision of Zionism looked so simple, so natural and necessary, when translated into action it was immediately faced with innumerable obstacles and almost insurmountable difficulties, as it meant not merely a transfer of a people, but its complete transformation, not merely a return to a country, but its upbuilding. And what a people! And what a country! The Jews had to remake themselves and to remake Palestine. We must remember that Zionist colonization is possibly the only one, or certainly one of the very few examples of successful colonization not undertaken and not supported by a state.

We are still very far from our goal and are still facing the most difficult test of fulfillment. But our past achievement supplies us with confidence that it can be done and that we can do it.

Meaning of Past Achievements

At the end of the last war there were 58,000 Jews in Palestine. In 1941 there were over 500,000. They settled in villages and towns built by themselves. The area they occupy is about 1,500,-000 dunams—less than 1/17 of the area of western Palestine. The whole area of Palestine is some 27 million dunams, of which the Arabs cultivate some 7 million. More than 18 million dunams are still waste land.

Contrary to accepted economic dogmas, Jews in Palestine went from town to country; townspeople for centuries, they became tillers of the land. Over 30% of the Jews in Palestine live in rural settlements. Even more marked is their return to manual work. Of 500,000 people, 125,000 adults are members of the Labor Federation. As in no other country Jews in Palestine are engaged in every kind of work: in fields, factories, quarries, mines, buildings, roads, railways, harbors, fishing, aviation, etc.

Coming from all corners of the earth with diverse languages and cultural traditions, they are being welded into a new unit, Hebrew becoming their common language, the rebuilding of Zion their common purpose.

Living in their own villages and towns, providing for their own defense, education and social services, they developed a comprehensive system of local and national self-government, rooted in an independent economy and culture, and thus laid the foundations, for all practical purposes, of a Jewish Commonwealth.

What 500,000 Jews could do, six, eight or ten times that number can do. What was done on an area of one and a half million dunams can be done on six, eight or ten times that area. There is no truer, more abiding and convincing test of fulfillment than fulfillment. Zionism stood that test.

The test of nationhood came to the Yishuv four years before the outbreak of the World War, when the Mufti, acting on the instructions of Mussolini and Hitler, tried to destroy the Yishuv by starvation, by interrupting their communications, and by stopping their work and the arrival of newcomers by terror—indiscriminate murder of men, women and children. Never before did the economic independence and strength of the Yishuv, its valor and courage, its deep attachment to its ancient soil, its creative energy in face of the most deadly and constant danger, manifest itself more strongly than then. Not only was there no retreat or abandonment of the smallest position, but there was continuous and manifold development and expansion in agricultural settlements, absorption of new immigration, industrial development and conquest of the sea and in creating a military defense force which Palestine had not seen since the seventh century, when, under the leadership of Benjamin of Tiberias, Jews fought as allies of the Persians against the Byzantine oppressions.

An even severer test came to the Yishuv with the outbreak of this war. And I can best tell you how it stood the test by quoting a recent message from the man who now leads our political struggle in Palestine, Moshe Shertok:

"Amid this sea of pain and horror, Palestine today stands out as a rock of refuge, a lighthouse of hope to an agonized Jewry. Steeled in adversity in the four pre-war years, the Yishuv is now called upon to act in this war as the vanguard for the entire Jewish people, shouldering on its behalf three major responsibilities: The first and foremost is fullest cooperation in the defense of the country and in the Middle Eastern campaign by mobilization of all available resources for the distinctively Jewish war effort, in the military, industrial and agricultural spheres.

"The second is the utmost exertion in saving Jewish victims of the war.

"The third is preparation and bold efforts for post-war construction.

"The following are the landmarks of our progress:

"12,500 men and women are enlisted in the military service. Thousands of Jewish technicians and skilled artisans are engaged in essential war work in Palestine and in the Middle East. Jewish industry employs 35,000 workers, who are increasingly harnessed to war production. Its output for war has increased eightfold since 1940. Many plants are working day and night.

"The Jewish National Fund has acquired 113,000 dunams of land during the war period. Eighteen settlements were founded, breaking new ground for agricultural production and increasing space in the old and new settlements, whose manpower and resources are strained to the highest pitch. Despite the vicissitudes of war, tens of thousands of refugees entered Palestine since September of 1939. The Yishuv is bracing itself for a new, supreme effort in defense and production. Thousands of youngsters from the towns are on their way to work on the farms. Large numbers are being trained for defense duties. New contingents of recruits for the Army are being raised."

The Message of Palestine

In our building of Palestine we could not have altogether escaped the conflicts, contradictions, and evils of the present economic system. But it is not in vain that we struggled for many centuries to maintain our identity, that Jewishness which was molded in our ancient homeland, where our prophets bequeathed to humanity the still unrealized vision of human brotherhood and justice, love of neighbor, peace among nations. Without bloodshed, without coercion, by voluntary moral effort, assisted by the good will and sympathetic help of the whole Zionist movement, our khalutzim set up a new type of communal and cooperative settlement—K'vutzoth and Moshavim—embodying a new human relationship of free creative work, mutual help, common interests and a complete equality, and combining an ideal social structure with a sound economic foundation—so far found nowhere else.

This new type of society has stood the test of time (the first K'vutza was founded in 1910) and proved its superiority both economic and social to other types of settlement. It is a message of living faith for all Jews and for the world at large that a better society is not merely a dream.

Our present world finds itself in a terrible mess. This is the second World War in our generation. Never before was the whole of humanity threatened with such danger of complete and total slavery. Never before was our own people threatened with such complete and total annihilation. While the war goes on we must devote every ounce of our energy to a complete and total victory. But we must beware of the dangerous illusion that the destruction of Hitlerism alone will free the world from all ills and the Jewish people from its misery. There is something fundamentally wrong in present human society if a Hitler can bring the whole of humanity to such a pass, and there is something fundamentally wrong in the Jewish set-up, if whenever there is trouble, Jews are singled out as its first and most suffering victims. And a victory over Hitler will not be an end, but a beginning of a new set-up for the world and for ourselves.

Our past work and achievement in Palestine has a double contribution to make to the reshaping of human society and to the remaking of Jewish history. It will serve as the rock upon which to build the Jewish Commonwealth and a Jewish Commonwealth means a Commonwealth of Justice. To achieve a Jewish Commonwealth will require a supreme effort by the entire Jewish people in the Diaspora and in Palestine. As part of the great human cause, America, England, Russia and others, leading the battle of humanity, may be expected to help us. But we must do the job ourselves. Palestine will be as Jewish as the Jews will make it.

June, 1942

To Whom Does the Earth Belong?

by DOROTHY THOMPSON

IN THE security and prosperity of our beautiful America, we are living in a dream world. We, who gathered tonight in this great meeting, came here openly, with no fear that we would be arrested on the way, hurled into prison, or mowed down by machine guns —or rounded up, now, in this hall, and carried off for extermination. Before we came, each of us ate a good dinner. And when we go, all of us will return to warm shelter and comfortable beds.

Far away there is a painful war. There have been wars before. They have all been agonizing. But eventually we have won them. Then peace has returned, and the world has gone on pretty much as before.

That is still, in general, our comfortable attitude towards this war.

But this is not that kind of war. What is happening today, all over the world in greater or lesser degree, is not just a war. It is the collapse of a civilization. It is the liquidation of an epoch. If we wish to seek an analogy for these times, we cannot find it in the Great War of 1914-1918. We cannot find it in the revolutionary wars of the eighteenth century, when the French revolution mounted the Man on Horseback to override Europe, Africa, and part of Russia. We cannot even find it in the seventeenth century religious wars, which devastated large parts of Europe and left, they say, in Central Europe more wolves than men.

No, to find the parallel one must go much farther back to the cataclysms that shock the fourth and fifth centuries, when Rome, the citadel of western civilization, fell before the barbarians and a great culture plunged headlong into the abyss. We refer to those years as the years of the Migration of the peoples, when war and

---

(*An address delivered at Madison Square Garden on March* 21, 1944.)

121

ruin set adrift millions of men, and the whole face of the globe moved, like a scattered anthill.

This world we live in is in such a state of fundamental eruption. Whether we cast our eyes upon China, where millions of men, women, and children, have beaten a mass retreat into the interior of that continental country, in their flight to a place from where to take another stand; or whether we look at Europe, where ten million non-German Europeans have been gathered from all countries and transported to the factories and fields of Germany; or whether we look at Russia, where other millions have been moved from the western lands to the eastern to man new factories and plough new ground—everywhere we see this vast shift and stir, this vast migration of the peoples. "Scattered like leaves before the enchanter fleeing—pestilence stricken multitudes."

* * *

Yet among these uprooted and harassed moving masses, there lives in all the breath of hope. The Chinese family, thousands of miles from its original home, still squats and fights on Chinese soil. The Frenchman, toiling in a Silesian field, or in a Breslau factory, dreams of the gentle air of Normandy or Auvergne, and has faith that one day he will return and be gathered into the arms of his countrymen. Even in the seething underground movements which burrow under the surface life of Europe, men, holding their lives in their hands, know that they will pay for their deeds only with a few patriots' lives.

There is but one people of Europe, for whom no hope is offered. There is but one people upon all of whom the death sentence has been decisively passed. That is the Jews. From Oslo to Milan, and from the furthermost Polish border to Bordeaux, the arm of the Nazi reaches out for them. Their transportation does not mean work or imprisonment—with hope. Their transportation means death. Never, in the whole history of a persecuted race, have they been so trapped.

The extermination center for European Jewry is Poland. It has become the mass death cell for European Jews.

It was, before the war, the country with the largest Jewish population. There, in its Jewish quarters, and in its great cities, lived 3,500,000 Jews. For the most part they were very poor. For the most part they were half-outcasts even in the happiest times. Today they are treated like vermin, like roaches or bugs, to be exterminated.

I have seen underground reports from Poland, from Jewish and Polish sources. The story they tell dwarfs the accounts of Christian martyrs in the arenas and catacombs of ancient Rome. The reports are cold and statistical. "Last November, at Trawniki, all the men in a camp of 10,000 were taken out for the alleged purpose of digging air raid shelters. After two hours they were surrounded and machine gunned to death. 50 trucks then evacuated the women and children to another point, where they were also liquidated. The camp was then re-filled with new arrivals — Italian Jews."

Here is another. "Early in November the Germans began liquidating all the Jewish camps in Eastern Galicia, near the front. In Lwow, on Janowska street, they publicly executed a selected 2,000."

That is the story. The Polish Jews, interned in ghettos and camps, are being executed to make room for other European Jews, who then, in their turn, will be executed. The camps are in Eastern Poland. As the Russians advance all male Jews will certainly be liquidated, lest liberated by the Russians they join them as guerrillas. For even in their ghettos—in Warsaw, Bialystok, and elsewhere, they have not been hounded into a firing squad without a fight. With such weapons as they could smuggle in, through the Polish underground, and with their bare hands, and with fire, they have made S. S. men pay with many wounds and many deaths for their extermination. They have not died like bugs and roaches. They have died like men. But their resistance has been only for the record of Jewish heroism. They have died to prove that Jews are not worms. But they have died, just the same.

It is reckoned that of the 3,500,000 Jews originally in Poland, not a quarter of a million still live. Those who do are protected by non-Jewish members of the underground, or live, like cave men, in the Polish forests. They live to tell a story, not to save a people.

*   *   *

But those who live have learned one thing: A people without a homeland of their own is doomed. What Theodor Herzl preached long ago, while "the most highly civilized Jews" of Europe refused to listen, has been proved in our lifetime. And from one end of Europe to another, Jews sit down and weep, aye they weep, because they remember Zion. And I say: Their word should go out through all the earth and their cry to the end of the world. And there should be no speech and language where their voice is not heard!

Hear this cry! It comes from the remnant of Polish Jewry: "At this last moment before our death, we, the surviving remnant of the Polish Jews cry out to the world for rescue. We know that you sense the agony of our martyrdom but are powerless to help us. But we know also that there are those who *might* help if only they *would*. To them we say, For the blood of three million slaughtered, vengeance will fall not only upon Hitler's beasts but upon the indifferent who instead of action offered only words of sympathy."

The problem of European Jewry is not merely how to endure for the length of the war. The words I must say are bitter, but they are true. There are many who think that European Jewry will be safe everywhere after Hitler's defeat. Many count confidently on returning even to Germany. They are living in illusion. For of all the devilish schemes of the devilish followers of Hitler, his campaign against the Jews has been most successful. Children have had implanted in their minds, and not only in Germany, a fairy story about Jews, in which every Jew is the bogeyman. They have been taught to search faces for a Jewish cast of features; to fear from all Jews treachery and deceit; to see in kindness offered by Jews only a hidden knife. You cannot argue, my friends, with fairy stories! The Hitler campaign against the Jews enters the realm of the subconscious. It makes the person innoculated, insusceptible of reasoning. It is enormously augmented by a suppressed sense of guilt. Do you think that men love those whom they have wronged? Never. The sense of their own guilt would be unbearable unless they could rationalize some justification for their behavior. It will take generations to wipe out of the subconscious minds of Europeans the sense of witchcraft, the dark fears, that have been implanted there. Even our victory will not make Europe a pleasant place for the Jews. Even outside Europe, yes even in America, the subtle poison, dropped day by day, in tiny doses has begun to take hold.

The opponents of Zionism are hypocrites. They oppose the Jewish homeland on behalf of the Arabs. Very well, then. What Christian country, however underpopulated, is prepared to receive all who come? Will Canada—with a population of a mere eleven million, in a country that could support fifty million? Will Australia, with a population of seven million, in a country that could support thirty million? Will Brazil, larger than the entire United States, and greatly underpopulated?

Before this war, when it was possible to remove every Jew from Europe, the democratic nations held a conference in Evian, in France, to consider just this problem—of refuge for the German Jews thrown out of economic and social life by Hitler's Nuremberg laws. Did the conference accomplish anything? Were the then mere hundreds of thousands of threatened Jews offered homes anywhere on the earth? The answer is No. Only driblets were allowed into any countries, and under the most careful restrictions. Nowhere were they welcomed. Everywhere they were merely tolerated—as a sop to the democratic conscience.

The brutal truth is that the only spot on this whole immense earth where European Jewish refugees were and are received with open arms, and with acclaim; the only spot where they were received as assets, and not liabilities—is Palestine.

There, the occasional ships which unloaded Jewish passengers at the wharves were a cause of rejoicing, and however destitute those passengers may be, coming more likely than not with nothing but their bare hands and the clothing in which they stand, they are carried ashore with laughter and singing.

* * *

And have they a right to be there? My friends, I shall not go into the historic bases of Zionism this evening. I shall not go into the promises of the Balfour declaration, or into the ancient Jewish claims. All these things are as familiar to you as to me. There is a far larger issue involved than the issue of Jewish colonization in Palestine, and a far larger issue than legal rights and political promises. The issue which is involved transcends the Jewish problem. The issue lies in the answer to the most fundamental question of human society; To whom, anyhow, does this earth belong?

The great psalmist told us: "The earth is the Lord's and the fullness thereof; the world, and they that dwell therein." The earth is a gift of nature to man. Man did not create it. The fertile soil and the food that grows upon it; the forests with their resources for building shelter; the rivers and seas, teeming with edible fish, the rocks with their previous minerals—all those are the free gifts of nature. They were here when man first stood up from all fours, and discovered that he had a brain and hands, and that with hands and brains he could continue and improve the original creations of nature.

From immemorial time, it has been a law of human progress, that these gifts of nature serve only those who serve them. Wherever men have colonized waste places, or colonized potentially rich but unused land in conformity with nature's laws, great civilizations have been built. The land that previously supported savages, nomads or squatters in poverty, want, and fear, has blossomed and expanded and multiplied its fruits. So that where a dozen families once could dwell, a hundred could live, and five hundred, and a thousand. This is the law of the progress and growth of civilizations.

There is also a law of the decline of civilizations. Where men have neglected land that once was fertile; or where they have exploited it in contradiction to the laws of nature, then where a a thousand families once lived, only five hundred can subsist; where many hundreds only a hundred; and finally, the desert returns, and its inhabitants are nomads, driving their flocks from oasis to oasis, and wandering over the desolations their forebears have created.

Nature and human history recognize no legal titles to land in the long run. Nature and history do not accord to any race of people in the long run an eternal title to what they do not use. If history did, there would be no British Commonwealth and there would be no North and South America. These great and prosperous new civilizations have been created by colonists, who left overcrowded areas where there was no land or work for them and found undeveloped land, and settled on it, and put their backs into it, and civilized it.

Colonization and Imperialism are the opposite poles of man's efforts for survival. Imperialism is the exploitation of other lands and other peoples for the increment of one's own profit. The British, American, or French capitalist who erects a factory in India because raw materials are plentiful and cheap and labor cheaper than in Lancashire or New Hampshire, and who then sends the profits home, is dis-employing Englishmen and Americans and exploiting for his own personal and national purposes the lands and resources of others. The British or American company which seeks out and leases Near Eastern oil is adding the fees he pays to the pockets of Near Eastern potentates, but is draining the oil, placed in the ground by nature, far from its sources, and using it for himself and his own national ends.

But the colonist brings to a country his own hands, his own muscles, his own back, and his own capital. He ploughs it all into the country itself. He is not the exploiter; he is the enricher.

***   ***   ***

I have no patience with the argument that Palestine "belongs" to the Arabs, because they are the original settlers there, which by the way, is very dubious. If Britain had tried to colonize North America, Canada, Australia, New Zealand, or South Africa, on the basis of an immigration restricted to a certain proportion of the native inhabitants, they never would have been any United States or British Commonwealth. Yet, today, though many decry the British Empire, none decry the Commonwealth. For these British colonists have been true creators. They have redeemed wildernesses and made them into homes for civilized men. They have enriched the world.

If I try to delve into the basic causes for this terrible European eruption and for the Asiatic eruption as well, I come to one root cause: the overcrowding of populations in some parts of the earth, while others remain empty and barren.

And unless in the rest of this century, we can begin new great movements of colonization—the actual creation of new civilizations in the wasted and neglected portions of the earth—this explosion will go on exploding until the world is in ruins.

The Near East was once a great center of civilization. Scattered over its deserts, and amongst its impoverished villages, are the ruins of ancient cities—rose-red cities, half as old as time—that testify through their broken arches and scraps of mosaic to the memory of a time when fruitful soil and brisk trade supported populous cities and lofty civilizations. Then the cycle of decline began. And for centuries the Near East was a lost world, a land of eroded soil, sparse vegetation, undernourishment, disease, filth, degradation.

Only in our own times could this land be redeemed—and by the science of modern agriculture, and engineering.

But in the whole Near East only one people have done it— and that is the Jews of Zion. Leave out of account the sentimental considerations that created the Zionist movement. Say, if you like, that it originated in a romantic dream. Dreams are judged by their fruits. It was not the quest for soil that drove the Puritans to New England but the persecutions of the Restoration after Cromwell. But it was their hands which built America's most comely villages

and cities; it was their hands which built the fastest ships on the
seas of their times; which put cattle upon hills which were jungles;
which laid stones on the bare earth surrounding harbors; which
created life, order, civilization, law, education, and aspiration in
the howling wilderness. And because of their pioneering work,
millions of men, not of their religious belief and not of their race,
have enjoyed the fruits of America!

So it is with the Zionist Jews. They are taking nothing from
the Arabs. They are giving the most essential thing there is to give
to the whole Near Eastern world. For they are saving and re-
creating the land—the work that is nearer to the work of God
than any of which mankind is capable. When the first Jewish
colonists entered Palestine, there were 600,000 Arabs living in it
at a very low standard of living. Today there are 1,000,000 living
there at a much higher standard of living. If all the Jews of Europe
should settle in Palestine and its surroundings and do what the
original stonebreakers and builders of the soil have done, there
would not be fewer and poorer Arabs but more and richer Arabs
in the Near East. For that is another law of the growth of the soil.
People learn by example. When Peter the Great wished to civilize
Russia, he went incognito throughout Europe. When he found a
village where the people grew fine vegetables, or forests where
there were superior woodsmen, or dairy communities where there
were exceptionally fine cattle, he offered them free land, tax free,
and housing, and many advantages to transplant themselves intact
to the Russian Empire. Then the peasants around their settlements
watched and observed. First they watched with hostility. But as
they gradually saw that their neighbors were rich, while they were
poor, that their cattle lived, whereas theirs died, they copied them,
and the pattern spread, until everyone was richer and more prosperous and more civilized.

*   *   *

The earth belongs to its lovers and creators. That is the
law of nature. The earth must be opened again to the children
of men that they may serve the earth, and by serving it extend the

welfare of humanity. Far and above the Zionist experiment, of itself, this truth must be enunciated in behalf of the landless, the impoverished, the idle from the teeming centers of civilization. Palestine must be opened to the Jews in behalf of the peoples of Europe, and in behalf of the peoples of the whole Near East.

Vengeance is mine; I will repay, saith the Lord. Vengeance for the persecuted Jews falls daily upon the cities of Germany, toppling its proud towers and great industry. Vengeance for the insult of Nazidom to mankind is inexorable, for they who take the sword shall perish by the sword. But vengeance will not save Jewry. Only the Lord of Creation will save Jewry, he who is the God of Love to those who keep His commandments. The Jews of Zion have kept His commandments. What indifference and waste have taken from His Earth they have replaced. What ignorance and greed have neglected, they have supplied. And as long as they keep on building; as long as the creative spirit moves them in their great trek toward Palestine, he who stands in the way is halting the whole progress of man into the only true liberation: Liberation is work, and sweat, for the building of new homes, new cities, new civilizations, for and by the outcasts and the unwanted of the earth.

April, 1944

Palestine—A Jewish Commonwealth
by Moshe Shertok

WE HAVE reached a turning point in our history, perhaps the most decisive turning point since we were driven away from Palestine. This turning point came not only as a result of the war and of what it brought in its wake for our brothers in Europe. It came before the war, with the change of policy on the part of Great Britain as the mandatory power in Palestine in regard to the future of the Jewish people in that country. So long as the mandatory regime went on as it was conceived in the spirit of the Balfour Declaration and laid down in the Mandate, we could concentrate all our thoughts and efforts upon the practical job at hand of sending people into Palestine, of acquiring land in Palestine, of proceeding step by step from little strength to greater strength, without necessarily posing to ourselves the problem of our ultimate goal in Palestine as a question of the most immediate concern.

For many years we resisted and defeated attempts to concentrate Zionist attention on the question of our ultimate aim. We regarded such discussions as unwarranted and harmful. We feared that they would result only in the diversion of attention and energy from the practical, vital task before us to dreams and fancies which could in no way add to our actual strength. That was the state of things as long as we could be reasonably certain that the framework of the mandatory regime, narrow and restricted as it was, was something firm and unshakable, and that it would be kept up and give us an opportunity to show what we could do; and that in the fullness of time we would be able to achieve the desire which burned in the hearts of every one of us.

But an end was put to that regime. An abrupt, violent change took place in Great Britain's official policy, months before the war. In May, 1939, the question of our political future in Palestine appeared to be in the balance, and we had to face that problem. We had to take up the challenge and give our answer to it.

131

Before and since that change developments have taken place, all tending in the same direction, all working with a cumulative effect, and today, if we do not want to fail in our historic responsibility, we must put before ourselves four-square the problem of what is to become of us in Palestine, and what we are going to do in this generation—during the war, at the end of the war, immediately after the end of the war—in order to prevent the defeat of our historic aim in Palestine.

When the last war ended, one of the new things which it created on the constitutional plane of international arrangements was the concept of the Mandate. It was a wide concept, and quite a number of countries came under it. Palestine was only one of them, but country after country reached the stage where it was deemed worthy of independence, and Mandate after Mandate was abolished. Today the Palestine Mandate stands as an exception in that process. The question of the duration of the Mandate would have stood before us today as a consequence of this war even if we had not witnessed a change in the mandatory policy before the outbreak of war. But the Zionist content of the Mandate was liquidated, and the Mandate, instead of being an instrument of facilitating the achievement of the Zionist aim, became an instrument of defeating it. Moreover, as a result of the disturbances of 1936 to 1939, in fact as a result of the first phase of those disturbances in the year 1936, the whole question of Palestine was thrown into a melting pot. A major inquiry was held, a very authoritative body called the Palestine Royal Commission surveyed the whole field, and the most far-reaching conclusion that it reached was that the Jews in Palestine, in order to be able to work out their salvation, must be given political independence—that a Jewish state must be established. It is true that the Commission proposed that the solution of our problem should be applied only to a part of Palestine, and a very limited part at that. In quantity their conclusion was a bitter disappointment, but in quality it was a most far-reaching, positive step: they recognized that the world will not redeem its pledge to the Jewish people, unless we were restored in Palestine to the position of statehood, on terms of complete equality with other nations.

And last, but not least, the question of the relations between Palestine and the neighboring countries has been definitely put on the political agenda; the question of the interconnection between various states in the world, between groups of states, in various parts of the world, and between all states of the world, as forming one world unit, has been put on the order of the day. The final solution of Palestine's political problem thus becomes inescapable, and if we are not prepared with an unequivocal statement of our aims, our case is bound to go by default. The question of what is to become of Palestine will be decided in the not distant future, but it may be decided in accordance with the will of others, without taking into account our vital interests. Throughout the last twenty-five years we have increasingly felt the need for a more dynamic policy in order to make our work in Palestine possible; we have increasingly felt the need for governmental powers in order to be able to do what we had to do in Palestine; conduct immigration, undertake large-scale development schemes, bring in Jews, settle them, make life for them possible.

We have always said that our work is in its very essence a state-building enterprise. We knew very well that we must start from the very beginning. To us it has not been a question of formal independence alone. Formal independence alone would not have settled our problem in Palestine, so long as we were few and weak, as we were twenty-five years ago. We had first to acquire land, even to "create" land in Palestine, and bring in people. We had to build up these people, to make workers, producers and defenders of them. We visualized the attainment of independence as the ultimate goal, but in the process of the work we found that some power, some political means at our disposal, in addition to the financial means such as we possessed and in addition to the human energy that we were able to mobilize, were essential if we were to be able to make further headway.

Today, in the face of a policy which is diametrically opposed to our aims, as well as in the face of the unique chance for remaking the world which democratic victory in this war is going to bring about, we must put our case before the world in its entire magnitude. We must speak clearly as to what we believe should be done in Palestine. What we believe is possible in Palestine, is to transplant there very large numbers of Jews, perhaps all the surviving Jews of Europe. We must speak in terms of millions. We must speak in terms of years, not decades. The thing must and can be done quickly, more quickly and on a larger scale than we thought possible ever before.

Our experience in Palestine proves that. When we started our work in Palestine it was a poor, sparsely populated country. It was a country of emigration rather than of immigration. It was only contact between the land-hungry, homeless Jew and his native soil that worked the miracle of Jewish productivity. It is not because the best Jews in the world went to Palestine that they were able to do there what they could not do anywhere else in the world. It was not because Palestine was the best or the richest country that the Jews succeeded there more than they did in any other country, but because Jews are the people made by Palestine, and because Palestine is the country which alone in the world is a place which the Jew can call his own.

Our enterprise was laughed at, it was lightly dismissed and rejected by people who pretended to be great economic experts. All this, they said, is artificial, mere fancy, and it cannot lead to a great historic work of reconstruction. They argued that it was against the world trend to take a people of town dwellers and bring them back to the land: the general trend is a flight of people from the rural districts to the towns, and these people are trying to reverse the historic process. The general trend of migration is from poorer to richer countries, and these people are trying to set in motion a process of migration from rich countries into the poorest country imaginable. The trend of general human progress is in obedience to economic laws, and it is against those laws that people should base their lives not upon their economic interest, but upon some idea, some fancy, a remote recollection of their glorious past, or a very vague hope for the future.

Not only has our experience in Palestine given the lie to all these prophecies and shallow dicta of would-be experts, but it is becoming more and more evident that the trends of world development are pointing in the same direction. Under the complex condition of human life in the world today it is impossible to leave economics and social affairs to take care of themselves. Life must be organized and planned. At the root of that organization and planning there must be a national decision. A people, a nation, a class, any collective entity must ask itself: what do we want?—and it must plan accordingly.

We are fully aware of the fact that we do not live, and act, in a vacuum. The world is a very complicated organism. We know how it affects our life in the countries where we are today, and we have learned from bitter experience how it affects our chances of re-establishment in our own country. But difficulties are there to be overcome, not to be overlooked or to run away from. One great difficulty facing us is that the country to which we are returning is not an empty space. That is the cruel penalty we are paying for having left that country. There is no such thing as empty space in the world today. The laws of pressure operate in human society as they do in the physical world, and the country which we left empty in the course of centuries became populated. It is not fully filled, but still there is a considerable population there, belonging to a different people. It is perhaps natural for that population to resist our entry into Palestine, not to want to see Palestine change its familiar character. But we cannot help that. Our survival as a people, our rehabilitation as a nation are here at stake. The people who live in Palestine today, beside the Jews, are entitled to have their national aspirations recognized, but so are we; we are human beings, like other peoples on the face of the earth, and it is an elementary right of every human being to live in an environment that is congenial to him, to live together with his own people, speaking the same language, sharing the same feelings and shaping their environment in accordance with their ideas and tastes. That right cannot be denied to us, and the only place where we can achieve the fulfillment of that right is Palestine. The Arab people inhabits vast and potentially rich countries, much richer than Palestine. The future and the national development of the Arab people are more secure than of many other peoples in the world, apart from the Jews. No nation, no political unit achieves 100 percent of what it wants; even if the Arabs were to give up Palestine completely they would be achieving more than many other peoples, but they do not need to give Palestine up completely. We say that Palestine is our country, the only country that is ours. That does not mean that the Arabs who have lived in Palestine for centuries past and to whom that country is a home in the real sense of the term, should be asked to give it up, to give up the feeling that they are at home there. We believe that Palstine is the one country where Jews as a people are destined to achieve their self-determination. The Arabs as a people will achieve their self-determination in much larger territories and in much larger numbers than we shall ever have the chance of achieving in Palestine. However, the Arabs who live in Palestine are fully entitled to the preservation of their character. That need not interfere with the attainment of our goal, of converting Palestine into a predominantly Jewish country. That should not and need not interfere with our aim to see Palestine as a whole established as a Jewish Commonwealth.

What does it mean when we say, "we want Palestine established as a Jewish Commonwealth?" We want to bring as many Jews as possible into Palestine, and by that we shall certainly create there a Jewish majority. As we believe that this is the destiny of that country—because it is ours, and because there is no other to be the home of the Jewish people—we also believe that it is right and just that the policy of the government to be established there should be actively to promote that development, actively to make it possible for as many Jews as possible to settle in Palestine. The future of Palestine will forever be bound up with the future of the Jewish people in the sense that the Commonwealth which we want to see established in Palestine will be a Jewish Commonwealth. That does not mean that there will be, that there need be any discrimination, any difference as regards individual rights between Jews and Arabs. We cannot in one and the same breath claim equality for ourselves and deny equality to others. There must be a regime of complete equality of rights for all inhabitants of that country, but there must be a clear decision taken—a decision backed by the great powers, a decision which the conscience of the world should indorse—that this is the country where the Jews are to be given the fullest possible scope for working out their salvation, settling there in large numbers, striking roots in the soil, creating agriculture and industry, transport and commerce, and culture, so that the imprint on Palestine should be mainly an imprint of a Jewish country, of a predominantly Jewish country. That is the meaning of the term which we have launched into the world: a Jewish Commonwealth.

We are facing a three-cornered struggle today. We have to struggle with the world at large, to create understanding and sympathy for our aims. We have to struggle with the world immediately around us, in Palestine; we have to resist local pressure and to strengthen ourselves so as not to give in to that pressure. But we also have to conduct a struggle within our own ranks, among the Jewish people, and that last struggle is perhaps the most difficult of all. The struggle between brothers is always the most difficult and painful. We have to struggle with the assimilationism which dies hard; we have to struggle with Jewish cowardice, with Jews who are afraid to speak out as Jews, to face the world as Jews, to tackle the Jewish problem. We have to struggle even within Zionist ranks for the proper understanding of what the essence of Zionist policy should be at the present time, and that struggle is, again, world-wide. It has to be conducted in America, in England, and even in Palestine.

It is difficult for a people not accustomed to act together suddenly to gather under one banner and accept one central discipline.

We are a scattered people, everywhere a minority, and in the conditions of our life there is a very substantial measure of unity in Jewish ranks today. That does not mean, however, that we can rest content with that measure of unity, and that we can give up the struggle against very dangerous deviations from our central path.

Such deviations are manifest even in Palestine. A group of very important Jews in Palestine got together and formulated a political program, entirely divergent from the official Zionist program which has been endorsed in Palestine and in other countries. This group says: we also want immigration, we also want settlement on the land, we also want freedom for the Jews in Palestine, but we can achieve it in a different way; we can achieve it if we are less ambitious in our political claims, if we do not proclaim that we want Palestine to become a Jewish Commonwealth; if we do not ask for immigration to be regulated by ourselves.

What is the political program of these people? They say: Palestine should be a bi-national state; it should belong to both Jews and Arabs; Jews and Arabs must be on a footing of political equality, on a fifty-fifty basis. Some of them add: there must also be numerical parity—again the fifty-fifty formula—and they take it upon themselves to assure us that that is what the other party will accept, if we make the offer, and that this can be a basis for reconciliation and for peaceful development. They also say: we must declare from the outset that we are in favor of Palestine becoming a part of a larger system or Federation. They appeal to us: you are addressing yourselves to the world, but you should address yourselves to the Arabs. The conflict, they say, is not between you and the world, but between you and the Arabs; this is the problem which you must settle, and you are neglecting it.

What should our answer to that be? We ought to expose the fallacies underlying this trend of thought. It is true that the conflict is between us and the Arabs; it is not true that the conflict is not between us and the world. It is true that we must do our utmost to find ways of living at peace with the Arabs; it is not true that we shall find those ways by excluding the world from the problem of our relations with the Arabs. Ours is a *world problem.* If there is a people whose situation is a world problem in the fullest sense of the term, it is the Jews, and the character of this world problem places a very heavy responsibility upon the international factors. It places a responsibility upon England, upon America, upon Russia, and we cannot free the world from that responsibility; we must make it more and more conscious of it, and the Arab world must know that ours is a world problem, and that the great powers are taking a very direct interest in it. They must be made to realize that this country of Palestine is not a private domain of the Arabs, but that as a consequence of history—something that cannot be changed—this country is a focus of all Jewish hopes, that the whole world regards that country as being the focus of all Jewish hopes, and that if they are to approach the problem realistically they must face the fact that Palestine is rooted in the consciousness of the world as a country which the Jewish people considers its own.

By over-stressing the importance of the Arab factor in our problem we are not paving the way to Jewish-Arab unity, we are not making Jewish-Arab peace more attainable. If the impression is created among the Arabs that the Jews depend primarily on their good will in order to achieve what they want in Palestine, then we stand very little chance of achieving it. But if the Arabs learn that the whole world takes an interest in our problem, and that it is necessary for the world to solve the Jewish question, they will sooner or later adjust their policy to that new reality. It is a fallacy to suggest that we can offer the Arabs political peace on the basis of numerical parity with any hope of acceptance on their part. The Arab Nationalists fully realize the consequences that numerical equality between Jews and Arabs is likely to lead to; they are not prepared to agree to such a settlement unless it is imposed upon them by the world.

But can we say: "We are prepared to guarantee that our numbers in Palestine will not rise beyond a certain point; we shall just become equal in numbers with you and then our growth will stop"?

How can we bind a Jew to whom it will be a matter of life and death to enter Palestine, who will know that there is room for him there, and that there is no room for him anywhere else in the world, how can we bind him by our political agreement today that he should honor this obligation of ours and not save himself? He will ask: "By what manner of right did you take such an obligation upon yourselves? How can you bind me? It is my country just as it is yours. How did you draw the line? How did you separate the Jewish people into two camps, the fortunate ones who managed to get in before a certain figure was reached, and the unfortunate ones who happened to be too late and in whose face the doors were closed by a Jewish agreement?"

This is an impossible undertaking, and it would not satisfy the Arabs either. Another fallacy is to offer a federation of Palestine and the neighboring countries as something that will bring about immediate Jewish-Arab agreement. We should certainly welcome a process of development which would bring us into closer and closer connection with the neighboring countries. But we envisage this process on the basis of ourselves becoming numerous and strong in Palestine. It is only if we are numerous and strong that we can offer something important to the neighboring countries.

Instead of agreeing in advance to a federation without knowing what kind of federation it is going to be, what we should say is: "We are most certainly prepared to consider any form of unity between Palestine and the neighboring countries which will not be contradictory to our basic interests. But we are already strong enough in Palestine to make it impossible for any other factor to decide the fate of Palestine without our consent, and therefore if the neighboring countries want a federation and they want Palestine included in that federation, they must provide such a scheme that would satisfy our basic interests. Otherwise we shall not take part in it, and if we do not take part in it, the whole scheme will not work."

If we talk that language, if we assume that attitude, only then can we achieve something. The Arab people around us must realize that a new reality has been created in Palestine which affects the neighboring countries, that the over half a million Jews in Palestine form a compact and highly productive community, which has shown what it can do in the present war, a community backed by the Jews the world over, with political friends the world over; a community which has chances of winning over the sympathy of the great powers for a major solution of the Jewish problem in Palestine. If therefore our homeland is needed as a part of that federation, Jews must be negotiated with. The question cannot be settled behind the backs of the Jews. Palestine cannot be handed over to the Arabs, over the heads of the Jews. The Jews are a party, and the most vitally interested party. If it is put on that plane, then perhaps there is hope for a political arrangement that will be satisfactory to all sides. The war will one day come to an end through the victory of the United Nations. The approach of victory is already stirring the conscience of the world, and an atmosphere will be created which will perhaps present a unique chance, one in many generations, if not in many centuries, to put our problem before the world.

April, 1943

AMERICA

Charles A. Beard

Bernard DeVoto

Uriah Zvi Engelman

Hayim Greenberg

Robert H. Jackson

Jacob Lestshinsky

Kurt Lewin

Claude McKay

Nathan Reich

Marie Syrkin

Jacob J. Weinstein

Popular Superstitions About Jews

by Jacob J. Weinstein

DURING THE past few years I was invited to address some sixty non-Jewish forums, clubs and societies on the Pacific coast on the theme, "The Jew in the Gentile World." I made it a necessary condition of acceptance that there be a period of discussion following the lecture which gave an historical account of the rise and spread of anti-Semitism. This essay is based on the material of these discussions. In many instances the questions and statements were written. For the rest, I made it a practice to write down the questions asked immediately after the lecture.

The term "superstitions" is not used in a derogatory sense. It is intended to convey the meaning of a holdover from the past; and to intimate that some measure of reality is given to a superstition by the very desire of the people who hold it. Thus, there is no scientific evidence that the "mandrakes" mentioned in Genesis actually cured sterility, but it is more than possible that belief in them created a psychological receptivity helpful to conception. Above all, we wish to imply by the term superstition, that evidence of one fulfillment is worth a hundred denials. The hundred instances where no untoward accident has occurred after a black cat crossed one's path does not balance with believers the one instance where it has. So too, a hundred poor Jews do not wash out the impress of one rich one with those who hold the superstition that all Jews are rich. We must leave to the folk-lorists and the psychoanalysts the explanation of this phenomenon.

The Longevity of the Jew

Some Gentiles are convinced that the Jew is immortal. The conviction excites an admiration that turns into awe and often into fear. There is a slight resemblance to the belief in the nine lives of a cat—where the initial admiration for the toughness of the feline merges into a suspicion of traffic with the devil. As one person put it, "I can understand the Egyptians, the Babylonians, the Assyrians. They had their day and moved off the stage. I enjoy the records of their achievements in our museums. But I wouldn't want a mummy for my neighbor." Another discussant confessed that he would be glad to pay Ripley 25 cents to see a 300 year old man but he would feel mighty uneasy about having that man on the same block.

Some years ago, Viereck and Eldridge wrote a fantastic novel, "My First Two Thousand Years" in which the hero is the undying Jew who delights in corrupting the blood of the people in whose midst he dwells. We are dealing with folk lore where logic is not a very effective antidote. It is not very helpful to point out the fallacies of confusing a race with an individual, of identifying cultural continuity with physical persistence.

Even accounting for the three thousand years of Jewish cultural continuity is no easy task. It is hard for Jews themselves to understand the complex of positive and negative forces that has preserved their identity. Which of us knows where the positive pulls of religion, history, language leave off and the negative push of anti-Semitism begins in this elliptical field of force that bounds the tents of Israel?

The Jew as Anti-Christ

Among fundamentalist church circles, I often heard that the suffering of the Jew is just punishment for his refusal to accept the identity of God and Jesus. The Jews' plight is a warning to all infidels and heretics and back-sliders. Since this is a divine plan, you would imagine the fundamentalists would hold blameless the human instruments through which this plan of salvation is achieved. The material success and outward happiness which some Jews seem to enjoy are interpreted as subtler forms of punishment on "the higher they rise, the harder they fall" principle. The orthodox Jew who practices his mistaken faith, they believe, is more to be admired than the agnostic Jew—for the religious Jew has the capacity for faith and some day will be converted to the one true faith while the unbeliever is hopeless.

Only rarely did I hear the charge that the Jews killed Christ. Once when in answer to this charge I maintained that the Jews could not consistently be blamed for crucifying the Savior when the crucifixion was the predetermined climax of the divine scheme of salvation, my auditor replied, "The Jews should have been smart enough to pass the buck and let Jehovah pick some other suckers." Another fundamentalist in my audience once expressed his bewilderment, "If Jehovah thought enough of the Jews to pick the Savior from their midst, why didn't he command them to accept the true Messiah?"

I remember vividly my discussion of the Jewish problem with a group of young Christians at their summer camp. A young Tarzan, thick lipped, full nostrilled, a student at a theological seminary, was intent on blaming the Jews for corrupting the faith of Christians. The Jews, he insisted, through their movies, jazz bands, their passion for pleasure, lured the faithful from the narrow path. I recalled that Adonis smarting under the fetters of a grim faith, when I recently read this passage from Freud:*

"We must not forget that all the people who now excel in the practice of anti-Semitism became Christians only in relatively recent times, sometimes forced to it by bloody compulsion. One might say that they are 'badly Christened,' under the thin veneer of Christianity they have remained what their ancestors were, barbarically polytheistic. They have not yet overcome their grudge against the new religion which was forced on them, and they have projected it on to the source from which Christianity came to them. The fact that the Gospels tell a story which is enacted among Jews and in truth treats only of Jews, has facilitated such a projection. The hatred for Judaism is at bottom hatred for Christianity, and it is not surprising that in the German National Socialist revolution this close connection of the two monotheistic religions finds such clear expression in the hostile treatment of both."

If Freud is right, the Jew is indeed damned for a sheep and for a goat. He is cursed for not accepting Christ and cursed for having foisted him on an unwilling world. It is my opinion that the Freudian thesis offers only a partial explanation and applies

---

* Freud, Sigmund, "Moses and Monotheism," Knopf, 1939, pp. 144-5.

mainly to the behavior of religious fanatics. More general causes of anti-Semitism are implicit in the superstitions I shall now detail.

The Jews Are Clannish

In not one of the sixty discussions recorded was there failing the charge that the Jews are clannish. In the smaller communities they do not join the social life which is centered around the churches. In the suburbs of our larger cities they do not join the Garden Clubs, the sewing circles or the country clubs. "On Sundays," said a cultivated woman in Mill Valley, "instead of visiting with the neighbors, they invite hordes of their city friends who noisily poke fun at our quaint suburban habits." In the same discussion a gentleman volunteered a case history from his tennis club.

"We had about five Jews out of 200 members up till 1931. They were well liked and were considered as sportsmen and not as Jews. Then we had a drive for new members to cover the scars of the depression and we brought in seven more Jews among twenty others. Now these seven would congregate together in the locker room, take a drink together and tell stories that seemed to call for loud and sustained laughter. Before you knew it we were conscious of a Jew group in the Club. We unconsciously refrained from joining their tables and took it for granted that they always wanted to play together. We had prided ourselves on keeping our numbers down to encourage a congenial family spirit. We saw that breaking down with this new Jewish clique and so we decided to limit our Jewish membership in the future to five."

In a San Mateo audience, a discussant expressed resentment over the fact that his wealthy Jewish neighbors contributed large sums to Jewish hospitals, relief of Jews in Europe, and to the upbuilding of Palestine. "They give more money to foreigners just because they're Jews than they give to Americans from whom they make their money," he concluded. The influx of some thousands of German refugees has greatly intensified this reaction. Acts of charity and self-sacrifice are interpreted as manifestations of the Jews' secret pact to stick together. The wave of nationalism, sweeping the world, has provided a patriotic rationalization for the provincials' distrust of people outside his bailiwick.

In the discussion on this point whenever it came up, I posed the question, "Is the Jews' clannishness a cause or an effect of anti-Semitism?" The question proved most fruitful for it often spared me the trouble of making any defense of this charge. An active clubwoman in Sacramento bristled with this retort: "When it comes to cold facts, when we invite a Jew of wealth and high social position to join us and she refuses, we say she is clannish, but we do not consider it clannish on our part to refuse membership to Jews who are not in a position to add prestige to our organization."

Another woman in Fresno almost threw her knitting needles at a fellow auditor who expressed resentment at the herd solidarity of Jews. This woman it seemed had a daughter whose closest chum at high school was a Jew. On graduation, the two friends went to the State University. A prominent sorority pledged our discussant's daughter but refused to issue an invitation to the chum solely on the grounds that she was Jewish. "What could the Jewish girl do, but join a Jewish sorority? Here is a perfect proof that Jewish clannishness is an effect of anti-Semitism."

A man in a San Francisco audience asked himself why he did not resent the fraternization of Irish, Italians, Germans or Armenians but did object to the Jews sticking together. He knew that the same Jews who belong to the B'nai B'rith lodge are proprietors of small clothing stores on Market Street. Theirs was the most competitive business, he admitted. The Italians, on the other hand, have a practical monopoly in the fishing industry. They set and maintain prices on everything from crab to tuna. Yet he resented the Jew and accepted the Italian. "Maybe it's because I got an inferiority complex about the Jew. I figure if one Jew is so hard to beat, where will we come in if they should decide to get together."

Here, too, there are motives at work which are deeper than those recognized by the prejudiced. Freud, who believes that we inherit certain reaction patterns from our ancestors, maintains that Gentiles harbor a hold-over of the resentment felt toward the Jews when they first claimed to be the Chosen People of God. Circumcision, the rite which set the Jews apart, evokes a fear based on a castration complex, he also adds.

Whatever the motivations, we now are confronted with a vicious cycle. The Jews' sense of superiority made him hated. The hatred hedged him in, forced him to seek consolation with his own —to become clannish. This clannishness gives the Gentile a good excuse to discriminate against the Jew. The discrimination further ghettoizes the Jew—ad infinitum

The Jew as the City Slicker

Moralists tell us that the soil is the seed bed of piety. Religion hinges on the seasons, and the soul's intimacy with nature. The city on the other hand is the estate of the Devil. Ruled by the whore of Babylon, it has drained the country of its youth and corrupted it. Some economists say the city leeches on the country. Manufacturers' tariffs, protected prices and bankers' mortgages siphon the cream of the harvest, leaving the farmer a residue of bills and hate. Whatever the reasons, most sociologists admit that there is a more or less latent hostility between country and city. In many a farmer there lingers the feeling that a man who makes his living off of anything but the soil and its resources is, somehow, a swindler. And this feeling is shared by many city folk who have recently come from the farm and whose relatives are still on the farm. Their occasional visits to the folks in the country, their interest in the country fair and the garden they cultivate even if it is a tiny strip of lawn, is their vicarious atonement for the sin of dwelling in the Metropolis.

The Jew cannot make this atonement. For in the eyes of many Gentiles, he has never been on the soil. To them the Jew is indigenous to the teeming alleys of the city. Asphalt and cobblestone are his native milieu. In them he sows his ducats and reaps his golden harvest. Whereas other stocks weaken and ultimately wither in the sterile air of congested cities, the Jew thrives and multiplies.

I count in my records no less than seventy-five statements that clearly intimate that the Jew would be better thought of it he could establish a reputation as a farmer. Following my talk in Los Angeles, an auditor sent up a newspaper clipping telling of the arrival of twenty-two German refugees on a boat bound for the Canal. The reporter had interviewed the arrivals and found that they represented medicine, law, teaching, engineering and business administration, one a bank executive. Across this item in heavy black pencil, the auditor had written, "How many of these will become good Americans and do honest-to-God work on the soil? We have more than enough stock brokers, bankers, pawn shop proprietors, and second hand dealers. . . . Signed, A Patriotic American."

When I mentioned such groups as the colony of eighty Jewish families on the poultry farms in Petaluma, my questioners often replied, "That ain't real dirt farming. That's mere processing. You convert feed into eggs and fryers." Nor does it help much to explain historically how the Jew was driven from his land in Palestine where he was primarily a farmer, how he was denied the right of owning land by all Christian countries from the third to the seventeenth century, how he was forced into merchandising and moneylending by the Church and the feudal lords, and finally how these business skills were needed by the trade expansion which followed the Industrial Revolution. The average American feels, in spite of these facts, that the Jew has had a chance to establish himself on the soil in America and should show a greater inclination to do so.

Responsive to this sentiment, Jews are establishing Vocational Guidance offices in the larger communities to direct Jewish youth to skilled crafts, the forestry service and scientific farming. It is not, by any means, certain that this will solve the problem. It may merely relieve the pressure of anti-Semitism in the cities and introduce it into the country. With the farmer bearing the brunt of our economic dislocation, mortgaged to the neck, his sons forced to seek a living in the cities, he may be more than ordinarily riled by the traits which the Jew is said to have derived from his long urban experience.

The Rothschild Myth

In Pasadena, a Townsendite explained to me that the reason they had adopted the slogan "Ham and Eggs" was so that Jews would know that they were not included in the "Thirty Dollars Every Thursday" plan. When I asked why—he replied that it was those international Jew money-changers called Rothschild, who, through their henchman Morgenthau, were keeping this country from adopting this simple and sure path to prosperity. He admitted that he had gotten much of the proof for this conclusion from a magazine called *Social Justice* edited by Father Coughlin.

In forty-five of the sixty audiences which I addressed there were people who had been bitten by the Rothschild Myth. "Isn't it true," said one soft spoken young engineer in an Oakland audience, "that the Warburgs, Paul and Felix, were responsible for the World War? Did not Paul of Germany write to Felix in America 'While this war is causing much loss of life it will definitely strengthen our firm's position?'" Another in the same audience followed this lead by declaring, "It is well known that the Jews Baruch and Brandeis steered Wilson into the war and that Baruch, the confidant of both Hoover and Roosevelt, engineered the stock collapse of 1929."

One notices in these and many similar statements a peculiar combination of populism and anti-Semitism. Bebel called it the "socialism" of blockheads. The farmer, the petty merchant and the worker are confused by the complexities of high finance. The mysteries of stock promotion and pyramiding are the devices of Satan. But they are also believers in the American dream, the streamlined ladder of success, the rewards of initiative and ambition. The conflict is resolved by making the distinction which Hitler makes in "Mein Kampf" between Aryan or creative capital and Jewish or destructive capital. This permits the Gentile to swallow a Rockefeller, a Mellon, a Ford, a Morgan, a Dupont, but to gag at a Kahn, a Warburg, or a Baruch who, compared to the first named titans, are small fry indeed. When Singer, President of the United States Bank, was indicted for fraudulent practices, there was considerable rumbling throughout the nation about the sharp practices of Jews. When Mitchel and Whitney were indicted and convicted of grosser crimes, there was not nearly as much revulsion. There was in fact a good deal of commiseration and excusing: "They were just unlucky. They got caught at it. Whitney must have been trying to pay off a debt of honor. He certainly took his medicine like a sport. You gotta hand it to him." Anti-Semitism and other forms of prejudice are most sharply manifested in the leaway to breakers of the laws and mores of a group. One who is labelled as "not belonging" or not one of *us,* must toe the line. He is constantly on probation. This is a holdover of the tribal suspicion of the outsider.

The Jew as Non-Conformist

In times of crisis and of sharp transition, the various "we" groups who have accommodated themselves to one another, become shaken up and realigned. Demagogues supply them with dynamic symbols and scape-goats to further sharpen the "we" feeling. Differences, formerly accepted and enjoyed in the give and take of the social process, now become danger signals and pretexts of hostility. In the halcyon days, Americans enjoyed the playing of an Elman, a Heifetz, a Gabrilowitch and considered the admission price little enough for the privilige of enjoying the masters of art. Today, we hear a great deal about patronizing American art and artists. A concert pianist in one of my audiences stated: "The booking offices are Jew-controlled. Only Jewish artists with Russian names get a chance. It is time for Americans to develop an art of their own and encourage their own talented people." Here again a positive movement for national expression and a justified reaction to the idolatry of foreign names in art circles is sharpened and distorted by the infiltration of anti-Semitism. There is perhaps also an element of revolt against universal culture—always a part of national revivals.

Revivalists, whether religious or national, are lacking in humor. Grim crusaders of the White Camellia, or the black shirt cannot afford to laugh. Satire is anathema to the frenetic. But even the average citizen gets touchy about his national virtues, his occupational traits, his household sanctities. I detected in not a few instances an antagonism to radio and stage comedians such as Eddie Cantor, the Marx brothers, the Ritz brothers, Al Jolson, Fanny Brice and Jack Benny. As one auditor revealed in a letter which she wrote because she did not want to say this on the floor, "I am not denying the cleverness or the talent of the Jewish comedian. My children will forego their meals rather than miss Eddie Cantor. I myself laugh at his jokes. When I am done laughing however, I feel sort of uneasy. Then I get resentful. I say to myself 'What are we going to hold on to and believe in if we keep on making fun of chastity, marriage, faith and honesty in business?' "

Another discussant vented his spleen on Groucho Marx, "Why that fellow's brains work like a machine gun. He's too quick for any Gentile to follow. I always feel he is having a good laugh at us Yokels. The Jew is too damn clever for his own good." Still others resented the Yiddish-Hebrew expressions like kosher, kibbitz, gonef and goy which these comedians introduce in their speech. They think these words are used with a double meaning so that Jews may enjoy particularly nasty cracks about Gentiles.

Students of post war Germany noted a similar reaction toward Jews on the stage and not alone toward comedians, but to musicians, artists, and writers. The Jews were charged with undermining the staid old Teutonic national virtues in order that they might introduce their own modernistic, Semitic, international styles and values. This fear of the innovator is not confined to the realms of literature and art. It comes down to the zipper trouser and beach pajama. One of the discussants at a Los Angeles forum charged

the Jews, as the monopolists of the clothing trade, with deliberately inventing these skimpy, bizarre, outfits to stimulate business.
And she further accused Hollywood movie interests and the big
Jewish beauty lotion makers, like Max Factor and Helena Rubin-
stein, of complicity in this conspiracy to corrupt American taste
while rifling the Gentiles' pockets. "The first man to wear a cor-
setted coat is your Jewish traveling salesman. The first woman to
introduce a new style in dress to the public is some daughter of a
Jewish designer. Why should a foreigner from Poland tell Miss
America what to wear?"

One of the most pathetic instances of misunderstanding bred
in the tense atmosphere of crisis periods came to my attention
during a round table discussion with a small group of Gentiles in
a Marin County suburb. One of the members of this group, Mrs.
Ingram, let us call her, told me of her experience with the Rosens.
The Rosens had only recently moved into the community. He was
the manager of the neighboring town's leading store. Mrs. Rosen
was neighborly and cheerfully assumed her share of community
responsibilities. The Ingrams were happy about their new neighbors—for there were few congenial couples of their own age—
and it was not long before the Ingrams asked the Rosens to an informal dinner. Mrs. Ingram explained that she served just the
sort of dinner they were accustomed to have—broth, leg of lamb,
peas, potatoes, cold slaw, home made gooseberry pie and coffee.
After dinner the foursome had a pleasant game of bridge, topped
off with the exchange of a few opinions about things in general.
Three days later, the Rosens invited the Ingrams for dinner. And
the Rosens, it seems, put on the dog. They had the best company
silver. They served cocktails with a dazzling variety of hors
d'oeuvres. There was crayfish soup, broiled squab stuffed with
wild rice and an elaborate rum torte, coffee, brandy and good
Havana cigars. The Ingrams were offended. Mr. Ingram knew
that Mr. Rosen was earning no more than he. He considered such
a dinner a vulgar, pretentious display. Mrs. Ingram felt that it
may have been a not too subtle reflection on her hospitality. At

any rate it set up barriers. The Ingrams were not willing to enter into this kind of social competition. They decided that this dinner was the Rosens' way of saying: This is the kind of standard we prefer in our social relationships. The Ingrams decided that the Rosens were guilty of bad taste and began slowly but surely to drop them.

Now it so happened that I knew the Rosens. I knew that they had, at considerable sacrifice, sought a small community where they might escape the burden of being Jews. They wanted a place where their children could grow up with other American children and not be conscious of their Jewishness. They were so thrilled that the Ingrams who were old residents and socially prominent had accepted them. Mrs. Rosen, an excellent cook, born in a family where an epicure's table was a tradition, had merely exerted herself to celebrate what she hoped would be a life long friendship.

Now one must admit that the Rosens would have shown better taste by making their hospitality more like that which they had received from the Ingrams. But is it too much to expect the Ingrams to have understood something of this defense mechanism which is at work in every Jew and makes him overcompensate for the feeling of inferiority with which the world has imbued him? Is it too much to ask the Ingrams to understand the intensity and eagerness which hostility has bred in the Jew so that his reaction is greater than the stimulus requires? In the mental climate of our times this *is* too much to ask of even such good folk as the Ingrams. It is the Jews' difficult task to overcome his conditioning by extreme self-discipline while he works for the mitigation of those economic and political pressures which turn minor differences into barbed wire fences.

The Jew as Radical

The Nazi propagandists could vindicate their low estimate of the average man's intelligence by pointing to those whom they have persuaded to believe that Jews are a menace because they are the controlling international financiers and also the guiding brains of world communism. The fact is that few people are capable of thinking in terms of economic philosophies or monetary plans. My experience with Gentile audiences convinced me that the average man's fear of the Jew as a radical is not based on his comprehension of the economic goals of radicalism. It is due more to his feeling that collectivism, socialism, communism, involve a departure from, if not violence to, certain principles that have become the immovable fixtures of his mind. The relation between vested interests and fixed ideas is not as automatic as some Marxists believe. People who know that they might benefit from public ownership of utilities nevertheless fear socialism as a threat to their individual liberty. The identification of Jew and radical sets against the Jew not only the wealthy conservatives but all those who find in the cluster of accepted traditions their only anchorage in a fast shifting world.

In the San Francisco Commonwealth Club section meeting discussing the problem of the refugees, a successful businessman uttered his conviction that communism was the extension of the Jewish clan idea. He thought that the Jews' generosity in philanthropy was the outcome of his belief in sharing the wealth. "The way they take care of the sick and poor would bankrupt any government besides loading society with the unfit. A poor Jew has a right to demand from a rich Jew all he needs to set himself up in business on the threat of exposing him in the synagogue if he doesn't." Another discussant was inclined to believe that there was something to this Jewish Bolshevism business from the way Jews disregard privacy, their own or anyone else's, and from the way they let their mother-in-law's relatives barge in for breakfast, lunch and dinner. In Seattle, I heard a University of Washington athlete give this reaction to Professor Harold Laski's visit to the campus, "What's the University come to when it pays a Jew from the London Ghetto to come here to tell us Karl Marx has got more on the ball than George Washington?"

In Portland, a waterfront employer resented the Jew's prominence in the labor scene, "They may not be the topflight officials but they are almost invariably the legal advisors, the research men, the negotiators, the editors and publicity men for the labor unions. They occupy the key positions and are teaching the unions to take every advantage of the New Deal labor legislation—also inspired by Jews like Frankfurter, Cohen and Frank."

The reactions here recorded are typical of many others received from my sixty audiences. They illustrate the human hunger for a scapegoat. We kick the door in which we have jammed our finger. Forces set into operation by the Industrial Revolution are compelling changes which threaten the property and peace of mind of the comfortable. There are those who cannot understand the nature of these forces nor the complex social structure in which they operate. It is easier and more satisfy for them to create a personal devil, a scapegoat and blame that trouble on him. The Jew offers himself as the most available candidate.

What is the Jew to Do?

The Jew is harassed by conflicting counsel. If he tries to make himself inconspicuous by withdrawing from public positions he is accused of disloyalty and civic ingratitude. If he joins the organizations which promise to relieve the pressures in our system, he is called a communist. Jewish leadership is stymied before this dilemma.

The fact is that we are dealing with folk lore and superstition where reason and logic rarely apply. Men are freed from superstition as they gain greater mastery over their environment. Failure to meet the problem of distribution and organization has led to a cultural retrogression. The Jew is caught in the widening area of the cultural lag. He is not powerful enough to do much by himself, to counteract this process. But he can ally himself with those democratic forces who are trying to lengthen the economic bed for our growing body politic as against those forces who would cut the body to fit the procrustean bed. In this alone lies the chance of his salvation.

May, 1941

When Facing Danger

by Kurt Lewin

I.

THE WORLD is suspended in balance between peace and war. Sometimes there seems to be hope that war will be averted after all; sometimes it looks as if war would start very soon. Most people hate war because it is destructive and senseless. On the other hand, those who are interested in democracy realize that there is but one of two alternatives, either to live as slaves under Fascism, or to be ready to die for democracy. Thus the heart of every freedom-loving person wavers between two opposite poles, and even more so the heart of the Jew. If the Jew is not a dreamer, he realizes what additional horrors he has to expect from both war and peace. In every European war the Jews have fought and died for their countries, and in addition have been picked out for mal-treatment both by friend and enemy. I am afraid this additional Jewish plight will be worse than ever before. There is little doubt that the German Jew who has been deprived of all means of livelihood and is now carefully excluded from the army, will nevertheless have ample chances to die for this very German "fatherland" in the next war, as he did in the last. Already, German newspapers, in other words the German government, suggest the formation of special Jewish battalions to be used in places of particularly great danger. With German machine guns in back, they will have to fight the enemy in front. The situation of the Jews in Italy and Hungary will not be much different, and certainly they will be the first to feel the scarcity of food. I am afraid that the situation of the great Jewish population of Poland, a country which at present stands on the other side of the fence, will not be much better.

But how does peace look to the Jew, a peace in which one coun-try after the other seems to be gradually drawn into the orbit of

Nazi domination or Fascist ideology? Today Nazi Germany is, doubtless, the greatest European power, having swallowed Austria, Czechoslovakia, and one might add Italy, which for all practical purposes can be considered as ruled by the German Gestapo. In all these countries, including Hungary, the outlawing of the Jews has of course been firmly established. Not less disastrous is the spreading of Nazi ideology which in times of peace is easily disseminated. Today in every country of the world, not only influential Nazi agents, but also powerful groups of citizens believe in the Fascist creed, and the greater the economic difficulties in those countries, the greater the number of adherents to this gospel. As to the Jews, Fascism necessarily means persecution and, at least, the establishment of a ghetto. Jews have been recognized as human beings only since the ideas of the American and the French revolutions became dominant, particularly the idea of the basic equality of men. Jewish rights are inseparably bound to this philosophy of equality. A basic principle of Nazism is the inequality of men. It therefore, of necessity, denies equal rights to the Jews.

Thinking in this way of peace and war, what then should the Jew hope for? Should he hope for peace with the likelihood of the spreading of Fascism including torture and destruction of the Jew, or should he hope for the disaster of war? The Jews are but a small atom in a turbulent world, their fate is decided by all-powerful forces, which may seem beyond the sphere of their influence. Thus the Jew might well ask himself: What shall we do? Shall we fall down and cry aloud, "Shema Yisroel," as our fathers did again and again when facing death and destruction? Little else seems to be left to the Jews in certain European countries. But for the rest of the Jews there is still time for thought and action.

I suppose many feel as deeply as I do that action is what we need in Jewish life today. My generation in Europe has gone through four years of war, followed by years of grave economic disturbances and revolutions. It does not look as if the next ten years are going to be more quiet and comfortable. The Jewish problem will certainly be no less serious.

If it has ever been a question whether the Jewish problem is an individual or a social one, a clear-cut answer was provided by the S. A. men in the streets of Vienna who beat with steel rods any Jew irrespective of his past conduct or status. Jews all over the world now recognize that the Jewish problem is a social problem. Thus we will have to turn to sociology and social-psychology if we wish to get scientific help for its solution. Scientifically the Jewish problem has to be treated as a case of an underprivileged minority. In the Diaspora the Jew does not enjoy the same opportunities as the majority. The degree and kind of restrictions imposed upon him vary greatly in different countries and at different times. Sometimes he is practically outlawed. At other times the restrictions are merely social in nature, without much hindrance in occupational and political life. Frequently some parts of the Jewish population enjoy better conditions than parts of the non-Jewish population. By and large, however, the Jewish group as a whole has the status of an underprivileged minority.

It should be understood that any underprivileged minority is preserved as such by the more privileged majority. The emancipation of the Jews from the ghetto has not been accomplished by Jewish action, but was brought about by a change in the needs and sentiments of the majority. Today again, it can easily be shown how any increase or decrease in the economic difficulties of the majority increases or decreases the pressure upon the Jewish minority. This is one of the reasons why Jews everywhere are necessarily interested in the welfare of the majority among whom they live.

It has been recognized long ago that the basis of anti-Semitism is partly the need of the majority for a scapegoat. Frequently in modern history it is not the majority as such but an autocratic group ruling the majority which needs the scapegoat as a means of distracting the masses. The most striking recent example is Mussolini's sudden attack on the Italian Jews against whom practically no anti-Semitic feeling had existed before. The same Mussolini, who but a few years ago was favorably disposed toward

Zionism, found it wise to follow Hitler's example, or he may have been forced by Hitler to do so. Certainly nothing in the conduct of Italian Jewry has given the slightest cause for this change. Here again, the need of the majority or of their ruling "elite" alone has determined the fate of Jewish community.

The Jew might as well realize that these happenings are practically independent of good or bad behavior on his part. There is nothing more erroneous that the belief of many Jews that there would be no anti-Semitism if only every Jew behaved properly. One might even say that it is the good behavior of the Jews, their hard work, their efficiency and success as businessmen, physicians, and lawyers, which give momentum to the anti-Semitic drive. Anti-Semitism cannot be stopped by the good behavior of the individual Jew, because it is not an individual, but a social problem.

How little relation exists between Jewish conduct and anti-Semitism is well illustrated by the way the majority shifts its official reasons for maltreatment. For hundreds of years the Jews have been persecuted for religious reasons. Today racial theories serve as pretext. The reasons are easily changed according to whatever seems to be the most efficient argument at the moment. I have been told that in this country one of the most influential associations of manufacturers is working with two types of pamphlets. One of these pamphlets, used when a group of workers or middle-class people are approached, pictures the Jew as a capitalist and as an international banker. But if the same propagandist speaks to an audience of manufacturers, he uses a pamphlet which pictures the Jews as communists.

The Jew answering accusations should realize that they are but a surface, below which deeper social problems are hidden even in those cases when the argument is put forth in good faith. The need of the majority for a scapegoat grows out of tension, e.g. from an economic depression. Scientific experiments prove that this need is particularly strong in tensions which are due to an autocratic regime. No "logical" argument will destroy these basic forces. One cannot hope to combat Father Coughlin efficiently by telling everybody how good the Jews are.

More than words of self-defense are necessary to change social reality. Certainly Jews will have to try everything to ally themselves with any other force seriously fighting Fascism. Being but few in number it is incumbent upon us to try to win the help of other groups. However, the Jew will have to realize that for him as well as for any other underprivileged group the following statement holds: Only the efforts of the group itself will achieve the emancipation of the group.

There is one field of action left to the Jew, where the results depend mainly upon himself. This is the field of Jewish life.

II.

What makes the Jews a group and what makes an individual a member of the Jewish group? I know that many Jews are deeply concerned and puzzled by this problem. They have no clear answer and their whole life is in danger of becoming meaningless, as it has become meaningless for thousands of German half-Jews and quarter-Jews who must face fate without knowing why. Historically this problem is relatively new to the Jew. There has been a time, only one hundred and fifty years ago, when in Germany belonging to the Jewish group was an accepted and unquestioned fact. During the time of the ghetto Jews might have been under pressure as a group; the individual Jew, however, had a social unit to which he clearly belonged. The Jews in Poland, Lithuania and other Eastern European countries have maintained what might be termed a national life which gave to the individual a "social home." When coming to America, the Eastern Jews brought much of this group life with them. They have kept alive the inner cohesive forces of the group.

It is well to realize that every underprivileged minority group is kept together not only by cohesive forces among its members but also by the boundary which the majority erects against the crossing of an individual from the minority to the majority group. It is in the interest of the majority to keep the minority in its

underprivileged status. There are minorities which are kept together almost entirely by such a wall around them. The members
of these minorities show certain typical characteristics resulting
from this situation. Every individual likes to gain in social status.
Therefore the member of an underprivileged group will try to
leave it for the more privileged majority. In other words, he will
try to do what in the case of Negroes is called "passing", in the
case of Jews, "assimilation". It would be an easy solution of the
minority problem if it could be done away with through individual
assimilation. Actually, however, such a solution is impossible for
any underprivileged group. Equal rights for women could not be
attained by one after the other being granted the right to vote; the
Negro problem cannot be solved by individual "passing". A few
Jews might be fully accepted by non-Jews. This chance, however,
is today more meager than ever and certainly it is absurd to believe
that fifteen million Jews can sneak over the boundary one by one.

What then is the situation of a member of a minority group
kept together merely by the repulsion of the majority? The basic
factor in his life is his wish to cross this insuperable boundary.
Therefore, he lives almost perpetually in a state of conflict and
tension. He dislikes or even hates his own group because it is
nothing but a burden to him. Like an adolescent who does not
wish to be a child any longer but who knows that he is not accepted as an adult, such a person stands at the border-line of his
group, being neither here nor there. He is unhappy and shows the
typical characteristics of a marginal man who does not know
where he belongs. A Jew of this type will dislike everything specifically Jewish, for he will see in it that which keeps him away from
the majority for which he is longing. He will show dislike for
those Jews who are outspokenly so and will frequently indulge in
self-hatred.

There is one more characteristic peculiar to minority groups
kept together merely by outside pressure as contrasted with the
members of a minority who have a positive attitude towards their
own group. The latter group will have an organic life of its own.
It will show organization and inner strength. A minority kept to-

gether only from outside is in itself chaotic. It is composed of a mass of individuals without inner relations with each other, a group unorganized and weak.

Historically, the Jews living in the Diaspora were kept together partly by the inner cohesive forces of the group and partly by the pressure of hostile majorities. The importance of these two factors has varied at different times and in different countries. In some parts of Eastern Europe the positive attitude has been strengthened by cultural superiority to the environment. In this country the positive attitude is also strong as yet. We should not, however, be blind to the fact that for quite a number of Jews "being forced together" has become the dominant, or at least an important, aspect of their inner relation to Judaism.

I have heard Jewish students in the Middle-West say that they feel more like non-Jewish Midwesterners than like Jews from New York. Since the religious issue has lost importance for Jews and Gentiles alike, there does not exist an easily tangible difference between both groups. To preach Jewish religion or nationalism to such Jews is not likely to have any deep effect. To speak about the glorious history and culture of the Jewish people will not convince them either. They would not want to sacrifice their lives and happiness to things past. In places with a limited Jewish population, and particularly among the adolescents, one finds many who are utterly bewildered about why and in what respect they belong to the Jewish group. One might be able to help some of them by explaining that it is not similarity or dissimilarity of individuals that constitutes a group, but interdependence of fate. Any normal group, and certainly any developed and organized one contains and should contain individuals of very different character. Two members of one family might be less alike than two members of different families; but in spite of differences in character and interest, two individuals will belong to the same group if their fates are interdependent. Similarly, in spite of divergent opinions about religious or political ideas, two persons might still belong to the same group.

It is easy enough to see that the common fate of all Jews makes

them a group in reality. One who has grasped this simple idea
will not feel that he has to break away from Judaism altogether
whenever he changes his attitude toward a fundamental Jewish
issue, and he will become more tolerant of differences of opinion
among Jews. What is more, a person who has learned to see how
much his own fate depends upon the fate of his entire group, will
be ready and even eager to take over a fair share of responsibility
for its welfare. This realistic understanding of the sociological
facts is very important for establishing a firm social ground, especially for those who have not grown up in a Jewish environment.

III.

I have already mentioned that problems of an underprivileged
minority are directly related to the conditions of the majority.
Anxious to retain a friendly attitude on the part of the majority,
important sections of Jewry try to avoid aggressiveness and tend to
hush-up disagreeable events. The motive behind this policy is
partly—but only partly—correct. Jews should clearly distinguish
two situations, one dealing with friends and neutrals and the other
dealing with enemies. It is a clear symptom of maladjustment for
a person to relate everything to Jewish questions and to bring up
the Jewish problem in every situation. But to keep quiet in regard
to Jewish questions where it would be natural to discuss them, is
no less a sign of maladjustment. Experience shows that on the
whole, non-Jews are less sensitive to an over-emphasis of one's
Jewishness than to the tendency of aping things non-Jewish. A
member of a minority who emphasizes his belonging to it, obviously does not try to sneak over the borderline, and therefore
does not need to be rejected. Those members of the minority,
however, whose conduct seems to imply an effort to "pass", will
provoke immediate counteraction.

Loyalty to the Jewish group therefore furthers rather than
hinders friendly relations with non-Jews. Both natural relations
between human beings and the political interest of the Jews demand the establishment of friendly bonds with as many groups
and individuals of the majority as possible.

However, the Jews should also be clear about those situations in which friendly approaches are out of place. Friendliness is no appropriate response to an aggressor. In recent years we have seen in world politics how undignified, morally distasteful and unwise is the policy of appeasing an aggressor. It is both shameful and stupid to talk to a man who is determined to destroy you. For the enemy such friendly talk means only that you are either too weak or too cowardly to fight him. We should not be mistaken about the following point either: the onlooker, who is not yet prejudiced, might be won over and brought to sympathize with an individual or a group of people who fight back with all their power against an aggressor, while he will show very little sympathy for people who bow to an insult. Britain has felt the truth of this simple observation rather keenly within the last two years.

I hope that Jews in America will recognize this truth before it is too late. There are now many among us who adopt the attitude of "talking things over" and "getting together" without the necessary discrimination. This attitude is entirely correct and advisable with friends and neutrals, but not if we have to deal with groups which have made up their mind to destroy us.

The Jew will have to realize, and he will have to realize it fast, that in fighting Nazis and their allies it does not pay to be polite. There is only one way to fight an enemy, and this is to return blow for blow, to strike back immediately, and if possible, harder. Everywhere the Nazis have been careful to keep their actions inside the formal law with the purpose of depriving their enemies of the protection of the law. But aside from this, Jews can expect to get active help from others only if they themselves show that they have the courage and the determination to stand up for a fight of self-defense. Jews will have to adapt themselves to a new scale of risks in their daily action. The situation of world Jewry seems to leave only this choice open: The choice between living like the Jews in Germany, Austria, Czechoslovakia, which means living as slaves, doomed to starvation and suicide, or being ready to fight with all means required and, if necessary, to die in this fight for freedom and against extermination.

This choice is not a pleasant one, and it may seem particularly depressing to young people. But the young will understand that it is more honest, more dignified and more in line with the spirit of both Judaism and Americanism, to react promptly and vigorously against the first insult than to wait until the enemy has grown strong enough to impose his will by force. To overlook insult may seem generous to the sophisticated mind. But in a situation like ours, where the very existence of the Jewish people is at stake, we cannot afford the luxury of this gesture. Aside from the moral issue, a man who does not show backbone acts unwisely. He invites the bestiality of the mob which is always ready to have its brutal fun but is afraid to stick out its neck when it knows that it will be resisted.

Such a fight in self-defense would be more than a self-centered act. It would have a direct bearing upon the struggle of the majority for the solution of their economic and political problems. We have emphasized that the fate of the Jews is bound up with the economic welfare of the majority. Unfortunately, it will be impossible to solve the economic problem so long as under-privileged minorities can provide cheap labor and political scapegoats. As matters stand today, the Jews as a group can hardly do anything more for the economic welfare of the country than to prevent the forces of Fascism from using the suppression of the Jews as a stepping stone towards the suppression of other racial and religious groups and the masses of the people in general.

It would be a mistake to believe that the man who has made up his mind to be ready for any action and danger which fate might hold in store for him lives in a continuous stage of tension, anxiety and stress. The opposite is true. Anxiety is characteristic of one who is confused and does not know what to do. One who faces danger rather than waits to be crushed under the enemy's heel can again live in a clear atmosphere and is able to enjoy life even when surrounded by danger.

September, 1939

Forgery About Franklin

by Charles A. Beard

". . . For the Values of the Scientific and Humane Spirit . . ."

These are times when physical force is exalted. It is widely deemed old-fashioned, outmoded, and infantile to speak of an appeal to reason, to exalt toleration as a virtue in itself, and to believe that truth has any part in practical affairs. That this is the situation in which we find ourselves calls for no illustrations. They lie on every hand and come upon our vision from every angle.

Yet there are a few left in the world who have not surrendered to this spirit of the times. There are a few who still believe that force, lying and deceit are not virtues in themselves, and that no civilization worth having can be founded upon them. It is these few who propose to keep the channels of discussion open and to cherish respect for demonstrated facts and for the values of the scientific and humane spirit. They do not propose to surrender to wrath and unreason, but to do battle to the bitter end in the belief that hope, as Shelley says, can create from its own wreck the thing it contemplates.

Although the following paragraphs deal with a single issue in this conflict between force and reason, deceit and respect for facts, they illustrate all too vividly the nature of the struggle now being waged. They show the lengths to which force will go in efforts to gain its end, the chicanery to which it will resort, the depths of unreason to which it will sink. Still more significant, perhaps, it shows how wide a currency may be given to a palpable lie, wittingly or unwittingly, by the press and by men presumed to have honor.

CHARLES A. BEARD.

ON FEBRUARY 3, 1934, William Dudley Pelley published in his journal "Liberation" a passage purporting to be an extract from the "Private Diary" of Charles Pinckney, of South Carolina, in which Benjamin Franklin was quoted as denouncing

169

Jews in unmeasured terms, with all the savagery of a Hitler or Goebbels. Mr. Pelley declared that Pinckney, as one of the framers of the Constitution, had taken notes on "Chit-chat around the table during Intermissions," that he had published this diary, that General W. T. Sherman had ordered the destruction of private libraries during the Civil War, and that among the rare books sacrificed was Pinckney's diary. But, Mr. Pelley went on to say, a copy survived in the hands of a descendant in the southwestern part of Georgia, and that the extract in "Liberation" was taken from this copy. Where the copy is now, who has it, Mr. Pelley did not state; nor has any copy yet been discovered by extensive researches.

In August, 1934, the "Weltdienst," an international news service, anti-Jewish in bias, published in Erfurt, Germany, in three languages — German, French and English — issued this alleged statement by Franklin condemning the Jews. In so doing it did not mention the name of Pinckney, but ascribed the document to the journal of a delegate to the constitutional convention of "1789."

Later in August, the "Volksbund," a Swiss Nazi organ reprinted the alleged Franklin's "Prophecy" ascribing its source to "co-workers in Germany."

In its issue of the first week of September, "Der Stuermer," the fiery organ published by Julius Streicher, contained a dispatch from its New York Correspondent, J. L. MacCormick, quoting the alleged Franklin "Prophecy" and using it as an introduction to an attack on the Jews in the customary Nazi style.

On September 20, the Jewish "Daily Bulletin," in commenting upon the article in "Der Stuermer," referred to the alleged prophecy of Franklin, without quoting it in detail or inquring into its authority.

Five days later, September 25, 1934, Robert Edward Edmondson, who has been accused by Mr. John Spivak of being a Nazi agent in the United States, sent the alleged Franklin "Prophecy" to investment and brokerage houses, business men, and others interested in his program or subscribing to his "service." In the hands of Mr. Edmondson the document and its history take the following form. Although it is not exactly identical with the extract published with Mr. Pelley, it is the same in substance.

GREAT AMERICAN STATESMAN CREDITED WITH FORESHADOWING PRESENT POLITICO-ECONOMIC "RED CRISIS"

" 'Whatever country Jews have settled in any great numbers,' said Franklin, 'they have lowered its moral tone; depreciated its commercial integrity; have segregated themselves and have not been assimilated; have sneered at and tried to undermine the Christian religion upon which that nation is founded, by objecting to its restrictions; have built up a state within a state; and when opposed have tried to strangle that country to death financially, as in the case of Spain and Portugal.

" 'For over 1,700 years the Jews have been bewailing their sad fate in that they have been exiled from their homeland, as they call, Palestine. But, Gentlemen, did the world today give it to them in fee simple, they would at once find some cogent reason for not returning. Why? Because they are vampires, and vampires do not live on vampires. They cannot live on themselves. They must subsist on Christians and other peoples not of their race.

" 'If you do not exclude them from the United States, in this Constitution, in less than 200 years they will have swarmed in such great numbers that they will dominate and devour the land, and change our form of government, for which we Americans have shed our blood, given our lives, our substance and jeopardized our liberty.

" 'If you do not exclude them, in less than 200 years our descendants will be working in the fields to furnish them substance, while they will be in the counting houses rubbing their hands. I warn, you, Gentlemen, if you do not exclude the Jews for all time, your children will curse you in your graves.

" 'Jews, Gentlemen, are Asiatics, let them be born where they will, or how many generations they are away from Asia, they never will be otherwise. Their ideas do not conform to an American's, and will not even though they live among us ten generations. A leopard cannot change its spots. Jews are Asiatics, are a menace to this country if permitted entrance, and should be excluded by this Constitution.'

"On the statute books of the United States is the Asiatic Exclusion Law by which Asiatics are prohibited from entering this country on the ground that they cannot be assimilated because 'their ideas do not conform' to the American customs and principles.

"If Red revolutionary Jews are Asiatics, would it not be in harmony with the aforesaid law to deport them as aliens illegally in the United States?

"Col. E. N. Sanctuary, whose racial problem books have attracted widespread attention, is authority for the statements that out of 19 aliens arrested in the San Francisco general strike, 11 were 'Red' Jews—whose origin might well be Oriental."

"New York, Sept. 25, 1934, Robert Edward Edmondson" (Edmondson Economic Service, 80 Washington St., New York).

WHEN this release by Mr. Edmondson came into my hands, I was amazed by the document. As a student of the writings of Pinckney and Franklin, I had never seen anything like it, and on October 15, 1934, I wrote to Mr. Edmondson asking him to give me the source from which his Franklin's "Prophecy" was taken, as I desired to examine the original myself. To my letter Mr. Edmondson replied that he understood that the "copy" for the "Prophecy" "emanated from Mr. Madison Grant of New York City, unauthenticated." He added that several investigations were being conducted to determine its authenticity, and that he had felt justified in issuing it because mention of it in the Jewish "Daily Bulletin" had caused a widespread demand for the story. In short, Mr. Edmondson published the alleged statement and then conducted inquiries to determine its authenticity.

Since Mr. Edmondson referred to Mr. Grant as the source of the story, I wrote to Mr. Grant on October 20, asking him to be good enough to tell me where I could find the original document. In reply, Mr. Grant stated that some years ago he had received what "purported" to be a copy of Franklin's remarks before the convention in Philadelphia, but had "no information whatever as to the authenticity of the paper."

Although I was pretty well convinced by this time that the Franklin "Prophecy" was a pure fabrication, I had been taught by bitter experience the dangers of drawing a negative conclusion. It is not easy in historical writing to prove a negative in the absence of authentic evidence. So I wrote to an old friend of mine, one of the outstanding scholars in the United States, a man most familiar with the writings of both Franklin and Pinckney. Should I mention his name, his authority would be immediately recognized, but I must not bring him into this affair. To my inquiry this scholar replied that there are indications which make it almost certain that Pinckney did not keep a diary of convention proceedings. He added that there is nowhere any evidence that Franklin ever made such a speech and that it is inconceivable that he should ever have done so. In addition, my friend declared flatly: "The alleged Franklin document is merely a forgery, and a crude one at that."

Although convinced by this scholar's report that the Franklin "Prophecy" was a crude forgery, I still had the historian's suspicion that there might be somewhere in Franklin's writings one or more remarks derogatory to the Jews, which could furnish some slender basis for the fabrication. So, I searched Franklin's writings myself, and had searches made by scholarly assistants in the available records, including the vast collections of Frankliniana in Philadelphia. I have sought the alleged Diary of Pinckney.

All these searches have produced negative results. I cannot find a single original source that gives the slightest justification for believing that the "Prophecy" is anything more than a bare-faced forgery. Not a word have I discovered in Franklin's letters and papers expressing any such sentiments against the Jews as are ascribed to him by the Nazis—American and German. His well-known liberality in matters of religious opinions would, in fact, have precluded the kind of utterances put in his mouth by this palpable forgery. Had he or any members of the Constitutional Convention entertained such violent convictions it is scarcely possible that they would have allowed the opportunity to pass for putting a bar in the Constitution when provisions for the regulation of foreign commerce and for naturalization were up for consideration. The proceedings of the convention were secret and any member was free to speak his mind without fear of publicity. Franklin was then an old man beyond all earthly ambitions and spoke freely without thought of effects on his political career. In his writings on immigration, Franklin made no mention of discrimination against Jews.

So much for the negative evidence to the effect that Franklin did not utter the sentiments expressed in the alleged "Prophecy" or say anything which could be twisted to imply that he entertained any such views. On the other side there is positive evidence that he he'd Jews in high regard. When the Hebrew Society of Philadelphia sought to raise money for "a religious house," or synagogue, in Philadelphia, Franklin signed the petition of appeal for contributions to "citizens of every religious denomination," and gave £5 himself to the fund. If he held the views falsely ascribed to him, he would scarcely have given money and lent his influence in the promotion of the Society's project.

Strange as it may seem to the creators and circulators of this alleged "Prophecy," the only racial immigration which Franklin feared was the influx of Germans, and he did not propose to set up a bar against them. In view of the fact that German Nazis make so much of the Franklin forgery, it seems fitting to include here just what Franklin did say about the Germans in a letter written in 1753:

"I am perfectly of your mind that measures of great temper are necessary with the Germans; and am not without apprehension, that, through their indiscretion, or ours, or both, great disorders may one day arise among us. Those who come hither are generally the most stupid of their own nation, and, as ignorance is often attended with credulity when knavery would mislead it, and with suspicion when honesty would set it right; and as few of the English understand the German language, and so cannot address them either from the press or the pulpit, it is almost impossible to remove any prejudice they may entertain. Their clergy have very little influence on the people, who seem to take a pleasure in abusing and discharging the minister on every trivial occasion. Not being used to liberty they know not how to make a modest use of it. And as Holben says of the young Hottentots, that they are not esteemed men until they have shown their manhood by beating their mothers, so these seem not to think themselves free, till they feel their liberty in abusing and insulting their teachers. Thus they are under no restraint from ecclesiastical government; they behave, however, submissively enough at present to the civil government, which I wish they may continue to do, for I remember when they modestly declined intermeddling in our elections, but now they come in droves and carry all before them, except in one or two countries.

"Few of their children in the country know English. They import many books from Germany; and of the six printing houses in the province, two are entirely German, two half-German, half-English, and but two entirely English. They have one German newspaper, and one half-German. Advertisements intended to be general, are now printed in Dutch and English. The signs in our streets have inscriptions in both languages, and in some places only German. They begin of late to make all their bonds and other legal instruments in their own language, which (though I think it ought not to be) are allowed good in our courts, where the German business so increases that there is continued need of interpreters; and I suppose in a few years they will also be necessary in the Assembly, to tell half of our legislators what the other half say.

"In short, unless the stream of their importation could be turned from this to other colonies, as you very judiciously propose, they will soon so outnumber us that all the advantages we have will, in my opinion, be not able to preserve our language, and even our government will become precarious."

One more point should be made in respect of this "Prophecy" ascribed to Franklin: The phraseology of the alleged "Prophecy" is not that of the eighteenth century; nor is the language that of Franklin. It contains certain words that belong to contemporary Germany rather than America of Franklin's period. For example, the word "homeland" was not employed by Jews in Franklin's

time. It was created in connection with the Palestine mandate.
Furthermore the return to Palestine, or Zionism, was not a popular
movement at that time. Few, if anyone, dreamed that Palestine
could then be wrested from Turkish rule and made a homeland
for Jews.

What is, then, the upshot? This alleged "Prophecy" ascribed
to Franklin is a crude forgery, and his name should be cleared of
the crass prejudices attributed to him. There is in our historical
records no evidence whatever of any basis for the falsehood.
Whoever encounters this piece of propaganda should nail it at
once. If the gentlemen who have given it currency have any honor,
they will either produce their proof or publicly confess their
offence.

Those willing to attack character in the name of falsehood
may go their way, but unless the spirit of scholarship and fair play
is dead in America they will be challenged at every point in their
sinuous career.

March, 1935

Mark Twain About the Jews

by BERNARD DEVOTO

UNDER THE title of " 'Jewish Persecution' A Business Passion—Mark Twain" a leaflet is being circulated, ostensibly by one Robert Edward Edmondson, "Public Relations Counsel," P. O. Box 19, Trinity Station, N. Y. City. It is based on excerpts from an essay by Mark Twain called "Concerning the Jews." A vile and dishonest misrepresentation of that essay, it is as vicious a bit of propaganda as I have ever seen, and I take this occasion to get the facts in print.

The introductory paragraph says that Mark Twain, "it is alleged by Jews, was pro-Jewish." I do not know about that, but certainly he had a lifelong admiration for the Jewish people, which he frequently expressed. The paragraph continues, "his daughter married a Jew, the Russian-born pianist Ossip Gabrilowitsch." That is true. Then.

> Occasionally the humorist wrote in a friendly way about the Jews; but in the March, 1898, issue of Harper's Magazine, under the heading "Concerning the Jews," he compiled a devastating analysis of Jew activities, which article was reproduced in a volume entitled "The Man That Corrupted Hadleyburg" and other stories by Mark Twain, 1900 copyright. The last edition of this book was issued in 1928, copyrighted by Mrs. Gabrilowitsch— AND THE ARTICLE "CONCERNING THE JEWS" WAS DELETED. Why? Your guess is as good as mine! From the article published in Harper's Magazine in 1898 the following extracts are taken in review.

We shall see in a moment what kind of article "Concerning the Jews" is, but let us first examine the insinuation that it has been suppressed by Mrs. Gabrilowitsch. It is true that the article once formed part of the collection of stories and essays called "The Man That Corrupted Hadleyburg" and does so no longer. But it does form a part of another collection called "In Defense of Harriet Shelley and Other Essays," which is in print and is sold every-

177

where in America. This change was made in 1917 when Mr. Albert Bigelow Paine, Mark Twain's literary executor, was re-arranging the contents of the collected works. The change was made entirely on Mr. Paine's decision, for reasons which had to do wholly with problems of arrangement. The volume in which the essay now appears sells just as freely and just as often as the one in which it was originally published. It is not now out of print and, since its original publication, never has been. The essay is also separately published as a paper-bound pamphlet at twenty-five cents. This edition was first published in 1934 and has been on sale ever since.

Toward the end of 1897, while Mark Twain was living in Vienna, there occurred one of the periodic riots in the *Reichsrath* over the *Ausgleich* between Austria and Hungary. The govern-ment put a stop to it with military force and, as a result, more serious riots broke out in various parts of the country, especially in Bohemia. The facts can be found in any general history of Nine-teenth Century Europe—they read strangely like events of the last year—and our only concern with the episode is that, as always in such disturbances, certain elements used the political agitation as a cover for attacks on the Jews. Mark Twain wrote an account of the episode which, under the title of "Stirring Times in Austria," was published in *Harper's Magazine* for March, 1898. He mentioned the attacks on the Jews and various people wrote to him inquiring why the Jews, innocent parties in the political dispute, had been, as he said, "harried and plundered." In answer, he determined to examine the whole "Jewish problem" and wrote "Concerning the Jews," which was published in *Harper's* for September, 1899. (Not March, 1898, as the Edmondson leaflet says.)

The essays set out to explain anti-Semitism. It is not, in my opinion, a very profound or very searching analysis, but certainly it is extremely favorable to the Jews. The inquiry is devoted to six points. The first is the citizenship of the Jew, and Mark brings in this finding:

Summed up, they [the facts just examined] certify that he is quiet, peaceable, industrious, unaddicted to high crimes and brutal dispositions; that his family life is commendable; that he is not a burden upon public charities; that he is not a beggar; that in benevolence he is above the reach of competition.

The second subdivision undertakes to answer the question: Can ignorance and fanaticism *alone* account for his [the Jew's] unjust treatment? It is from this part of the essay that most of the quotations in the Edmondson leaflet are taken. Many of them are disgustingly garbled and all of them are wrenched from their context in such a way as to completely obscure Mark Twain's essential point, which was his conviction that the Jews are the most intelligent people in the world and that the persecution of the Jews has been due, throughout history, to the inferiority and consequent envy of other people. Thus Mark writes, "If he [the Jew] set up as a doctor, he was the best one, and he took the business." In the Edmondson leaflet the sentence appears, "If he set up as a doctor, he took the business." What has been omitted here is the essence of Mark's argument, and it is repeatedly omitted as the leaflet goes on selecting parts of the essay that can be twisted to its use.

Thus the leaflet quotes as follows:

In Berlin a few years ago I read a speech which frankly urged THE EXPULSION OF THE JEWS FROM GERMANY. And the agitator's reason was this: "Eighty-five per cent of the successful lawyers of Berlin were Jews; and that about the same percentage of great businesses of all sorts in Germany were IN THE HANDS OF THE JEWS. THE MOTIVE OF PERSECUTION STANDS OUT AS CLEAR AS DAY.

What Mark Twain actually wrote is:

In Berlin a few years ago I read a speech which frankly urged the expulsion of the Jews from Germany; and the agitator's *reason* was as frank as his proposition. It was this: that *eighty-five per cent* of the successful lawyers of Berlin were Jews, and that about the same percentage of the great and lucrative businesses of all sorts in Germany were in the hands of the Jewish race! Isn't it an amazing confession? It was but another way of saying that in a population of 48,000,000, of whom only 500,000 were registered as Jews, eighty-five per cent of the brains and honesty of the

whole was lodged in the Jews. I must insist upon the honesty—
it is an essential of successful business, taken by and large. Of
course it does not rule out rascals entirely, even among Christians,
but it is a good working rule, nevertheless. The speaker's figures
may have been inexact, but the *motive of persecution* stands out
as clear as day.

In other words, the leaflet omits entirely what Mark Twain
considered the entire explanation of practically all persecution of
Jews, their superior intelligence and honesty. Or, as he put it in a
letter to Twinchell, "The difference between the brain of the
average Christian and that of the average Jew—certainly in
Europe—is about the difference between a tadpole's brain and an
archbishop's." Or, as he put it in a notebook, "The Jews have the
best average brain of any people in the world. . . . They are peculiarly and conspicuously the world's intellectual aristocracy." That
is the whole point of this part of his essay. He decides that the
envy of inferior but more powerful peoples has been the real
cause of the persecutions of the Jews. The Edmondson pamphlet
is using the familiar technique of suppressing essential portions of
an argument in order to misrepresent it for use as propaganda.

Mark then addresses himself to the question: Will the persecution of the Jews ever come to an end? His conclusion is that
dislike of the Jews will probably continue, for "by his make and
ways he is substantially a foreigner wherever he may be, and even
the angels dislike a foreigner." But persecution, he thinks will
end, in fact is ending (in 1898). "That is, here and there in spots
about the world, where a barbarous ignorance and a sort of mere
animal civilization prevail [persecution will continue]; but I do
not think that elsewhere the Jew need now stand in any fear of
being robbed and raided."

In view of the tragic failure of that prophecy (though perhaps it is not a failure after all, considering the reservation "where
a barbarous ignorance and a sort of mere animal civilization prevail") it will be interesting to quote the final paragraph of the
essay, to suggest on which side Mark Twain would be enlisted if
he were living now:

If statistics are right, the Jews constitute but *one per cent* of the human race. It suggests a nebulous dim puff of star dust lost in the blaze of the Milky Way. Properly the Jew ought hardly to be heard of; but he is heard of, has always been heard of. He is as prominent on the planet as any other people, and his commercial importance is extravagantly out of proportion to the smallness of his bulk. His contributions to the world's list of great names in literature, science, art, music, finance, medicine, and abstruse learning are also away out of proportion to the weakness of his numbers. He has made a marvelous fight in this world, in all the ages; and has done it with his hands tied behind him. He could be vain of himself, and be excused for it. The Egyptian, the Babylonian, and the Persian rose, filled the planet with sound and splendor, then faded to dream-stuff and passed away; the Greek and the Roman followed, and made a vast noise, and they are gone; other peoples have sprung up and held their torch high for a time, but it burned out, and they sit in twilight now, or have vanished. The Jew saw them all, beat them all, and is now what he always was, exhibiting no decadence, no infirmities of age, no weakening of his parts, no slowing of his energies, no dulling of his alert and aggressive mind. All things are mortal but the Jew; all other forces pass but he remains. What is the secret of his immortality?

"Concerning the Jews" is not, I have said, an exhaustive analysis of the history of anti-Semitism. But certainly it is a warm-hearted expression of Mark Twain's lifelong liking and admiration for the Jews, and certainly the Edmondson leaflet has completely perverted it. There are in the Mark Twain Papers, of which I am now the custodian, many unpublished expressions of this same liking and admiration. I will see to it that they are published, but meanwhile the leaflet in question should be denounced as a lying and contemptible misrepresentation, and those who are interested in knowing Mark Twain's true attitude toward the Jews should go direct to the essay which it perverts.

May, 1939

For Group Survival
by Claude McKay

IN THIS twentieth year of the Russian Revolution, fifteenth year of Italian Fascism and the fourth year of Nazism, it should hardly be necessary for any Negro to advocate the aggregate organization and development of his group against the passive Uncle Tom and Do-Nothing policy of integration.

If a scheme is put forward to establish something beneficial and exclusively for Negroes, such as a hospital, a school or a bank, the black cry of segregation is heard. No sane Negro believes in or desires legal segregation, in which his racial group will be confined by law to ghettoes. For such a system of segregation will inevitably result in congestion and increased crime, disease and filth.

But it is one of the most natural phenomena of human life everywhere that people possessing special and similar traits will agglomerate in groups. And it is a physical impossibility to compel two different groups of people to live promiscuously together against their will. Different groups agglomerate for different social reasons; such as a common nationality, a common religion, a common language, class interests, or special characteristics of race or color.

It would seem a most elementary law of self-preservation and survival that wherever a distinct group of people is living together, such a people should utilize their collective brains and energy for the intensive cultivation and development of themselves, culturally, politically and economically. The intellectual leaders and professional members of such a group should be zealous in promoting the special interests of the mass of their community. For it is the living reality of the common mass which makes possible the more cultured existence of the intellectual leaders and the professional members of the community.

The United States of America are uniquely a national composite of various groups. In the so-called "melting pot" we have distinguishable groups with special interests, who are none the less American and proud to be identified with the general interest of the nation. There are Italians, Finns, Irish, Scandinavians, Jews, Chinese and others, all more or less living together in groups. These people in building up themselves fraternally, culturally, politically and economically as groups are contributing their special part to the greatness of the American nation as a whole.

To these diverse groups must be added the Negro group. The Negroes, who were emancipated from slavery before the great waves of European immigration swept into America, still remain the lowest group of Americans, socially and economically. Ever since its emancipation from chattel slavery the Negro group as a whole has been hopelessly divided and half paralyzed by the ideology of segregation. The difference between an aggregated group of people and a group segregated by law has never been defined, clarified and explained by Negro leaders. Unique efforts to establish institutions for the special benefit of the Negro people have encountered opposition because of the ideology of segregation. Handicapped by the fear of segregation, the Negro group has never launched out in confidence to develop the positive potentialities of its position as a special group.

When Booker T. Washington founded the great institution of Tuskegee as a practical demonstration of what Negroes might accomplish for themselves, culturally and economically, as a people, he was opposed by leading Negro intellectuals of the North. Yet although Mr. Washington may have followed a mistaken lead in national politics, his social basis was sound. He did not fold his arms and whine and wait for integration. He accomplished something different. He attracted national attention because he had something different to offer. Tuskegee Institute stands a fine monument to him and is perhaps the greatest all-Negro institution in the world.

The Negro group still has a long way to go and a great deal to learn. Of all the groups in America the Negro might learn most from the Jewish group. The American Jewish group is a conglomeration of Jews from different countries, such as Russia, Poland, Germany, Hungary, the Balkan states. Similarly the American Negro group has been augmented by Negroes from the various West Indian islands and from South America.

Not all Jews live in Jewish communities, but the majority of them are socially conscious and aware of the necessity of aggressive group organization and the development of Jewish community life. There are Jewish Youth organizations, a Jewish Historical Society, Jewish Publications Society, Jewish Physical Culture, Jewish Legion, Jewish War Veterans, Jewish Occupational Committee, etc. There are a Jewish Agricultural Society, Jewish Labor Committee and, perhaps the most important of all, the United Hebrew Trades with its militant membership—an integral part of American organized labor. In the national field there exists the B'nai Brith, a society organized in 1843 for Jewish unity. In the international field there is the *Alliance Israelite Universelle,* which was organized in 1860 for the emancipation, education and defence of the Jewish masses in all lands.

Jews organize Jewish hotels, theaters, clubs, stores, printing establishments, colleges and hospitals, without segregating themselves from national institutions. In fact they have broken down 100 per cent barriers of American prejudice and discrimination by building up institutions inferior to none which are a credit to the entire American nation . . . I am not trying to present the Jewish people as one harmonious whole. There are differences among them as there are among all other groups. The interests of Jewish capitalists are at variance with the interests of Jewish workers. Yet Jewish labor has won such concessions as it has from the Jewish employer class and put itself in the front ranks of the American labor movement, because the moral sentiment of the majority of the Jewish community was on the side of the workers.

The Irish, the Germans, the Scandinavians, the Italians, the Jews—all the European immigrants who poured into America, were not from the wealthy classes. They were, in the majority, poor workers and peasants fleeing from class prejudice, poverty, aristocratic and royal exploitation in Europe. They came here as individuals and in families. They had to start from the bottom to build themselves up. They also had to face prejudice and discrimination, although not in the same degree as the Negro. Those who had a common nationality or religion or language found it necessary to develop group unity to fight for and find a place in the national life.

After their emancipation the black people found themselves up against white prejudice and discriminatory laws and practices. The possessing white majority would not yield any solid ground in their social system to the dispossessed black minority. For over half a century Negroes remained good Lincoln Republicans. The Negro group was practically the ward of the Republican Party. Perhaps its leaders could not understand that guardians do not like to have wards on their hands forever, that they expect their wards to grow up sometime and think and act independently. But a few choice plums were distributed to outstanding Negroes and the Negro group applauded. Uncle Tom slave, Uncle Tom free!

The Negro people remained a special group. They were excluded from trains and trams, hotels and restaurants, schools and theatres and other public places. They were kicked out of the Christian churches. They were effectively segregated. But the only thing more than any other that Negroes started out to build exclusively for themselves was the Negro church. Because the Negro people are so profoundly religious-minded, they have always neglected their material interests for the spiritual.

Despite constant discrimination and virtual segregation leading Negroes declare: We want integration. Now I believe that all sane Negroes want integration. But how are they going to get it? Can the integrationists demonstrate to the black minority how they may be integrated into the white majority? Can they point to a group of blacks blissfully integrated in the white Utopia? Why do the integrationists preach integration and yet practice segregation by residing in the Black Belt, while most of them represent Negro concerns and institutions. The Negro group is *not* integrated because a few Negroes are employed here and there in white institutions according to their intellectual attainments; or because some have special places in the Republican, Democratic, Socialist and Communist parties.

The integration of a minority in a majority group depends entirely upon the goodwill of the majority and not upon the desire of the minority. I can see no indication anywhere that the white majority is ready to let down the barriers to include the black minority. The few philanthropic white individuals and organizations interested in Negro welfare do not represent the will of the white majority. The Communists have a program of local autonomy and complete social equality for Negroes, but they are only a small minority. There is the great organized labor movement. Yet the integrationists are not visualizing the Negro group as integrated in a new order of proletarian society, but in the present set up of capitalist society.

Organized labor, just as white in complexion as white capitalists, is not indulging in a pipe-dream of integration in the capitalist control of society. The advance guard of organized labor makes a militant fight. Much more an integral part of this nation than the black minority, militant labor has its own banks, schools, printing establishments, clubs and cooperatives.

The educated Negro has long labored under the illusion that he could ignore and neglect his own group and find the place in white society for which he thought his education entitled him. But thinking Negroes should realize that we are living in a changing world under a new era and that the age of individualism is dead. Thinking Negroes must realize that in this age of the radio, the control and direction of the masses is the big problem alike of democracies and dictatorships.

And what of the Negro masses? Must they remain abandoned
to the fine theory of integration and the care of white philanthropists? Is it possible that the educated Negro can feel no kinship
with his own people? Certainly if the Negro leaders abdicate
their right to leadership of their own people others must step in.

With the world's attention fixed upon events in Hitler's Germany today, it seems to me that the attitude of the Negro apologists
of integration is not merely defeatist, but also criminal. The German Jews had come closer to integration and assimilation than
Jews in any other country. As a group they were not strongly
organized for emergencies. They were fairly unorthodox, intermarried freely with the best German families. They were
tolerated and accepted by the majority of Germans.

Yet now under a political change of regime, the Jews of Germany are being systematically reduced to the status of Negroes
in America. Perhaps if the German Jews had been more strongly
organized as a group, they might have been better prepared to
fight against the evil of Nazism. Perhaps some Negroes fondly
imagine that in the event of a reactionary change in this nation's
government, they will be treated better than the Jews of Germany.
But Jews at any rate have this advantage over Negroes. Thousands
of them cannot be differentiated from white Christians.

It seems to me that the argument for the intensive group organization of Negroes is a very simple and elementary one.
Negroes must organize as a group to obtain the utmost out of
their special situation. Negro leaders should get together and plan
to lead their people out of their present state of apathy and confusion. As a group we are the most supine to ruthless exploitation by others. There are numerous Negro associations. It seems
to me that what the group lacks is coordination of organization
and leadership and a definite purpose.

A Negro community may be likened to any uncongenial small
town where a businessman may be compelled to reside for business reasons, even though he prefer to live in a large up-to-date
city. Such a person would naturally be interested in the town as

a whole; the fire department, streets, housing, lighting and police. Because if there is a fire, an epidemic or a riot, he or a member of his family may be a victim. Similarly any group-conscious Negro should be interested in the intensive development and advancement of his community.

This excerpt from an article by a Jewish intellectual might be pondered with profit by Negro leaders: "Today no minority group has a right to consider itself adjusted to the life of the majority unless it is economically assimilated. To be economically differentiated means to be denied protection of one's right to live by leaving one's livelihood at the mercy of the majority group."

That is the real issue the Negro has to face—the economic issue upon which integration depends. Negro leaders who evade the practical issue of group organization and development to shibboleth the empty slogan of "integration" without being able to demonstrate a practical plan of integration are not only betrayers but lynchers of the soul of the race.

October, 1937

Do Jews Shun Manual Labor?

by DR. URIAH ZVI ENGELMAN

AT THE beginning of the 19th century there were only about 3,000 Jews in the United States. Only during the decade of 1840-1850 did Jews begin to come in considerable numbers. These were mostly German Jews of the lower middle class who were possessed of little culture but of much pluck.

The United States, at the time of their arrival, was pushing its frontiers to Florida, Louisiana, the Pacific Coast and Mexico. New settlements were springing up all over the continent, while on the Atlantic seaboard all sorts of new industries were arising. The latter created an active demand for a class of itinerate merchants who would advertise and sell the commodities manufactured in the East to the pioneers in the thousands of new settlements which dotted the sparsely populated stretches of expanding 19th century America. In those days railroads did not yet span the continent, national magazine advertising by means of such mediums as the *Saturday Evening Post*, *The Ladies' Home Journal* or *The Country Gentleman* had not yet developed, while the ubiquitous radio and automobile were yet to come. The German-Jewish immigrants, who were petty traders in their old home, thus found in America a virgin field for their trading. Together with the non-Jewish Yankee trader they followed the frontiersman: since, at the time, they performed an important economic function, they were successful and prospered.

Towards the close of the century, the East European Jews began to arrive. They came in multitudes, and soon exceeded in number all the previous arrivals put together. What did these East European Jews do when they came here? Unfortunately, there is no statistical information available on which to base a direct and accurate answer to this question. However, we have sufficient data telling us what they were on landing in America, and some data, which may serve as straws in the wind, pointing to the occupational lines they followed on their arrival in the country.

Between the years 1899-1910, a total of 1,074,422 East European Jews entered the country. According to the occupational classification of these immigrants by the United States Immigration Commission, 36.8 per cent were skilled workers, comprising tailors, masons, carpenters, shoemakers and others; 17.4 per cent were engaged in miscellaneous occupations, 45 per cent had no occupations, and 0.7 per cent were professionals. The professional group consisted mainly of Hebrew teachers, musicians and rabbis.

The non-occupational class, which claimed 45 per cent of all the Jewish immigrants, consisted largely of women and children. If we deduct the number of Jewish women and children from the total number of Jewish immigrants and confine the analysis only to the male occupational group, we find that the skilled workers formed 67.1 per cent of all Jewish adult male immigrants. This is a very high proportion. According to the United States Commissioner of Immigration, "all races contributed not only much smaller proportions (of skilled workers) than the Jews, but very much smaller absolute numbers to the total body of skilled laborers." The proportion of unskilled workers among the Jewish male immigrants in the occupational group was 11.8 per cent; servants, 11.1 per cent and farm laborers only 1.9 per cent. If we add up all these figures we find that the proletarian element made up no less than 91.9 per cent of all the Jewish immigrants reporting occupations.*

This is what the Jews were, in the main, when they came to the United States—a nation of workers, of proletarians. What have they become here? Three factors shaped the course and des-

---

* This analysis was in the main corroborated by the findings of the late Dr. Rubinow who in a monograph prepared for the U. S. Government many years ago, came to the same conclusion, though using different data. He used data of the Russian Census taken in the year 1897, and also the data collected by the Russian-Jewish society for the advancement of agriculture and crafts among Jews.

tiny of Jewish labor here in the United States at the end of the 19th and at the beginning of the 20th centuries. These were:

(1) The United States ceased to expand. The era of the frontier was closing. By the time the Jews of Eastern Europe came to America, the railroads cut across the continent in many directions, rural mail delivery was established, big mail-order houses were organized, and national magazine advertising became the vogue. The rural mail delivery and the railroads could do now the work of the itinerant merchants more efficiently and cheaper. The peddler became a declassed being. His was no longer the gate to wealth, but the road to poverty.

(2) The majority of the East European Jews who came to the United States were skilled needle workers; 36.6 per cent were tailors, 10.0 per cent were seamstresses and dressmakers. Including the closely allied trades, such as hat and cap makers, milliners, etc., the needle workers composed practically one-half of the entire body of skilled Jewish labor. In proportion to the non-Jewish immigrants, Jews claimed twelve times as many clothing workers, while the proportion of tailors among Jews was 25 times larger than among non-Jews.

(3) In the eighties, at the time the Jewish immigrants skilled in needle work came to America, the manufacture of clothing (I use the term in a broad sense, including men's and women's wear, underwear, hats and caps) was emerging into a great American industry.

Till the Civil War almost all clothing was made by hand. During the War, soldiers' uniforms began to be manufactured on a large scale for the first time. Inventions multiplied, the sewing machine was invented and improved, also the cutting knife. Fashions became simplified. The manufacture of clothes for men became a national industry in the years 1870-80. Ready made women's clothes followed later.

The demand for men and women to run the machines of this expanding industry was very great, and industrial agents awaited the immigrants on the pier and directed them into the clothing shops.

Mr. George Cohen, in his book "The Jews in the Making of America," says: "The reason for the Jewish preponderance in the clothing industry is not far to seek. Tailoring is a sedentary occupation and therefore has an appeal to the Jew who is unfit for the heaviest kind of manual labor." This is a ridiculous explanation of a great historic phenomenon.

The Jews of Russia and Poland took to tailoring not because it was a sedentary occupation but because it was one of the few occupations they were allowed to engage in. The Jews of Russia and Poland were forced to make a living from a few occupations, and they overcrowded them all. Almost all the blacksmiths of the Russian Pale were Jews, and so were most of the traders in grain. The first occupation required physical strength and muscular exertion, the other a business brain.

There were many tailors in the Russian Jewish towns, because tailors were needed. Tailoring was done by hand. There were no machines. Hence there was a larger demand for tailors to supply clothing.

To say that the Jews went into tailoring because it was a sedentary occupation is first false to facts and explains a phenomenon by one of its attributes. It is like explaining why Negroes work on the cotton fields by saying that they love to work outdoors under the Southern sun, neglecting entirely the many historical forces which displaced them from their native soil and planted them on the American cotton plantations.

Since then many years have passed. The Americanization of the Jew proceeded at a fast past. Depressions followed boom periods, and boom periods followed depressions, till the great Coolidge Era arrived. In the meantime American industries grew, American commerce expanded, the number of industrial technological inventions multiplied, and the American ways of doing business and producing commodities became increasingly mechanized. The cumulative effect of all these changes generated a growing demand for technical and professional workers, office clerks, accountants, stenographers, typists, salesmen, saleswomen, and agents of all sorts. As a consequence the flow of Jews, as of non-Jews into the industries was checked and was re-directed into the professions, the arts and the white collar occupations.

How big was this demand for office workers? In 1870 there were 366,752 persons engaged in office work of all sorts; in 1930 the number rose to 7,949,455 an increase of 2,167.5 per cent. In 1870 the office workers formed but 2.9 per cent of all people gainfully employed; in 1910—10 per cent, 1930—16.3 per cent. Or expressing the same fact in another way, we learn that in 1870 there were 1,926 typists, accountants, clerks, etc. for every million inhabitants. In 1880—2,999; in 1910—16,569; in 1920—26,691 and in 1930—30,336. Almost a sixteenfold increase in office help in relation to population.

A large increase in the number of people employed as salesmen and saleswomen had also occurred during these years. In 1870 there were 6,139 clerks (in stores) for every million inhabitants; in 1920 the number increased to 14,565 and in 1930 to 19,469, a threefold increase in relation to population.

There was a similar increase in the number of people in the professions that are related to the industries (and which professions today are not related to them?). In 1860, twenty chemists were recorded for every million inhabitants; in 1930 the number was 302. In other words, chemists have relatively increased fifteen times as fast as population. Very large increases proportionately to population took place also in the legal and other professions. In 1870 there was 1,057 lawyers and judges for every million inhabitants; in 1930 there were 1,308. The number of people engaged in the medical profession in relation to population growth, contrary to all current notions, did not increase, but shrank. In 1870, 1,618 physicians and surgeons were recorded for every million inhabitants; in 1920 there were 1,372, and in 1930 1,253. The relative decline in the number of physicians is probably due (1) to the growth of hospitalization, (2) to the concentration of the population in urban centers, and (3) to the introduction of the automobile, which enables the doctor of today to treat many more patients than his colleague of a few decades ago was able to.

The oft repeated cry that the medical field is overcrowded, and hence that there is no room for Jews is utterly baseless. In a study made by the committee on Costs of Medical Care, Chicago, 1932 (University of Chicago Press) we read: "One thousand individuals with incomes under $1,200 a year had 1,931.9 home, office, and clinic calls by physicians, compared to a desirable standard of 5,649.5. They also received days and 117.9 units of dental care instead of the 1,000 required."

The Jews, who are mainly concentrated in the industrial centers, where the demand for clerical and professional services is strongest, naturally responded to this demand, as did the non-Jewish inhabitants of the industrial cities. It was not a matter of choice. It was an economic compulsion made imperative by the development of American industries.

In addition to the stimulus of an expanded demand for professional, clerical and sales help, which directed Jewish young men and women into the white collar occupations, there was yet another factor which accelerated the process of alienating the Jewish workers from the factories. This factor, which I will discuss at greater length later, was the general shrinkage of the field of labor as a source of income. The extent to which the number of Jewish workers had decreased in the industries as a result of the two aforementioned factors, is difficult to ascertain. Neither the United States Census Bureau, nor the United States Bureau of Labor Statistics abstract employment statistics by race or religion, while private Jewish research organizations which would collect Jewish occupational data are yet to be organized.

However, there is some information which may serve as indicators, pointing the direction Jewish labor is headed for. These indicators are the Jewish membership data in some of the Jewish unions. The International Ladies' Garment Workers' Union controls an industry which employs about half a million wage earners.

In 1924, the Jewish membership in the union was 63.8 percent, and the non-Jewish was 36.2 per cent. Today the non-Jewish membership in the Union in the city of New York is 62 per cent and the Jewish is 38 per cent. Outside of the city of New York the Jewish percentage is still smaller.

A Jewish labor leader, who ranks high in union circles, recently remarked that in the unions known as Jewish because of the large Jewish membership, an abnormal situation has evolved: the leadership has still remained Jewish, while the rank and file, the workers, are no longer Jewish, but Spaniards, Italians, Negroes and native Christian Americans.

The Jews have thus lost important labor positions during the last period of America's industrial and commercial expansion. Will they regain these positions?

All human beings, Jews and non-Jews, in search for bread and shelter engage in any and all available occupations. The question is then not whether the Jews will re-enter as workers in shops and factories, which they have left when called upon to fill the offices, but rather whether the shops and factories wil re-absorb them.

American industries, because of numerous technological improvements have been progressively employing less labor, while increasing their productive capacities at the same time. Technocracy recently made this new trend famous in American economic life. We tried to laugh it out of court, but, how big really is this big, bad wolf—technological unemployment—which seems such a monster on the American horizon, ready to devour our jobs and leave us with no pay envelopes?

In 1880, in the production of women's clothing, there were employed 8,045 tailors, seamstresses and milliners for every million inhabitants; in 1910 the number increased to 10,712. But since then the number of people employed in this industry proportionately to population has been steadily declining. In 1920 only 6,662 were employed for every million inhabitants, and in 1930 it was but 4,421. In other words, the number of people engaged in the production of women's apparel for every million inhabitants decreased during the decades of 1910-1930 by 6,291 or 58.7 per cent.

Similarly in the production of men's clothing, the importance of labor in relation to the productivity of the industry has been declining yearly. And taking the year 1926 as the standard year, as 100, we will have the following graphic picture of the decline of labor's weight in the industry.

1923	118.6
1924	106.9
1925	103.1
1926	100.0
1927	97.8
1928	92.2
1929	91.9
1930	80.4
1931	74.6
1932	65.3

Another indication that the industry of men's clothing is losing ground as a source of labor income is also given by the following fact. The average annual earnings of a worker in the men's clothing industry in 1900 was 376.23 dollars, in 1921 it was $1,222. Since then the average earnings of the workers in the industry have been continuously on the decline; in 1930, it was but 873.85 dollars. And this decline, it is well to bear in mind, began many years before the depression had set in! The reason for the decline is on the surface. The worker's skill is being replaced by machine operations and the increasing use of power. In 1899 one horse-power was used for every 8.4 workers in the clothing industry; in 1919 one horse-power was used for every 5 workers. I could find no data for later years, but one may safely assume that the use of power by the industry has increased in recent years.

The situation in the tobacco and the cigar industry is not much better. Many Jews are employed in this industry. In 1880, 1,536 people were employed in the manufacture of tobacco and cigars,

for every million inhabitants; in 1910 the number increased to
1,826; in 1920 it declined to 1,707 and in 1930 it declined again
to 1,017. Thus 814 less people were employed in this industry
in 1930 than in 1910 for every million inhabitants, a decline of
44.5 per cent.

The textile factories also employ many Jews. The process of
rationalization in this industry started late. But it is on the way.
In 1850 the industry employed 1,925 people for every million
inhabitants; in 1920 the number grew to 9,097 but in 1930 it
dropped to 7,796, a decline of 1,301 workers per every million
inhabitants.

In the shoe and boot industry, Jewish representation was
claimed to be large. In the Russian Pale almost all shoemakers
were Jews. Many Russian Jewish immigrants found employment
in the United States as shoemakers. . But rationalization of the
industry is fast putting them out of business. In 1850, 5,644
people were employed as shoemakers for every million inhabitants;
in 1930 the number so employed dropped to 2,482, a decline of
3,162, or of more than 56 per cent in the number of people engaged in the shoe industry for every million inhabitants.

On the other hand, one has to point out that certain occupations in which Jews are employed have been gaining strength in
the last decades. Take, for instance, the baking industry. In 1850,
when every household did its own baking, only 615 people were
employed in this industry for every million inhabitants; in 1930,
the number of bakers increased to 1,147 for every million inhabitants. The same is the case with several other occupations. In
1870, there were 2,208 painters, glaziers and varnishers for every
million of inhabitants; in 1930 there were 4,261. In 1870 there
were only 65 paperhangers per million inhabitants, while in 1930
it had increased to 231. Also the number of upholsterers increased
from 149 in 1870 to 419 in 1930. Likewise the number of
plumbers, gas and steam fitters had increased from 289 in 1870 to
1,613 in 1910, to 1,956 in 1920 and to 1,937 in 1930. The
number of plumbers, gas and steam fitters, it seems, had been rap-

idly increasing till 1920. But since that year their number for every million of population has remained stationary, and even slightly declined by 1930. The number of laundry workers has doubled between 1920-1930, while the number of people engaged in pressing, cleaning and dyeing has more than quadrupled. Also many more people are working today in garages, apartment-hotels, and restaurants and beauty parlors.

We find thus two processes taking place in American industry. On the one hand, due to technological advance, less labor is employed in the older industries. On the other hand, new industries arise in response to new wants. But when we strike one against the other we find that the accounts do not balance. More labor is deprived of employment than is being absorbed in new industries, and a large reserve of unemployed people is being created. And in the formation of this reserve, Jews constitute a very large share.

Summarizing the above discussion, one arrives at the following conclusion. In the years after the war, especially in the decade of 1920-1930, the economic life of the Jews was greatly influenced by two factors operating in the economic life of the country. One was the increasing demand for office help and professional workers, the other was the shrinkage of the field of labor as a source of gaining a livelihood. The concurrence of these two factors resulted in a departure from the labor ranks into the white collar occupations, professions and arts. It was an irresistible process decreed by the onward course of America's industrial development. It was a question of following the course or starving. An attempt to explain this process as an expression of the Jewish "spirit," or by reference to specific Jewish abilities, aversions or racial characteristics, blinds one to the true historic causes.

What of the future? The future will depend on whether America will develop along the narrow lines of autocratic nationalistic capitalism or whether it will choose the broad highway of economic and political democracy. On the choice America will make depends the future of the Jews and of Jewish labor in the United States.   January, 1938

Jewish Occupational Problems

by NATHAN REICH

G IVING ADVICE is an old Jewish habit and Jews have been only too prone to offer the world all sorts of counsel on how to run its affairs. But the Jewish people as a whole is now atoning for it by being, in turn, the most advice-ridden people of modern times. Among the periodic admonitions addressed to the Jewish masses the most persistent one refers to the supposed vulnerability of the economic structure of American Jewry. Over and over again, Jewish as well as non-Jewish intellectuals have taken time out to point out that the Jewish economic structure is unsound; that Jews tend to concentrate in relatively few areas of economic enterprise; that these Jewish occupations are of doubtful economic security and of suspect social productivity; that such concentration, apart from undermining the soundness of the Jewish position, is a potent factor in feeding the flames of anti-Semitism; and that unless the Jews are prepared to effect a drastic reshuffling of their occupational pattern they are inviting a crisis which will bring down upon their heads incalculably disastrous consequences. The gradual deterioration of the status of many Jewish communities in Europe in the last two decades, accelerated by the savage onslaughts of Hitlerism upon the very existence of millions of Jews in more recent years has lent new vitality to the preachments of economic doom and panaceas of occupational restratification.

The fact that the occupational distribution of the Jewish people differs markedly from that of the composite American population is beyond dispute. The Jewish community in the United States is characterized by a threefold concentration. Geographically, Jews tend to gravitate toward large urban settlements. New York City and Chicago house one-half of the entire Jewish population of this country. Perhaps ninety per cent of the Jewish people live in cities of one hundred thousand or over. Economically, Jews tend to concentrate in commerce, consumers' goods industries, professions, clerical occupations and certain service trades. While there are no precise, comprehensive statistical data on Jewish occupational distributions, fragmentary studies made by private agencies and individuals, and general observation, permit the rough generalization that while 14 percent of the general American population is engaged in trade, 7 in the professions, and 26 in manufacturing industries, among the Jews of America 40 to 50 percent are engaged in mercantile pursuits, 10-12 percent in professions, and perhaps 15-20 percent in industry, both as employers and employees. In New York City, the home of the garment industry, the proportion of industrial wage-earners is considerably higher. The proportion of Jews who depend upon commerce as a source of livelihood is probably three times as high, that in the professions twice as high, and in the manufacturing industries somewhat less than the corresponding proportions among the general population. It is common knowledge that Jews hardly figure in American agriculture, or in the heavy industries, mining, and railroad transportation. Moreover, within the few major areas in which Jews operate, there is further concentration within relatively few subdivisions. Thus, Jews in trade are found largely in the retail branches; within the consumers' goods industries they are prominent only in the garment, fur and millinery branches, and, to a lesser extent, in the food products and printing industries; and within the professions, Jewish participation is heaviest in law, medicine, pharmacy, dentistry and, to a lesser degree, in teaching, with only a minor representation in the engineering professions.

While the occupational one-sidedness of the Jewish people is beyond dispute, it is the interpretation put on these economic facts and the conclusions drawn from them that are open to serious challenge. First, it should be borne in mind that this so-called abnormality is not an exclusively Jewish phenomenon. In the United States, every immigrant group of fairly recent origin displays an abnormality of its own. A close examination of the occupational patterns of Americans of Norwegian, Italian, German and Slavic origin would probably reveal that each group differs from the general American population in occupational structure. Norwegians loom largest among sailors; Italians among construction workers, truck-farmers and the restaurant trades; Germans were, and probably still are, dominant in the brewery industry; Welshmen are heavily represented among miners; and Slavic groups supply large numbers of agricultural laborers, and unskilled and semi-skilled labor. Every immigrant group brought with it certain occupational habits and skills, and, upon coming to this country, sought, wherever possible, to adjust themselves to the new conditions with a minimum of friction. Likewise, when Jews arrived at these shores, they naturally looked for occupations which came closer to the pattern of life they had pursued in the old country. Most of the Jewish immigrants hailed from cities and towns; the bulk of them were craftsmen, petty traders, semi-professionals and young city folk without any particular training, but easily adaptable to a variety of urban, industrial or commercial, occupations. A few years of "Americanization" were sufficient to transform the tailor from Warsaw into the dress manufacturer of Lower Broadway, the petty merchant from Minsk into the owner of an emporium in the Bronx, and the talmudic scholar from Vilna into an attorney at the American bar.

The fact that a certain "abnormality" of economic structure is common to all immigrant groups does not of itself answer the other charges levelled against the occupational pattern of the Jewish people. First, are the occupations followed by the Jews unwanted? Did the Jews impose, so to speak, their vocational preference upon an unwilling American economy? Or did they simply distribute themselves in response to the requirements of the American economy? The best way to answer this question is to take a quick backward glance at the main economic trends as they are reflected in the decennial inventories of American society. An examination of occupational trends of the last seventy years reveals a continuous shift of population from rural to urban industrial and commercial occupations. Thus, while in 1870, 53% of gainfully employed Americans were engaged in agriculture, the percentage in 1940 was only 17.5. The proportion of those engaged in manufacturing industries remained fairly stationary, between 25 and 28 percent. But the percentage of those engaged in trade and transportation rose from 9.1 to 23, that of professionals from 2.7 to 6.8, clerical occupations from 4.6 to 10.3 percent of all those gainfully employed. Stated in absolute terms, this means that while the economically active population quadrupled, the agriculture group rose by only a little more than half, the manufacturing group merely held its own, but the trade group increased almost twelve times, the professional group eleven times, and the clerical group seventeen times. The figures reveal that it was precisely those groups which registered the greatest rate of expansion that attracted the largest number of Jews. In other words, Jews did what millions of other Americans did; they distributed themselves economically, in response to the economic opportunities of the time. They simply obeyed the dictates of the market, the ultimate arbiter of the American economy. The fact that the vocational and social preferences of the vast Jewish immigrant masses coincided with the general trends in the American economy accounts for the rather successful adjustment of Jews to the conditions of the new world.

Moreover, this occupational shift in favor of trade, professional and service groups is not the exclusive characterisic of the American economy, but is the common experience of all modern industrial countries. The nature of modern large-scale industry based on specialized production requires an ever-increasing army of administrative, technical and distribution personnel. Specialized production increases the distance between producer and consumer, in terms of both space and time. The greater the distance between the act of production and that of final consumption, the larger the army of people who mediate between the producer and consumer. Large-scale production could hardly function without the services of the shipper, the salesman, the billing-clerk, the wholesaler, the retailer, and a host of other auxiliary personnel. It is true that these functions add to the final cost of the article, but they are indispensable to the functioning of a large-scale and low-cost manufacturing system. The price of a pair of shoes in the past, purchased from the shoemaker across the street, contained practically no distribution cost; the prices of shoes today, manufactured thousands of miles away and bought at the neighborhood store, includes about 40% of distribution cost. Yet the total price is lower than would probably prevail were we to eliminate the distributor and return to the handicraft age.

A proper appreciation of the complexities of the modern system of production puts the function of that much-abused middleman in a different light. His function is as indispensable as that of the actual maker. A pound of coffee in Brazil is without value unless it is packed, transported, safeguarded, warehoused, insured, packaged, displayed and delivered to the kitchen door. All factors participating in the long journey of the product are creators of value. In a sense all people engaged in economic activities are middlemen. The farmer mediates between the minerals of the soil, his skill and the produce dealer; the manufacturer mediates between the producer of raw materials, the seller of labor and the distributor and so on along the line.

It is true that our society may suffer from an excess of middlemen in some instances and that the elimination of some might and frequently does result in lower prices, but any economic group may become overgrown. There are just as likely to be too many farmers or bricklayers as too many merchants. The belief of early socialists that the man engaged in distribution is a parasite fattening at the expense of the "maker" of things, is based on a misreading of the nature of values. Even a socialist society, as long as it is based on specialized production, would require the services of a large army of distributing personnel. Whether it would succeed in reducing the army of distributing functionaries would depend on its efficiency.

If the foregoing analysis is correct, the whole argument about the "unproductive" character of Jewish occupations fades away.

The further charge that areas of activity in which the Jews function are less secured is just as untenable. This argument is usually popular with those who advocate a return to the soil. Farming, the source of producing the prime necessities of life, is said to offer greater security than city occupation. But there are serious flaws in the argument. As a source of livelihood, agriculture is relatively shrinking. Mechanization and scientific cultivation of the soil have severely limited its absorptive capacity. The type of agricultural work which does offer economic security of a sort is the European type of diversified, self-sufficient, but relatively unproductive peasant farming. But the American farmer, with his one-crop cash-farming, exposed to all the risks and vagaries of the market, is in fact a produce manufacturer. The experience of recent years dramatized by threats of wholesale foreclosures of farm properties and the exodus of the Okies, the heroic efforts of the Roosevelt Administration bolstering the weakened agricultural economy should lend little encouragement to those who urge the Jews to seek refuge behind the plow.

Nor would Jews enhance their security by transfer to the heavy industries. These industries, such as steel, mining, lumber and construction, are most sensitive to depressions, whose first manifestation is a decline in investment, a cessation of factory expansion and industrial construction. Moreover, there is a substantial body of economic opinion that American economy now grown to maturity is likely to witness a shift of emphasis from the production of heavy capital goods to that of consumption goods and services, as experienced in the older countries, such as England.

Now what of the claim that economic concentration and substantial material success of many Jews provide easy targets for anti-Jewish attacks? The causal connection between the age-old phenomenon of anti-Semitism and the occupational position of the Jews, while widely held, is by no means established by fact and historical experience. It appears extremely doubtful that the stubborn manifestation of xenophobia can be "appeased" by a mere occupational reshuffling. It is a strain on one's credulity to believe that a non-Jew who turns away from a Jewish shopkeeper, or dentist or pantsmaker, will embrace a Jewish farmer or miner in a flush of brotherly love. As a matter of fact, the first step by European anti-Semitic politicians was to deprive Jewish tillers of the soil of their land holdings. For Jews to vacate their present economic positions in which they function fairly well, for positions for which they would be less suited by traditions, habits and social predispositions—all for the sake of a highly hypothetical degree of toleration—is a poor bargain.

The economic argument does not dispose of the issue of restratification as a prerequisite to the development of a well-rounded balanced national existence in a national homeland. Nor does the present discussion imply that American Jews are not faced with any problems of economic adjustment in this country. Ours is a dynamic economy. Within the major areas in which Jews operate some occupations become congested. Established skills become obsolete and new ones bid for recognition. New forms of distribution (e.g. the chain stores) press hard upon the heels of the small independent store-keeper. Some professions become overcrowded and new ones appear on the horizon. The growth of economic concentration narrows the scope of individual enterprise and many young Jews will be forced to seek employment with corporations. Economic discrimination is a grim reality which cannot be argued away and which requires the utmost attention of Jewish as well as non-Jewish public opinion. All that this discussion seeks to convey is that by and large the occupations pursued by Jews are productive by the accepted standard of productivity; that Jews, in choosing occupations, did what millions of other Americans did, that is, flock to expanding areas of economic opportunity; that their sources of livelihood are at least as secure as any other operating within the framework of capitalist enterprise; that Jews probably would and should continue to seek employment opportunities in industries offering good economic prospects; and finally, that a voluntary surrender of economic positions will not appease local anti-Semites.

The main economic problem facing American Jewry is not restratification, but rather helping preserve the principles of equality of opportunity, which would continue to permit Americans of all origins to make any vocational adjustment dictated by changing economic realities.

April, 1942

My Son Who Is a Jew
by MARIE SYRKIN

My son is dark:
The gang on the corner can spot him at a glance.
My son is bright:
He studies late for marks and knowledge.
My son has seen a vision:
He goes to meetings and marches in parades.

Shall I say to my son,
"Dim your eyes, and your hair, and your gladness"?
Shall I say to my son,
"Close that book"?
Shall I say to my son
"Let others carry the banner"?

World!
What of my son?

June, 1939

Too Many Students?

by Nathan Reich

AT THE turn of the century there were approximately one hundred and sixty thousand students enrolled in the colleges and universities of the United States. The number rose to two hundred and sixty-seven thousand in 1910, four hundred sixty-two thousand in 1920, nine hundred twenty-four thousand in 1930 and to over one million three hundred thousand in 1938. This seven hundred percent increase in student population compares with only a seventy per cent increase in total population. The spectacular growth is strikingly revealed in the fact that while forty years ago there was one college student for every four hundred and forty people, ten years ago there was one to one hundred and thirty-three, and in 1938 the proportion rose to one student to every one hundred people. Comparing the growth of student enrollment with the total population of college age level we find that in 1900 there was one student for every twenty-five youths between the ages of eighteen to twenty-one inclusive, but in 1938 the ratio was one per every seven youths of that age. In the case of the Jewish youth, enrollment at colleges and universities grew at an even faster rate. Private estimates reveal that in 1915-16 the number of Jewish students was approximately ten thousand. A similar estimate made in 1935-36 places the number of Jewish students at over one hundred thousand. This gives us a tenfold increase within a space of twenty years during which period the general Jewish population increased by less than fifty per cent. There was one Jewish student for every three hundred Jews in 1915-16, while in 1935-36 there was one Jewish student for every forty-seven Jews. The ratio of Jews to the general population in the United States was about less than three per cent in 1916 and about four per cent in 1936, but the ratio of Jewish students to the total student population rose from about three per cent to about nine per cent during the same period.

The rapid increase of student population, while indicative of the growing intellectual maturity and the economic progress of America, has caused some concern to many thoughtful observers of the American scene. Until the present war emergency with its attendant shortages of every kind of professional skills temporarily shoved the problem into the background, voices were heard that the expanding flow of college graduates swelled the ranks of the professionals and tended to create a serious problem of congestion in the market of professional services. It was pointed out that young people, armed with college degrees but unable to find employment in the professional field and for reasons of "prestige" unwilling to stoop to manual or mechanical work, were filling the ranks of the discontented army of dispossessed intellectuals. It was pointed out that in Italy and Germany such armies provided the most fertile recruiting ground for the Fascist and Nazi movement. It was feared that the continued reckless graduation of tens of thousands of young people without regard to the absorptive capacity of the professions, for which most of them prepared, would result not only in many wrecked careers of individuals, but would also produce explosive material threatening our socio-economic order. The concern was felt even more strongly in Jewish circles in view of the traditional tendency of Jewish students to concentrate in relatively few professions and in view of the discriminating practices barring the entry of Jews to many professions. Many Jews feel that the congestion of Jews in some professions is a factor in the rise of anti-Jewish feeling.

The question is: Are these fears justified? What is the relation of the growing supply of professional aspirants to the likely course of demand for professional services both in terms of general and specific Jewish problems? Now, economic predictions are extremely hazardous. Economic prognosis at its best expresses mere probabilities rather than certainties. Needless to say that no more is claimed for the attempt undertaken in this essay.

The proper comprehension of the problem requires an understanding of the reasons underlying the rapid rise in student enrollment—a phenomenon which incidentally is not confined to the United States but has to a varying degree been a part of experience in practically all countries of the world. A world-wide study made in 1934 lists four factors: advance in economic welfare enabling more families to finance the college education of their children, the trend toward fewer children per family enabling the expenditure of more money on education per child, the social prestige attaching to the exercise of white collar and professional work as contrasted with manual and mechanical work, the higher average earnings of professional workers as compared with those of farmers and industrial workers, and the relatively more rapid growth in the demand for professional services as compared with that for most other occupational groups.

The last mentioned is undoubtedly the most potent factor both in explaining the expansion in current student enrollment and in evaluating the future relation between supply of, and demand for, professional services. A glance at the census informs us that the professional group enjoyed the most rapid rate of growth in the occupational structure of the American people. In 1870 the number of professionals amounted to three hundred thirty-two thousand one hundred and seventy-nine or 2.7 per cent of the total gainfully employed population, and in 1940 to approximately three million six hundred thousand or almost seven per cent of the total. In other words, while in 1870 there was one professional per every one hundred and eighteen people, in 1940 the proportion is one to thirty-seven, a relative growth at a rate three times that of the total population.

The reasons for the rapid expansion of the professional group are rooted in the dynamics of modern economy. First and foremost is the fact that modern economic life is characterized by a growing professionalization of its many economic functions and services. The growing complexity of modern life brings an ever widening range of activities within the province of specialized knowledge and skills. The building of homes done by home grown carpenters and builders under simple conditions of an earlier era, today requires an army of architects, draftsmen, interior decorators. The emergence of new industries, the mechanization of industrial processes and the application of scientific methods to agriculture, fed the demand for a wide variety of professional services. The growing institutional complexity of modern living and the consequent widening range of public control over social and economic life called forth a host of public administrators requiring a varying degree of professional training. The universal extension of educational facilities and an increasing awareness of health problems continue to accentuate the demand for persons with professional training. The second source of demand for professional services is the growth of national income which, with the exception of the setback experienced in the depression of the early thirties, characterized the last hundred years. It is common knowledge that the demand for professional services is more flexible than that for other necessities such as food, clothing and shelter. As income increases the proportion of money spent on so-called cultural or social services such as education, health, recreation and entertainment rises faster than the expenditure on necessities. Consequently, as incomes of American families were rising, the expenditures allotted to these cultural services—which in a large measure represent professional services—were rising at a faster rate than the incomes themselves. The growing importance of professional services in economic life is reflected in the shifting proportion of income claimed by the professional group in relation to the total national income. Thus, while the relative shares of agriculture and manufacturing industries declined between 1919 and 1938, the share of national income claimed by professional groups was from 9.3 per cent to 13.7 per cent of the total income during the same period. The sustained demand for professional services is also reflected in the earning record of the leading professions. Thus in 1929 the average income of physicians was well above $5,000 per year, of lawyers and engineers, over $4,000. It is true that in the depression years they were considerably reduced, but with recovery in the middle thirties they rose again. In 1938, the average income of practicing physicians was $4,400, of dentists $2,900, of lawyers $4,000, of engineers $3,000. These are of course, averages including some whose income is many times the average and some who hardly make a living or are without income at all. Considering that the average wage of gainfully employed industrial employee was about $1,300 in the prosperous year 1938, and that considerable social prestige attaches to the exercise of professional work, it is easy to appreciate the powerful attraction held out by professional work to young people in search for a career.

Now, what are the prospects of absorbing the vast army of college and university graduates? Assuming a stabilization of college enrollment at approximately present levels, what is the present absorptive capacity of professional vocations?

The demand for new entrants into the professions is fed from several sources. The largest source is the replacement rate as measured by the annual withdrawal of present practitioners through death, retirement and shift into other occupations. Experts estimate the average active life span of a professional person at between thirty to thirty-five years. An estimate of three per cent of annual replacement rate would appear a fairly conservative amount. According to the 1940 census the number of professionals in the United States is around three million and six hundred thousand. A three per cent replacement rate on the basis of that figure would yield an annual demand for one hundred and eight thousand new entrants, merely to fill the ranks depleted by death and retirement. The second source of the demand for new professionals is presented by the net annual natural growth of the population. The population of the United States is still growing, though at a decreasing rate. Between 1930 and 1940 the net average annual addition amounted to roughly nine hundred thousand. Assuming an annual rate of increase of eight hundred thousand for the next ten years and applying the ratio of one professional to every thirty-seven people, we obtain a demand for twenty-two thousand new entrants.

Thus even if the average annual national income should only stay on the level of the years preceding the war boom, the professional market is in a position to absorb about 130,000 new entrants without detracting from the established professional earning levels. But in the past, growing national income provided an additional source of demand for professional services. It is, of course, extremely difficult to estimate the course of national income in the coming post-war years. Some economists fear a post-war economic collapse; others anticipate a period of prosperity, initiated and sustained by the accumulation of an enormous pent-up demand during the lean and priority-ridden war years. The author is inclined to the latter view, reinforced by the belief that the post-war social climate will not permit the spectacle of idle machinery, idle resources and idle men. On the assumption of a progressively rising income at least approximating the rate of growth of the period 1900-1930 we may expect an annual increase of two to three per cent in addition to the normal three per cent replacement demand giving us a total annual demand of about two hundred thousand new recruits to the ranks of professionals. The extent of unfilled socio-cultural needs due to low income is enormous. It is estimated that thirty-eight per cent of the people are without dental care; a study of a group of families revealed that of those earning less than $1,200 per year, only very few received any dental care, but of those earning $2,500, fully three-fourths received such care. The census of 1930, for instance, reveals that twenty per cent or five million and seven hundred thousand children between the ages of six to seventeen were not in schools. An extension of schooling facilities to this group would alone increase the demand for teachers by tens of thousands. A downward extension of schooling to kindergarten age is a further potential demand for professional workers. If this analysis is correct, the annual absorptive capacity lies somewhere between a minimum of one hundred and thirty thousand per year in case of a stationary per capita income and a possible maximum of two hundred thousand, should income resume its rising trend exhibited prior to the depression of the early thirties.

Should the annual supply exceed the minimum or maximum demands under the two respective economic conditions, the excess newcomers could be absorbed only at the cost of intensified competition with established professionals, probably leading to lower professional fees and salaries and lower earning levels.

How does the estimated demand compare with the supply of professional candidates? The total enrollment in colleges and universities was over 1,300,000 in 1938. More significant for our purposes is the number of those who complete their studies and go forth annually in search of careers. The numbers of college graduates receiving degrees (bachelors as well as professional degrees) amounted to 189,000 in the same year. Of these 100,000 received professional degrees. In view of the rise in freshmen enrollment in the years immediately preceding 1940, the number of graduates would have been expected to increase in the early forties, had not the war emergency intervened with its reduction in student enrollment due to draft and defense work. If we assume that all graduates immediately seek occupations in professional work, the supply would definitely exceed the demand for newcomers. But, of course, not all students attend college with professional intent. How many do, is difficult to know with any degree of accuracy. Assuming that only those graduating with a professional degree aspire to a professional career, the supply of graduates does not at all appear to exceed the possible absorptive capacity of professional field. There is even considerable leeway in allowing for additional entry into professional work of a goodly portion of those who pursued a general arts course.

It would thus appear that the widely felt concern that our graduates are facing hopeless odds in fitting themselves into the professional structure are not justified by the facts and probable prospects. Young people able and willing to prepare themselves for a professional career face prospects which are at least as good in professions as in any other vocational groups. Indeed, in case of rising national income the prospects in the profession are probably considerably better than in most other groups; in case of a stagnant or declining national income they are not any worse. It should be noted that this analysis deals with over-all estimates and in no way disposes of congestion in specific professions, i.e. law, or the local overcrowding of the medical profession in metropolitan, and the scarcity, in rural areas.

In approaching the problem facing Jewish students, the prognosis becomes even less certain. The outlook is complicated by several factors. First, Jewish students tend to concentrate heavily in relatively few professions. Thus while Jewish enrollment amounted to over nine per cent of total student body in 1935-36, they comprised twenty-six per cent in dentistry, twenty-five per cent in law, twenty-two per cent in pharmacy, sixteen per cent in medicine, but only six per cent in engineering, three per cent in education and only 2.5 per cent in agriculture. Consequently conditions of over-crowdedness in the legal profession may affect the Jewish student body to a greater extent than the rest of the student youth. Secondly, the professional distribution of Jewish students tends to follow the lines of geographical concentration of the Jewish people in large cities, where the competitive scramble for professional work is probably keener than in other areas. Some degree of geographical scattering seems to be indicated. Thirdly, vocational prospects of Jewish students are affected not only by the strictly economic consideration of the demand for their services, but by the political factor of discrimination. It is obviously difficult to appraise the future course of anti-Jewish discrimination in this country. It is likely that a continual pressure of Jewish youth into professions coupled with attempts to spread out in search of wider professional opportunities will increase the resistance of non-Jewish professional circles and perhaps intensify social friction. On the other hand, it is clear that in a considerable measure anti-Semitism has received a powerful impetus from the advancing Fascist powers in Europe. It may, therefore, be reasonable to hope that the military destruction of Fascist powers and the reinvigoration of the democratic world, tested and consolidated in the fire of battle and committed to the idea of equal treatment for all, would lessen the inter-racial and inter-religious tension and on the whole enhance the opportunity of the component Jewish professional worker. But whatever the course of future events, the fear of discrimination must not be made the controlling factor in the vocational policy for young Jewish people. Personal ability, integrity, a willingness to work hard and do well still remain the paramount consideration. The young Jew entering upon a professional career must accept the possibility of discrimination as another professional risk. If he actually comes face to face with it, he must accept it as a challenge to be overcome. In a democratic and expanding economic world he should be able to meet the challenge as effectively in professional work as in any other vocation. In a world ridden with social and religious discrimination or in a world of shrinking economic opportunity he will have a dismal future in any walk of life.

June, 1942

A Jewish Economic Problem

by JACOB LESTSHINSKY

I S THERE a specific Jewish economic problem? Are not Jews an organically integrated part of the economic body of the United States?

Although everyone would answer in the affirmative to the second question, we have to offer an equally categorical affirmative reply to the first one as well. One need not go far afield to prove the existence of a specifically Jewish economic question. It is enough to point out that Jews are almost the only group among whom one hears of discrimination, and abnormal social and professional composition in order to conclude that, economically speaking, something is wrong with American Jewry. Nor was it the Zionists, who are suspect of seeing a Jewish problem wherever a general social ailment manifests itself, that were the first to call attention to the weakness. On the contrary, it was other elements, generally inattentive to specific Jewish manifestations, that pointed out the ailment. So much more reason to suspect that the malady is serious.

It might have seemed that immigrants from dozens of different nationalities and states would rid themselves of their old heritages and begin a new and common historical chapter in the country of their adoption. It is true that all the immigrants together lent a hand to the upbuilding of the United States. But it is equally undeniable that every immigrant group brought to these shores a great and influential socio-psychological heritage which to a great extent determined the present social and economic position of the respective groups. Jews brought with themselves a heritage older than that of the others and hence a more potent one. But the Jewish heritage is, by its very nature, one that bears the potential seeds of all those ailments whose collective name is "the Jewish question."

Jews assimilate easily and rapidly, but never completely. Other peoples too manifest a tendency to create ghettos, concentrate in separate quarters and crowd into a definite group of preferred professions. But among no people does this tendency assume such broad scope or such an enduring and nationally binding character. The Jewish ghettos in the United States are more crowded and heavily ballasted with specific national content. They therefore last longer and exert a more powerful influence on the second and third generation than is the case among other immigrant nationalities. When comparing the Jews with the central and northern European nationalities—groups with whom the Jews have much in common so far as professional and social composition and cultural standards are concerned—it becomes apparent that although American Jews have shown no disinclination to compete with the above mentioned groups for the higher social and economic positions, they have not succeeded in attaining the desired goal. It is true that many individual Jews, of the more recent Russian-Polish immigration as well as those of the older German immigration, have almost succeeded in hurdling the barrier into the dominant class. But in their overwhelming majority Jews were economically stranded midway.

In the very midst of this process the depression occurred, became a permanent condition and hurled all elements of the population a couple of steps down the economic ladder. The crisis of necessity affected more severely that segment of the Jewish population that was in the midst of a process of economic transition. The number of those who were already well advanced up the economic ladder decreased. Further progress became even more difficult for those who did not succeed in becoming firmly entrenched in economic positions they had but recently attained. The percentage of enterprises among Jews that crashed was therefore considerably greater than the percentage of failures among corresponding economic groups of the other elements of the population. While this may have partly been caused by the known tendency on the part of Jews to undertake greater risks and to engage in less firmly grounded enterprises, it was mainly a result of the simple fact that the larger Jewish enterprises were of more recent origin and therefore less able to withstand the shock of the crisis. As a result we may today find among American Jews a considerable number of economic "had beens," mostly older people whom it is difficult to readjust. But their children can be rehabilitated, especially after the lesson they had learned from their parents' experience.

However, the above discussed element constitutes only a small part of American Jewry. A much larger segment consists of people who were not goaded by high economic ambitions but, on the contrary, orientated themselves on the economically less privileged national groups in the country. The many millions of Slavs, together with whom the Jews came to the United States, whose language and habits they knew, became a source of livelihood for a large part of American Jewry. In the Polish, Ukrainian, Czech and other quarters of the large cities, commerce is largely in Jewish hands. House to house peddling and selling on the instalment plan is also to a good extent engaged in by Jews. Frequently such sections of American cities give one the impression that they had been bodily transferred from a Polish or Lithuanian city and placed on the American scene. The only difference is that the Polish laborer in Detroit earns more than his compatriot in Bialystok. The Jewish merchant in Detroit consequently also earns more. But the division of economic functions is the same and the mutual relations are frequently also very similar.

The above mentioned section of American Jewry is numerically the largest and in many cities places its stamp on the physiognomy of the entire Jewish community. In the smaller towns the Jewish communities consist almost exclusively of such merchants and peddlers. And while even in the smallest communities in eastern Europe at least a third of the Jews was engaged in handicrafts, this element is almost altogether lacking in the United States. In contrast to the eastern European town the non-Jewish population in the American towns is larger and wealthier while the Jewish population is relatively smaller, hence also better off economically. A small and scattered Jewish community will always find a livelihood in trade. It is also true that not all trade in the American towns is in Jewish hands, as had been the case in Poland, for instance. But unlike Poland or Lithuania, nearly all Jews in the American towns are storekeepers and traders. Eighty to ninety per cent of the Jews in the small towns engage in trade. The remainder is in the liberal professions. The laborers and independent artisans can be counted on the fingers of one's hands and are generally considered to be failures who had not attained a higher economic plane through their own fault.

In the medium sized cities the proportion of traders is somewhat smaller and ranges between sixty and sixty-five per cent, but the number engaging in the liberal professions is greater and reaches twelve to thirteen per cent. By their quantitative strength alone these two groups give its character to American Jewry. When we bear in mind that a storekeeper or a lawyer is more prominently displayed to catch the public eye than a laborer, it is easy to understand why the surrounding non-Jewish population is convinced that all Jews engage either in trade or liberal professions.

In the very large cities it is likewise true that the bulk of the Jewish population engages in commerce. It is difficult to express this fact in terms of percentages since the data available is meagre. But even as in the smaller cities this section occupies a central place in Jewish life and gives the impression of being *the* Jewish people. There are tens of thousands of Jewish laborers and even more professionals in the large cities. The latter, however, must be considered a part of the middle class. The composition of the Jewish communities in the very large cities, which only two or three decades ago bore such a distinct proletarian stamp, is increasingly becoming more middle class.

It is quite possible that this impression of the economic composition of Jews in large cities is often exaggerated due to the following factors. The native born Jews who are employed in industries often referred to as "non-Jewish" are in a small minority and are therefore not noticeable. On the other hand, the number of Jews employed in the so-called "Jewish trades," trades in which they were once in the majority, is constantly decreasing. Many thousands of Jews still work in the needle trades but this mass of workers no longer constitutes the heart of Jewish life as they did a brief quarter century ago, nor do they now appreciably affect the general impression created by the Jewish community.

Jewish workers in America are not as segregated as they were in Europe, neither are they as isolated from the non-Jewish workers. This fact still further reduces their influence on Jewish community life as a whole. Jewish commercial enterprises, on the other hand, are concentrated in Jewish residential sections and lend the tone to its general appearance. Again it is necessary to stress that there are also Jewish stores in non-Jewish neighborhoods but hardly any non-Jewish mercantile establishments in Jewish sections. Despite the existence of considerable numbers of workers the one-time proletarian aspect of New York Jewry is gradually vanishing.

The above observations lead to the following conclusion: if we include the professionals and white collar workers in the middle class, then this class constitutes the overwhelming majority of American Jewry. Even if we should classify the white collar workers among the proletariat, the wage earning element among Jews would still be only half as large as among the American population in general. Seventy per cent of the economically active population in the country are wage earners; among Jews this group constitutes only about forty per cent. Furthermore, while seventy per cent of all wage workers among non-Jews are engaged in physical work and only thirty per cent in clerical office work, this proportion is reversed among Jews. Since Jewish white collar workers are mostly connected with mercantile rather than with industrial enterprises, it is not surprising that they are actually and psychologically closer to the middle class. A large part of them eventually leave the proletarian status altogether, the women after marriage and the men through setting up in some business independently.

Let us briefly consider one process within the non-Jewish world which is of great and direct significance to the subject under discussion. We have already pointed out that the ascent up the social and economic ladder has suffered a severe set-back among the entire population. This results in an ever increasing number of people who remain within the middle class and the professional *intelligentsia*. In the coming years the number of candidates for this class from the non-Jewish population will still further increase. The cultural level of the immigrants from backward countries is rising and their children and grand-children seek higher education in ever growing numbers and provide a mounting contingent of competitors for professional and middle class positions. The rise of a professional class within any section of the population is always a harbinger of other middle and petty bourgeois elements to come to the fore. It is a symptom of cultural advance which is followed by social advance, if they succeed in becoming economically entrenched in their new vocations.

The native middle class and professional element has good connections with the established population which stand it in good stead. The rising middle class from the immigrant masses is closely related to the mass of workers in many industries from which it arose. The competitive struggle within the middle class throughout the world is sharper than that within any other economic group. The reason for this is that the middle class, and especially the professionals, suffer from a malady almost unknown among either the very high or very low economic strata—the contradiction between ambition and opportunity. The top economic strata have unlimited opportunities; the lowest have limited ambitions. The middle class longs for more than it can attain. This explains why in a country like Poland lawyers and doctors were even more anti-Semitic than workers or unemployed. The middle class and *intelligentsia* were the bearers of the most savage anti-Semitism in Austria, Germany, Czechoslovakia, Hungary, Rumania and Czarist Russia. This was the case despite the fact that in the above countries the non-Jewish middle class also came in contact with Jewish workers and even farmers.

The conclusions are obvious. The middle class, to which such a great majority of Jews in this country belong, is and will become even more crowded through an influx from two sources—those elements in the population whose social and economic rise was retarded by the depression, and the growth of a corresponding group from among immigrant masses from backward countries and Negroes. This situation is not likely to arouse optimistic thoughts. Of course, it is not an unbreakable law that the competition between various middle class groups must assume the same forms in all countries, especially since conditions in America are so different from those in Europe. But those who wish to console themselves with the illusion that Jews would become unrecognizable and that it would be impossible to single out the Jew in the American melting pot, should be reminded again that Jews assimilate easily and rapidly, but never entirely.

June, 1940

The Myth of Jewish Parasitism

by HAYIM GREENBERG

IN THE anti-Semitic propaganda which has been flooding every country since 1933 a very prominent place is given to the old charge that Jews are parasites in the world's economic order. As the economic problems in each country become more accentuated and increase in complexity, the average man has more difficulty in finding his bearings in this maze, and easily accepts the charge as true. It even influences people who have until lately been comparatively free of anti-Jewish bias.

Jews also have been considerably influenced by the notion that they constitute an unproductive, or even a destructive force, in the world's economy. We speak of Jews as essentially a people of *luftmenschen* engaged in *luft-parnosses* that is, individuals whose occupations are unsubstantial, who are exploiters, speculators and traffickers in the labor of others.

Signs of this self-condemnation first appear in the literature of our "enlightenment." Jews who felt spiritually emancipated from the civilization of the ghetto even before they were emancipated from its legal disabilities, developed a great admiration for European culture and were in no small degree affected by its anti-Jewish prejudices. Certainly they shared the European's disdain for the Jew as a trader. During the past hundred years or so wealthy Jews have always been ready to help in the proletarization of Jewry. But their motives were different from those of the Zionists or the nationalists. The latter see in Jewish economic restratification a means to insure a more rounded national existence, or a better chance of weathering crises, while the former view the transition of many Jews from urban to rural life or from trade to manual labor mainly as a way of wiping out a blot on the Jewish name.

The views of many Jewish socialists in regard to the economic role of the Jews have also been tinged by a certain anti-Semitic

223

bias. This is especially true of Jewish socialists who are not interested in Jewish survival. Not that every Jewish Marxist has actually read Marx's essay on the Jewish question where Judaism is made synonymous with capitalist exploitation, greed and usury. But some of the spirit of that shocking accusation is to be found in the attitude of the average Jewish Socialist.

Non-Jewish socialists, and not necessarily Marxian socialists, have tended to look down on the Jew in the world's economy. The Russian *Narodnaya Volya* of the late nineteenth century which glorified the peasant and was more thoroughly humanist than any other socialist or reformist movement of modern times* could be expected to be immune from anti-Semitism. Nevertheless, the *Narodovoltzi* once issued a proclamation to the peasants calling on them "to burn the mansions of the nobility, to rob the estates, and to beat up Jews." This was not, as some believe, a mere demagogic device to rouse the peasants to revolt by appealing to their prejudices. The authors of this proclamation would not have issued it if they did not, at least vaguely, entertain the idea that the Jew was essentially a "bloodsucker." Socialists and other reformers who stressed the agrarian problem and who saw in the peasant the chief potential carrier of their ideal, generally tended to see in the Jew the extreme expression of urban life and of the iniquitous exploitation they associate with the city man. This also explains Tolstoy's rather unfriendly attitude towards the Jews, an attitude most eloquently expressed by his repeated failure to speak up on behalf of the persecuted Jews. Tolstoy had the peasant's primitive notions of enonomic life, the peasant's narrow outlook in judging economic values and the peasant's suspicion of urban sophistication as mere crookedness.

The literary influence of Tolstoy, and the influence of some schools of Socialist propaganda are largely responsible for the tendencies of self-deprecation and self-condemnation so common to many Jewish socialists and Jewish intellectuals.

---

* The *Narodnaya Volya*, that is People's Freedom or People's Will, was the forerunner of the Social-Revolutionary Party, prominent in the revolutionary movement until October, 1917.

Nor is Zionism free from its share of responsibility. There was a time when it used to be the fashion for Zionist speakers (including the writer) to declare from the platform that "to be a good Zionist one must first be somewhat of an anti-Semite." One can sense this attitude in some of Pinsker's writings; there is a great deal of it in Syrkin and in Borochov, the two main theoreticians of the Labor Zionist movement; A. D. Gordon, the author of the idea of the Religion of Labor (*Dat ha-Avoda*) wrote, in a spirit of extreme contrition, about the national sins of the Jews which must be atoned for by manual labor; I. H. Brenner, the nearest to Dostoyevsky in Hebrew literature, indulged in a masochistic self-flagellation. To this day Labor Zionist circles are under the influence of the idea that the Return to Zion involves a process of purification from our economic uncleanliness. Whosoever does not engage in so-called "productive" manual labor, is believed to be a sinner against Israel and against mankind.

When addressing the non-Jewish world we become exceedingly apologetic and talk of extenuating circumstances to explain our supposedly incriminating economic position. We quote the Bible to prove that as a nation we were born honest toilers on the soil, and that it was the Canaanite, the Phoenician, who used to be the trader of antiquity. We do not dispute the basic fact contained in the accusation against us. We admit, expressly or by implication, that we constitute a useless and an unlovely element in the economic set-up of every country. We merely blame it on our tragic history, on the persecutions and on the disabilities we have suffered.

Our apology is based on ample evidence. There is no doubt that no religious literature (with the possible exception of the ancient Chinese) contains so much glorification of manual labor as do the Bible and the Talmud. Nor can there be any doubt that our history made us a people of traders in a much larger measure than we would have become under normal circumstances. In contrast to the Greeks who looked down upon manual labor as an occupation for slaves, the Talmud takes the view that manual

labor is ennobling. Even Plato and Aristotle adopted the dominant Greek attitude, but the Talmud says that if labor was good
enough for God when he created the world, it ought to be good
enough for anybody. The number of passages one could cite from
the Talmud which express the same view is legion, and we have
a right to be proud of that attitude. But that does not mean
that a man who works hard for his living as an honest store-
keeper has reason to be ashamed of his occupation or to feel constantly apologetic. In medieval feudal Europe, manual labor and
particularly agriculture were so intimately bound up with the
Church that for a Jew in many countries to take to the plough
meant assuming distinct obligations toward the Catholic Church.
There are many other reasons for the change in Jewish occupations
during the Middle Ages. The recitation of these reasons fills our
apologetic literature.

The present economic structure of the Jews may not be ideal,
but there is nothing shameful or unethical about it. In the first
place, we have more manual workers than is commonly believed
and their numbers have increased in the past few decades. In the
second place, there is nothing evil or parasitic about useful work
which is not manual.

Useful or productive labor does not mean only manual labor, or
labor engaged in producing things which can be seen and touched
and which have physical dimensions. Any work which satisfies
human needs or is socially useful is productive work.

Of all great thinkers of modern times Tolstoy probably went
farthest in stressing the virtue of simple manual labor. At one
time he was under the influence of a homely moralist by the name
of Bondarev, who preached the doctrine that only work which
helps produce bread is morally good. A peasant who ploughs and
reaps corn is a good man, but a farmer who plants oranges or
bananas is a *darmoyed* who eats the bread of idleness, since he
wastes his time on producing unnecessary and evil luxuries. At
about the same time, Tolstoy was under the spell of another home-
grown philosopher, a Swede, who taught that every man must

produce the grain for his own food. This Swede reprimanded Tolstoy for drinking tea. Drinking tea, he said, encourages the Chinese peasant to plant the ungodly weed and neglect the cultivation of life-giving rice, thus bringing about famine in China. One day when Tolstoy offered his Swedish friend a glass of milk, he refused, saying, "My mother has been dead a long time, and the cow you have milked is some one else's mother." Tolstoy was tremendously impressed by the argument. Most of us think it ludicrous. But it serves to illustrate the absurd extremes which may be reached by the consistent application of the idea that only work immediately resulting in prime necessities is socially and economically useful.

Modern socialism is free from such extravaganzas, since its object is not to limit human needs, but to expand them. The doctrine that man may enjoy only that which he himself produces is alien to a system which looks forward to an abundance requiring an increasing complexity and differentiation of labor. But for many years socialist theory has stubbornly clung to a dogma that stresses the worth of the producer and the relative worthlessness of the intermediary between the producer and the consumer. A "logical" deduction from such a view would declare the milk wagon driver a parasite, and the cow the only producer in the milk industry.

Bernard Shaw was justified in ridiculing this primitive notion. His illustrations are the country boy who shoos away the birds from the seeded field and who performs by his unsubstantial noises the same functions as the village carpenter who builds a gate to keep the cows away from the same field, or the housemaid who has nothing of physical substance to show for her hard labor except an occasional broken dish.

No one is a parasite who engages in work which makes life more agreeable, more comfortable and more abundant for his fellow-men. In our modern society, the distribution of goods is indispensible to their enjoyment by the largest possible number. Anyone engaged in distribution—the exporter, the importer, the sailor, the wholesaler, the retailer—is doing useful work. We may hold the view that nationalized commerce is more socially beneficial than private commerce. Yet in principle, there is no moral difference between a merchant operating his own store and an employee of a workers' co-operative or of a Soviet state store. Both earn their livelihood, provided they do their work honestly and conscientiously, and provided they do not resort to cunning to extract a remuneration which is not commensurate with their service.

Each one of us owes it to society to do some useful work in order to pay for the things he enjoys as the result of the work of others. But among our creditors, so to speak, are not only the farmer, the tailor and the mason. There are hundreds of people who produce nothing that is tangible, but without whose labor our life would be much harder or would at least lack many of the amenities and the pleasures which we prize. There is the milkman, the grocer, the bus driver, the waiter in the restaurant, the actor, the writer, the radio announcer—even the exterminator of vermin.

Take any typically Jewish occupation which has long been the butt of our moralists and satirists. I, for one do not approve of the institution of *shadkhoness,* that is, professional match-making. But, after all, this is a matter of taste, and no one forces me to pay for the services of a *shadkhan* if I do not employ him. There are others who do, and what right have I to impose my attitude upon other people? Or take the Jewish clerics—the rabbi, the *khazan,* the *mohel,* the *shamash,* types whom our "enlightened" literature has presented in a most uncomplimentary way—again it is a matter of the point of view. Millions of Jews require the services of these functionaries and are willing to pay for them. Compared to the numerous clerics, monks and nuns of other denominations the Jewish religion has been neither overstaffed nor overpaid. In Poland, before the war, we had several hundred *"einiklech,"* that is, grandsons of famous hassidic rabbis, and we have some of them in this country. These people who trade on their pedigrees constitute to my knowledge the only specific class of unproductive Jews. But then, they are no more so than Siamese twins, or the Dionne quintuplets.

The point I am trying to make is that we have no reason to feel morally apologetic about our economic position. I do not mean to say that all Jews are saints. Nor do I deny the need for a thorough restratification of our economic life. But this restratification ought not to be motivated by a sense of collective guilt. We have to reconstruct our economic life because the present status is fraught with dangers to our well-being, and because a fuller national life requires a more balanced economic set-up. We are not economically wicked. We have not eaten unearned bread all these centuries. And under the conditions of modern society, we have been fulfilling a useful economic function.

I have no reason to be proud of the Jewish saloonkeeper in this country, or of his antecedent in Eastern Europe. But I know they have their counterparts among non-Jews. There is nothing edifying about the Jews in the Ukrainian villages under the feudal system who held the keys to the village churches and opened the churches only when the peasants paid the rent. But the keys were placed in the Jews' hands by the greedy and lazy Polish nobility. We are, on the whole, neither better nor worse than others.

The question may well be asked, what of our Labor Zionist ideology? What of our propaganda about ruralization, the dignity of labor, *khalutziut?* These principles are still sound. A reshaping of Jewish economic life is a historic necessity, and it cannot be accomplished without the popular enthusiasm that Zionism generally and Labor Zionism particularly have aroused for these aims. There is nothing wicked in being a middleman, but it is not sound for a whole people to consist of middlemen. We are building a new nation in Palestine, and we cannot succeed unless we make its economic life varied and many-sided and thereby relatively complete. It requires no effort and no propaganda on our part to create a Jewish merchant class in Palestine. But the emergence of a Jewish agricultural class cannot be a spontaneous process. At this juncture in our history, the creation of a class of Jewish farmers in Palestine is of paramount importance and justifies the expenditure of moral and mental energies that have gone into the effort. Sometimes the enthusiasm of the Palestinian pioneers appears to us at a distance as being too naive and narrow. But taken in its historic perspective this exaggerated glorification of manual labor and its achievements is necessary.

I am not oblivious of the desirability of a restratification of Jewish economic life outside of Palestine, say in the United States of America. I know that our top-heavy economy contains some dangerous possibilities. But mere preaching will not accomplish the desired change. I am not an economist, but I question the feasibility of effecting a complete change in Jewish economic life in the present state of capitalist development in this country. How can we produce large numbers of farmers, coal-miners and metalworkers? If present conditions make such a feat impossible, there is nothing to be gained by continuous moralizing. If it is possible, it ought to be done. But let us stop apologizing for ourselves.

March, 1942

Louis D. Brandeis

by ROBERT H. JACKSON
Associate Justice of the Supreme Court
of the United States

THE LAST decade of Justice Brandeis' life was saddened. Relapse of whole peoples, under Fascist influence, into a course of torment and plunder deeply offended his sense of justice, as it offends that of all right-thinking men. But to him it was more than abstract injustice. He saw the Jew, again as of old, on the rack of persecution in Europe and saw those of his own stock become refugees from resurgent barbarism.

Flight from home itself is bad enough, but these were in flight with no destination. It seemed that everywhere those who had first gotten to free land had closed the door to later migrations. Everywhere people had lost their old self-confidence in the presence of strangers and were too preoccupied with their own fears and troubles to extend any general right of sanctuary. The world's livable spots seemed pre-empted, frontiers were all closed, and the days of easy migration were no more.

In these circumstances Justice Brandeis' foresighted interest in a Jewish National Home in Palestine was strikingly vindicated. While "ancient historic connection" no doubt stirred his sentiments, very practical considerations had guided his efforts. He had gone to that old and neglected land and had seen the work of men and women who had returned there. He saw them building new cities, establishing new industries, draining swamps and watering the desert, and making the countryside to prosper again. There, at least, was a land with capacity to absorb refugees, and there was opportunity for their resettlement. There he wanted those of his blood to have opportunity to renew their national existence and to resume their modern culture on its ancient foundations.

231

Papers and speeches in which he outlined this vision and pleaded this cause recently have been collected and published. It would be sheer presumption for me to attempt additions to what he made complete or interpretation of what he made so clear. In a foreword to that book a discriminating Judge says that Justice Brandeis is "the moral symbol of Zionism throughout the world, notwithstanding the judicial insulation of his life." If I could help you to penetrate this judicial insulation, the qualities of the man would be the strongest buttress of the cause he championed.

The great work of his life, to which all else was prelude, was as a Justice of the United States Supreme Court. The character of such work is, to laymen, obscure and elusive. It does not lie on the surface, nor does it thrust itself upon lay attention. Even for lawyers, unless they follow the work of the Court closely, it is difficult to appraise. A Justice officially expresses himself in the technical language of the law, and he is as remote from the lay world as if he wrote in a dead language. When he speaks for the Court, his opinion is depersonalized by the necessity of adapting it to the several minds for which he speaks. While legislators may act as they want to act, judges often act as statutes tell them to act and render judgments that are the law's judgments rather than their personal ones. Oftentimes, too, the judge is legally bound to base his conclusions on facts as they are decided by some one else. As a result he appears to approve a good deal that in truth he has no say about.

Then, too, in many fields of law where there is no controlling legislation, judges must usually submit to the guidance of precedents. Justice Brandeis never carried regard for precedent to a worship of them. But he did accept, as all judges should, certain traditional restraints on personal judgment. Laymen often fail to see why this should be. The law is, after all, a rule for men to live by. They must have some way to find out how they should behave in order to avoid liabilities and punishments and troubles with the law. When there is no known rule except the personal will of the judge one happens to come before, one can never know how to conduct himself. Bentham said that judges, when they assume to make the law, do it "just as a man makes laws for his dog. When your dog does anything you want to break him of, you wait till he does it, and then beat him for it." I think we must agree that there is uncomforting truth in this criticism of judicial law-making, and that it is to be avoided so far as possible consistently with the view that law is a living and progressing body of learning.

The device by which judicial action is made at all predictable is the precedent. It is the doctrine that a court will give a word or phrase in a contract or statute the same meaning tomorrow that it did yesterday, that it will resort to the same principles to fashion future judgments that it employed in past ones. Of course, even at its best the endless variation in the facts of cases makes any prediction from precedent an imperfect one. But in its absence, or before judges with no regard for the true function of the precedent, there is no law but that day's opinion of the judge who perhaps accidentally gets the case. Brandeis, it seems to me, came near the golden mean in his attitude toward the precedents. He examined them patiently and followed them in the absence of grave reasons for a departure. If he departed, as he never feared to do, he paid his profession the respect of a searching, candid, and unequivocal opinion giving his reasons.

I often hear it said of Brandeis as if it characterized his life's work, "He was a great dissenter." Let me warn you against this popular but badly mistaken standard of appraisal. Dissenting opinions, of course, have a way of better pleasing those who read as well as those who write them. They are apt to be more individual and colorful. Opinions which must meet the ideas of many minds may in comparison seem dull and undistinguished. In the past few years a dozen, or perhaps a score, of really important decisions of the Supreme Court have been overruled. In consequence, minority opinions won belated vindication. The drama of a high court reversing itself has news value, and some have come to regard dissent as something worthy in itself.

Brandeis had no such delusion. It is not the number of his dissents, but the quality of his dissenting opinions, that is outstanding. The fact is that of the dissents that have been written in the history of the Court only a trifling proportion have later become law. The same is true of the dissenting opinions of individual Justices. In judicial thinking as elsewhere two good heads will average better results than one, and time more often vindicates majority opinions than minority ones.

The great work of Brandeis was done, not in opposing the Court, but in leading it. He was its spokesman in many difficult and complicated problems which covered the wide range of issues that come before it. It was for the Court that he wrote the greater number of his five hundred and twenty-eight opinions. They interpret the great life-giving clauses of the Constitution, pioneer in administrative law, deal with the law of public utilities, patents, monopolies and restraint of trade, labor relations and civil rights. In these he patiently gathered up the facts of record, examined the arguments of counsel, reconciled the views of his associates, and set forth the conclusion of the Court in clear, illuminating and unadorned language.

It was this constructive type of work on the Court for which his career at the bar peculiarly fitted him. His work as a lawyer was constructive, practical and bold. He pioneered in fields lawyers seldom entered and more rarely were distinguished in, and always he was building—building—building. I shall not dwell on these early activities. In them Woodrow Wilson with singular vision detected the making of a constructive jurist. He named lawyer Brandeis to the Supreme Court, fostered the nomination through a stormy confirmation, and gave to his country Mr. Justice Brandeis.

The period of his service began June 5, 1916, and ended by retirement February 13, 1939. In that almost quarter century unprecedented things came to pass. The United States went through the ordeal of one world war and stood on the precipice overlooking another. Between the two we harvested crops planted by a century of industrial revolution—speculation, extravagance, and inflation, with its aftercrop of depression, deflation and disaster. Paul Freund, one of the closest friends of the Justice, has recorded that when Brandeis was asked in the dark days of 1933 whether he believed the worst was over, he answered almost cheerfully that "the worst had happened before 1929."

This period of rapidly fluctuating price levels and economic chaos, of social unrest and upheaval, of political transition and experimentation, brought to his Court an unprecedented grist of difficult problems. Some of them the Court did not meet too well. On important occasions he was a vigorous and sometimes solitary dissenter. In earlier days he was sometimes joined by Justice Holmes, and later by Justice Cardozo, Justice Stone and Chief Justice Hughes. The message to Congress in which President Roosevelt proposed to reorganize the Court brought on some of the most critical moments of its long and not always tranquil history. Brandeis had protested some, though not all, of the decisions that had aggrieved the President and many others. In general the attack in the court fight was against decisions that he had opposed in the Court. But while he was always ready to struggle within the Court, he would have no hands laid upon the institution from the outside. It mattered not that the outside hands would in the main uphold his views and would rebuke those with whom he had long and often disagreed. Brandeis valued the Court's *independence* of decision even more than *rightness* of decision. He joined with Chief Justice Hughes in a letter to Senator Wheeler which did more than any one thing to turn the tide of the Court struggle.

I mention this because it revealed the man. I suppose perhaps eighty-five per cent of those who followed and revered him were in the camp of the President. I think ninety-five per cent of those who disliked or scorned him were in the opposition. But Brandeis did not determine his principles by counting heads. He simply thought his friends were wrong and his foes for once were right, and that was an end of the matter for him. He believed with all the intensity of his being that the country needed the institution he served, and that a court of courage, character and independence could exist only in an atmosphere of freedom from political pressures. But he believed the Justices maintain it by self-restraint and openmindedness, by unbiased, patient and accurate application of the law, and by freedom from political ambition or partisanship.

The handiwork of his opinions measured up to this standard. He mastered completely the facts of his case, respecting facts for the stubborn things that they are. He set them forth with fidelity to the record and with unbiased emphasis. He analyzed them in the light of research, not only in the law, but in economics, science and history. As Mr. Freund, who served as his law clerk, tells us, when he had finally completed the many revisions of an opinion he said, "The opinion is now convincing, but what can we do to make it more instructive?" And instructive his opinions are. When one comes upon an opinion by Brandeis, it is like finding bedrock upon which it is safe to build.

He was not an ornamental writer. Clarity and simplicity were his aims, and so well did he achieve them that style never steals attention from the substance. He did not have the apt and cutting phrase that Holmes wielded so devastatingly. But while Holmes illuminated a subject like a flash of lighting, Brandeis illuminated it as does the noonday sun—steadily, evenly, completely. Chief Justice Hughes summed up his workmanship by describing him as "the master of both microscope and telescope. Nothing of importance, however minute, escapes his microscopic examination of every problem, and, through his powerful telescopic lens, his mental vision embraces distant scenes ranging far beyond the familiar worlds of conventional thinking."

Justice Brandeis greatly influenced many young men. He found time in some way to cultivate their acquaintance. His modest home on Sunday afternoon often gathered those who wanted to see him or to whom he had extended an invitation. He would draw them into conversation, fortify their courage if he found it failing. He saw life as it was lived by aspiring young men. He gave no encouragement to those who came to whine over their bruises. He sought no easy way to lift even men he liked into positions they had not earned. He did not tell every lad he could do great things, but he made them all feel they could do useful things, and he urged them to do well whatever task they had in hand. He urged them after enlarging their experiences and broadening their viewpoints to go home, to fill places in their own communities.

Brandeis has been called a reformer, and he had the passion for betterment that lies at the root of reform. But he never went off on any plan for making men into angels. His aim was only to make better men, and content if only a little better. Crusader, some called him, and he had the zeal, the consecration and the courage of one. But he stuck to practical jobs and left windmill-tilting to those whose emotions outrun their judgment. Friend of the poor and champion of the disadvantaged he was, but always he planned ways for them to help themselves and never sought to relieve them of work or responsibility, which he thought to be great educators. He was in no sense a collectivist or believer in centralized control of life or of industry.

Brandeis was labelled as a "liberal," and labels are tyrannical things. Because Brandeis had been a liberal in politics, many expected him as a judge to sustain all that was done in the name of liberalism. Those reckoned without knowledge of his high concept of his judicial office. He feared and distrusted large, unconfined and irresponsible power, whether in private or public hands. He would never accept it as wholesome merely because found at the time being put to good use by good hands. He knew that the powers which evil men misuse are often acquired because lodged in the hands of men on the argument that they were good men.

In the "Hot Oil" case and the N.R.A. case he joined in striking down as unconstitutional acts of Congress sponsored by the Administration and identified with its program of economic recovery.

Although few were more sympathetic with debtors in the depression, he concurred in holding unconstitutional state legislation which deprived the creditor of all effective remedy, and wrote the opinion holding the Frazier-Lemke Act for the relief of farm debtors unconstitutional. In the Tennessee Valley Authority litigation, while he agreed that the Act was constitutional, he would have refused to decide the point because he thought it not properly presented. Later he would have refused judgment sustaining the old age benefit provisions of the Social Security Act as constitutional. In all of these matters he refused to yield his ideals of what was constitutional or as to appropriate procedures because of his political sympathies with the causes involved.

What was the general philosophy of this man? It is safer to seek it from his own words. Many admirers have tried to make Brandeis over in their own image. What he stood for is perhaps better and more shortly stated in his famous letter to Robert Bruere than any one could do for him. Hence, I quote at length what I think could wisely be the basic creed of the modern liberal:

"Refuse to accept as inevitable any evil in business (e.g., irregularity of employment). Refuse to tolerate any immoral practice (e.g., espionage). But do not believe that you can find a universal remedy for evil conditions or immoral practices in effecting a fundamental change in society (as by State Socialism). And do not pin too much faith in legislation. Remedial institutions are apt to fall under the control of the enemy and to become instruments of oppression.

"Seek for betterment within the broad lines of existing institutions. Do so by attacking evil *in situ;* and proceed from the individual to the general. Remember that progress is necessarily slow; that remedies are necessarily tentative; that because of varying conditions there must be much and constant inquiry into facts . . . and much experimentation; and that always and everywhere the intellectual, moral and spiritual development of those concerned will remain an essential—and the main factor—in real betterment.

"This development of the individual is, thus, both a necessary means and the end sought. For our objective is the making of men and women who shall be free, self-respecting members of a democracy—and who shall be worthy of respect. Improvement in material conditions of the worker and ease are the incidents of better conditions—valuable mainly as they may ever increase opportunities for development.

"The great developer is responsibility. Hence no remedy can be hopeful which does not devolve upon the workers participation in responsibility for the conduct of business; and their aim should be the eventual assumption of full responsibility—as in cooperative enterprises. This participation in and eventual control of industry is likewise an essential of obtaining justice in distributing the fruits of industry.

"But democracy in any sphere is a serious undertaking. It substitutes self-restraint for external restraint. It is more to maintain than to achieve. It demands continuous sacrifice by the individual and more exigent obedience to the moral law than any other form of government. Success in any democratic undertaking must proceed from the individual. It is possible only where the process of perfecting the individual is pursued. His development is attained mainly in the processes of common living. Hence the industrial struggle is essentially an affair of the church and its imperative task."

Such was the philosophy, such the tough fibre of his mind, such the qualities which make his work pre-eminent among the many powerful men of his time.

These are the qualities he brought to guidance and advocacy of a national home in Palestine for his people after centuries of exile, dispersion and persecution. What true American would not rejoice to see fulfillment of Brandeis' vision that men of his stock should resurrect the life and culture of the people of the Bible in that little land where our faith was founded? If the stock of Brandeis is of one fibre with him, their modern oppressors will find, as the Egyptian taskmasters found of the Children of Israel, that "the more they afflicted them, the more they multiplied and grew."   July, 1943

The Yellow Badge and Mrs. Grossman

by Marie Syrkin

WHENEVER I come across the suggestion that the free Jews of America should don the yellow badge as a symbol of solidarity with the suffering Jews of Europe—to transform the symbol of shame into a symbol of honor—I think of Mrs. Grossman. I know how aghast and bewildered Mrs. Grossman would be at such a dramatic demonstration. And yet Mrs. Grossman is a symbol, too; in her way, a very significant symbol.

At present Mrs. Grossman is looking for a plastic surgeon. Not that she's having her face lifted. Heaven forbid! Mrs. Grossman is a sensible woman and she has no illusions as to the value of the effects obtained. Above all, Mrs. Grossman detests an artificial smile. And every woman knows how set and expressionless a "lifted" face can be. Nor is Mrs. Grossman planning to have her nose "reconstructed." She would be the first to admit that she is no longer as young as she used to be; besides she is not planning to crash Hollywood. Harold likes her well enough the way she is, so why undergo an expensive and painful operation merely to remove a slight droop? All this indicates that Mrs. Grossman is the acme of good sense. Her zeal in seeking for a competent face remodeller is motivated not by vanity but by maternal love. She needs a surgeon for Peter, her seventeen-year-old son. Peter has not been disfigured by a baseball bat swinging the wrong way, nor has he been mauled beyond recognition in a football game. He has the same agreeable young face that he has always had. But his nose is "Jewish." It is not as short and as straight as Mrs. Grossman would desire. Not that the organ in question outrages any beholder. Peter is no Cyrano de Bergerac, and his mother is not swayed by aesthetic considerations. She is driven by solicitude. Despite Boas and other anthropologists, Mrs. Grossman is convinced that any departure from absolute rectitude in a nose is a

240

Semitic lapse. And Mrs. Grossman reads the papers. She wants to shield her son from Coughlin, from Hitler. What mother wouldn't? And so there must be no incriminating beak, or hook, or curve, be it ever so slight.

Peter is going to college next fall, probably to one of the bigger and better universities. He is bright, studious and has an exceptional record; even Harvard looms as a possibility. But his intelligence, industry and excellent character are not enough. He has to be adequately prepared for the great day by two amputations: his name and his nose must be foreshortened.

There once was a simple era in American Jewish life when Peter would have faced the world as Milton, and Grossman would have naively shrunk to Gross. But those days are gone. Mrs. Grossman's revisions are more ambitious and sophisticated. Just now she is toying with the idea of "Gregg"—Peter Gregg! The evolution of Grossman into Gregg was almost axiomatic. There are rules for all types of circumcision, including those of family names. It must always be remembered that under no circumstances would Mrs. Grossman consider throwing her name wholly to the winds and boldly assuming "Sheridan" or "Hughes." That would shock Mrs. Grossman. She wants no alias. Something of the original issue must remain, and the steps that led to "Gregg" followed a definite pattern. The first step is always the dropping of the last syllable. Step number two is the vowel change: "Gross" becomes "Grass" as "Levy" becomes "Lave" (what's a vowel among enemies?), but Mrs. Grossman didn't like the anaemic implications of "Grass," or the uneuphonious foreign quality of "Griss" or "Gruss." So the consonant change is invoked. Thus Gross becomes "Gregg." The family initial appears in triplicate. The link with Grossman is unbroken, even reinforced. It's really the same name, as "Shoenberg" is "Belmont" and "Goldberg" is "Ormont." Mrs. Grossman is satisfied with the solution. She has denied nothing, she has made no fundamental change. She has merely sent her child into the world better fortified to cope with an unjust and hostile environment.

And once Peter Grossman is Peter Gregg he must be equipped
with a suitable nose. That slight aquiline curve might not worry
a Boston blue-blood, but it disturbs Mrs. Grossman. No dubious
nasal inclination must impede Peter's progress through life. A
nose by any other name may smell as sweet—but Mrs. Grossman
considers more than the functional aspects. A nose must not only
smell; above all, it must not tell. It must not tell of the great-
grandfather who was a Rabbi—the one from whom Peter is supposed to have gotten his brains. It must not tell of the
grandmother whose name was a by-word for piety and kindliness.
It must not even tell of Mr. and Mrs. Grossman, upstanding
Americans, whose energy, ability and sense of values make Peter's
prospective career possible. Mrs. Grossman has always been a
good mother. When Peter was born, she was careful to honor
the Lord's covenant with Israel in the prescribed fashion, and
now that he is seventeen she is prepared to offer further slices
of her son's person on the altar of anonymity.

Fortunately there are not too many Mrs. Grossmans. "Cutting
off your nose to spite your race"—to repeat the classic witticism—
is neither easy nor cheap, and not many will go to these lengths,
or abbreviations. But Mrs. Grossman represents a sufficiently distinct trend in American Jewish life to merit comment, particularly
these days when the cries of Hitler's victims can be heard even on
our shores.

At best, without invoking larger issues of courage and dignity,
how kind has Mrs. Grossman really been to Peter? In college, in
one of his courses, he is bound to hear the anecdote of the famous
biologist who studied the inheritance of acquired characteristics
by cutting off the tails of successive generations of mice. Finally
one new-born mouse, still boasting a tail despite the loppings to
which its ancestors had been subjected, arose and confounded the
scientist with, "You cannot shape our ends, rough-hew them as
you may." While the class howls with glee at the professorial
quip, will Peter's nose redden? He will know, having studied

genetics, that he owes a confession to the maiden of his dreams. He will have to announce that he does not come to her intact— otherwise she may be aggrieved at the unexpected appearance of an aquiline nose among her offspring. So Peter will have a guilt-complex. And what about his name? Having lived seventeen happy successful years as "Grossman" will he ever be wholly at ease in "Gregg"? How will he introduce his mother to his friends?

Americans recall the stir made some years ago when one Slav, called Kabotchnikoff, petitioned a New England court to have his name changed to Cabot. A cry of outrage arose among the Boston Brahmins—the Lowells who speak but to the Cabots, and the Cabots who speak but to God. If Kabotchnikoff had to change his name, why did he have to choose so "exclusive" an appellation? However, Kabotchnikoff, being free, white and twenty-one, remained undaunted and emerged as Cabot, with all the privileges pertaining thereto.

Louis Adamic has recently commented on the sequel to this episode, and brought to light a curious denouement. It seems that after a lapse of years, the same Kabotchnikoff—Cabot again appeared before the court and petitioned to have his name changed back to Kabotchnikoff. The explanation he gave was that he had never really felt at home in the guise of Cabot, and now, that he was growing old, he preferred to join his ancestors in his original state of Kabotchnikoff. Had he been more articulate, he must have been able to voice something that no doubt stirred obscurely in his soul—the feeling that though Cabots speak only to God, God speaks only to Kabotchnikoff.

I meditated on Mrs. Grossman's Peter and on Kabotchnikoff when I read Rabbi Magnes' recent proposal that all Jews don the yellow badge as a symbol of solidarity and protest. The great Yiddish poet, Leivick, had expressed the same idea earlier in his profound poem, "The Yellow Badge:"

"Punish me because I do not don,
Of my own will, the six towered shield of David
And the round emblem of the Yellow Badge,
To hearten Israel in the hangman's land,
To praise and exalt throughout the world
The arm that wears the glory of this crest."

But how could Mrs. Grossman, who is ready to snip off a
piece of her son's nose to prevent his identification with Isreal
begin to understand such an idea? And those far greater num
bers, who hope by shuffling the alphabet to propitiate the furies
of prejudice and folly, who come bearing syllables to Cerberus
how will they rise to the call to 'hearten Israel in her hangman's
land?"

A few days ago, on a Saturday afternoon, while walking along
Fifth Avenue, I noticed a drunk among the women shoppers.
The drunk bent towards a Jewish woman near me and whis
pered, "Sarah." *In vino anti-semitas,* but I wasn't sure of the
significance of "Sarah" till I heard him shout a few feet
later to another woman, who stopped to look into a shop-window
"Go in, it's kosher." So the drunk had learned. He had learned
from the Christian Front, or its equivalent, that the beautiful
biblical name of Sarah could be an epithet of insult. And Jew
had helped him learn. Every German Jew called Sigmund, and
every German Jew called Hedwig, who winced at the compulsory
addition of "Israel" and "Sarah" to their names, had given the
drunk a weapon. Some German Jews committed suicide to escape
the "shame" of the specifically Jewish name. But there were some
who couldn't be hurt—not in this fashion at any rate. The Jews
called "Schlomo" or "Hayim" or "Israel" had, in a psychological
sense, defeated the Nazi tormenter. You can't debase a man who
proudly calls himself "Israel" by affixing another "Israel" to his
documents. Such a Jew had instinctively made of the badge a
shield.

It is this that Mrs. Grossman must learn: That the *Magen*

David means the shield of David, not only etymologically; that it can be a shield of pride to shelter even her beloved Peter; that, best of all, a shield can be borne into battle. Otherwise, Peter will be defenceless despite the most skilful plastic surgery. And as to expressions of solidarity with one's people—instead of the sorry stampede of syllables, let all the bright strong Peters stand up and be counted. That's one way of making common cause against the common foe.

December, 1941

To a Christian Friend

by MARIE SYRKIN

There is something between us now:
The cry you did not raise.

You have washed your hands again.
Put down the pitcher.
This water will flow between us.

Give me back Jesus;
He is my brother.
He will walk with me
Behind the gray ghetto wall
Into the slaughter-house.
I will lead him into the lethal chamber;
He will lie down upon the poisoned stone;
The little children pricked with the death-bubble
Will come unto him.

Return to him the yellow badge.
Give me back Jesus;
He is not yours.

March, 1943

At War

EDITORIAL

SINCE PEARL HARBOR, the intellectual and emotional content of our lives has undergone a great simplification. We are aware of a few truths, so elementary that they hardly need stating: We are Americans, so we know that Hitler and his satellites must be overcome if our country is to survive. We are citizens of a great democracy, so we know that fascist aggression must be crushed, if a free world is to emerge from the agony of this war. We are Jews, so we know that the triumph of Hitlerism means the enslavement of every oppressed people. American Jews have a triple stake in the outcome of this struggle—as lovers of their country, as lovers of liberty, and as members of a religious and racial minority which was the first to feel the full infamy of the Nazi attack on civilization. Jewish suffering was the weathervane which foretold the fury of the tempest that was to overwhelm the world. The fate of the martyred Jewries of Europe, as the fate of Ethiopia, bore the character of an unwilling prophecy—a prophecy which went unheeded. We are the chief witness against the criminal before the ultimate tribunal of historic justice, and we have no illusions as to what befalls those who testify against gangsters, if the gangsters escape sentence.

If America is to make good the costly errors of the past—the tragic delays and obstructionism of appeasers and isolationists—she needs the full energy and devotion of every man and woman in the land. Just as there can no longer be any evasion for the country as a whole, so can there be no evasion for the individual citizen. The time for subleties and argument is past. There is no escaping the grim and difficult task before us. In the great marshalling of man-power upon which the United States is entering, every person's will to victory and readiness for sacrifice will count. No American, Jew or Gentile, should sit back and wait till he is reached by the civil or military draft. There are no valid excuses for any American; there are particularly no excuses for American Jews. We say, particularly, because as Jews we have the melancholy advantage of understanding even better than other sections of the community what a catastrophe for every human value an Axis victory would be. We have good company in comprehension. The Poles of Warsaw, the Dutch of Rotterdam, the Greeks who saw the swastika defile Athens, every tortured people of the world whose sole sin was to be defenseless before bombs and tanks, shares our knowledge, but we still enjoy advance information of a special sort. We must act in the light of this knowledge.

To those past military age, we say: If the proper authorities will have you, take your place as an air-raid warden despite your lumbago or your fear of a chill. Enroll for a first-aid course even if accidents make you faint. Donate blood even if you are not husky. These are obligations which cannot be transferred or delayed. Such contributions may not be tremendous, but they matter in the total effort.

Of the young, the strong, the able-bodied, greater things are asked. As long as the United States Government is calling for volunteers in any branch of the service, our young men should enlist without waiting to be called by the draft board. We know that Jews are enlisting in as large numbers as any other group. We hope they will enlist in numbers far exceeding their proportion of the population. There may be no Jewish army through which the Jews of Palestine and the Axis-held land will be able to participate as a people in the struggle against the common enemy. But since the Axis attack on the United States, every American Jew has the opportunity of giving expression to both his American patriotism and his sense of outrage as a Jew. We can help wipe away the foulest blot on the page of history. Our dignity as human beings demands no less. We are no longer impotent. The sense of helplessness before mounting horrors which paralyzed us for so long, is over. All our indignation, our anguish, our hope for a free world can at last be transferred into effective action. The Axis neo-barbarism has paid the Jew the honor of identifying him with the democratic order which it is sworn to destroy. Such an honor carries it with it not only dangers but responsibilities. Jews who have been in the front ranks of the victims will march in the front ranks of the fighters against the fascist conspiracy. We can offer no greater service to our country.

THE EDITORS.

January, 1942

PALESTINE

DAVID BEN GURION

LEON BLUM

ABRAHAM DICKENSTEIN

HILLEL GILEADI

BEN HALPERN

ABBA KHUSHI

BERL LOCKER

EMANUEL NEUMANN

SHULAMITH SCHWARTZ

MOSHE SHERTOK

ARTHUR WAUCHOPE

Building a Nation

by BERL LOCKER

I.

ON HANUKKA, 5680 (December, 1920), the workers of
Palestine, in number somewhat less than 4,500 (the majority
of whom had arrived in the country after the world war) proclaimed the foundation of their all-embracing organization *Ha'histadrut ha'klalit shel ha'ovdim ha'ivrim b'Eretz Yisrael"* (General
Federation of Jewish Labor in Palestine)—known by its common
abbreviation, *Histadrut*. The Jewish population as a whole num-
bered at that time some 65,000-70,000 souls. Organized Labor
accounted for between 6 and 7 per cent of the *Yishuv*. If we
include their children, this figure was nearer 8 or 9 per cent.
Today the population of the *Yishuv* is about 500,000. The membership of the *Histadrut* is over 120,000. The *Yishuv* has grown
more than sevenfold; the *Histadrut* membership has multiplied
itself almost 27 times. One in four Jews in Palestine is a member
of the *Histadrut*. Including members of families ineligible by
age for membership, the number doubtless reaches some 200,000
souls—40 per cent of the *Yishuv*. The unprecedented growth both
of the *Yishuv* and the *Histadrut* is the result of immigration.

II.

The history of the *Histadrut* does not, however, begin with
the history of the Jewish Labor Movement in Palestine. The
foundation of the *Histadrut* is the most important, the most decisive, landmark of this story which began with the commence-
ment of the so-called second *Aliyah* (*i.e.,* the second wave of
Jewish immigration) in 1940. This *Aliyah* consisted mainly of
workers and young men and women who came into the country
with the aim of becoming workers on its soil and thus laying the
foundations of a rejuvenated Jewish life.

The pre-history of the *Histadrut* can be traced back to the *Bilu*—pioneers who, at the beginning of the eighties in the last century, came to Palestine as part of the *first Aliyah,* with the idea of becoming agricultural workers and of creating collective forms of settlement—and, still further back, to Moses Hess, who, in 1862, in his "Rome and Jerusalem," proclaimed the fundamental identity of Judaism's social teachings with the ethics of socialism, and envisaged the restoration of the Jewish people to its homeland—a Jewish, therefore a socialist, homeland.

III.

The pre-history as well as the history of Jewish Labor in Palestine are closely interwoven with the different *Aliyoth.*

The men of the *first Aliyah* made the earliest attempts to create a Jewish Labor Movement in Palestine. In 1886, a "Workers' Association" was founded in the plantation settlement of Rishon-le-Zion; in 1891, an organization called "Land and Labor" was established; in 1897, a "Workers' Organization" came into being. These attempts provoked the hostility of the colonizing bureaucracy of that period and of certain well-to-do planters. They were, on the other hand, defended by the more enlightened circles of the *Khovevei-Zion* (Lovers of Zion). These organizations were, however, short-lived; the number of workers was too small, the general conditions of the *Yishuv* too primitive.

The *second Aliyah,* which brought to Palestine a more substantial number of workers and young people aiming at a life of productive physical work, created the nucleus of a real working class. They built up a permanent Labor Movement, fashioned the instruments and founded the institutions for the achievement of its aims, and took the first concrete steps to promote independent Labor colonization.

It was during this period that the Palestine Labor Movement, in constant clashes of ideas of its component parts, each influencing the other, struggled through to a clarification of its conceptions and ideals and of the path to their achievement. The Socialist

Poale-Zion ("Workers of Zion") brought with them the traditions and ideological inheritance of the Russian Revolution and
the European Labor Movement. They introduced the economic
analysis of the Jewish problem, the conception of class differences
and class interests within Jewish life and even in the process of
Palestine settlement, and the idea of an interconnection between
the aims of Jewish Labor in Palestine, both with the fate of the
Jewish Labor Movement in the countries of the Diaspora and the
great struggles on the world front of Labor.

The *Hapoel Hatzair* (The Young Worker) party, created by
the idealistic immigrant groups of *Zeire Zion* (Youth of Zion),
laid primary stress on *Kibbush ha'avodah,* whose meaning is far
wider than its literal translation "conquest of work" for the Jewish worker, embracing also the idea of the conquest of Jewish
youth for a life of work—especially of agricultural labor. It was
their most important teacher, A. D. Gordon, who coined the
phrase "Religion of Labor" as the moral basis of the movement.
In practical work the two groups co-operated with each other and
with the considerable section of "non-partisan" workers. The most
important organization of agricultural laborers, *Histadrut haklait,*
was the outstanding product of this co-operation.

All agreed on the fundamental necessity of creating a Jewish
land-working class, both by gaining a foothold as wage-earners in
the old private settlements and by creating independent small-
holders' and cooperative settlements (Sedjera, Merkhavia, Kinnereth, Degania). In the theoretical and political education of
the Zionist movement toward the recognition of the co-operative
principle in national colonization there was full agreement; there
was, too, community of purpose, if not always direct co-operation
in execution, in the spheres of land policy (national ownership and
self-labor), cultural work, in the endeavor to overcome the unpro-
ductiveness and backwardness typical of the pre-Zionist Jewish
population in Palestine and introduce democratic principles in the
conduct of public affairs. There was no water-tight separation in
other fields, although the Poale-Zion initiated and was the direct-

ing spirit of the famous organization of self-defense and protection of Jewish work and property, "Hashomer," and in the creation and leadership of the urban Trade Union movement.

IV.

The beginning of the *third Aliyah* coincides with that period of tragic crisis in the World Labor Movement created by the unsolved problems left by the war and marked most distinctly by the creation of the Communist International and its disintegrating action which broke the unity of most of the European Labor movements. The Jewish Labor Movement in the Diaspora was not spared this crisis. Both the *Poale-Zion* World movement and the anti-Zionist Bund had to experience division in their ranks on their attitude towards communism or democratic socialism. Palestine alone of the countries with a considerable Jewish Labor movement remained almost immune; moreover, just at that time there began a process of unification in the movement, which went through many stages and has not yet ended. The first step in this direction was only partly successful. It was early in 1919 that, at a general conference of the workers' delegates, the Zionist Socialist Union *Akhdut Ha'avodah* (Unity of Labor) was created. This organization was conceived as the one all-embracing body of organized Labor, uniting within itself all the functions and activities of the working class, political party, Trade Union movement, cooperative movement, colonization agency, and cultural centre. In other words, it was to be the working class in action. This will to unity was dictated by the feeling of urgent responsibility for the anticipated and eagerly awaited mass immigration as a result of the Balfour Declaration.

This unification was enthusiastically hailed by the *Poale-Zion*, Agricultural Workers' Union *Histadruth haklait*, non-partisan workers and groups, and the members of the Jewish legion and the first newcomers of the *third Aliyah* who had arrived, after extreme difficulty in leaving Soviet Russia, Poland, and Roumania, and in entering the country, which was still legally closed to immigrants. But of the *Hapoel Hatzair,* only a section was prepared to accept this total unity. The majority of that party refused to give up their separate existence and decided to retain their identity, cultivated and developed over more than a decade, of which they were proud, and in whose basic truth they continued to believe. Thus the maximum of unity was not achieved. Against its own will, *Akhdut ha'avodah* became a party. Before the movement as a whole two roads alone remained open: either to achieve unity on a less ambitious scale, but still embracing the most vital aspects of the whole movement, Trade Union and co-operative activity, social and cultural work, immigration, colonization, and certain political work—or to face the danger of growing friction, which could even lead ultimately to total disruption. Realism and a sense of responsibility dictated the choice of the first path. And so in 1920 the *Histadrut* was founded.

With this act, a period of unification began within the Zionist-Socialist movement the world over. Its culminating points have so far been in the amalgamation, in 1929 of *Akhdut ha'avodah* with *Hapoel Hatzair* into the Palestine Labor Party, and the unification of the corresponding world organizations into the *World Union of Poale-Zion and Hitakhdut,* in 1932. The Palestine Labor Party is now the major force in the conduct of the whole range of activities of the *Histadrut.*

V.

The activities of the *Histadrut* are dominated by one central aim: to make Palestine the home of the Jewish people. It is the organization of those who have already returned to their home and to their work. Its task is to make this return permanent, and to create conditions for an ever-increasing stream of newcomers. These in turn will themselves participate in this great task, broadening the scope for the absorption of further immigrants, and so the process must continue until the goal is reached—a Jewish people, reestablished in its national home, rooted in its soil, performing all the functions of production in agriculture and industry, commanding the resources of its country, ensuring the full political, economic and social equality of all its members, creating its own culture, enjoying the privileges and fulfilling the obligations of free nationhood. The Jewish working community in Palestine thus regards itself merely as a beginning, as pioneers and trail-blazers for those still to come, holders of a sacred trust, to live and work in the national home-in-the-making, to ensure its steady growth and development by new waves of immigration.

The meaning of Jewish immigration to Jewish Labor, and indeed to the whole Jewish population of Palestine and the world Zionist movement, is perhaps best symbolized by a striking linguistic usage. There are two different terms in modern Hebrew for general immigration, and for Jewish immigration into Palestine. General migration is denoted in Hebrew by the term *Hagirah,* whereas the Hebrew word for Jewish immigration into Palestine is *Aliyah,* whose literal meaning is "ascent." Immigration into Palestine is looked upon as an ascent from Diaspora to the homeland, from dependence to freedom, idleness to productivity, humiliation to personal and national dignity, from the uncertainties of life as a permanent minority to the status of nationhood.

The *Histadrut* has thus not only to secure the interests and improve the conditions of life of its present membership, by Trade Union, co-operative, political, educational, sport, and self-defence activities. It fulfills all these duties faithfully and with considerable success. But it has also to assume a great range of functions and activities unknown to the Labor movements of other peoples.

The working classes of all other peoples have been brought into being by the natural economic development itself. The Labor movement begins once the working class has come into existence by the process of history. The Jewish working class in Palestine, however, is to a very large extent *self-made;* it has come and continues to come into existence by the purposeful resolve of masses of youth in the Diaspora to change the basic conditions of life of the Jewish people by becoming workers in Palestine. They are imbued with the conviction that the realization of Zionism depends on making labor in agriculture, industry and all branches of economic life the dominant factor of the new Jewish life in Palestine. Becoming a worker is for them the fulfillment of a great mission in the history of their people.

It is this ideal of work which the Palestine Labor Movement and its allied forces, the Zionist-Socialist parties and the *khalutz* pioneer youth movements the world over, are seeking to implant into the Jewish youth in the Diaspora. It is this ideal by which Zionism succeeded in creating new values in the economic life of the Jewish people in Palestine; in the transformation of barren stretches of sand, stone, and swamp into fertile fields and fruitful orchards; and the transformation of scores of thousands of young people, estranged from the soil and from manual labor by centuries of Diaspora life, into enthusiastic toilers in the agriculture and young industry of the national home. It is this ideal of work and this pride in becoming a worker, this consciousness of the high mission of labor in the regeneration of the nation, which has enabled these young people to become builders of roads and bridges, hewers of stone, drainers of swamps, workers laboring on roads and railways and ports, and the afforestation of hills. It is this ideal which inspires them in the daring attempt to create the nucleus of a new economic and social order in the midst of a world built on the conception of personal advantage as the dominant driving force and incentive of economic success. It is this ideal which has made possible the collective and co-operative settlements based on the principles of solidarity, and which has brought into being industrial and transport undertakings created and administered by the workers themselves and by their institutions. It is this ideal which inspires the youth and these workers to *khaluziut*—"pioneering"—which involves the surmounting of all difficulties of external conditions as well as of tradition, upbringing and Diaspora background, and the constant preparedness to meet new difficulties, undertake new tasks, open new vistas of work and building for themselves and for those who await their turn to come to the land of Israel.

March, 1941

Communal Settlements in Palestine
by ARTHUR WAUCHOPE

I DARE SAY some of you are surprised that I should have chosen as the subject of my talk today "The Communal Settlements in Palestine" and not, as an old soldier might be expected, deal with some aspect of the war.

I have chosen this subject for two reasons:

First, I feel you all know just as much about the war as I do, but after having lived for nearly seven years in Palestine, I believe I have a more intimate knowledge of these communal settlements than most people.

My second reason is this: We are all interested not only in the war, but also in any social or economic changes that may take place after the war, especially those needed to bring about a more equal distribution of wealth.

Many economic changes have been proposed, but some of these suggestions seem to me rather theoretical than practical. I cannot myself believe that any form of Utopia will follow on immediately after the war.

But I thought it might be of some general interest were I to explain today how these 30,000 Jewish settlers have, not only in theory but in actual practice, solved the problem of equal distribution of wealth by the simple, if drastic, method of having none.

Not that I suggest that this system, whereby no man or woman may own or acquire any personal possession, is in any way suited to the spirit of this country or to the traditions and ideals of my countrymen; but I do suggest if changes in our social or economic structure are to be discussed, then it is worth while to consider, if only for a few minutes, the one example of such a system where people actually do live on an equal economic basis. And this example is of a people who can be judged by their deeds rather than by their theories, and who have made a success of their life for more than a generation.

Address delivered at the Overseas League, London.

As you know, similar experiments have been attempted mainly in America and Australia, but none has succeeded. I do not count any experiments that are being made in Russia, for little is known of them except that they are State-controlled; it is questionable if they are purely communal, and the one fact we can be sure of is that their future is very precarious.

The earliest experiment I know of was made nearly 2,000 years ago in the Early Christian Church: it is best known to us by the story of Ananias and Sapphira who, you remember, came to rather an abrupt and painful end. The members of this early Church held all things in common.

I will read how that society is described in the Acts of the Apostles:

"They held all things in common.

Neither was there any among them that lacked for anything.

For as many of them as were possessors of lands or houses, sold them, and brought the prices of what they sold to the Apostles;

And distribution was made unto every man according as he had need."

Though we hear no more of this communal life in the Early Christian Church after the death of Ananias and Sapphira, I have recalled its existence because the principles of their method of living seem to have been very similar to those of the communal settlements in Palestine which I speak of today.

It is generally said that without the incentive of personal gain little work would be done, many would die, others remain incompetent to carry out their duties, and the people of such a community would soon starve.

But the very reverse of this has happened and is happening today in Palestine, as even a most cursory study of the condition of Jewish agricultural settlements shows.

During the last 20 or 30 years the Jewish immigrants have proved most successful farmers. The villagers generally prefer mixed farming. They own many herds of dairy cattle, the number of their sheep and poultry increases every year. They produce over half the oranges grown in Palestine.

At this season of the year the valleys and foothills are covered with green fields of young wheat and barley and lucerne—with many vineyards and orchards, so that the country now occupied by Jewish settlers more than justifies the words of those spies who long ago reported to Joshua that Canaan was a land flowing with milk and honey.

Some 200 of their farm settlements are run on ordinary lines of individual ownership, the land usually being divided into small holdings, and the produce sold for the profit of the individual cultivator.

But in over 80 well-established settlements the land is held in common; and not only the land, but also the produce, the means of production and transport, are all owned by the community as a whole.

For no individual owns a field, a cow, or a hen; no worker receives any wages, no man gains profit from the fruit that he gathers; no woman from the cow that she milks. But whatever is needed is shared equally by all the villagers, and the surplus sold for the good of the community as a whole.

In other ways these settlers live much as our villagers do in this country. All the grown-up people work over eight hours every day, bar the Sabbath, which is kept as a much-needed day of rest.

Indeed they live laborious days, and as women work in the fields with the men, the small children are looked after in communal nurseries by trained helpers; all the young boys and girls spend the whole day with the school teachers till the evening comes, when the day's work is done, and they all very happily rejoin their fathers and mothers. I have often been witness to these meetings. The children's cries of joy and their unrestrained signs of affection show at once that the daily separation during the hours of labor causes no lessening of devotion on one side or the other. On the contrary, I believe the relationship between parents and children is peculiarly happy in these communal communities.

Each year a committee is elected by popular vote, and this committee decides how the profits of the past year shall be spent, and determines what tasks shall be allotted to each laborer for the coming year. The first profits of a new settlement are usually spent in building the school and communal nursery, for care of children is one of the noticeable features of these communal villages.

In succeeding years, additional farm buildings and equipment, tractors, the purchase of new herds, the planting of new orchards —all add to the productive capacity of the community. The villagers I speak of look on wealth not as a snare, but as an illusion so far as happiness is concerned.

There is, of course, no compulsion. A man is free to join either a communal settlement or a settlement where the principle of individual ownership is maintained—just as he pleases. And should he find after experience that the communal life does not suit him or his family, he is always free to quit. And if he quits, he has no bother about settling accounts or packing up his goods, for he has no impediments to trouble him.

We may consider the economic idea of these people fantastic, but I can assure you they are very human. For instance, if a young man feels he wants an outing for a few days, the committee will give him a pound or two, provided he does not ask too often. Or, if a girl wants a new frock, if she is a good worker, she will get one. In fact, an annual holiday of a week or ten days is quite usual in most of these settlements.

As you may imagine, when the community is first formed the hardships are great, the labor severe, and as for luxury or comfort, there is little or none. The settlers live not to be sheltered from dangers, but to be fearless in facing them. Hardship is their garment, but constancy their shield. Their manner of living compels them to bear and forbear. No people carry out so thoroughly that precept of the Talmud which says that he who fails to teach his son a trade teaches his son to steal. The sacrifices of personal wealth, the surrender of personal possessions having once been made, then all must of necessity work and their children taught the need and dignity of labor.

But as the years pass, the land is improved and where necessary irrigated, more vegetables are grown and the resources of the villagers increased. The settlers can then afford to build a library or village hall for meetings, concerts, lectures or occasional dances. Amenities are naturally far greater in a settlement after a dozen years of labor and constant cultivation than when it was first founded by the pioneers.

It is easy to understand how much self-sacrifice is needed for this method of living and how much each individual must give up to share in this communal life. But without visiting and talking to the settlers it is harder to realize how much they gain by their disregard of personal wealth.

They have no fear of want; no envy of another man's possessions; if labor is arduous it is regular; there is, of course, no unemployment, and a livelihood for every family is assured.

For there is more gained than only material advantage. These people are free to form and live up to their own set of values. They are not bound by those shackles that grip many whose chief aim is wealth and great possessions. Freedom of thought is far from leading to anarchy. If it be better to give than to receive, then perhaps more happiness comes from living for the good of the community than for self alone.

As I said earlier in this talk, in other countries and in other centuries similar experiments have been tried and all have failed. But, as we say in Scotland, "Facs are chiels that winna ding." Facts that stare us in the face cannot be brushed aside. These communal settlements increase in number and prosperity every few years. Formerly a good many members grew dissatisfied and walked out, for every man is always free to do so; but now few quit, and many sons follow in their fathers' footsteps or form new communal settlements.

What is the reason for this astonishing success? The reason is to be found in the spirit of the settlers. The spirit that fills them is the faith of a people believing themselves to be more happy leading a simple life without money, than if they joined in the general world struggle for wealth and yet more wealth.

Such a faith demands great unselfishness in the individual, as well as great devotion to the community.

Should that faith ever fail, should they ever, like Lot's wife, look back, then will this economic experiment in plain living also fail; it would soon prove to be but Dead Sea fruit.

And so will it be in whatever form of reconstruction may be made after the war in this country. Faith in our country and our ideals is essential. Wealth must be the servant, not the master of the people. As Mr. Winant, the American Ambassador, said the other day: "People in the future must either co-operate, dominate, or perish."

These communal villages in Palestine are an example of co-operation working in its extreme form. Not the best form suited for this country, but worthy of study as a society where wealth is unknown, but where "Distribution is made unto every man according as he has need."

We shall win this war by our determination to see it through. By that same spirit of determination, I am confident, we shall bring about, in one form or another, a just settlement of our social and economic needs after victory has been gained.

October, 1941

Palestine's Economic "Absorptive Capacity"
A Common-Sense View

by Ben Halpern

THE OFFICIAL defense of British policy in Palestine was once based chiefly on the contention that the country is economically incapable of absorbing large numbers of immigrants. This line of argument has not been as boldly or as frequently used since the publication of the White Paper in May, 1939. There is good reason for the change: The White Paper, contumaciously enforced in spite of the disapproval of the Permanent Mandates Commission and the protest of public opinion, has itself erected the most formidable barriers to economic development in Palestine. It has set a rigid political quota for Jewish immigrants, and thus blocked the influx of labor and capital which was the chief cause of Palestine's phenomenal advance. It has burdened land transfers with discriminatory decrees by which Jews are *absolutely forbidden to buy land from Arabs in almost two-thirds of the country; forbidden except with special authorization, in almost one-third; and allowed to buy land freely only in one twentieth of Palestine:* to wit in the small fraction which they have already settled. These "laws" are unconstitutional, being specifically opposed to the Mandate; they are flagrantly unjust on even more basic "legal" grounds, by contravening the principles of freedom and of equality before the law upon which all democratic orders are founded; and the White Paper policy, finally, in setting up a Pale of Settlement for Jews in Palestine such as obtained in old Czarist Russia, imposes artificial, unnatural limits upon economic progress. It remains to be seen whether such a retrograde economic plan can "successfully" be carried out; but in the meantime its official advocates are naturally disinclined to argue their case on the economic plane. They have taken refuge in the sphere of *Hochpolitik* and military strategy and there, as we are given to understand, the common people must not intrude with impertinent questions—particularly so long as the war continues.

Although temporarily shelved, the "absorptive capacity" argument has not been entirely discarded. It reappears occasionally, as for instance in the High Commissioner's recent broadcast announcement of post-war reconstruction plans for Palestine, in the course of which reference was made to the "congestion" problem, and to "what little remains, after many years of insufficient attention, of the soil of that country." Such phrases also abound in the various reports by British expert commissions, including the latest one, of the Woodhead or Partition Commission, which was followed, in due course, by the White Paper. It is no more than natural that such statements, issued by official sources and under the warrant of expert authority, have had their effect; so that even persons responsive to the tragic fate of the Jewish people and unimpressed by the *Hochpolitik* of low expediency are shaken, and begin to doubt whether, after all, there is room in Palestine for more Jews, if the country is as "congested" as the experts claim.

It happens, however, that the experts have been singularly out of luck in Palestine. Sir John Hope Simpson, a seasoned administrator of refugee and resettlement movements, spent several weeks investigating Palestine in 1930, and solemnly concluded that there was not enough room left in the country to swing a cat. Those were his very words. In less than ten years after the Simpson Report, the Jewish population of the country was almost tripled, chiefly by the admission of refugees, and the Arab population continued a rate of natural increase without parallel anywhere in the world. Sir John himself was singing another tune by 1939:

"This small country (Palestine), probably not exceeding 10,400 square miles in area, a land devoid of obvious natural resources, has become for a large section of the refugee community one of the most important areas of refugee settlement in the world. This fact is due to the religious enthusiasm of the Jewish race and to their genius for development."

Other investigators, including American experts sent by Jewish sponsors as well as British observers sent by the Colonial Office, have been as badly mistaken. An American expert survey back in 1927 advised the Zionist Organization to prepare for the social and economic collapse of the collectivist rural settlements—which subsequently throve and prospered and grew to unprecedented strength. The advice of these same experts, mistaken as they were in this point, has nonetheless been followed with profit in Palestine in many another important point. Out of a long experience with experts of all sorts, the Jews in Palestine have, in fact, developed a very sane, common-sense view on the subject. The view is expressed on page 160 of the Minutes of Evidence of the public sessions of the 1936 Palestine Royal Commission, in the testimony of Mr. H. L. Wolfson. This witness, an official of the non-political Palestine Jewish Colonization Association (PICA) stated that geologists (like other experts) could be safely followed when they stated where and at what depths water would probably be found, but experience had shown them to be frequently mistaken when they declared that it was *impossible* to find water in a given location. In the same spirit, Jewish pioneers in Palestine have not been impressed by the gloomy prophecies of failure issuing both from interested and disinterested expert oracles, but have utilized their positive suggestions, and, as is the way of pioneers everywhere, they have failed and failed again, and eventually succeeded.

To what conclusion does this lead? That no person of common sense should accept as valid a specific figure of the maximum population which Palestine can absorb, no matter how many experts lend it their authority. No expert is entitled to state a maximum beyond which further increase is impossible, even though so many of them do it. Plain logic warns us that all generalizations and deductions hold only within conditions specified in advance, or within stated premises. When conditions or premises change, the old conclusions cannot hold. In the case of Palestine, nobody can know today what may be the eventual conditions which will determine how large a population can be absorbed. It is certain only that they will not be the present-day conditions. The Jews, at least, will never rest until they have tried every avenue that holds a promise of economic expansion.

No common-sense opinion can be ventured on the question of how many people Palestine can ultimately hold. Nor is the question important. What we are really interested in knowing is how many people Palestine can absorb in a short time after the war; or rather more specifically, can Palestine rapidly absorb the number of Jews it must admit in order to become truly the Jewish National Homeland: *viz.,* the five or six hundred thousand or more needed to create a Jewish majority; or the one or two million it may be necessary to admit in order to solve once and for all the Jewish problem in Europe?

Resources

The discussion of Palestine's absorptive capacity has been based almost exclusively on the question of whether there is any unused or inefficiently used cultivable land left in the country. One of the reasons why the economic arguments in favor of stopping immigration are no longer emphasized in official statements—a reason, also, why the White Paper has adopted a political rather than an economic criterion for restricting immigration—is that the answer to this question is clear beyond cavil. Nobody really doubts that there is unused cultivable land in Palestine, or that much of the land now cultivated could be greatly increased in productivity.

It is true that British statements repeatedly make subtle references to "agricultural congestion"—if not now, then for future generations; and, also, that according to the statistics still officially accepted by the Palestine Government, there is no "cultivable" land in the country which is not already being "cultivated." But these statistics are based on assumptions which make them completely extraneous to the question at issue. When the British Government says all the "cultivable" land in Palestine is being "cultivated," they are talking double-talk in the strictest possible sense. "Cultivable" means, according to the statistical glossary of the Palestine government, *"land which is actually under cultivation, or which can be brought under cultivation by the application of the labor and financial resources of the average individual Palestinian cultivator"*—that is, the Arab.

We may forget about the second clause in the definition when discussing official Palestinian land statistics—because it finds no application. The figures of "cultivable" soil cited by the Palestine Government were compiled not by soil chemists but by surveyors, and not in the course of soil analysis or geological survey, but of a survey for purposes of taxation. The rough and ready criterion of cultivability which had to be used by the Government surveyors was no more and no less than the then state of the soil—whether it was actually under cultivation or not. What does it mean then when, on the basis of statistics so compiled, it is claimed that all "cultivable" soil is being cultivated? No more than the tautology that all the cultivated soil is being cultivated. And sometimes even less, because in the time since the tax survey of Palestine much officially uncultivable soil has actually been put under cultivation—although, in most cases, the Government's statistics have not yet been adjusted accordingly.

The fact of the matter is that the Palestine Government has simply refused to investigate seriously the question of how the soil and water of Palestine can be most effectively utilized if capital and modern techniques are applied. Moreover, they know very well that if they were to make such a study—which their obligation under Article 6 of the Mandate "to encourage . . . close settlement by Jews on the land" would seem to require—it would surely reveal that there is much cultivable land unused, and that modern techniques could substantially raise the productivity of the land now being cultivated. A frank admission of this fact is contained in the Report of the Woodhead Commission (p. 30) which states:

> "There is no doubt that Palestine could support a larger agricultural population if better methods of cultivation were

adopted, if the area under irrigation could be extended and if markets for the increased produce could be found."

For an authoritative estimate of how much larger the agricultural population could be under the above conditions, we must consult Jewish Agency experts, for they are the only ones who have devoted themselves to a study of this question. Their conclusions have been stated by Dr. Chaim Weizmann with all the caution of a scientific mind:

> "Adding together the large uncultivated area south of the Gaza-Beersheba line, the irrigable free stretches in the Jordan and other valleys, and the Maritime Plain, and allowing for some intensification of agriculture, in the hills, it is hardly overoptimistic to say that at least 100,000 more Jewish families can be settled on the land."

Markets

The estimates by agricultural experts of how many more farm families Palestine's soil can support depend largely on calculations concerning the areas that can be reclaimed, improved, and brought under cultivation, and also concerning the amount of water available for intensifying farm practice by irrigation—after allowing for the needs of power production and other "civil and industrial" requirements of the population. In other words they are estimates based on calculations of productivity, under given improved conditions. They assume, therefore, that the increased product can be marketed, and at prices sufficient to maintain the enlarged population at their present or an improved standard of living.

However, we need not rely on assumptions alone in this question, because it has been made the subject of specific analysis by Jewish Agency experts. The premises upon which this study has been based are appropriately conservative. The pre-war market for the agriculture and industrial products of the Yishuv was chiefly the Jewish population itself. It is assumed that this will be even more overwhelmingly the case in the post-war period.

In 1936 a substantial part of Jewish agriculture was devoted to citriculture, essentially an export industry. The Agency plans for the future contemplate only a slight increase in the citrus industry. The growth of the farm population is expected to depend almost entirely on the intensification of agriculture and the devotion of a larger proportion of the land to dairy and vegetable and similar products, as far as possible under irrigation. These products of Jewish farms, in pre-war days, were sold almost exclusively to Jews. However, earlier blue-prints for Palestine's development always planned to take advantage of Palestine's climate in order to produce early-ripening vegetables and fruits for export. Successful beginnings in such an export trade were already made before the war and there are good prospects of new cultivations for export, such as pharmaceutical plants and seeds. The conservative Agency post-war plan assumes, however, that only 6% of the value-output of Jewish farming (excluding citriculture) will be disposed of by export; none will be sold to the Government or the Arabs; and the rest will be taken up by the expanded Jewish population itself.

The "home market" is also the chief reliance of Jewish Agency experts for the disposal of the output of Jewish industry. In 1936, only 6% of the industrial output was exported, and 15% sold to the Government and to Arabs. The remainder was bought by Jewish consumers and producers. Future plans indicate a reduction of the share of export to 5% of the output of Jewish industry, and of Arab and Government purchases to 10%. The growth of the industrial population is predicated mainly, therefore, upon the growth of sales to an expanding Jewish population. Jewish Agency plans anticipate that industrial growth will go substantially ahead of other economic branches, and that the industrial population will be a relatively larger proportion of the total than in pre-war days —at the "expense" chiefly of parts of the population now living on their own incomes or on incomes contributed by relatives abroad.

This change will also, it is planned, remedy a certain disharmony in the Jewish foreign trade of Palestine. The persistent large difference between the value of imports and exports to Palestine has often been pointed out as a defect in its economic structure. It has as often been noted in reply that the "unfavorable" balance of trade is merely an apparent "deficit," Palestine's international payments being balanced by the import of capital—chiefly by Jews—and by other "invisible exports." Such capital imports, reflected in an apparent "unfavorable" balance of trade, are a normal phenomenon in countries of pioneer settlement. In the years before the war, Jewish capital imports alone were covering 80% of that so-called deficit. However, only half of this sum was spent for actual capital equipment; the remainder was expended in the purchase of foodstuffs and manufactured articles which could very well be produced in Palestine itself at competitive prices, after the necessary investments had been made.

Jewish Agency plans for expanding the Yishuv's industrial population—thus helping also to provide the expanded market necessary for post-war agricultural settlement—envisage the replacement of such imports by local products. Actually this aim has been substantially achieved under the pressure of wartime necessity. The goal—an economically rational goal—is to reduce the "unfavorable" balance of trade to the amount of capital import expended on new investment material which cannot be produced locally; to import in addition to this only raw materials, foodstuffs, and manufactured goods which cannot be locally produced at fair competitive prices, paying for these purchases by the value of the Yishuv's exports; and to substitute for the remainder of the Yishuv's trade "deficit" local products. This scheme, while based on the necessary increase of the Yishuv's self-sufficiency, is thus far from a plan of "autarchy." On the contrary, since it envisages a continued expansion based on capital imports, and a development of Palestine's natural advantages for export purposes, it means an expansion of Palestine's foreign trade and a large absolute, if not a relative, increase in the value of its imports.

The plan is essentially conservative for it is based on the intensive development of Palestine's own resources by the influx of settlers and capital, and on the utilization primarily of the internal market so created. As a relatively short-term plan, calling for the settlement of less than a million and a half settlers and the investment of less than a billion dollars, it does not take account of the possibilities of expansion which may open up if world trade in general expands, and particularly if there is large-scale development in the regions of the Middle East, and the even broader hinterland to which Palestine is so conveniently placed.

Necessary Political Conditions

It is of course obvious that none of this plan can be achieved under the White Paper. For any development of the country, Jews must be permitted to purchase land; they must be allowed to bring in capital; and, above all, immigration must continue.

There is, moreover, no prospect of economic succor for the insupportable position of the Arabs themselves if the White Paper is maintained. The Palestine Government likes to insist that the economic troubles of the Arabs are immediately caused by Jewish development—even though their underlying causes, as the Government recognizes, are poor methods of cultivation, an irrational system of land-holding, the merciless extortion of Arab moneylenders, etc. It is true, as a matter of fact, that since the Jews came in, population has so increased that the old methods of cultivating the soil may not provide for a further increase; also that many Arabs have become dependent on Jewish employment and customers; and—a factor which the war has even further enhanced—the Arabs now expect more than they did before the Jews came. The Arabs have been set on the road to economic advancement and cannot be stopped. The government recognizes this, and is preparing, on the basis of the White Paper, development plans for the "Arab" reservations in Palestine at the expense of a Treasury to which Jews primarily contribute.

Apart from the political objections to the White Paper, it is subject to the very economic arguments for which the Partition

Plan was rejected. The country "devoid of obvious natural resources" is certainly too small to be divided into zones of economic freedom and reservations of economic stagnation. An economic development of the Arab zone not based on the stimulation of economic enterprise and progress and regulated not in the interests of justice but of an outmoded economic order is hardly probable. However, the abrogation of the White Paper and the end of the mediaeval economic discrimination between Jew and Arab in Palestine does offer a way of economic succor to the Arabs as well as the Jew. This has been pointed out to the Palestine Government not only by Jews but also by the Woodhead (Partition) Commission itself (p. 30):

> "The future for the Arab population is already menacing— *unless Jewish immigration and Jewish imports of capital are allowed to continue.*" (italics ours)

But the abrogation of the White Paper is not enough. The Jewish Agency is preparing flexible plans and concrete projects for the settlement of one to two million Jews in Palestine in a relatively brief period after the war. It is the only agency anywhere in the world which is in a position to prepare and is actually preparing real plans for the permanent economic rehabilitation of European Jews after the war. Its projects are of a complex, though practical, nature which require that the authority which will determine Palestine's economic policies in the post-war world shall be of a character which will itself adopt and see to the implementation of these plans.

October, 1943

Going Down to the Sea

by David Ben Gurion

I F I SHOULD be asked what event looms most important in the history of Palestinian colonization during 1936, I should unhesitatingly answer: neither the disturbances nor the riots, but the inauguration of the Tel Aviv port. I am convinced that a review of events, judged in historical perspective and unaffected by press ballyhoo, would reveal the real milestone in the past year to have been the creation of the Tel Aviv port. That innovation has indeed a permanent value which promises to give a new turn to our political and resettlement program.

For the Tel Aviv harbor is a starting-point which leads up to the much larger maritime question. We should never forget the all-important fact that Palestinian Jews constitute only a picayune percentage of the Jewish people scattered throughout the world. And yet (barring one or two clusters of Jews in Persia and Iraq) we have no way of maintaining connections with the rest of the Jewish world, save by means of the sea. And in turn, no Jews— except those living in Syria, Mesopotamia, Turkey or Persia—can possibly reach us other than by boat. Now inasmuch as communication with the Diaspora plays a vital part in our work, our sea predicament creates a grave danger. Observe what happened during the riots. We suffered not only from the Arab "strike," but from terrorist gangs, recruited not from local Arabs but in major part—if not numerically, at least from the point of view of their viciousness—made up of neighboring Syrians and Iraqi imported from bordering countries. These murderers had a direct land route for both entrance and egress. But Jews who arrive to create, cannot come by land. They must take ship to enter Palestine. And yet, though sea communication is so all important to us, Jews have no ships of their own. The many Jews in the Diaspora constitute an appreciable power and possess economic, financial and in some cases even political influence. New York boasts an enormous Jewish population of two million which can sometimes turn the tide in mayoralty elections and which is no mean factor in determining the outcome of a hotly contested Presidential campaign. It possesses financial power and controls many institutions and industries. But in one particular economic enterprise—that of the sea—Jews are complete outsiders. And yet the realm of the sea is neither an empty one nor an unpopulated desert of water. In its own way, indeed, it is an inhabited area, an immense economic resource, the main artery of communication for humanity. On this vast expanse we have staked out no holding. Jews conduct many businesses throughout the world. They own factories, banks and corporations—but on the boundless sea teeming with transports, freighters, passenger vessels, fishing yawls, tourist and scout-boats, we cannot find even one Jewish launch. Of their own volition, Jews have excluded themselves from this potential economic activity. And this self-elimination has taken place despite overcrowding into various occupational fields, vain searching for new trades, and grasping for new means of livelihood.

Why have Jews neglected the mighty mart of the sea which promises economic openings to thousands and tens of thousands of Diaspora families residing in coastal cities? Must Jewish workers in America, for example, devote themselves entirely to indoor shop work? Why should not some of them enter maritime occupations. The same holds true of Jewries in Holland, England and similar lands. Why perpetuate a self-enclosed *terra firma* ghetto?

And can we afford to resign ourselves to this situation? We who have undertaken the great and arduous task of gathering together a dispersed people and of bringing it back to the land by sea—can we submit to having the sea locked in our very faces? Even under the best of political conditions—we could not risk continuing in this predicament. Certainly at the present time, when not one of us knows what the morrow holds in store for us, we dare not accept a self-imposed injunction which excludes us from the major part of the earth's surface and leaves us without an independent link between the concentration of Jews in Palestine and the Jewish dispersions in other parts of the world. Somehow we must win our rightful place in maritime economy, the main artery of world communication. Does such achievement lie beyond us?

A sound historical instinct led our movement to use as its point of departure the wish to return to the soil. Hence from the days of Bilu to those of Hekhalutz, we were all dominated by the desire to strike roots in the soil. Though we have achieved much in this direction, our agricultural conquest remains in its incipient stage still. And now, when we heed the call of the sea, we certainly do not aim to weaken or diminish our agricultural development. We do not propose to substitute seacraft for farming, nor do we urge self-dedication to the sea at the expense of agriculture. We intend only to include maritime activities in their proper place in our economic program. For clearly our future as a creative people and a militant labor movement is bound up with our sea-strength no less than with our skill in working the soil. The time has come to expand our economic conquest and structure. We shall not budge one jot from our determination to inaugurate and develop more and more points of settlement on the land. But in addition to these land colonies, I foresee upon the sea highly promising, valuable elements of economic growth. Every Jewish sailing vessel will be both a "colony" and a source of strength. A Jewish boat means Jewish deckhands, sailors and naval officers. Further, it implies not merely a Jewish boat, but a workers' boat which, for me, is fully as much a labor settlement of economic, cultural and political value as any rural or urban center. Indeed the very mobility—its moving at will—increases its importance and strength. This fluidity does not suggest shiftlessness but on the contrary indicates a flow of power and might.

At this time, above all, when we are forging the tools of self-defence and rallying all our physical and economic forces to ward off the terrible dangers which beset us, we must embark on the high seas and undertake the high duty of establishing a solid maritime economy. This we can do only if our movement rouses all its latent powers of conquest and recognizes its new noble mission—to conquer the sea with the same strength displayed in winning the Emek. The very effort has its own validity—even apart from its significance to our difficult political position. Extension into marine activities portends new economic possibilities and further opportunities for immigration, additional absorptive power, settlements and generation of further strength. We must build up Jewish shipping, and as much as possible make it a proletarian Jewish marine. We need Jewish labor vessels not only for commerce and travel but also for broader reasons. First of all we must create a merchant marine: tens and hundreds of Jewish ships manned by Jewish workmen but under the tutelage of the Jewish labor movement—must sail the sea. These ships will drop anchor in the ports of Roumania and Poland to embark thousands of pioneers. This is not beyond our attainment since we have at our disposal pioneer forces the like of which no other national movement perhaps has ever enjoyed. True, we are not familiar with nautical trades and maritime economy. None of us ever sailed before the mast. Yet how many Emek colonists farmed before they came there? There is no trade which we cannot learn to master. Without vital impetus, however, without throwing behind this endeavor all our movement's enthusiasm (and by the movement we do not mean individuals or isolated groups, but the creative spirit of all Zionism), without this, I say, it will be impossible to attain our great goal. For we are land-bred and alien to the sea. As yet the lore of the waters is a closed book to us. But neither have we yet exploited all our hidden talents. We ignore the wide extent of our own competency. The Histadrut is an instrument with infinite capacity and resources which have not been exhausted, not by a long shot. In a short time we have erected numerous institutions, every one playing a specific role in our society. But each of our institutions has obligations beyond its own needs. In addition to its specific functions each bears a direct relationship and responsibility towards other elements in our movement. Once we view our going down to the sea as a matter of great historical moment—parallel to our own entrance into agriculture—the necessary strength will be found and the effort will be forthcoming. The Histadrut institutions represent great potential resources. Also we may draw on the strength of the entire Zionist movement, whose character, purpose, method and will largely depend upon us. Just as we directed the Zionist movement toward the acquisition of national wealth, pioneering, agriculture—and we have not yet completed this difficult task which runs counter to traditional Diaspora psychology—so we must now orientate the Zionist movement toward a new goal and begin to muster will power and wherewithal for the great nautical project required for us.

Our entry into sea-commerce presents this additional advantage: It neither involves conflict with Arab competition nor limits us within the confines of Palestine. The sea lies open, free and almost without bourne. Not only the Mediterranean at our door but all "the seven seas" of the world, the gigantic expanse surrounding the six continents. Nothing hinders our having ships docking at all ports of Europe, the Americas, Asia, Africa and Australia, just as nothing prevents the ships of all other nations from calling at our ports. Jewish boats will make Palestine known everywhere. By carrying the Jewish Palestinian flag to all corners of the earth, they will forge a new, living, heartening link between the *Yishuv* in the homeland and scattered Jewish communities everywhere. Our boats shall bring tidings of Jewish labor and Jewish settlement to all dispersed Jewry which may thus also be stimulated to engage in maritime work.

We may use the ocean to batter down the walls between Palestine and the Diaspora. We can build Jewish ships not only in Palestine but also in Latvia, Roumania, Holland and England. Land settlement can be effected only in Palestine. But Jews may penetrate into the sea from any land. Our movement at all times aimed at synthesis, at bridging Palestine and the Diaspora, and the sea alone constitutes such a material bridge. American-Jewish workers can share only metaphorically in agricultural resettlement. But nothing can deter their actual participation, not only by financial contributions but by their own labor, in a Jewish proletarian maritime scheme. Jewish deckhands in England, America and elsewhere may join the company of their seagoing Palestinian fellow-workers. Just as we acquire and build ships here, our comrades in other Jewries may do the same in their respective countries. The maritime profession may thus form an economic framework including all branches of the Jewish people, all our workers and pioneers, wherever they may be.

May, 1937

Planned Economy in Palestine

by ABRAHAM DICKENSTEIN

RECENTLY THE Labor agricultural marketing cooperative "Tnuvah" celebrated the opening of the most modern dairy plant in the entire Near East in Haifa. The installations in this plant cost nearly a quarter million dollars. This celebration was transformed into a festive occasion for the entire workers' community in Palestine. The figures that were cited in the various speeches concerning the growth of cooperative mixed farming were a source of great encouragement during these depressing days.

These figures were particularly encouraging since only recently all sorts of "specialists" declared that this type of cooperative agriculture in Palestine was doomed to failure. A few years ago, during the so-called prosperity period, when so many people sought quick riches from orange raising, the assorted specialists jeered at the "impractical" workers' cooperatives which engaged in mixed farming, a branch of agriculture that barely paid a day's wage and brought in no profits on invested capital. Many will remember the stormy debates at Zionist Congresses when the so-called "middle class" Zionists demanded the cessation of "wasteful" labor colonization. These colonists were then frequently described in derision as "boarders."

The above historical facts are cited here not out of any desire to renew an old controversy or to be able to declare proudly that "we told you so," but merely in order to clarify the practical conclusions that should be derived from the experiences of recent years. The devotees of private initiative declared only a few years ago that the Jewish people as such need not buy land nor bother with organizing colonization. These things will take care of themselves, they said; Jews will come to Palestine, buy land and settle on it and develop industries. The "people" need only encourage, help and advise.

It is not hard to imagine what the Jewish position in Palestine would have been during the past four years had the Zionist movement followed this sagacious advice. It may be maintained with certainty that had such a policy been followed, the Jews coming to Palestine would have devoted themselves largely to land speculation and to some extent to orange growing. Only when we consider the purpose of the struggle which Palestine labor organized in the Histadrut conducted these many years for a planned economic development, is it possible to grasp the cause of the strength of organized labor. The Histadrut frequently had to depend on its own efforts solely in order to carry out the most elementary dictates of Zionism—the transformation of the Jewish nation into a people creating the products it consumes and the development of Palestine into a land that can provide for the needs of its inhabitants. For this reason the Histadrut has fought for three decades for the right of Jewish labor to be employed in private enterprises and for the development of mixed farming on nationally owned land. Difficult as that struggle has·been, the results have fully justified it. 35 million litres of milk produced annually in the Jewish cooperative farms provide for the entire demand. This is a striking achievement when we bear in mind that only a few years ago the Jewish community was dependent for milk upon the Arab villages and upon the German settlements which during the years of terrorism served as nests for brigands. Today one of the leaders of the German settlements in Palestine has been stationed by Hitler in Poland where he is actively engaged in the work of annihilation.

For the processing of dairy products, "Tnuvah" has established three central dairies in Jerusalem, Tel Aviv and Haifa which surpass in technical facilities and organization anything of this kind previously built in the near East. Through scientific breeding and care the labor settlements have succeeded in multiplying the production per animal eight fold over that of the native stock. In addition over 50 million eggs and tens of thousands of tons of vegetables, hay and grains are produced annually. These achievements in the field of mixed farming have been attained after a great expenditure of energy, determination and self-sacrifice. Nor would this have been possible were not these settlements backed by a powerful organization, the General Federation of Jewish Labor in Palestine, which guided economic development on a basis of systematic planning.

With the outbreak of war, various food products disappeared from private stores. This apparent shortage was not due to any real lack of such products as flour, sugar, etc. It was rather a result of hoarding on the part of wholesalers who refused to sell because they were speculating upon a sharp rice in prices. The only stores in Palestine which continued to sell at regular prices and in usual quantities were the consumers' cooperative stores of "Hamashbir Hamerkazi" which announced that they had enough reserves for several months.

This cooperative retail organization had the foresight to store up reserves during the fat years and to encourage various types of production which could provide the needed goods during times of unrest and uncertain communication with the outside world. As a result of the excellent organization of the transport cooperatives there have been no interruptions in communication within the country and sufficient gasoline as well as spare parts have been stored away to provide for possible needs over a long period of time.

The workers' sick fund "Kupath Kholim" continues to provide medical aid to 150,000 people without an increase in membership dues despite the rise in the prices of supplies on the private market. The foresight of the unemployment fund of the Histadrut, which created a reserve of hundreds of thousands of pounds, and the establishment of the society "Bitzur", whose function it is to carry out public works to alleviate unemployment, have enabled the Jewish Agency to continue colonization work with the national funds instead of having to divert them for purposes of assistance to the needy. The financial institutions of the Histadrut are among the most powerful in the country. The Workers' Bank which was founded in 1920 pays a regular dividend of 4% to its shareholders and, in addition, has built up a reserve amounting to 60% of the paid up capital. Together with its twenty-five branches which are registered as cooperative loan and savings societies, the bank has succeeded in concentrating a sum of over 5 million dollars which are at the disposal of planned and constructive enterprise.

Deficiencies in the economic organism of a country are seldom keenly felt in more or less normal times. The ordinary citizen is seldom aware of what goes on about him and is not very concerned where the goods he consumes come from and how they are brought to him. It is only when upheavals occur and communications are disturbed that he becomes aware of these problems. But while this is true of the individual, the representatives of a people must feel compelled to provide for all needs while there is time. It is regrettable that aside from the Histadrut few Zionists gave these problems sufficient attention. Only when we understand the role of the Histadrut in building a planned national economy in Palestine do we realize its full import.

January, 1940

Post-War Plans for Palestine

by DAVID BEN GURION

On March 22, 1943, the Palestine Government announced the appointment of Sir Douglas Harris as Reconstruction Commissioner to prepare a coordinated scheme for post-war agricultural and industrial development and reconstruction and social security in Palestine. On March 23, the High Commissioner for Palestine broadcast over the Jerusalem Radio a message to the people of Palestine, in which he commented on the new appointment and stated the Government's post-war reconstruction program for Palestine. The next day, David Ben Gurion delivered the following address at a joint meeting of the Elected Assembly of the Yishuv and the Zionist General Council, analyzing the High Commissioner's newly proposed Reconstruction Scheme against the background of the White Paper policy.

WE HAVE been visited by three successive disasters: the White Paper, the War and the massacres of European Jewry. The second was greater than the first, and the third greater than the second; and there is a danger that the latest of them may divert our attention from those preceding it, that our preoccupation with a new front may lead us to forget dangers which have been threatening us long since. This danger is all the more acute in that we have stood alone in all these misfortunes, and have no one to rely upon but ourselves.

By the *White Paper,* a blow was administered to us by the Government of the only people that had extended aid to us as to a nation, since the beginning of our dispersion.

When *the War* broke out it had seemed to us that we were standing side by side with our Allies, together with all the nations fighting against Hitler; but even here, there is discrimination against us. Despite the fact that we are the first and the most tragic victim of the Nazi regime, even the nations that are fighting for freedom, for national and human rights, do not recognize our elementary right to serve as a fighting nation. We alone have been denied the status of an Ally.

And *the Massacres.*—They are directed at the destruction of he Jewish people and of the Jewish people alone. We have re-eived words of condolence from many friends, but by words lone, our children cannot be rescued from the assassins. The act is that in this appalling triple disaster that has befallen us, we ave been left to our fate.

We must not give up hope in the conscience of mankind. In world where wickedness rules supreme, there will be no hope for s. But the conscience of humanity will not become aware of us f the Jewish will and Jewish strength are not brought to ex-ression. We shall be helped only if we help ourselves.

But even the Jewish nation is not free as a whole to work for ts salvation. In the enemy-occupied territories, Jews are in a hope-ess trap—languishing in prisons, done to death by assassins. Even n the free countries, in the British Empire, in America and in ussia, Jews are not free to take action as Jews. Whether they real-ze it or not, they are subject to the will of the national majority mong which they live, bound to a political course which is not he outcome of Jewish needs, to laws enacted by others. They annot, and very often do not even wish to act as Jews and as ews alone, in accordance with Jewish interests and with a Jewish pproach to the general situation, even as other nations act.

There is only one small Jewish community in the entire vorld, the Jewish Community of Palestine, which is not subject o the will or policy of others. Only here can the Jew act as a Jew, ven as the Russian is a Russian and the Englishman an English-nan. The Yishuv is therefore in the van of the work for the re-lemption of the whole nation. The Yishuv cannot exist on its wn if that hope is not realized, and that hope has nothing firm n which to rest outside the Yishuv. Without the Jewish nation broad, we are but another of the dispersed Jewish communities, nd we shall be faced with the fate of Polish Jewry. But as the nstrument of the national vision of renaissance, and as the ucleus of national independence in the homeland, we have a pecial status and a special mission.

Palestine's Future at Stake

Let us remember that we must fight on many fronts. We ar
immersed in the war effort, and are also engaged in a desperat
effort to rescue the remnants of Jewry from annihilation by th
Nazis. But we dare not allow ourselves to be blind to the new, o
rather renewed attack now launched against us by the Whit
Paper Government.

There are people who say that at the present moment there
only one task before us—to fight Hitler, and to save Jews from
destruction. The political future of the country, they say, can b
left for discussion at the Peace Conference. But it is absurd an
dangerous to suggest that we should wait for the Peace Conferenc
to secure our future in Palestine. In the first place, who know
whether there will be a Peace Conference at all? And wh
has promised us that at the Peace Conference they will listen t
the voice of the Jewish nation? And whence comes this certaint
which has as yet no foundation in fact, that the Peace Conferenc
will discuss the fate of Palestine?

It is only through our blind assumption that what has hap
pened once will happen again that we talk today about a Peac
Conference after the war. One can say, indeed, that a Peace Con
ference is already taking place, while the war is still on. Whe
Churchill met Roosevelt at Casablanca, that meeting was part o
the Peace Conference. When Eden, together with our friend Lor
Halifax, held discussions with Cordell Hull in Washington, th
was one of the sessions of the Peace Conference. When represen
tatives of the Anglo-Saxon world meet representatives of Sovi
Russia, this, too, is part of the Peace Conference. The provisio
of the post war settlement are being planned now, not only i
London, Washington and Moscow, but also in Cairo, Baghda
Jedda and Jerusalem.

We forget that, in fact, the new order to be introduced i
Palestine is entirely ready, that it bears the imprint of that Britis
authority which rules in Palestine today and, it can be safely a
sumed, will rule in Palestine after the war as well. There is
declared British policy in Palestine, and this declaration, unlil

others, does not exist only on paper, but is being applied here energetically, consistently and with determination. It is the policy of the White Paper. There is no use blinding ourselves to this fact. A real danger does not disappear if you bury your head in the sand.

The Peace Conference is proceeding in the very midst of war, and the provisions for Palestine's future are also being made during the midst of war. The fate of this country is being shaped by the creation of political, military and economic facts. In accordance with the policy laid down in the White Paper, Palestine is being transformed into a bi-national state: an Arab-State with a Jewish ghetto.

Where Jewish Cooperation Is Required

The Jews of Palestine cannot, in present circumstances, be converted into a permanent minority, that is to say into inhabitants of a ghetto, without assistance on the part of Jews themselves, or at any rate without their tacit consent. For here in Palestine, Jews represent an economic, political and physical factor which possesses the strength to frustrate the designs harbored against them. The work of giving effect to the White Paper cannot succeed without Jewish cooperation. They do not need Jewish assistance in evolving the abstract formulae. Only we Jews are keen about formulae and slogans. Others content themselves with creating facts, and they do not care by what name these facts are called. Now an attempt is being made to secure our participation in the creation of facts by which the policy of the White Paper will be implemented. And in truth they have chosen an excellent opportunity for their purpose.

For they know that we are very occupied at the moment with our desperate efforts to overcome our misfortunes. The White Paper Government thinks—and possibly not without reason—that if it gives its schemes the high-sounding name of "reconstruction", we Jews who have devoted all our lives to the reconstruction of our country will be pleased at the sound of it. And especially if that is done at a time when we are engrossed in the war

effort and in our efforts to rescue our people, and if no mention
is made that these schemes are in any way connected with the
White Paper. The Government springs this scheme on us at a
time when we are cooperating with Great Britain despite the
White Paper policy. We shall certainly continue that cooperation, because this war is no less our affair than it is the affair of
Great Britain or Russia. Nothing that can be done by the White
Paper Government can ever divert out attention from the danger
threatening the world and the Jewish nation as long as Hitler
exists. We shall play our part in this holy war, with all our
strength and resources, in body and in spirit, because we do not
desire, and we must not permit, that a job which is ours to do
should be done by others.

They assume, and possibly not without reason, that it will
not be easy for Jews to make a distinction between the England
which is fighting against Hitler and between the Government
which is enforcing the White Paper, particularly if they give the
actions of this Government a nice name, attractive to Jews, and
especially to the Zionists. And so they have put forward this
scheme for the "reconstruction" of Palestine.

Only the naive could have believed that, under the stress of
war, the implementation of the White Paper policy would be
shelved for the time being. If we ourselves refrain from discussing the future of this country, it does not prevent others from
doing so. In fact, very lively negotiations are proceeding between
Baghdad and Cairo, between Jedda and Jerusalem. No one has
consulted us in the matter, indeed, though we have heard reports
of certain Jewish circles, who consciously or unconsciously, are
acting as instruments of the White Paper policy and of the White
Paper Government. Yes! There are even Jews in Palestine who
are trying to persuade us that we should give up the idea of Jewish independence, and that we should put up with immigration
restrictions, and give our consent to a scheme under which Palestine would come under the rule of Syria, Iraq, or Saudia, and
who call this scheme "a Federation." But all these suggestions

reach us only from Jewish quarters. The Government has never put any suggestions or demands of that kind to us.

The authorities seem to believe that they do not need our cooperation in giving effect to the political provisions of the White Paper policy. But there is also an economic aspect to the White Paper policy, and it is not so easy to implement this economic policy without the consent and cooperation of the Jews. So yesterday they were good enough to ask us to cooperate in planning the post-war "reconstruction" of our country. Thus the discussion of the future of this country has been raised officially and publicly, and we cannot avoid it. Nor can we ignore the appeal which was made last night in the speech of His Excellency the High Commissioner.

The high authority of the speaker, and the serious content of the speech compel us to analyze this document carefully and frankly.

Point By Point

We must analyze two things: what the speech contains and what it omits. Both aspects are of equal importance. Let us begin with the first:

The country has been promised a development scheme, and to work out that scheme a special Commissioner for "Reconstruction" has been appointed, a man who is not unknown to us, at all events so far as his career in this country is concerned. The speech referred to two things: (a) positive schemes, (b) the limiting provisos to the schemes.

The positive schemes are as follows:

1. The development of public services, wider facilities for education and public health, insurance against the disabilities of old age, sickness and unemployment.

2. With regard to industry, the selection of those branches which have "a reasonable chance of survival" in conditions of peace, and which will be allowed to exist after the war.

3. The Government undertakes to continue after the war, though not on totalitarian lines, the Government control of several branches of the country's economic life.

4. The Government proclaims the urgent need of planning for irrigation, drainage, water supply, terracing of hillsides, etc., with a view to preserving "what little remains, after many years of insufficient attention, of the soil of the country."

5. "Insuring the marketing of citrus products to the best advantage."

His Excellency does not leave any room for illusions and tells us that "it is not to be supposed that (this) program can be carried out in full within the space of a few years."

The limiting provisos on which His Excellency dwelt are but few. The most important of them is that of financial difficulties. "Either the money (needed for the scheme) will have to come from resources which have accumulated locally or it will have to be borrowed from elsewhere, for instance on the London market." The prospects of an external loan are restricted, in the High Commissioner's opinion, as we shall "find ourselves in competition with most of the countries of the world; and let it be remembered that the great majority of them have suffered infinitely more than Palestine. The urgency of their needs will, indeed, be overwhelming, and no more than a very limited issue may be possible for Palestine."

We must now examine the meaning of this scheme from the Jewish point of view—and I do not intend excusing myself for making this examination from the point of view of the Yishuv. Let us examine the scheme clause by clause:

1. As the High Commissioner has stressed, preference will be given, under the "reconstruction" scheme to public services such as education, public health, etc. His Excellency did not forget to mention on this occasion that "the Jewish public here has already done much on these lines," while "the Arab is less well provided for in this respect." And this means that, just as in the past, the Government will devote the means at their disposal to the improvement of the public services among the Arabs, while we shall have to supply the means required for British officials to satisfy the needs of our neighbors.

2. The second item is industry. This is of the greatest concern to us, as the industry now existing in this country is to an overwhelming extent Jewish. In this respect we are told very plainly that the Government does not intend to increase and expand industry, since "Palestine is essentially an agricultural country." On the other hand, what the Government does propose is to lop off those branches of industry which, in its view, have no prospect of surviving in peacetime conditions. A special officer will be entrusted with the task of making a selection of those industries which should be protected and encouraged. "It would be useless," the High Commissioner has said, "to attempt artificially to bolster up an industry which was doomed to collapse in the depressed conditions of the post-war era, and far more preferable to divert the available manpower and energies into more fruitful fields." Sir Douglas Harris, whose skill has been employed for seven or eight years in the development of agriculture without any of us being able to see the results of his efforts; but who has distinguished himself in a certain kind of attitude towards what we Jews are trying to do in this country,—he is the man who is now entrusted with the task of deciding the fate of the industries we established. The whole of our enterprise in this country, both in agriculture and in industry, was doomed in advance by a few experts who did not understand why and how we were conducting our work. Nor do we know what is Sir Douglas Harris' special authority, nor what are his attitude and intentions in respect of Jewish industry which we have established with our own capital, our own initiative and our own work to meet our own needs and to serve our future.

We do not think that this country must remain essentially an agricultural country. All industrial countries were once mainly agricultural. It seems to me that Britain was once mainly agricultural. Yet in Britain a great industry was built up and still exists. Palestine was once a purely agricultural country and agriculture will continue to play an important part in her future. In our own Jewish settlement work we have always given and shall continue to give priority to agriculture; but our plans call for industrial development, because we need the expansion of sources of livelihood and the means of absorbing masses of immigrants. But our ruler has now given us the assurance that after the war an "expert" official will decide which factories are to survive and which will have to close down.

3. As to the State control that we are promised after the war though not "upon the totalitarian model"—we cannot conceal our apprehension that this control will be directed towards shackling our economic initiative and restricting the pace of our settlement work. Wartime needs necessitate control, but that control has not always been employed in accordance with war needs. The Government is guided by its desire to implement the White Paper policy, perhaps even more than by its desire to implement a war policy. As to the continuation of state control after the war, we see in it very little utility. On the contrary we have good reason to suspect that the real motive is to continue to shackle Jewish initiative and to strangle the "National Home."

4. As to the schemes for irrigation, drainage, water supply and terracing, they could be a blessing for both Jews and Arabs and for the country as a whole.

This time His Excellency did not state expressly that these schemes were intended mainly for the benefit of the Arabs, as he did in respect to the general social services. Such an indication would, indeed, have been superfluous, for according to the Ordinance which came into force in February, 1940, the Jews are restricted to residence in the towns and in a small area along the seashore, namely to places where there is no need for terracing, reforestation, drainage or any of the other things promised by the High Commissioner. The program of the Government for agricultural development—if it is realized at all—covers those areas from which Jews are forbidden to derive benefit. The hill region, the plains of the Negeb, the Jordan and Jezreel valleys are closed to Jews. Our task will be to supply Sir Douglas Harris with the money necessary for irrigation, terracing and reforestation; but we shall not be permitted to derive any benefit from the reforested and terraced hills and from the irrigated soil, for in that area (which comprises ninety-seven per cent of the whole of Western Palestine) Jews are forbidden even to rent a home in which to live. Latterly a new law has been made according to which Jews are not even allowed to enter that area for the purpose of enjoying a walk in the countryside, unless they keep to the roads, the use of which is still permitted to us outside our own "Pale of Settlement."

But even as regards the "Arab" area we have been told that we are not to expect plans for the development of the vast stretches of waste land in the south, in the hill region and the Jordan Valley, for His Excellency found it necessary to point out that the plans for irrigation, terracing, etc., were meant to preserve "what little remains, after many years of insufficient attention, of the soil of the country. Without this the congestion problem will become more and more dangerously acute."

White Paper Assumptions

In view of the Government there will be no influx of capital into the country from abroad for the purpose of development after the war. Jewish immigration will come to an end in accordance with the White Paper; and Jewish immigration was almost the only source of the influx of capital into Palestine from abroad. Government is also of the opinion that there will be no possibility of raising a loan abroad for the development of the country, for there are countries in greater need which have "suffered infinitely more than Palestine." The High Commissioner, naturally, does not take into account the fact that there is a people which has suffered infinitely more than any other people, that this people has some relation to this country and that so far it has been the main, almost the only contributor to the development of Palestine. The High Commissioner passes this over because he is faithful to the White Paper policy, the declared aim of which is to cut this link and to separate the problem of Palestine completely from the problem of the Jewish people.

Thus the money for the development scheme of the Government, and we have already seen for whose benefit it is intended, if it can be realized at all, will have to come from resources which have accumulated locally. I am neither an economist nor a financial expert but I have been living in this country for over thirty-six years and I have never heard of money accumulated locally, apart from the surplus accumulated until a few years ago from taxes paid by Jews. But on the other hand I know that a large amount of capital has been brought into the country by Jewish immigrants and by Jewish funds and institutions.

Only a small proportion of the deposits in the banks of Palestine is the result of local accumulation. For the greater part, these deposits belong to Jewish immigrants from Poland, America, Bukhara, Britain, Germany and all the other countries where Jewish refugees were able to save part of their assets and bring them to Palestine. Government has assigned to this capital the function of carrying out the "reconstruction" scheme on the lines of the White Paper policy.

We have been told, also, by the way, that there will be unemployment here after the war; and this prophecy is indeed not without foundation. Since the Government is basing its plans on the White Paper policy, there will be a complete stoppage of Jewish immigration into Palestine after the arrival of the twenty-nine thousand children promised us a few weeks ago by the Secretary of State for the Colonies. The gates of Palestine will be slammed tight against Jews, and the stoppage of immigration will undoubtedly result in unemployment. The only way out which Government sees is building, for industrial activity will be reduced and there will be no more Jewish settlement. Yet the Government leaves building mainly to private enterprise.

Though the Government does not undertake responsibility for unemployment, it finds it necessary to issue the advance warning that there will be unemployment in this country after the war, in order to disillusion some naive people who might possibly permit themselves to believe that Palestine could serve as a refuge for the remnants of Israel.

In the High Commissioner's speech we were given an even more serious warning. Speaking of the plans of agricultural development, His Excellency told us that there exists in this country a problem of rural congestion which will become more and more acute.

Though His Excellency did not quote his authority for his statement, we remember having heard about the problem of "congestion" from the author of the White Paper, Mr. Malcolm Macdonald, in a speech made by him in the House of Commons on March 6th, 1940. Defending the Land Restrictions Ordinance, Mr. Macdonald told hundreds of M.P.s who had never seen Palestine that the areas prohibited to Jews, such as the Negeb for instance, were "over-populated," and that there was unemployment and a shortage of land in those areas. The majority of the members of the House of Commons who do not know the conditions prevailing here swallowed this amazing fabrication concocted by the then Secretary of State for the Colonies. But it is to be regretted that the experts of Government have misled the High Commissioner by supplying him with such absurd information. Do the Government experts really not know that over two-thirds of the land of Palestine—of Western Palestine alone—have not been under cultivation for the past few centuries, and are uninhabited and desolate? Has it escaped the attention of the experts that in all the southern half of the country — over fourteen million dunams—there is not a single inhabited centre, agricultural or urban, and that this vast area is entirely unpopulated apart from a few thousand Bedouin?

But the important aspect of the speech we heard last night is not what is actually contained therein, but what is omitted. If we consider this aspect we shall more fully understand the significance of the surprising statements which were made.

This was no mere improvisation, but a carefully prepared speech of a ruler, and not on any trifling subject, but on the future of this country after the war. Yet this speech failed to mention several "unimportant" matters: the special status of this country; the peculiar conditions prevailing in it; its association with the Jewish people in the past and in the future; the special obligations undertaken by the Mandatory Government; the rights of the National Home; the historic link between the Jewish people and Palestine which existed even before the British Empire came into being; the terrible disaster that has befallen the Jewish people; the place which this country occupies in the life of this people and in its hopes for the future; the reconstruction work that has already been done by the Jewish people here and the ability displayed by the Jews to revive the desolate areas of this country; the great benefits that Zionist work has brought to the country—all this the High Commissioner has deliberately and significantly failed to mention.

When one reads the speech, one gets the impression that the rulers of this country have never opened their Bibles, never heard anything of the Balfour Declaration, never heard the clauses of the Mandate, never visited a Jewish settlement, never met a Jewish pioneer and, naturally, never heard of the existence of a Jewish Agency for Palestine which has been entrusted under the Mandate with "assisting and taking part in the development of the country."

We Shall Not Lend a Hand

We must not be ungrateful for the compliments bestowed on us in the speech, the compliment to the Tel Aviv Municipality for planning for the future, the compliments to the Jewish community which has done so much in the field of public services, education and health. But in expressing our thanks for those compliments let us be frank and tell the Government openly and clearly that there will be no cooperation between us and the White Paper Government, neither today nor after the war. We shall not lend a hand to the implementation of the schemes announced last night, for all those schemes are based on the stoppage of Jewish immigration, on the segregation of the Jews in a Pale of Settle ment, on the implementation of the White Paper policy, on robbing the Jewish people of its right to a homeland. And because of all this, we shall assuredly fight the White Paper and everything connected with it, to the bitter end.

We are certain that this so-called "reconstruction" scheme is based on a fundamentally false premise. This country will never be able to achieve its reconstruction and to rise from its desolation by its own capacity and financial resources. Its soil, as the High Commissioner has pointed out, has been neglected and left uncultivated not only for years but for centuries, ever since the time when we were exiled from our country. And what has been done in the spheres of agriculture and industry in this country during the last sixty years has been done by returning exiles. It was not money accumulated in the country, but pioneering capital and pioneering labor, bearing with them the vision of Jewish revival, which built Petah Tikvah on the swamps of Yarkon River, Rishon Letzion on the sand dunes of Ain Hakoreh, Moza on the rocks of Jerusalem, and Hanita on the heights of Galilee; it was they that made fertile the neglected and desolate Emek, and created the Potash Company, the Electricity Corporation, "Nesher," "Lodzia," "Ata" and "Assis" and hundreds of settlements and industrial enterprises.

In none of the neighboring countries, neither in Egypt nor in Syria, neither in Transjordan nor in Iraq, have such advances been made in the development of agriculture and industry in the past twenty years as this country has witnessed in that period. And all this has been achieved not by the Government but by Jewish immigration and Jewish settlement. It has been achieved not with money accumulated in this country, but by the Jewish National Fund, the Palestine Foundation, the Palestine Jewish Colonization Association and by private Jewish capital that streamed into Palestine as a result of immigration. It has been achieved not as an outcome of the plans of Government, but as a result of the initiative, the enthusiasm, the perseverance and the pioneering work of the people who bore with them the vision of the Jewish revival. And without Jewish immigration the Government will do nothing after the war, just as it did nothing before the war.

Our rulers have not asked themselves why the soil in this country was neglected and insufficiently cared for. Well, let us reveal the secret to them. Western Palestine, like Eastern Palestine, Syria and Iraq, does not suffer from overpopulation, but from a lack of population. The existing population had apparently so much land at their disposal that they could afford for many years to neglect the soil and to cultivate only part of it. And they will go on doing so, even after the proclamation of the "reconstruction" program and the appointment of Sir Douglas Harris. About eight years ago that particular expert was appointed Development Officer, and till this very day we have not seen the villages he has developed, the swamps he has drained, the hills he has reafforested and terraced, the irrigation schemes he has created. Developments in those fields have taken place during these years. They were not accomplished with the help of the Development Officer, but in spite of constant obstruction from him and his colleagues in power.

Our Post-War Plans

We shall not cooperate in any schemes connected with the White Paper policy. The development of this country and its economic future concern us certainly to no smaller degree than they do our ruler. We were preparing plans for the post-war period even before we heard the proclamation of the Government's "reconstruction" program. But our plans differ from those of the Government. They are based on two fundamental facts.

(a) The land of this country is for the most part desolate. Over eighteen million dunams in Western Palestine alone are uninhabited and wholly uncultivated. Even the eight million dunams which are under cultivation are only partially cultivated. Even in the inhabited and cultivated area there is room for the intensification of production and for a denser population—as we have proved in our settlement work in the past. If we make use of all the resources of water—rain water, rivers, springs and underground water—we shall be able to irrigate millions of dunams and to settle hundreds of thousands of new farmers, enabling a far larger number to derive their livelihood from crafts, industry and maritime work.

(b) There is in the world one people without a country of its own, which has been bound since its existence to this, its ancient homeland. There is no salvation for this people but to return and settle in its homeland. Whether it will have in its hands an official scrap of paper called an immigration certificate or not, it will return here. Because it is to its own country that it is returning, and its immigration is dependent on right and not on sufferance— a principle which was recognized by the British people and by the whole civilized world, including the representatives of the Arab people at the end of the first World War. And the terrible disaster that has now come upon this people will become a tremendous stimulus of creation and reconstruction if it is given back its homeland and achieves the independence of a free nation.

We, too, have considered the problem of finance. We know that there is no money in this country; that the country is poor. We know, too, that the majority of the Jewish people is being destroyed and pauperized, but there are still a number of countries where Jewish capital exists. In addition, we hope for an international loan. If the High Commissioner is right in saying that, as regards loans those who have suffered most must be given preference, then our claim is strong, for there is no other people in the entire world which has suffered more than we have, or as much as we have. We are not asking for charity. We have had experience in this country and we know that our enterprise has the seeds of blessing in it, that it bears fruit and maintains itself; we know that capital invested in the development of Palestine will return dividends.

Such are the plans we are preparing, and we shall be glad to cooperate with all men of upright heart in the redemption of the Jewish people, and for the benefit of this country, and all of its inhabitants. But we reject the assumption that there is only little land left here for development, when three-quarters of the country are awaiting reclamation. We reject the assumption that this country is overpopulated, when we know that it suffers from a lack of population.

Palestine's Post-War Regime

Our program is the maximum development of this country in agriculture, in industry and on the sea, in order to prepare for a maximum immigration within the shortest possible period of time. To that end, there must be an international loan and a new regime which will have the capacity, the will, the perseverance, the enthusiasm and the vision to rebuild the ruins of a nation and its homeland. An alien regime, however conscientious it may be, will never accomplish that task. Officials who are today in Tanganyika, tomorrow in Palestine and the day after in the Sudan, officials who have no real connection either with the country or with its inhabitants, either with its past or with its future, will not succeed in reconstructing this country and achieving the advancement of its inhabitants. This great and difficult task can be accomplished only by a regime which identifies itself wholeheartedly, body and soul, with the country and the revival of its people.

The history of the last twenty-five years is proof of it. There has been a British Civil Service here, and they were entrusted with the task of helping the establishment of the Jewish National Home. The British have had more experience in colonization and settlement, perhaps, than any people in the entire world. The regime here had all the necessary power—and it has failed. And we Jews, who have had neither authority nor power, nor experience, and only very little means, have done things and succeeded in them. And the reason is that we have had the historic vision, the need and the will to accomplish it. We believe in our planning, but we reject the schemes of our rulers. There is a gulf between our plans and theirs, the White Paper serves a barrier between us.

Let us leave no room for illusions: There is no possibility whatever of our acquiescence in the White Paper policy.

There may be "realists" in Norway who said: Hitler is perhaps a bad thing, and Norway's independence is a good thing, but we have to face facts, and the fact is that Hitler is strong and victorious. There were "realists" not only in Norway but even in Britain, who advocated the conciliation of Hitler. Small wonder, then, that among us, too, there are "realists" who say: The White Paper is a fact, the regime is strong, and we have to accept "realities." These "realists" are blind, they think that a scrap of paper is stronger than the distress of a people, the will for regeneration, the longing for a homeland and the vision of redemption! . . .

The conflict between the White Paper and the will-to-live of the Jewish People need not necessarily involve a conflict between us and England. Not only for the duration of the war shall we cooperate with fighting England. I assume and I hope that this cooperation for the solution of one of the most difficult and urgent problems in the world will continue after the war. But in order to make such cooperation possible, we must destroy all illusions about the possibility of cooperation between us and the White Paper policy, which denies the Jewish people its homeland and its right to be free.

This Is Our Reply!

At the beginning of 1939, at the London Conference, we were told for the first time of the proposals of the White Paper. The Jewish delegation at that conference included not only representatives of the Zionist Organization and the Jewish Agency, but also representatives of the Agudath Israel and some Jewish members of the House of Lords. That delegation unanimously informed His Majesty's Government that the Jewish people would not cooperate in the implementation of those proposals and would not cooperate with the Government.

And when the White Paper was published in May, 1939, the Jewish Agency issued the following statement:

"The new policy for Palestine laid down by the Mandatory in the White Paper issued on May 17th denies to the Jewish people the right to reconstitute its National Home in its ancestral land. It hands over the government of the country to the present Arab majority and places the Jewish community of Palestine at the mercy of that majority. It decrees the stoppage of immigration as soon as the Jewish inhabitants of the country have become one-third of the total population. It sets up a territorial ghetto for Jews in their own homeland.

"The Jewish people regard this breach of faith as a surrender to Arab terrorism, a delivery of England's friends into the hands of its enemies. It widens the gulf between Jew and Arab and destroys any prospect of peace in the country.

"The Jewish people will not acquiesce in such a policy.

"The new regime envisaged in the White Paper will be a regime of mere coercion devoid of all moral basis and contrary to international law. Such a regime can only be established and maintained by force.

"The Royal Commission invoked by the White Paper indicated the dangers inherent in such a regime.

" 'Convinced as they (the Jews) are,' they wrote, 'that an Arab Government would mean the frustration of all efforts and ideals, that it would convert the National Home into one more cramped and dangerous ghetto, it seems only too probable that they would fight rather than submit to Arab rule. And to repress a Jewish rebellion against Britain would be as unpleasant a task as the repression of the Arab rebellion has been.'

"The Government has disregarded this warning.

"The Jewish people has shown its desire for peace even during the years of disturbances and was not provoked into retaliation by the prolonged Arab terror. But the Jewish people did not and will not yield to terrorism despite His Majesty's Government's decision to reward the terrorists by jettisoning the Jewish National Home.

"It is in the darkest hour of Jewish history that the British Government proposes to deprive the Jews of their last hope and to bar the way back to their homeland.

"This cruel blow is doubly cruel because it is delivered by the Government of a great Nation which extended its helping hand to the Jews and whose position in the world rests upon the foundations of moral authority and international good faith.

"This blow will not subdue the Jewish people. The historical connection between the Jewish people and the land of Israel will not be broken. The Jews will never accept the closing of the gates of Palestine to them nor will they let their National Home be converted into a ghetto.

"The Jewish pioneers who for the last three generations have shown their strength in rebuilding their desolate land will now likewise prove their strength in defending Jewish immigration, the Jewish homeland and Jewish freedom."

This is our reply. There is no other.

August, 1943

Organizing Arab Workers

by ABBA KHUSHI

WHAT HAS been done by the Histadrut to organize Arab labor, to help Arabs win better living conditions and to create a *modus vivendi* between Jewish and Arab workers in Palestine?

The general public, and even the average Jewish worker in Palestine, knows very little about the subject, partly because of lack of interest and partly because some aspects of our activity cannot at this stage be given publicity. It is not a matter of common knowledge that the *Confederation of Palestine Labor* (*Brith Poale Eretz Israel*), an organization of Arab workers federated with the Histadrut, has carried on an almost uninterrupted activity since 1929, even through the turbulent years beginning with 1936, throughout the disturbances and the war, to this very day.

To be sure, there have been ups and downs. Membership in the Confederation has fluctuated between several thousand in its heyday and several dozen during the height of the terror when Arab workers had to risk their lives to belong to an organization connected with Jews. But the thread binding the Jewish worker and his Histadrut to the Arab worker and the nucleus of his organization has never been severed.

Within the Histadrut itself the proper methods of activity among Arab workers have been a matter of debate for years. According to the view of some, the organization of the Arabs should be undertaken with the same methods as those employed in organizing Jewish workers; the supporters of this view claim that all that is necessary for achievement is a strong will and the required means. At the opposite extreme it has been argued that the comparatively small number of Jewish workers in Palestine and the preoccupation of the Histadrut with its own problems, as well as

304

the immaturity of the Arab worker, make the organizing of Arabs a premature undertaking.

But the test of the value of those arguments came with the actual attempts at organizing Arab workers and with our gradual familiarization with the language, customs, mentality and way of life of the Arab masses. An examination of the various attempts made to establish Arab labor organizations from time to time is instructive.

I.

Arabs themselves were the first to try to set up labor organizations. Thousands of Arab workers comprising different sections and trades belonged to these groups established at various times in Haifa, in Jaffa, Jerusalem, Nazareth, Migdal and Nablus. But sooner or later these organizations, which had been launched with considerable fanfare, disappeared almost without trace. Here and there there may still be a chairman or a secretary, but the life of the organization is gone. The Arab worker, lacking in endurance and in genuine interest, failed to put his shoulder to the wheel and would soon leave the organization.

The explanations for this failure were several: Not all such bodies were created with an honest intent to organize the Arab worker and to seek to better his living conditions. Some of them were tools in the hands of Arab nationalists, others were the creatures of ambitious persons using the labor organization as a stepping stone to their own advancement in Arab society.

The initiators of these organizations were neither workers nor socialist intellectuals, but individuals and circles alien to the worker such as Levantine intellectuals, employers and members of the landed aristocracy.

Some of these Arab attempts at organizing Arab workers were closely enough observed by us to enable us to draw conclusions about the reasons for their failure and derive lessons for the future. For the present, however, we shall merely note the fact and devote some space to the discussion of unsuccessful attempts made by Jews to organize Arab workers.

Jewish Communists tried at different periods to organize Arab labor. They were not handicapped by lack of funds, nor one must admit, did they lack an idea. But all that their vas efforts and generous use of money produced was a few paid agents who exerted no influence on the Arab labor movement. The failure of the Jewish Communists can be explained by the same two reasons as the failure of Arab organizers: the organization wa merely a means to an end, and the leaders did not enjoy the con fidence of the masses. The Arab worker could not and would no trust individuals who betray their own people and join hands with its enemies.

II.

On the basis of our experience in organizing Arabs during the past twelve years or so, I have come to the conclusion that the only way is the slow, patient and honest way. The only right polic is the policy of the Histadrut with the Confederation of Palestin Workers. So far it is the only attempt which has not failed and which points to ultimate success.

The policy of the Histadrut in the Confederation of Pales tine Workers consists of assisting the Arab worker to liberat himself from economic, spiritual and political subjection; of help ing him to organize in a form most suitable for his national an individual character, in order to raise his standard of living to human level, to improve his working conditions, to combat ex ploitation and subjection both by his employers and by his politica and national leaders, and, finally, to educate him to take his fat into his own hands.

We want to help the Arab worker found an Arab labor or ganization which will have a fraternal bond with our Histadrut We do no intend to make a Jew or a Zionist out of the Arab an more than we mean to conceal our Zionist aspirations from him We tell him quite candidly that we have come to Palestine to re deem our people and build a Homeland, and that we are neithe able nor willing to forego this aim at his or at anyone else's reques Only by being truthful about our Zionism will it be possible fo us to find the way to the heart and the mind of the Arab worker and *fellah*.

This road is long and difficult, but it is sure. We tell the Arab worker that though we have not come to Palestine for his sake, our coming has helped him better his position, and that the organizational, economic, cultural and political power of Jewish labor has been a decisive influence in the steady improvement of the Arab worker and the Arab *fellah*.

Arab workers have benefited by the fight of the Histadrut for an eight hour working day for Jews, and in some economic sectors an eight hour day has been achieved for the Arab worker as well (e.g., in the postal service, in the harbors, in international companies). The wages and the working conditions of Arab labor in Palestine are far ahead of any neighboring country in the Middle East, including Egypt and Turkey. In some occupations workers enjoy sick leave and paid annual vacations, which are unheard of in the neighboring countries.

The beginnings of social legislation in Palestine, though far from satisfying the demands of the Histadrut, are for the Arab worker who benefits by them little short of a miracle. But this miracle did not come from heaven; it is the result of a long fight by the Histadrut.

An Arab worker who is one of the veteran members of the Conferederation said in a speech to new members: "Just as the sun spreads numberless rays of heat and light upon everything around us, even so the Histadrut, by its very existence and struggle, radiates heat and light without end upon the Arab worker." Indeed, the very existence of the Histadrut was bound to arouse in the Arabs a desire for labor organizations.

III.

What can the Histadrut do, and what methods ought it to follow, in organizing Arab workers?

1. The economic areas which lend themselves to useful activity by the Histadrut among Arab workers are (a) government proj-

ects; (b) international companies; (c) private enterprises connected with the above two classes of work; (d) projects of mixed
municipalities; (e) industrial undertakings and workshops owned
by Arabs.

2. Arab workers in the above-mentioned areas ought to be
organized in permanent trade groups which will in time grow
and crystallize into a basis for regular trade unions. Taking into
account the special nature of these economic areas and the
peculiarities of the Arab worker, it would be advisable to have
these trade unions organized on a vertical plan, by industries.
Such groups should be formed only in places of permanent employment or in places whose stability is assured for a reasonable
period of time. Before a group is formed, a nucleus of serious-
minded workers must be created so that it may act as the executive
committee or the leading body of the group. A great deal of educational work is required for the creation of such a nucleus.

The organizational activity must proceed very cautiously to
avoid being frustrated by the manufacturer or the building con-
tractor who will stop at nothing to destroy the new and weak
organization. The Arab worker, like all immature workers, is prone
to be over-enthusiastic at first and thoroughly disillusioned soon
afterwards. At any rate, he can easily be frightened away from
his labor organization. For that reason it is necessary to cultivate
the nucleus of the active and responsible members and to carry
on the initial stages of the work underground, taking care to have
substitutes ready for any members of the nucleus or for all of it,
who may be unable or unwilling to go on in the face of pressure
from outside. Before the existence of a group and the names of its
members are made public, it is well to have a period of experience
behind it.

Collaboration is possible between Jewish and Arab workers
in places where there is mixed employment, such as government
projects, international companies and municipalities. Practical
questions of wages and working conditions can be discussed at
joint meetings which should also be called from time to time for

the express purpose of fostering good will. In such places it is necessary to have a few Jewish workers who speak Arabic and who are willing to assist in the furthering of the work of organizing Arab workers through the Confederation and its methods. Here, too, a nucleus of Arab workers must be formed to be prepared for the task of spreading propaganda among the mass of Arab workers.

3. Cells must also be organized in the industry and crafts of the Arab economic area. This is a particularly difficult task and is full of obstacles. Arab employers are quick to react to any attempt at founding a labor organization and are ruthless in their methods, discharging or bribing any one active in it.

A great deal of caution and understanding is required in dealing with the workers themselves, who must be warned against expecting speedy and spectacular results and against hasty actions. They must be made to understand that a strike is to be used as a last resort and that education and negotiations are required with employers just as they are with workers, and that a strike, if inevitable, must be the consummation of long and careful preparation. A great deal of time will have to be devoted to forging a solid body of workers ready for sacrifices and risks.

4. The medical service rendered the Arabs by the *Kupat Holim* is important both as a means of attracting them to the Histadrut and as an educational force. The poor Arab, whose medical needs are entirely unprovided for, is grateful in the extreme for medical assistance given by the *Kupat Holim,* and for the spirit in which it is given. Many times a whole village has been won over to the Confederation because a child of a *fellah* has been helped by the *Kupat Holim.* The members of the Confederation are greatly appreciative of the friendly attitude and the readiness to help shown by the management, the physicians and the nurses of the organization.

The question of fees for medical service presents a difficulty, since the Arab worker is as yet unaccustomed to the idea of a substantial monthly contribution. For the time being, the practice of the Confederation in imposing a small fee for each visit is the only wise one under the circumstances. However, with the increase of the number of Arabs enjoying its services, the *Kupat Holim* will find its burden too heavy and the necessary financial resources will have to be found to take care of it.

5. Wide opportunities for future activity are to be seen in the attempts recently made by the Confederation in Haifa to create instruments for mutual help among Arab workers in the form of a Savings and Loan Society and a fund for emergencies. This attempt was made possible by the fact that for several years the Savings and Loan Society of the Histadrut has been extending help to Arab workers and that the idea of similar projects for members of the Confederation has been disseminated among Arab workers by a concerted campaign. To be sure, the assistance of the Histadrut is required in such efforts both financially and organizationally.

6. Clubs are important as social and educational agencies especially among a people like the Arabs who like to be together. In any Arab quarter or village one can always find a group of people sitting together engaged in a discussion or listening to one of their members reading a newspaper or listening to the radio and an impromptu commentator in the group. A club organized by us would become the center of social activity in the neighborhood, if it is properly organized in accordance with the customs of the Arabs.

7. Joint activities in sport and youth organizations are possible and desirable. The *Hapoel* has already succeeded in meeting with some Arab sport clubs, and while the chauvinism of many teachers presents an obstacle, it can be overcome by direct appeal to the pupils.

8. Organized outings, if attended with a view to establishing friendly relations with Arabs, can be of great assistance. The presence of Jews familiar with the Arab language and customs and due regard for Arab sensibilities are of paramount importance.

Jewish rural settlements can be extremely useful in strengthening friendly relations with rural Arabs. Emulation of Arab hospitality and the organization in each Jewish settlement of a small unit of Arabic speaking Jews to act as unofficial liaison officers are important. The rendering of medical assistance and instruction in the improvement of agricultural methods will help in the establishment of close relations. But here too a guiding hand is needed and the work must be co-ordinated. Furthermore, one must not expect immediate and spectacular results. One must take the long view.

December, 1942

Leon Blum Salutes the Histadrut

I am happy to salute your work for Jewish labor in Palestine on the occasion of the 15th anniversary of the Histadrut.

In how many fields has not the Histadrut displayed its extraordinary activity! It seems that there is no field absent.

In the first place, in its organization of workers: in the course of 15 years, the membership has risen from less than 5,000 to approximately 90,000 and soon it will probably celebrate the 100,-000 mark. This is a proud record. Of yet greater importance are its various institutions: the rural and urban economies, the cultural institutions, the youth work, sports, and so forth. Not many organizations can boast such activity. And what a feeling of international solidarity! The Austrian occurrences have amply shown it in a particularly emphatic way. The membership of the Histadrut displayed an overwhelming enthusiasm in the aid extended to the fighters against Austrian fascism.

In Arab-Jewish relations the responsibility devolving on Jewish labor is tremendous. The present sad events have shown how well the Histadrut understands its mission. For it is altogether likely that in some places Arabs have not allowed themselves to be influenced by reactionary and feudal incitements and have shown humanity to Jews, thanks to the work of the Histadrut. This is certainly an indication that the development of the *Yishuv* in Palestine has also brought benefits to the Arab laboring masses; but without the work of the Histadrut it would have been more difficult to weaken the demagogic incitement.

I wish you greater successes for the Jewish working class in Palestine. At the same time, I wish the Histadrut success in its great historic mission of rebuilding the Jewish National Homeland in Palestine on the basis of labor, international solidarity and peace with the Arab masses.

Léon Blum.
June, 1936

Defense—Not Revenge

THERE HAVE BEEN many outside of Palestine who wondered how long Havlaga—the self-imposed restraint of the Jewish Community in the face of repeated outrage—could endure. There have even been some who doubted the wisdom of this discipline. When the first act of retaliation took place; when six Arabs were shot on November 14th by the Jews, it was feared that the long, tragic endurance of the Palestinian community had at last snapped. However, there were no grounds for this fear. The immediate reaction of the Yishub showed that we were faced with an isolated anti-Jewish, as well as anti-Arab, act, which in no way indicated a change of temper or conviction on the part of the Jewish community as a whole. Every responsible Jewish body in Palestine condemned the killings in terms which left no doubt as to the stand of Palestinian Jewry in regard to Jewish terrorism. The Jewish Agency and the Vaad Leumi, the Jewish National Council, expressed their abhorrence of such retaliation in statements of moving eloquence. The memorable words of Dr. David Yellin, whose son was slain by an Arab terrorist a few weeks before, spoke for Palestine Jewry: "When an Arab was killed after the slaying of my son, my whole family was shocked for we all felt that the murder of one innocent son cannot atone for the murder of another innocent son. We are proud that even in the most difficult days an Arab could pass unafraid and unmolested in Tel-Aviv itself and in Jewish quarters of other cities." These are noble and magnanimous words. What is perhaps even more remarkable than the moral grandeur of one individual, is the fact that this utterance represents the ethical stature of 400,000 people tortured and goaded for nearly two years. It is easy enough for us who sit apart in safety to understand that terror must not be fought with terror; that it is neither righteous nor politic to combat violence with a counter-violence which strikes not the perpetrators of the crime,

but the innocent. It would also have been possible for us to understand, though not condone, a wave of retaliatory acts. Unwillingly,
we would have understood the bitterness which drove a desperate
community to the madness of vengeance. But we have been spared
the necessity for this understanding. We have been spared the
graceless task of counselling fortitude and calm to human beings
on the firing line. We have been spared the shame of urging lofty
sentiments on the victims of evil. The shock evoked by the first
Jewish outrage to occur in almost two years, shows clearly enough
how profound a part the conception of Havlaga plays in the spiritual life of the Palestinian community. It is more than strategy—
a fear to let loose uncontrollable forces on the population—though
the element of common-sense naturally figures. It becomes obvious
on reading the Palestine press that the sense of horror felt by the
Jewish community was evoked not merely by the criminal folly
of the Jewish terrorist, but chiefly by his brutal immorality. No
innocent son must be slain to avenge another innocent son.

There is little doubt that the Arabs were killed by a political
group which has more than once endangered Palestine and Zionism by its reckless disregard of the discipline and will of the
Yishuv. Jabotinsky knows well enough that they "hit back." They
hit back with valor and intelligence every time that they are openly
attacked. A raid on a kvutzah is not met meekly. But there can be
a question only of hitting, not of hitting back, when a shot is
fired at random, when its purpose is not to repel an assailant, but
vengeance. Self-defense is one thing; anonymous revenge is another. Palestine Jewry has not sunk to the level of jungle savagery
and desert blood-feuds. It has not striven to emulate or equal the
Arab terrorist. It has created its own noble and heroic pattern of
conduct, a pattern which is, in a sense, a contribution to the spiritual history of man. The overwhelming majority of Palestine
Jews who have achieved the difficult mastery of themselves under
agonizing provocation have the right to expect a similar self-
conquest from others. Jabotinsky has done harm before, but the

opportunities for havoc which now offer themselves to an irresponsible and inflamed mind are infinite.

In this connection one should remember that a considerable part of the Arab press has also protested against continued violence. Both Al Jamia al Islamia and Ad Difaa have come out with protests against terrorism as a method of struggle. This attitude, together with the appeal issued jointly by the Arab and Jewish merchants of Jerusalem is a hopeful sign. Perhaps the indignation of the Jewish Community at Jewish terrorism has had an effect. Agriculture is not the only contribution which the Jew may make to the reconstruction of Palestine. The municipal council meetings of Palestine now begin with a roster of the dead fallen in the past week. And the roster concludes with the words "may these be the last." We too repeat as we read the lists of the victims, "may these be the last." And if these be not the last, we know that the Jewish struggle will continue fearless, but pure, as before.

January, 1938

Twenty-Four Hours

by HILLEL GILEADI

IT WOULD be a pity not to take note of such an historic incident as the one which occurred yesterday, Sunday, March the twenty-first. Perhaps it would suffice to say only that on such and such a day the dream of the two *kvutzot*, Massadah and Ein Hakoreh was realized, and that they finally settled on the soil which is associated with the name of Chaim Arlosoroff. For to describe the act of the "ascent" upon the soil of the hundreds of comrades who took part in it requires a great artist, one who would be able to express all the emotions we knew, standing there on the edge of the desert, at the shores of the Yarmuk. I shall attempt to recount the facts alone.

In Dagania B a joint conference of all the *kvutzot* of the Jordan Valley with the assistance of Comrade Hartzfeld of the Agricultural Center took place on Saturday, March 13. Again and again the difficulties connected with the "ascent" of the two *kvutzot* came up. Of the eight or nine thousand dunams of land known as the Miphal Arlosoroff, only about two thousand are in one stretch, and even these are cut through by two strips of land belonging to Arabs who refuse to exchange them for better soil closer to their other possessions.

We said: Of course we shall not stop, even though there may be some Arab strips of land right in the center. True, the country is restless. All roads are dangerous, and we are settling far away, on the very brink of the desert, with the "peaceful" Bedouins as neighbors. Into the bargain, it is the eve of Nebi-Mussah. Who knows, it may become somewhat "jolly" again. And there are no roads, not even a telephone. Shall we depend on the police? Such and other difficult problems confront us, but speculations are of no help. We have waited long enough for peaceful times. Only with our coming will the region cease being a desert, only with our

316

oming will there be peace, only with. . . . Thus all doubts are
ushed aside. It is decided that a week hence, March 21, the
ettling will take place.

We all sit close to Hartzfeld who starts pointing to a map:
Here there will be two *kvutzot*. . . . Here two Irgunim. . . . Here
even. . . . And more here. . . . And here. . . . Until we shall
ave surrounded the wild desert with a strong chain of new,
owering settlements. . . ."

It is Sunday morning. The work is almost finished. Details
ave already been worked out. And suddenly the frightful news
f Kefar Hacoresh and Jabniel reaches us. Five new victims.

Committees are elected. One is dispatched to the funerals in
Kefar Hacoresh and Jabniel, and the other goes to work on the
lans for the settlement of Massadah and Ein Hakoreh. The plan-
ing starts immediately. What shall be built the first day? How
any people? Who are they? Where to get building materials,
ansportation, etc.? Time is so short. Only one week left. It was
ecided that in both *kvutzot* the following structures must be built
n Sunday: A double wooden wall filled with sand so thick that
o bullet would penetrate it, a fourteen meter tower with a pro-
ctor on top, a dynamo, a double barbed wire fence, and within
is fort three cottages for the members, a dining room and
itchen, and other essential buildings. And all this must be com-
leted in one day. Materials, men, machinery, automobiles. . . .
he head goes in circles, but some inner voice whispers: We shall
ealize it all. . . . To work!

And the work started. This one is going to buy machinery.
hat one to bring materials. This one. . . . It seems a mess. But
o, everything happens in order. The calculations show that we
hall need about 300 men in order to build everything in one day.
We have no fear of this. In our Jordan Valley we have Kinnereth,
Daganiah A, Dagania B, Beth-Zerah, Afikim and Gesher. We
ay have to issue a command that all settlements stop their work
or one day, although this is the season of work everywhere. And
f we still lack men, then we will just whisper over the telephone

to the Emek, to Upper Galilee, Lower Galilee, and we shall b
overrun with voluntary workers. There will be automobiles too
Quite simple: we take all the autos from all the *kvutzot,* and als
from the Ruthenberg Naharaim hydro-electric plant.

The days fly. They are too short, and we must borrow hour
from the night. Everything goes as we imagined. The trucks fl
from Haifa with materials. The machinery is all purchased. Th
projectors are delivered. Voluntary engineers who want to tak
part in this good deed of the Aliyah arrive. Letters are posted t
all the *kvutzot,* informing them of the number of people they ar
expected to send. They only have to send us the lists of names, s
that we may organize the work accordingly.

Tuesday and Wednesday are long past, and Saturday is here
Who can tell what may happen tomorrow. Until today we hav
prepared everything secretly, so that the Arabs may not know
about it till the very last moment. Yet the entire Jewish neighbor
hood is consumed with joy, even Tiberias. The whole city speak
only of this event. Is it possible that "they" have not noticed th
holiday mood? Or are they perhaps preparing a "jolly reception
for us? Everything must be well organized. The plan is ready. A
command is issued that every settlement must provide three "Gaf
firim" (special guards). A special car with "Gaffirim" will guar
the roads all Sunday. In every place, on the highest point a scou
will watch. Sky rockets are prepared. And finally, on the place it
self will be a special automobile with first aid, "Gaffirim," and
doctor. Nothing has been forgotten.

It is Saturday. It is somewhat easier to breathe. All the *kvutzo*
have already sent their lists of names. But trouble again. Th
telephone keeps on ringing constantly with the same excited repri
mand: "Why haven't we been invited? It's of no use. We ar
coming." "All right," I reply, but inwardly I think: "Where wil
we put them all?" Well, it does not matter, I decide, we shall pu
up an extra cottage. "Come, comrades, come. It is a joy for all o
us." And the telephone keeps on ringing. "Who is talking?
"Ayelet Hashakhar and Kefar Gileadi. We are coming tomorrow.

"Come, we are waiting." The telephone again. "Who?" "The old colonies, Kinnereth, Milhamiah. We too are partners. We are coming tomorrow with our sons and daughters." "Come in the name of the Lord." Again the telephone. "Who?" "Naharaim. The women, too, demand work. The Ruthenberg station will work with a minimum of people. We are all coming. Make arrangements." God Almighty! I already have a list of more than three hundred and fifty people, and we can get along with two hundred and fifty. Well, it does not matter. The telephone again. "Who?" "Jabniel. In spite of the fact that tomorrow we have a memorial meeting in honor of our recent victims, we have decided to come and take part in the work, till midday, at least. The memorial service will take place in the afternoon. About twenty or twenty-five of us are coming."

Two jobs are still before us. First, we must take a trip to the place and parcel out the soil at the two points. This we have decided to do the very last moment lest the Arabs see it and then destroy our sign posts. Secondly, we must organize the work of about four hundred people, so that it will be productive throughout, and so that each one will know his place and task the first thing in the morning. But we have all night for this.

It is four in the afternoon. The truck is filled with "Gaffirim" and some twenty other comrades, and we start out.

Truly speaking, the heart does beat faster, not with fear, but with a feeling that we are going to the desert. Something may surprise us though all seems quiet. We reach the Yarmuk, the very place where tomorrow there will be two new settlements. The mountains of Gilead and Horan have come closer. You can almost reach out to them. At their foot are pitched brown, parched Bedouin shacks. Here and there you see some crops coming up. But otherwise everything is desolate, so full of thorns that you walk with difficulty. Only in the West are seen our green fields and our white buildings. The sight of this disperses one's uneasiness. We start working. "Such will be the general plan for the houses. This is the direction of the wind. And here it will be well to rest on hot days and nights. Here will stand the fort, and here we erect the fence. Here will be the tower, in the very center. And here the cottages." The gigantic hammer pounds upon the sign posts. We do not notice how the sun approaches the mountains of Galilee and is about to descend. Uneasiness comes over me. I begin to hurry my comrades. "Enough. Everything is ready for tomorrow. Let's go home." We feel somewhat unsafe. "They" can come from behind every thistle or rock, and we don't feel like spoiling tomorrow's holiday. Although the soil has been paid for long ago, it is still not ours. Only when we are settled upon it do we feel that we are safe.

And now the last task. The division of the work for tomorrow. There is hard and light work. It is bad that the women demand the more difficult work. Midnight, and we have not yet finished. We'll have to rise earlier and complete it. One's head is too dull now. According to the plan all are to meet in Afikim, the nearest point to the new settlements. I lie down and promise myself to fall asleep immediately. One is rather tired after such a week. But it can't be helped. I awake every minute. First, a dream filled with shots, and then one about difficulties in transporting the gravel. It is already three o'clock, and I decide that it is time to get up. The East pales in the distance. The great day is approaching. In an hour everything will be ready. At last I hear the gong. From every room the noise of speedy rising is heard. Everybody is afraid of being late. Exactly on time. Everybody is on the trucks. We drive. No one utters a word. At half past five everybody is in Afikim. Everyone wears working clothes, but a holiday spirit is prevalent everywhere. We are divided into groups, each one headed by a commander. Each group gets into a separate truck. In a corner two rows of our Gaffirim stand with the commander-in-chief at their head. A command rings out: "Take seats!" We all hurry to our places. The packed trucks line up in a single row with the Gaffirim truck at the head of the line. In addition, two or three Gaffirim with loaded rifles are stationed also in each separate truck. Another command and the whole caravan starts out. Everyone is silent. Only the comrades whose lot it is to remain behind, shout with envy: "Shalom. Shalom."

The morning breeze whistles cheerily. The first rays of the spring sun begin to appear. And we are going Eastward!

The sun has risen when we reach the place. The sign posts are here. The entire gang scatters like locusts. Everyone in his place. The trucks are unloaded in a minute. No lack of experts. They can be depended on. Everything will be in the best of condition. One board after another, one word after another, and the thing begins to grow. The hammers pound, the ropes are pulled, and the tower begins to rise. The autos are still in search of new roads among the thorns. And behold, a new, smooth road appears. I take a flying trip to Ein Hakoreh. I am attacked on all sides: "You have assigned more people to Massadah than here. That is why we see their tower in the distance, and we are only starting on ours." "Be at ease." Everything will be all right. Rest assured." And the hammers keep on pounding. And I fly back to Masadah. I am attacked there too: "You have stationed more men in Ein Hakoreh. That is why we see the walls of their forts rising in the distance, and we are only starting on ours." And the hammers keep pounding. One wall after another, and they grow larger and longer. One knock after another, and the barbed wire is stretched out. It is already eight o'clock. It's coming up. It's growing. The trucks now run fast on new flattened roads. Just command them. Or rather, just say one word: "Gravel here. Boards there. Machinery here." And they start running like the devil. There is really no time. Everything should be finished by three, so that we have enough time for some celebrating. Massadah again. Hartzfeld harangues that the work somehow isn't moving, and that going at such a pace we may be finished by next year. "It's already nine o'clock. In Ein Hakoreh the cottages are up and here, why here, hardly a nail has been driven. Shame, shame." Well, I don't move from here before I see the first roof up. But you don't even have to urge the comrades. It is not they who work, but some demon within them. "Shalom, Tanchum, what are you perspiring about? It does not seem so hot." He smiles, but does not answer. He has no time. "And you, Ben-Zion, you are not entirely well yet. What's the rush about?" And here is an old farmer from Mena-hemiah dragging a long board. His old wife is helping him. I notice that she wipes her eye hurriedly. But not he. It's a weak-ness on the part of his old woman, and does not befit him. He lifts his eyes to the sky and mumbles something. It seems to me that he is uttering the blessing "Shehekheyanu." The hammers keep pounding. It is ten. The work is progressing. No difficulties encountered. The Gaffirim have scattered all around the camp in a large chain, occupying the most suitable positions. They stand there without doing a lick of work and enviously look at the new settlements growing. Nobody is tired. The women serve food and drinks. We all eat in a hurry, like the Israelites during the exodus from Egypt. There is no time. The day is short, and we are overwhelmed with work. We grow more and more perturbed. It is almost noon, and there is still enough to do. True enough, the forts are erected, the towers are seen from the distance, the motors hum, but the cottages must be finished. It is impossible to leave these comrades without a roof over their heads. The plan must be carried out. If not by three o'clock, then it will be by four. But we need more help. Oh, this is fine. New people are coming. The ones who stayed behind were unable to remain there long enough, and came on their own account after dinner. "Help, com-rades, help. We must finish." The gravel is poured in between the boards, the hammers are pounded over the roof tops, the pro-jectors are already fastened to the towers. Another blow, and yet one more. It is four. It is growing quieter. Here and there you can still hear a final blow: now everything is done. The forts stand fast, full of gravel, the projectors turn on top of the towers, though it's full daylight. And the cottages too, stand erect, all surrounded by a double barbed wire fence. Here and there a window or a door is missing, but still these are dwellings.

Between the two new settlements everybody gathers in one large circle. The old Tiberias Rabbi delivers his blessing in the name of the community. He says that we Jews have always had the lot of fortune and misfortune going hand in hand. Tears rise in the eyes of many of us when the old Rabbi mentions the fresh graves. "No, no, we must not become weak. We must keep silent and continue building." Arlosoroff is mentioned, and somebody makes the wish that Massadah and Ein Hakoreh may be worthy of his name. We assure the new *kvutzot* that they shall always have our comradely help both in times of joy and in times of sorrow. The great day comes to an end with "Techezaknah" and the "International." And then our hands and our hearts are tied in a Hora.

The sun is setting. It is almost night. Well, dear earth, we promised yesterday and fulfilled today. Are you satisfied?

A last handshake and we part from our new neighbors.

It is dark. We are home. We are beginning to feel tired. It is unbelievable that all of it is true. Maybe it was only a dream? I hurry to the roof and strain my eyes towards the East. No, it is not a dream. The projector casts large rays from Ein Hakoreh towards the wild mountains. Massadah signals that everything is safe. Two new settlements in one day, on the brink of the desert. Now it is certain that every night they will illuminate the distance.

No, not only Massadah and Ein Hakoreh, but all of us have ascended that day.

June, 1937

Murder on the Black Sea

EDITORIAL

WE DEMAND to know the names of the British officials in Jerusalem or in London or in both capitals who are responsible for the death of the seven hundred and fifty Jewish men, women and children on the *Struma* in the waters of the Black Sea. Whoever they may be, the British Government owes it to the public opinion of the world to disclose their names so that they may be branded as murderers and removed from their positions and adequately punished for their cold-blooded crime.

Should the London Government fail to act, it will assume the responsibility for a deed which is bound to fill every decent person with a feeling of indignation against those who stand at the helm of the Empire. Those seven hundred and fifty nameless people who had been wandering about for weeks on the four hundred ton boat, could have been saved. All that was needed was one word from the British colonial officials. The permission to land could have been given in accordance with the provisions of the Macdonald White Paper or it could have been done in violation of that disingenuous document. It hardly matters when the lives of unfortunate refugees are at stake.

The refugees, fleeing from massacres in Rumania and the Gestapo in Bulgaria, like the passengers on the *Darien* last year, believed that outside of Hitler's world there was still a human world. Like the *Darien* passengers they set out for Palestine on a fishing boat and wandered for weeks without being permitted to land anywhere. Their entreaties were of no avail; in vain were the pleadings and assurances of the Jewish Agency which was ready to agree that the number of the refugees admitted should be deducted from the immigration schedule. The Joint Distribution Committee of America offered a financial guarantee. But the British colonial officials refused the unfortunates the right to save their lives. The captain of the *Struma* warned the authorities that both his vessel and its cargo were no longer seaworthy; that the passengers were hungry, sick and hysterical and that some of them had already gone insane. But the Turkish officials and the British officials were adamant in their refusal. The vessel was denied passage through the Bosphorus or a landing on Turkish shores. The refugees had their choice of two courses, either to go back to destruction in Rumania, and Bulgaria, or to seek salvation in the bottom of the sea. A stray mine brought the second alternative to pass.

To be sure, the Turkish authorities are not free from responsibility in this matter. The fatality took place only a few miles off the Bosphorus, at a place where it was the human duty of the Turkish officials to save the lives of the passengers by permitting them at least temporary shelter.

But one cannot expect of sophisticated modern Turkey the old-fashioned hospitality of its Islamic rulers of old—of Bayazet the Second, of Selim the First and Suleiman the First, who offered asylum to the Jewish exiles from Spain and Portugal. Certainly, Turkey cannot be expected today to show greater concern for Jewish refugees than the Empire which solemnly pledged itself to facilitate the establishment of a Jewish National Homeland in Palestine.

Moreover, Turkey has not assumed any responsibility for the moral order of the world; her Premier does not parade any Atlantic Charter, nor does he speak in the name of democracy and of Christian civilization, nor call upon all the oppressed to revolt against Hitler and to help create a better world.

The excuses offered by the British officials are hypocritical and revolting. Some of these officials fraternized with Hitler's henchmen and emissaries as recently as three years ago, and their "fear" of Nazis among Jewish refugees sounds ludicrous in the face of the keen awareness of the Palestine Jewish community who may be relied upon to spot any spy or saboteur in their midst. It is preposterous to pretend that another thousand or two thousand souls would aggravate the food situation in a country which has enough to feed its million and a half inhabitants plus the military forces stationed there. The argument becomes even more preposterous when one bears in mind the fact that many of the refugees could help to fill the shortage of agricultural labor caused by Jewish enlistments in the British army.

The colonial officials have used these ludicrous arguments before to explain the inexplicable. They still use them in regard to the eight hundred men, women and children imprisoned in an internment camp in Palestine. These people are neither criminals, lepers nor vagabonds. They are refugees who arrived in Palestine on the ship *Darien* in March 1941. Most of them are Rumanian Jews, fugitives from the Antonescu massacres of January 1941. About one third are Bulgarian Jews fleeing from the fury of Hitler's New Order in a once friendly country. There are among them also survivors of the *Salvador* which sank in the Sea of Marmora in November 1940. Nearly all the children aboard and many adults, several hundred in all, perished in that disaster. The survivors arrived on the *Darien* and were confined behind barbed wires together with the rest of the passengers. These refugees are still in Palestine only because the Palestine Administration cannot at this time find ships to deport them to the distant islands of the Indian Ocean.

A similar excuse was offered by the British colonial officials in November 1940 in the case of the passengers of the tragically celebrated *Patria*. It was only after the ship exploded in the harbor from a still undetermined cause and several hundred people lost their lives, that the survivors were admitted. Of these over one hundred later volunteered for the British army!

But the tragedy of the *Struma* exceeds all that the vicious and dull-witted colonial officials have done so far to make a mockery of Britain's pledge to the Jews and of the principles proclaimed in the Atlantic Charter and in Churchill's speeches.

Wherever the culprits may be—in the Colonial Office, in London or in the High Commissioner's residence in Jerusalem—the British Government must disclose their names, whatever their position in the administration or in society. The higher their positions the more shocking the crime and the greater the blot on the fair name of England.

Respect for England and confidence in her Government are essential to the morale of the public in this war. The task of maintaining that confidence and of inspiring faith in the oldest democratic country in Europe devolves in the first place upon the British Government.

Public opinion in Britain has properly been aroused by this shocking iniquity, and voices have been raised in protest demanding the resignation of the Palestine authorities and of a change in the British policy in Palestine.

"The New Colonial Secretary must examine the policy of the Palestine Administration and tell its officials that either the policy or the Administration itself will have to be changed," the *Manchester Guardian* declared editorially.

The British Government must realize that one cannot wage war for the destruction of Hitlerism with the help of colonial officialdom which is itself infected with Hitler mentality.

March, 1943

The Palestine Jewish Units in Italy

by MOSHE SHERTOK

I WAS IN Italy for eleven days. From the day I disembarked in Bari on April 11 till I left from Naples on April 25, I spent day and night among Palestinian Jews. Never have I experienced anything so strange and wonderful: it was as though a complete section of our Palestinian Jewish life had been transplanted to a strange place, where it continued to flourish powerfully and beautifully. In all earlier ages, Jews have been exiled from Palestine, while others returned to the land. But the thousands who today have left the country went not as exiles but as liberators, not as weak victims but as strong rescuers, not in submission to fate but as volunteers for a mission—to fight shoulder to shoulder with the men of other nations against the enemy of all the world. For the first time in thousands of years, Jewish soldiers have appeared on the field of battle as the men of a rooted people. They proclaim the beginning of our national rebirth, and by their devotion to duty they lay claim to our right as one of the United Nations. Small as their number is among the Allied forces, the organization of Jewish units has enabled the Jewish soldiers to leave a distinct impression of their special qualities. The Star of David is painted in blue and white on their machines. "Palestine" is sewed upon their shoulders. Though there are ten times as many Jews scattered among the various Allied armies, only the Palestinian units make a distinct impression.

I visited all the units in Italy. Except for the group of women auxiliaries, they are all commanded by Palestinian officers, three of whom are native-born, and two of whom rose from the ranks to the position of major. They are all healthy and look well

From a radio address by the head of the Jewish Agency Political Department upon his return from a visit to Italy.

Many of my own good friends, at least, have noticeably improved in health and appearance. Most of the units are in barracks, the rest in tents. Wherever they are, each unit is a true reflection of our Palestinian lifeforms.

*   *   *

I first visited the broad encampment of a transport unit. The commander is a former member of the *Egged* cooperative bus company. Machines bearing the Star of David insignia pass in and out. There is great tumult and activity in the shops. The reputation of the unit is such that the Headquarters Staff send it all their cars for repair. The office staff works busily. Officers and ensigns hurry on urgent missions. In a large reading room, a few drivers of the night watch take their ease. The library is in charge of one of the early settlers of our labor colonization, a man who developed the vision of the large collective settlement. Gradually one perceives the rhythm of the group's activity. One is surrounded by men who have been in service for three, four, and five years. Sharp orders ring in the air, brisk calls of "Good morning!" "Yes, Sir!" The Hebrew language prevails—in commands, signposts, wall bulletin, and painted signs. The pride of the unit are its chorus and orchestra. Their fame is widespread, and when I visited the unit they were preparing a performance to be given at the Opera House before a large audience from all the Allied armies.

Another transport unit was headed by a Jerusalem boy who had graduated from an English university. This was my first visit to the unit, even though it was four years old. All that time it had been in the Libyan desert. The unit had done vital work in the campaigns—both in retreat and on the offensive. When they were sent to Italy, the soldiers had not seen Palestine for two years. They know full well they have a long road to travel before they return. For some reason the unit was certain they would be the first of our men to enter Rome, and they were already planning to pass in review by the Arch of Titus.

I remember particularly a visit with a unit assigned to a special technical function at the front. The group was divided into a number of teams. The commander, a Tel Aviv municipal engineer who graduated from the "Herzlia" school, took me in his car to a point fifteen miles from the front. At nightfall all teams that were free to do so gathered on a hill slope in the open air. One team had not come at a late hour, and finally we learned that at the last moment they had been called in for an urgent night assignment. During the talk, while watching the faces of my young audience, I sought in vain for traces of the shattering effect of the bombing, strafing, and shelling they had experienced. To that time they had been fortunate enough not to lose a single man. But it is certain that they too will travel a long road before returning. The unit belongs to the Eighth Army and proudly wears, together with that Army's emblem, the insignia of their country.

In one city in the center of the liberated area, far from any danger zone, I met a group of twenty-five of our women auxiliaries, the PATS. One of them made me promise to remember them to their families when I spoke on the radio. I am now keeping that promise. In truth, they all look well. They are excellently housed, and Palestinian Jewish soldiers from far and near as well as American Jewish boys are frequent visitors. Near the town is a tent encampment of a Palestine engineers' unit. After I had talked with the PATS at their camp, they were permitted to make the trip to the engineer encampment to be part of my audience there.

There is one problem that worries practically all the encampments. At the PATS's camp, one girl said to me, "I am a German immigrant. I came to Palestine alone. I am single and have no parents. I left a good position in order to enlist. What will happen when I return? I know, of course, that you cannot promise me another position here and now. But will there be anyone to deal with such a problem, anyone to whom I can turn?" The same problem disturbs all the Palestinian units. In each unit groups have organized and plan to settle on the soil. I remember that in an infantry unit I once visited in North Africa, 280 out of 900 men belonged to such settlement groups; and that was in addition to the large number of recruits who came from already established farm settlements. But there are other soldiers who do not have such plans. Our appeal for volunteers implies large-scale community assistance to our recruits after the war. Our soldiers certainly deserve this all the more in that their enlistment turned into so providential a support for Jewish internees, as happened in Italy.

*   *   *

Much has already been reported concerning the rehabilitation work by Palestinian soldiers among internees and liberated Jews. Since the impressive scale of the accomplishment of Jewish soldiers in this field is already somewhat known, it may be even more in place to stress that the men of our units are, first and foremost, soldiers who carry out every demand of military discipline, and who tirelessly, devotedly, and successfully perform their military duties. Their skill, efficiency, and discipline have won the recognition of high officers. A section commander in Italy told me: "Your units are the best in my section. Their education is far higher than the army average. Their discipline is exemplary. There is no such thing as drunkenness among them. I couldn't wish for better soldiers." At another section command post, too, I heard the service and deportment of our soldiers praised. A certain officer once came to one of our North African units which I visited on my way home from Italy. His plan called for a ten-minute inspection; he stayed for three-quarters of an hour, because he was so interested by the internal organization of the camp. What caught his attention was not only their military smartness and efficiency, but their educational plan, their artistic interests, the men themselves.

Thus, what our men did in rehabilitating refugees was done in their free hours, on furlough, in haste and under pressure, by men who carried the full burden of military duties. With tremendous initiative our men sought out individual refugees over the whole length and breadth of the land, and organized an ambitious program of relief. They brought tidings of liberation to internees and renewed their bond with Palestine. Our soldiers set aside part of their own rations to feed the needy and gave their shirts to clothe them. Out of their own pay, the Jewish soldiers raised funds for relief, and for work and retraining projects. They created a new community spirit among the refugees. They devoted all their human understanding, social experience, managerial skill, and education to the work. In short, they came in the spirit of national responsibility, as the representatives of Palestine Jewry, to the first part of Europe where survivors of the decimated European Jews were saved from annihilation. Thereby they realized a dream which was implicit in our recruiting drive from its beginning.

There is not a single Jewish unit which does not employ refugees in its various services; but many units do much more. In one repair shop I found a group of wonderful boys, twelve to fourteen years old, who had been adopted by the soldiers for the duration. They spend half-days working as apprentices in the shop, and for half a day they study. In that same place, a young soldier approached me and introduced his father who was employed there as a laborer. The boy had come to Palestine from Germany with the Youth Aliya. In Italy he found his father who had been left behind in Germany, had passed through the seven cycles of Hell in concentration camps, escaped, and was interned in Italy until liberated. Father and son had a simple request: if I should return to England, would I seek out their wife and mother and tell her I had seen them alive and reunited?

The crowning achievement of our soldiers are their retraining farms. It was incredible. There are four groups in training, two of young people, two of adults, on abandoned Italian properties. The men have organized these groups on the lines of collective living, the study of Hebrew, systematic work, and psychic and physical recuperation. All this was done on the initiative and through the contributions of soldiers. Boys and girls were delivered from enforced idleness to labor, from confinement to the open fields, from helpless depression to the joy of production. Their lives have been given direction.

In the internment camps and among the scattered refugee groups the advice of our soldiers is eagerly sought after. From organizing craft cooperatives whose products are bought by our units, to providing Hebrew text books and homemade song books —in everything our soldiers are active participants. The very organization of the refugees draws its strength from their moral authority. To be sure, the Zionists among the refugees successfully maintained their organization through years of flight and internment camps. But their strength was redoubled by the bond which was created between the soldiers and the refugees. Today Zionist education is being conducted in all the camps, branches of WIZO (Women's International Zionist Organization) exist, and work is being done for the Jewish National Fund.

* * *

Of 5,500 Jewish refugees in the liberated area less than 2,000 are now in internment camps. The rest are scattered and have found commercial employment. I visited the three main camps, one near Bari, one near Santa Maria in the heel of Italy, and one at Ferramonte di Tarsio. Ferramonte, the best equipped camp, was taken over from the Italians. The refugees, by the way, are full of gratitude to the Italian people, including their minor officials, for their humane attitude. At present, they are under the care of Military Government. The British and American officers in charge fully understand that only a permanent haven, not relief and temporary shelter, solves their problem. Under the best conditions, the life of a refugee is one of persistent depression, especially in a temporary camp. At this time the first group of about five hundred persons with visas for Palestine is being organized. Those fortunate enough to be included are awaiting the day of departure impatiently. Others hope to get additional visas. Many have grown-up children, and some even wives and infants in Palestine.

In all the camps and wherever else refugees are encountered, one is overwhelmed by their gratitude for our soldiers' faithful, generous, and understanding assistance. I doubt whether the

name of the Palestinian soldier enjoys as much respect anywhere
else in the world as in those Italian camps; whether any other
Jewish group is as well qualified to appreciate the significance of
our Palestinian voluntary mobilization as those refugees. I have
seen the esteem with which our men are regarded by their non-
Jewish comrades, the love and gratitude of the refugees towards
them, the deep impression they have made on other Jewish soldier
in the Allied armies—and I thought: these marks of recognition
belong to all our volunteers wherever they serve. It is a mere
accident that only the present group of Palestine soldiers, that
these and no other units were assigned to Italy. All our units, all
our volunteers—wherever they may be, abroad or at home, from
the Persian ports to Tripoli—all share in the achievement and the
honor. What would have happened if the Jews in Palestine, by
some stroke of ill fortune, had not undertaken this vast campaign
of voluntary mobilization? What if we had not fought successfully for the organization of most of our men in Jewish units?

*   *   *

I must conclude. I will relate only one more incident. I
arrived in Ferramonte late in the evening. For some reason, we
followed a very roundabout route and even in a speedy, light jeep
the trip took eleven hours. A captain, formerly a member of the
"*Hamanhig*" cooperative bus company in Tel Aviv, drove the
whole way himself without relief. Upon arrival, we found that
most of the Jews in the camp—they number 800—had assembled
in general meeting to greet me. The meeting lasted until after
midnight. In the morning I made a tour of the camp and its
various institutions. There, as well as in Santa Maria and elsewhere, I saw the children of our people.

Where were these children born?

This is the story: the camp includes the members of two groups
of refugees who once took ship for Palestine without visas. One
boat was wrecked at sea somewhere on a desolate Aegean island
The passengers were saved. They were taken to Rhodes and im
prisoned for two years. Then they were removed to Ferramonte

An order of deportation to Poland long hung over their heads, but was not issued. The other group reached Benghazi. They tried to find a way from there to Palestine but were not permitted because war broke out; they too were sent back to Italy. On all these journeys and in all the ports, children were born: on vessels, in Rhodes, in Benghazi, and in Ferramonte. I saw them, and was told where each one was born. I still cannot understand how Jewish mothers were able to rear these children of wandering and internment—through perils, congestion, and dire want.

That morning at Ferramonte I saw this spectacle: a car came from one of the Jewish units to fetch a group of refugees to work on a military project. As the machine with the Star of David appeared, it was immediately covered with a swarm of gleeful, shouting tots. The driver stood in his machine, bronzed, powerful, broad-shouldered, and with a beaming face. The children clambered upon the car and the driver, felt in his pocket for candy, climbed into his arms and on his shoulders, clung to him on all sides. He stood, braced and happy, in the midst of the mob of youngsters, all brimful of energy and life.

I did not know him, nor did I ask who he was. He seemed at that moment like the unknown Jewish Soldier, the hero of this suffering and fighting age in Israel. The children seemed like symbols of all the wandering children of Israel, rescued from the slaughter in ghettos, hiding in Polish forests, sheltered by kindly non-Jews all over Europe—and, after all the horrors they had witnessed, still remaining in their innocence and beauty the harbingers of a happier future. And it seemed to me that, at any moment, the Unknown Driver would take his place at the wheel of the car with the Star of David, and drive it over hill and dale, splitting the sea like a sword, and would bring the children of our people's future, the precious remnants of our hopes, safely into the gates of the Homeland.

July, 1944

Seder Service—Palestinian Version

by Shulamith Schwartz

E VEN THE curt Associated Press cables a few weeks ago
pointed out that the banners carried in the Palestinian protest
demonstrations against the new land restrictions all bore Biblical
quotations. For those who know Jewish Palestine there is nothing
surprising in the fact that the plasterers' and waiters' unions, the
Palestine Symphony Orchestra, the bus cooperatives, the League
of Working Mothers, the Labor Athletic Groups, and all the
other marchers turned to the Bible for appropriate expression of
today's sentiments. The Bible is in the air this so predominantly
secular-minded community breathes. Always the link with Palestine, always a sort of literary substitute for the missing earth, the
Bible has been given new life by the modern resettlement of the
country. Living in the same geographical, climatic, and, in some
respects, political conditions as those the Bible reflects, has tele-
scoped the centuries and given the old words an oddly current
significance. Sentences that for centuries were merely so many
staid and respected accumulations of words leap out of the page at
you now and seem to be part of the editorial in this morning's
paper. What could be more topical than the recurrent prophetic
themes of the gathering of exiles from the four corners of the
earth, brought back home sometimes against their own will; the
conversion of desolate land into blossoming gardens; the finding
of water in dry land; the planting on rocky mountains of trees that
"will bear fruit for my people Israel."

One might easily say that, in general, tradition seems to be
taking the place in Palestine that it occupies in any normal group.
It is not only the Bible that has suddenly become so close and
meaningful. Words, beliefs and practices that were for centuries
essentially a carefully guarded repository of memories and hopes,
now have so much vitality, so clear and accepted a relation to the
present, that changes are made in them in a very natural manner

and without impairing their essential values. They are just as eagerly awaited and happy pauses in the working year as they once were in Eastern European towns and cities, but, by and large, the emphasis has shifted in practically every case, from the liturgical and ceremonial aspects of the occasion to the historical and the agricultural and seasonal. Thus Passover—to take the example nearest at hand—is quite as much the "Spring Festival" as it is a commemoration and prophecy of national redemption. It is no accident that most villages and many urban groups compose their own Haggada each year, retaining the most striking passages and best beloved songs and psalms in the traditional service but adding material that reflects the forces which are shaping modern Palestinian life. It would be hard to find more interesting evidence of the creative acceptance of Jewish tradition than that offered by those Haggadas read at crude but festive Seder tables throughout the country.

A recent Givat Brenner Haggada is a perfect case in point. It includes, as most of them do, those noble passages on "the bread of affliction" we eat now as slaves but "next year . . . as free men"; on the duty incumbent upon each individual to realize that, historically speaking, he, too, was delivered out of Egyptian bondage; on the divine promise which enables our ancestors and us to survive "for not only one hath risen against us to annihilate us, but in every generation hath an adversary risen against us to destroy us." It includes also the psalm on Israel's marching forth from Egypt and the Lord's returning "the captivity of Zion," and it ends with the inimitable "Chad Gadya," but it leaves out much of the traditional text and makes its own little anthology of appropriate and illustrious poems culled out of ancient and modern Hebrew literature. Carrying out the agricultural motive, Rachel's twentieth century "Aftergrowth" jostles the "Song of Songs"

Rise up, my love, my fair one, and come away,
For lo, the winter is past,
The rain is over and gone;
The flowers appear on the earth;
The time of singing is come,
And the voice of the turtle dove is heard in our land. . . .

Centuries apart, there are two tender and lovely pronouncement
on the return to Zion: Jeremiah's voice of Rachel weeping for he
children who are not, and Judah Halevi's famous "My heart is i
the East and I at the end of the West" poem. And on the way
between Judah Halevi and "Chad Gadya" comes a long pros
passage beginning: "And these are the words of the scroll of ou
tenth year," which in nobly archaic language recites a ver
modern tale, the story of the international and Palestinian scen
summed up by a disillusioned but heroic generation. Non-inter
vention, starting with Ethiopia, was responsible for the tragedy o
Spain, Austria, Palestine, for "when the wicked saw that ther
was no retribution after he had removed the borders of th
Ethiopian people and taken unto himself the inheritance of a
ancient folk, his pride waved exceeding great." And so Israel'
oppression was multiplied, his staff of bread was broken, and h
was cast into prison cells. "And he lifted his eyes to the moun
tains of Zion, but that mighty Kingdom which ruleth over man
nations . . . left the gate only partly open and was powerless t
overcome tiny bands. . . . Yet we, a handful returned from exile
have held our ground against our enemies, have even burst ou
boundaries and pitched our tents in the far north and the fa
south of the land. And so on this eve of the festival of freedom
we send out blessing to our brothers who are conquering th
wilderness with labor and blood, from those who guard th
northern border at Hanita to those who are digging wells in th
dry southland."

An Ain-Harod Haggada, also written before the end of th
riots, is even more ambitious. Beginning with a plea reminiscen
of the traditional memorial prayers—to remember "those who ar

far and lonely and defenseless, every solitary comrade, every exposed and tiny settlement,"—it goes on to give elaborate directions for a ceremony only briefly alluded to in the Givat Brenner Haggada. Now that there are once more sheaves of grain to be waved, the brief injunction in Leviticus to bring the Omer, "a sheaf of the wave offering," on Passover has evolved into a new and lovely ceremony practiced in varying forms in many villages. The directions in the Ain-Harod Haggada are very explicit. On the eve of Passover all work is to stop at four in the afternoon. At five a bell rings and a double procession is formed. Marching from their schoolhouse, the children pass between the two rows singing:

> In Sharon and in Galilee
> The fields and gardens grow,
> And there is song upon the lips
> Of those who plant and sow.

The smaller, pre-school children join the procession and a new song follows:

> Trust in the seed that you have sown,
> Know the tree you planted shall not die!

The whole public in answer chants a verse out of Deuteronomy, "Today you shall cross over into a new land," and then sings the Psalm of the returned captivity of Zion, and finally that very modern song

> We have come to the land to build,
> To build and to be rebuilt.

Adults and children together go down to the field of new grain where the first sheaf, or "Omer," is to be reaped. Scythes and pitchforks are wielded, and meantime those who are watching sing a song with words by Moshe, Ain-Harod's own poet, a young boy born and brought up there. It has strangely traditional overtones:

> "Has the sun gone down?" the reaper asks
> "It has, it has," the people say.
> "And shall I reap—and with this scythe?"
> "Yes, yes!" the people say.

To the music of the flute the little girls dance, and then the children heap up the grain they have reaped while songs of reaping and binding are sung. Each child is given a sheaf to carry and wave—that far-off "wave offering to the Lord" out of Leviticu.—and all return to the communal dining room. The children march around the room and present the sheaves to the adults.

That mixture of very old—and yet entirely recast—agricultura ritual and very new pioneering characterizes the rest of the Haggada as well. At the seder itself, most of the passages of the traditional Haggada read at Givat Brenner are included. In addition there are "four questions," but four questions never asked before at Passover:

"Why is so much blood shed in our world today?"
"Why must Jews be persecuted everywhere?"
"When will they return at last to their land?"
"When will all the land bloom as a garden?"

Then come passages from the Bible elsewhere dealing with the first redemption and Moses' rebuilding of the nation—the psychological as well as the physical redemption, that is. God speaks to Moses out of the burning bush, and centuries later, in David Frishman's words, He asks Moses: "Do you know how to form a people? Take those who toil and are broken and weary, all those that groan and are afflicted and have nothing but deep-feeling hearts. They will not understand you when you tell them that they are enslaved and wretched, but against their will you will open their eyes and redeem them. And you will turn worms into men, men into a nation, sand into a country."

Moses standing on Mount Nebo, Bialik describing the "Dead of the Wilderness," Isaiah prophesying the second redemption follow each other around the village Seder table, until finally the high seriousness of: "And it shall come to pass at the end of days" gives way to the strong, traditional rhythms of "Chad Gadya," the one only kid linking the stubborn, persistent ghetto ancestors with the new fields of Emek-Jezreel.

April, 1940

Americans in Palestine

by SULAMITH SCHWARTZ

ORDINARILY THE United States Consulate in Jerusalem seems placid enough; it has a pleasant lawn and strong, stone walls and the colorful American flag flying on Sundays and American holidays—to the delight of the tourist's heart. During periods of stress in Palestine, however—1921, 1929, 1936—the American Consulate is suddenly and clamorously urged to safeguard the life and property of many more American citizens than it is usually conscious of. Vice-consuls scurry about the country in the face of all sorts of dangers, and statistics on investments, holdings and population begin to appear in the press. There are, it would seem, about 10,000 American Jews in Palestine, a larger number than most of us would have expected. And the ten thousand vary so greatly that there is probably no one person acquainted with all the various types and classifications. They run all the way from the red-lipped and crimson-nailed woman I overheard speaking Bronx American on Jonah the Prophet Street in Tel Aviv to the two young girls with American graduate degrees and teaching experience who have joined a German-Polish *kibbutz* near Haifa and turned out (as one of the members of the *kibbutz* publicly testified) to be the unifying Hebraic and communal-minded factor in the entire group.

Though there are a few hundred ardent young Americans in various *kibbutzim* and *kvutzot,* I am very much afraid that the crimson-nailed woman is nearer than they to the general run of Americans in Palestine. The exigencies and ideals of Palestinian life have forced most immigrants to alter their way of life radically—to become farmers or manual workers, to speak and read Hebrew, to adopt that anomolous thing, Palestinian citizenship. Not so with Americans: they hold on to their past for many reasons. Whereas the majority of other immigrants are young—somewhere between eighteen and thirty—the majority of Amer-

icans are middle-aged business people with families and some
capital (even if very little by American standards), retired widows
and widowers, old parents whom their children have established
comfortably in Tel Aviv, Haifa or Jerusalem apartments. Obviously, such Americans—with the important exceptions we have
already indicated and shall indicate later—are not proletarianized
in Palestine, and many thousands of them continue to lead an
almost American existence in apartment houses which, as often as
possible, have running hot water and a pretense at central heat-
ing and built-in closets. They possess those greatest of Palestinian
luxuries, electric refrigerators and radios, and send their children
to private rather than public schools. On Thanksgiving Day you
may see the American flag out of more than one apartment
window and canned cranberries carefully served on many a table.
There are even spiritual and cultural imports: American Jews have
brought to Tel Aviv—name and all—something that grew up on
the sidewalks of the East Side and Brooklyn, the punctiliously
orthodox Young Israel society.

As for language, they learn Hebrew more slowly than almost
any other group, for English is, after all, one of the official languages of the country and can always be used in government and
business offices. Moreover, while bitter opposition kills all attempts to publish German or Yiddish dailies, Americans, unable
to read Hebrew fluently or at all, have access to a daily newspaper in their own language, the *Palestine Post,* intended, its able
American-Jewish editor insists, for the benefit of the thousands of
British soldiers and officials in the country and not for Jews who
ought to learn to read the Hebrew press. Oddly enough, the fact
that English is the Government language often makes those very
persons who spoke Hebrew or Yiddish at home in America,
proudly flaunt their usually questionable English and feel somehow superior to their ignorant fellow-Palestinians.

Differences in living standards and languages are perhaps less
important than the differences in the matter of citizenship. Only
a very few, highly enthusiastic individuals have voluntarily given

up American citizenship to become Palestinian subjects; the bulk of American Jews in Palestine renew their passports with loving care, even if, as naturalized citizens, they must return to the United States every few years. They may be ardent and self-sacrificing Zionists but most of them, having a fatherland so different from Roumania, Poland, Yemen or Nazi Germany, cherish their old as well as their new ties. Besides, it is convenient to be an American and to have America in the background as a possible refuge. I can remember a typical snatch of conversation in front of a Tel Aviv apartment-house at the time when the Ethiopian situation was becoming particularly threatening. "Oh, yes, Mr. Levine used to own this house. He came here from America in 1930 after his business failed there. But now the newspapers talk about war in the Mediterranean and conditions are better in America, so he sold the house at a £5,000 profit and went back."

Perhaps Mr. Levine represents a minority—but this business of being able to have one foot in Palestine and one outside of it is a general matter and one that, along with the other circumstances, naturally irritates the rest of the population. A further cause for irritation and for the failure of so many American Jews to understand and sympathize with the prevalent mood and philosophy of Jewish Palestine, is the fact that they belong by past associations and present occupations to the middle class. That is, they are members of the petty middle class, who are real-estate operators, agents for American firms, owners of shops, orange groves, small factories, *pensions,* or little banks, importers of last-season's American models in clothing or household equipment, and in all of these capacities, they run up against the all-powerful Histadrut, which imposes labor conditions naturally more galling to small entrepreneurs than to large ones. Incidentally one must not forget the erstwhile American housewife's troubles with the unionized and critical domestic "assistants" who are none too easy to deal with. One of the most curious aspects of the situation is the fact that many of the most vociferous American opponents of the Histadrut voted nothing but the Socialist ticket in America:—being suddenly

344 JEWISH FRONTIER ANTHOLOGY

transported to the highest economic stratum (for lack of any other, to be sure) is evidently a severe test for purely theoretical radicalism and results in no inconsiderable degree of snobbishness. English and South African Jews are similarly affected, and I have even seen a former rising young star in the Fabian Society turn real-estate man and bitterly anti-Labor in Palestine.

No generalizations about the group of American Jews living in Palestine can be correct unless they are supplemented by a description of the various groups within the group. American interest in the industrial development of the country has long been notable and is given practical expression by those American economic experts who conduct the affairs of the Palestine Economic Corporation and the American Economic Committee for Palestine. There are several larger factories founded by American Jews, at first certainly with little prospect of profits: the Artificial Tooth Factory is one such that does more than make both ends meet and export to many Asiatic and European countries; the Meshi silk factory as admirably equipped as its owner's Paterson New Jersey plants still has many tariff and merchandizing difficulties to meet but is producing silk that local dress manufacturers prophesy may be able to compete with the Japanese. Dress-manufacturing, incidentally, is a distinctly American-Jewish contribution to a country where the seamstress' rule is just beginning to be shaken, and there was a good deal of difficult pioneering involved when about ten years ago a more than middle-aged New York manufacturer wound up his successful affairs to start a new and not too appreciated industry in Tel Aviv.

American business-men with American methods and connections, naturally want American-trained secretaries who can write literate English and not the stylistic atrocities of the average Palestinian secretary who inevitably claims "perfect knowledge" of at least four or five languages. Efficient girl secretaries from any number of American cities form a distinct class in Palestine for many a young tourist has seen the opportunity to come and work for a year or two—and the news spreads to others. The

Imperial Chemicals Industries and the Iraq Petroleum Company alone have harbored many American girls, a goodly percentage of whom marry Palestinians—of many origins, to be sure—and stay in the country. Some of them come in the first place, because they married Palestinians studying in America; their adjustment to their new home varies, and there are even a few who are distinctly unhappy. However, whether or not they become really Palestinian, their husbands remain permanently part-American and share the American group's enthusiasm for the *New York Times*, English speaking films (for which most of the Palestinian public has little respect), and American election campaigns.

Many factors are responsible for the coming of these industrialists, shop-keepers, investors and secretaries. Zionist feeling was in many cases the sole or the chief reason, but the economic depression or, in the case of the younger people, the desire for adventure and change, as well as the existence of jobs in Palestine must very often have turned into reality what might otherwise have long remained a vague plan and aspiration. There are certain groups, however, whose entire cultural life was always so thoroughly Hebraic and Palestinian that their settling in Palestine is the logical outcome of years of psychological preparation. Consider teachers and Hebrew poets, for example.

America has a small group of what are called scientifically trained Jewish educators, and their efficiency in administration and classroom management has already made a contribution to the formal and external aspects of Palestinian education. Back in 1920 when Miss Szold organized the Zionist Department of Education, she brought American experts with her, and up to two or three years ago the head of the Department of Education was an American who battled valiantly with budgetary difficulties, Governmental interference, and unsympathetic teachers suspicious of the English accent in his Hebrew and the substitution of Teachers' College for Talmud in his education. The American influence on Palestinian education, rather ungraciously welcomed though it is, is further strengthened by the fact that American Hebrew teachers have subsidized a chair in Education—filled by an American—at the Hebrew University. Furthermore, a number of former teachers in American Hebrew high schools and a number of Palestinians who did graduate-study in education in America are, as it were, conspiring together to make Palestinian teachers more conscious of the values of discipline and regularity. An American and an American-trained Palestinian have even founded a Junior-Senior High School with elective subjects, vocational guidance, some progressive methods and other American innovations which astonish and irritate the old-guard of believers in the Russian-German type of *gymnasium*.

As for the poets, they are members of a group of hardly more than a dozen individuals who have always had a disproportionately large influence on American-Jewish cultural life; with the exception of one or two who were born in America the rest, born and educated abroad, came here in their late teens or early twenties, still young enough to receive a thorough Western education. One by one, they have been going to Palestine—a phenomenon which caused a distinguished Palestinian poet to remark with some justice that the only immigration restriction he favored would be the refusal to admit any poet unless he brought at least a thousand readers with him. However that may be, the American poets, who generally held fairly good positions in Hebrew education here, are occupied with many tasks besides the writing of poetry; most of them become teachers of English and (in what spare moments are left after correcting themes) translators of novels and plays—by D. H. Lawrence and W. H. Hudson, Shakespeare and Galsworthy and even of such works as "Love on the Dole." One of the poets, a writer of delicate and thoughtful lyrics, has departed from the general pattern and entered upon a way of life which, if he is able to cope with the many difficulties it presents, may prove very fruitful from the literary point of view: he and his family are cultivating their own small orange grove and farm in one of the less centrally located villages.

The lyricist's transition to a new, genuinely Palestinian type of living makes him representative of that considerable minority of American Jews in Palestine who have become an integral—and often significant—part of the Palestinian community at its hardworking best. There are the young Americans who fit successfully into the life of *kvutzot* and *kibbutzim*—as for instance at Naana, Kinneret, Mishmar ha-Emek, or the American Shomer ha-Zair group at Hedera. There are the boys who drove the family-car at home and, by investing a few hundred pounds, now become members of bus cooperatives. By imperceptible degrees they begin to conform to the usual type of Palestinian chauffeur,—those tanned, vigorous, polyglot, highly skilful, intelligent and self-possessed young men whose cooperatives are unusually well-managed and prosperous and who made history quietly during the riots. There are, too, the hundreds of middle-aged Americans who banded together in the United States, who had land bought and cultivated for them cooperatively, and who settle in their homes when their orange groves and fields are beginning to be productive. Their adjustment to agricultural work and new social and climatic conditions is difficult enough, but they are much more fortunate than the usual Palestinian settler in being able to finance the first difficult stages without running hopelessly into debt and wearing themselves out working on their own farms and as hired laborers, simultaneously. The cooperative basis of their settlement is typically Palestinian, but they are not merely remaking their lives according to Palestinian models. On the contrary, they, more than any other American group, are actually bringing some of the best in the American tradition to Palestine.

The outstanding examples of this process are of course Herzliah and Raananah, the Akhuzah settlement in the Sharon. Based on private ownership and hired labor, they yet come much closer to political and economic democracy than any other Palestinian village or town, with the natural exception of the *kvutzot* and *moshavim*. Raananah, the more homogeneous of the two, is popularly referred to as Palestine's model colony, and an example of what may be accomplished even within a capitalistic framework.

Most of the Americans at the head of the Raananah local council were formerly teachers in Hebrew or Yiddish schools (their letters to the press sound impressive even when dealing with roads or sanitation or other prosaic details), but they seem practical enough for all that, and sufficiently strong-willed to carry out their principles. One of the most important of these, the employment of only Jewish labor, is very unusual for a colony specializing in citrus growing, and goes hand in hand with a good relationship with the nearby Arabs.

Raananah is consciously trying to build a Jewish working society in Palestine and that consciousness pervades all phases of its communial life. For instance, it grants the right to vote to every man and woman above the age of twenty-one, whereas there is a fairly high property qualification (in the form of amount of taxes paid for the residence occupied) elsewhere, except in the Labor settlements, of course. The local school is free to every child. In this respect the colony is paralleled only by Tel Aviv where this has been the practice for the last two years. Again, every Raananah settler, whether employer or employee, is enrolled in the Workers' Sick Fund of the Labor Federation so that socialized medicine is the rule in the colony. Many other details of Raananah life have real significance for Palestine but the influence of American universal suffrage and free public education and what the Raananah leaders themselves call the democratic spirit is particularly important as evidence of perhaps the best American contribution to the growth of Palestinian life.

February, 1937

Jordan Valley Authority

by BEN HALPERN

"One may say that man has degraded, profaned the nature of the universe. For what has man done with the elements, the fields, the gardens, the plants . . . ? What do these mean to man . . ? So many measures of grain, of vegetables, of fruit, of wood, of meat, of skins, of feathers, so much working power, and all for a certain price? . . . There must be a radical change in all forms of human life—in dress, homes, workshops, schools, cities, villages, as well as in . . . man's way of gaining a living—in order that man may become integrated into nature. Whatever man does upon, or to the earth—planting, drilling, excavating, building— everything must heighten rather than diminish the beauty and majesty of nature."　　　　　　　　　　　A. D. GORDON.

WHAT WE MAY CALL the conservationist philosophy is a natural attitude for all life, man included. Carnivorous animals rarely kill for sport. Even humans who live on what they kill are careful and conservative in their hunting; they spare females with their young. Primitive tribesmen have a pious awe of the animals they hunt, reverencing them as sacred beings, and performing elaborate rituals in order to make the game, the totemic deities increase. Piety toward nature is equally characteristic of pastoral and peasant peoples. Both pagan Greeks and God-fearing Jews honored the elements, the soil and the springs. Even in war the Hebrews were forbidden to destroy the forests, and in peace they were commanded to observe the ritual of a sabbatical year of rest for their fields.

Yet the history of man is full of destructiveness, of waste and parasitism depleting the earth. The movements of peoples and the fortunes of war have frequently given mastery of urban or peasant civilizations into the hands of nomadic conquerors. Ignorant and scornful of the arts which had conserved the resources of their new subjects, the conquering vandals inevitably brought ruin in their wake. In modern times, exploitative industrialism, heedless of the need to restore to the earth equivalents for the resources its withdraws, often succeeds in wreaking the same havoc as those ancient barbaric invasions.

One of the cardinal points in an effective post-war order will certainly be the conservation and rational use of the world's natural resources, for the common welfare of all the world, as well as of the localities whence they are extracted. This is, above all, an essential part of any plan intended to prevent a new global war. It is also an economic necessity. Through modern transport and finance, mass production and world trade, the resources of every part of the world have become vital to all the rest. Waste, improvident exploitation of the soil, of mineral deposits, of oil, of water, and, not least of all, of human life causes losses felt not only by the country directly involved, but by all those others who depend upon it. This is coming to be realized more and more clearly.

The United States and the other United Nations have subscribed in the Atlantic Charter to the principle that the resources of any region must not be thriftlessly expended solely in the narrowly conceived interest of its immediate owners, but conserved and used in a cooperative program of world-wide development. How far this principle will be put into effect only time will tell. It has already brought about a significant awakening of interest in world resources in all countries, and also among forward-looking Americans.

*   *   *

*Palestine, Land of Promise,** a new book by Walter Clay Lowdermilk, is a product of this interest. Dr. Lowdermilk is the assistant chief of the Soil Conservation Service of the United States. In 1938-9, he was sent to Europe, North Africa, and the Eastern Mediterranean in order to study the effects of wasteful

* Harper & Brothers, 236 pp.

resource exploitation and the problems of soil and water conservation in those centers of ancient civilization.

In Palestine, as in Egypt, Iraq, and North Africa he found that wasteful land use and sheer destructiveness had ravaged the countryside. However, he also found that, unlike the other centers of ancient civilization in the Middle East, large sections of Palestine were being steadily restored by devoted and intelligent care. In Zionism, the force which was accomplishing what he called "the most remarkable (reclamation) we have seen while studying land use in twenty-four countries," Lowdermilk discovered an articulate philosophy which expressed the implicit credo of his own kind of American conservationist and liberal. In Zionism he found a program of action to which he felt he must contribute. And in the plan for a Palestinian counterpart of the Tennessee Valley Authority, which is outlined in his book, Dr. Lowdermilk does indeed make his substantial contribution to the Zionist program, as well as to the further development of Palestine.

The Lowdermilk plan proposes to establish a Jordan Valley Authority, with an assignment similar to that of TVA, for the "unified development" of the Jordan Valley drainage area and the Palestine coastal plan. The most important physical characteristic of the Jordan Valley is that it is the deepest cleft in the earth's surface, running far below sea level for most of its length. The steep drop of the Jordan River itself is already being utilized for hydro-electric power production by the Palestine Electric Company. However, after pouring through the turbines of the power plant on the Jordan, the fresh river water can no longer be used for irrigation at levels above the river bed. If this water were not needed for power, it could be conducted through canals along the hills above the Jordan and Jezreel Valleys, and then brought by gravity to irrigate fields in the valleys below. Lowdermilk's plan proposes to free this fresh water for irrigation by using the water of the Mediterranean Sea for power production purposes. Since the Jordan Valley is only about twenty miles west of Haifa, it is quite feasible to conduct sea water by way of a cement-lined canal and tunnel through the Jezreel and Beisan Valleys to a point 1,200 feet above the Jordan water surface. By setting up hydro-electric plants along this fall, and by using the power potential of the various irrigation schemes proposed for the Jordan River, Palestine could have a supply of at least 1,000,000,000 kilowatt hours of electricity per year. This would supply the needs of "well over a million of additional population."

Like the program of TVA, Lowdermilk's plan calls for "unified development" of all the resources of the region. It provides not only for power and irrigation in the valley, but for soil conservation, swamp drainage, reforestation, improved farming and grazing practice, and industrialization. A rounded program of this type, says Lowdermilk, "will in time make possible the absorption of at least four million Jewish refugees in addition to the 1,800,-000 Arabs and Jews already in Palestine and Trans-Jordan." (p. 227.)

> "If the forces of reclamation and progress Jewish settlers have introduced are permitted to continue, Palestine may well be the leaven that will transform the other lands of the Near East. Once the great undeveloped resources of these countries are properly exploited, twenty to thirty million people may live decent and prosperous lives where a few million now struggle for a bare existence." (p. 229)

• • •

An increased population in Palestine and the Middle East depends on a development plan such as Lowdermilk outlines. *On the other hand, the present population of Palestine or Iraq is neither large enough nor sufficiently skilled to carry out such a program or to operate or even maintain the productive capacity it could develop.*

Palestine and the Middle East were once far more productive and populous than they are now. Instead of one and a half million inhabitants today—after half a century of intensive development by Zionism—Palestine had, at a conservative estimate, a population of three million in ancient times. The decrease in Iraq from the days of ancient Babylon is greater still. The decline in population and culture in the Middle East is so striking that certain geographers have come to the conclusion that some great physical change must have occurred in the area. Ellsworth Huntington* suggests that the ancient Middle East enjoyed a greater rainfall than Palestine and Irak today. He explains the decline of those areas by a climatic change which has made them semi-arid.

Contrary to this supposition, Lowdermilk found no evidence in his studies in the Middle East of a change in climate. Archaeologists showed him ancient water supply installations which still fit present-day water levels and quantity.† Though rainfall has not decreased substantially, the methods of cultivation in use have radically altered. The ancient canals of the Mesopotamian irrigation system have not been tended, and they have become clogged with silt. The terraces of Palestine have been neglected, its forests cut down or ruined by grazing goats. The result has been disastrous soil wash, far greater than would have occurred if terrace cultivation had never been started.

Let us suppose then, that some international agency were to finance and restore the irrigation system of Iraq; or that a Jordan Valley Authority developed a capacity of 1,000,000,000 kilowatt hours yearly, installed irrigation for almost 1,000,000 acres of additional land, resurrected terrace farming, and developed grazing on modern lines in Palestine. The only result, *if we assume that all this were done solely for the present population,* would be a tremendous waste of money. Not only would the present population of Iraq be unable to make full use of the restored canal system but they would be unable to maintain it; and the system would gradually deteriorate again. In Palestine, if immigration were cut off, there would be nobody ready to buy the increase of electric power, to use the irrigation water, or keep the terraces in repair.

The essential basis for any scheme of "unified development" of all the resources of the Middle East—and not merely for the for-

---

* Ellsworth Huntington and S. S. Visher, *Climatic Changes, their Nature and Causes,* New Haven, 1922.
† *Palestine, Land of Promise,* p. 82 ff.

eign exploitation of its soil—is a considerable local increase of population. The Jordan Valley development plan for Palestine is feasible only because we anticipate continued, large-scale Jewish immigration after the war.

*   *   *

In his recent account of the Tennessee Valley Authority, David E. Lilienthal, chairman of that remarkable agency, ascribes much of its success to the intelligent drafting of the statute by which it was chartered and its powers and functions were defined.* The development of Palestine has been both advanced and, in some ways, hampered by the nature of the international compact under which it is administered, the Mandate for Palestine.

This is not the place to examine the language of the preamble to the Mandate or of the Balfour Declaration which it embodies. It may be that in 1922, before it had been clearly demonstrated that the Jews had the will and ability as well as the need to establish themselves rapidly and in large numbers in Palestine, the League of Nations could not have been expected to set down in precise language the main purpose of the Mandate: the creation of a Jewish Commonwealth after Jews should have become a majority. In any case, in the actual administration of the Mandate, British officials evidently did not feel themselves committed to a full-scale development program or to cooperation with the Jews. Their view, apparently, was that it was up to the Jews to prove that such development was possible. The Mandate provided for the creation of the Jewish Agency, the body through which the Jews were to work in making Palestine into a Jewish National Home. The British Administration soon began to act as though it conceived its own function to be the preservation of the *status quo* against alteration by the Jewish Agency.

The Mandate says (article 6):

"The Administration of Palestine, while ensuring that the rights and position of other sections of the population are not prejudiced, shall facilitate Jewish immigration under suitable conditions and

---

**TVA—Democracy on the March,* New York, Harpers, 1944, p. 167 ff.

shall encourage, in co-operation with the Jewish Agency . . ., close settlement by Jews on the land, including State lands and waste lands not required for public purposes."

How the Palestine Administration "facilitated" Jewish immigration into Palestine, has been a subject of much bitter comment, and need not be gone into here once more. The close settlement by Jews on the land was encouraged in the following ways, *inter alia:* the administration did little or nothing to discover water in unsettled parts of Palestine; new Jewish settlements found it very difficult to get roads built to them, and often did this at their own expense; squatters on land newly bought by Jews were given such consideration that a regular racket was developed by some Beduins of driving their herds onto any land Jews bought in their neighborhood and extorting large sums in compensation before they would remove themselves and permit Jewish settlement. As to the use of State lands, wherever Jews and Arabs both applied for concessions to develop such lands, the Arabs got them. Then after failing to improve their concessions, they sold their land to Jews at highly inflated prices, and the improvement finally began.

Such an antagonistic attitude to the Jewish Agency may have been inevitably involved in the way the administration conceived of the Palestine Mandate. It looked at the whole thing as a sort of contest, with itself as umpire. But the umpire in this contest had placed his bets against the Jews—encouraged to do so, to some extent, by the terms of the Mandate. Article 4 of the Mandate empowers the Jewish Agency to act in "such economic, social and other matters as may affect the establishment of the Jewish National Home and the interests of the Jewish population in Palestine, and, subject always to the control of the Administration, to assist and take part in the development of the country." The only thing not included in the terms of reference of the Jewish Agency was to advance the interests of the *non-Jewish* community—and this the Administration took as its special province, interpreting its assignment, often enough, as to protect Arab vested interests against "too rapid" progress by the Jewish Agency.

No "unified development" plan can operate under such conditions. If the TVA had been placed in a similar position, very likely its directors would all have resigned—and with reason. The Jews, however, accepted these terms and they built up whatever parts of the country they could drive their stakes into. But the method can no longer be used. The stage has been reached in Palestine where further progress demands an all-over program for developing the whole country and its essential natural resources. A definite understanding must be reached, redefining the competence of the Jewish Agency on lines similar to the TVA, and endowing it with adequate powers for full development of the soil and water resources of the whole region, and for the reclamation, resettlement, and industrialization of Palestine.

The minimum requirements for the public authority or corporation—to use the TVA set-up—which must do this job are these: First, it must have sole rights, in cooperation with existing local communities and enterprises, to develop all Palestine's resources. It must not have to compete against other concessionaires. Second, its development projects should not be held up by petty racketeers pretending land rights on the basis of one day's grazing, or by individuals refusing to transfer necessary land for a damsite, or a canal, or a swamp drainage scheme. Like any public utility, the corporation should be entitled to buy land through condemnation at a price established by courts. Third, since the importing and training of labor power will be an essential element in the development of Palestine, the corporation directing the whole work must have the right to bring in as many Jewish immigrants as it feels it requires at any stage of its program. Fourth, since the scope of the corporation's program will include improving existing Arab localities as well as new Jewish settlements, its funds cannot all be contributed by Jews or by international agencies aiding Jewish refugees. As in the case of the Huleh development scheme, where a similar situation occurred on a smaller scale, the Palestine government must provide a proportionate part of the necessary means.

The public corporation charged with developing Palestine will obviously have, in addition to the present functions of the Jewish Agency, the duty of raising the standard of production in Arab settlements in conformity with the general plan. It is obvious, therefore, that the Agency will have to revise the policy previously adopted by Jewish bodies with respect to the Arabs. The old policy was based on the restricted authorization given to the Jewish Agency to develop Palestine with respect to areas of Jewish re-settlement, which, at that time, were relatively limited. When given a new charter, both broader and more specific, after the war, the Agency will have to apply generally a type of policy adopted by agreement between the Jewish National Fund and the Palestine Administration in construction work in Arab sections. In such cases a proportionate number of local residents are employed. Like the TVA it will have to cooperate in the resettling of persons, Arab as well as Jewish, who may have transferred their land to make way for development projects. It will have to stimulate by precept and example the adoption of improved forms of cultivation and better social services and living conditions among the Arabs.

To work out methods of cooperation with Arabs in raising their standard of living and production will be an essential task of the Agency. Despite the obvious difficulties, past experience points to two elements which favor success. The development of Palestine will create markets for much greater production; and where this has been the case in the past, Arabs have shown considerable ability to adjust to the new opportunities. Moreover, the plan will establish modern farming and industrial settlements in close proximity to Arabs; and in the citrus and other industries, Arabs have shown the ability to adopt, in due time, the improved methods which the evidence of their own eyes showed to be more profitable than their own old techniques.

The Agency will also have to have an entirely different relation with the Palestine government. The corporation charged with carrying out such a Jordan Valley development plan as Lowder-milk envisages need not be the government of Palestine, but it certainly must have a very close working arrangement with the government. As a development corporation, the Agency will naturally operate during a transition period, long or short as the case may be, and in areas undergoing development. Its ultimate purpose is to hand over to the Palestine government a region supplied with plant for the most efficient use and conservation of its resources, with a better trained population, and social services on a higher level.

In order to accomplish this task, it needs a government fully in sympathy with its goal. Tariff and tax, fiscal and social policy, every phase of government activity must contribute to the goal of development. The old situation, with the Palestine Administration regarding itself as essentially a guardian of vested interests and a necessary check upon the "enthusiasm" of the Jewish Agency, can certainly no longer be tolerated. The government of Palestine during the development period cannot be one which, *ex officio*, questions whether the plan will succeed; it must accept the plan as its own purpose, and direct its own activities upon the assumption that the plan must and will be accomplished.

The first requisite for the acceptance of this viewpoint by the Palestine Administration—and by the Palestine Arabs as well—is the explicit statement that a Jewish majority is to be rapidly settled in Palestine. Without such an understanding the whole Jordan Valley Authority plan has no basis.

May, 1944

Economic Regionalism in the Near East

by EMANUEL NEUMANN

I.

A DISCUSSION such as ours today is necessarily projected against the background of the coming post-war settlement. It is, in fact, inspired by the transcending importance and increasing urgency of that problem. The questions which concern us here must therefore be viewed in perspective and in the wider setting of world reconstruction.

Since World War I we have made some progress in our thinking on international problems. Without accepting the German thesis that Versailles was an unmitigated mixture of malice and stupidity or embracing the Marxist dogma which would reduce all history to the clash of economic forces, it is well to admit and to repeat to ourselves in the light of experience that one of the serious weaknesses of Versailles was its almost total preoccupation with military and political questions to the neglect of vital economic considerations. Actually the only economic provisions of the Peace Treaty were those relating to the exaction of reparations which never materialized.

The neglect of basic economic factors was reflected in the treatment of dependent territories. Thus in establishing the mandate system, the statesmen of the period gave more thought to ensuring equality of commercial opportunity for member states of the League of Nations in the countries to be placed under mandate, than to the problem of promoting the rapid development and economic progress of the mandated territories themselves. Proceeding in practice—though not in theory—on the notion that colonies

(*Address delivered at Conference on Economic Problems of the Near East, under the auspices of the Institute of World Economics, January* 30, 1943, *Roosevelt Hotel, New York City.*)

and mandates were milch-cows, everybody was concerned about securing free and equal access to the cattle without bothering to consider how they should be fed that they might be milked to better advantage.

Today there is a much clearer realization that peace is not a static state of bliss but a dynamic process requiring continuous effort and adjustment—a process in which economic growth and change play a vital if not decisive role. We are beginning to understand that in our contracting world the economies of all peoples everywhere are increasingly interrelated and interdependent, groping their way toward ultimate organic integration. We should therefore welcome the emphasis which forward-looking statesmen and publicists are now placing on the economic aspects of the new world order, on the famous "quart of milk," on the "century of the common man," on raising the subsistence levels of masses of humanity, on the education of backward peoples and the industrial development of backward countries. They are indicative of a deeply fortunate trend that may lead to a final break with an outworn political outlook which saw states but not peoples, which saw nations but not the human beings who composed them, which was hyper-sensitive to splashes of color on the political map, to boundaries and frontiers, but was utterly blind to the homely but vital needs of parched soils, eroded fields and the undernourished humans who tilled them. Surely, the statesmen of the new age must be something more than political cartographers. They must be social and economic engineers in the broadest sense. They must strive to release the energies of man and set his creative forces in full motion, so that social and economic security as well as political security may come to be within the reach of all.

II

These considerations apply with particular force to the continent of Asia. Permit me to quote from a recent address by one of the few American statesmen who know Asia at first hand

—Senator Elbert D. Thomas. He said: "The coming century is likely to be the century of Asia. By that I mean, that in the generations which are to come we shall witness a mighty reawakening of that Mother of Continents which now shelters almost one-half of the whole human race. There is no power on earth which can arrest this process. I for one shall welcome the progress of the peoples of Asia and the attainment of their full stature. But it is a matter of the greatest concern to the Occident and to civilization as a whole that this development shall proceed along democratic lines; that the new Asia which is being created shall be the understanding partner of the Western Democracies in our new world order."

For centuries many Asiatic countries and peoples have been exploited. The blame attaches not to the imperialist powers alone. It attaches in large measure to the inherited social structures, social institutions and traditions and the character of native leadership which have obtained in many parts of Asia and Africa. Consider for instance, the socio-economic implications of the fact that in Egypt today ½% of the population own 57% of the tillable land! The impoverishment of the masses, the stagnation of native agriculture, the decline of native handicrafts, moral and social deterioration where they have taken place—have been too often the joint product of imperialist domination and native exploitation going hand in hand. Progressive Western Powers became involved in a tragic contradiction: strongholds of democracy at home, they were frequently driven by the relentless logic of the imperialist system to align themselves with the forces of reaction in their colonial possessions. If there is to be a genuine change, if we would help Asia attain her full stature as one of our great partners in the world of tomorrow, the unholy alliance between occidental democracy and oriental reaction must be dissolved wherever it may exist. A fresh start must be made predicated upon a community of interest between us and the common people throughout the East and full collaboration with such democratic forces as have been germinating.

Let us now bring into focus the particular corner of the world with which we are concerned today. From the papers already presented it is abundantly evident that the Near East, considered as a region, is richly endowed with natural resources and with great potentialities for agricultural development, industry and commerce. There is plenty of oil and coal. There are large deposits of iron, copper, chrome, potash, magnesium, bitumen, bromine, phosphates—to name only some of them. There are vast stretches of fertile but uncultivated land and the water with which to irrigate them. However, despite its natural wealth and immense possibilites, the region taken as a whole is still underpopulated, underdeveloped, with large masses of its inhabitants constantly ravaged by disease and perpetually on the brink of starvation.

It is not only in the interest of the indigenous populations but of civilization as a whole that these conditions be altered. Any region so richly endowed and so strategically situated at the juncture of three continents—but also so weak, so backward and so underpopulated, is bound to constitute a low pressure area generating international storms. For centuries it has, in fact, offered a standing invitation to military and political adventurers from Alexander the Great to Hitler the Mad. It will continue to be a danger zone and a source of septic infection in international relations unless it is strengthened through social and economic regeneration and stabilized by its mounting strength.

Despite the importance of this task from the broad international point of view, little constructive thought has been applied to the problem thus far. At Versailles and thereafter the solution of the Near Eastern question was conceived in political terms, leaving the basic and underlying economic problems almost untouched. To be sure the political settlement itself represented a great advance and gave a certain impulse to economic life, even though indirectly. But the rate of progress has been slow and wholly incommensurate with the possibilities. Turkey alone broke its fetters and as a result of the Kemalist revolution forged ahead at an astonishing pace. Something similar, though on a modest scale, happened also in Palestine through the efforts of the Zionist movement and the enterprise of Jewish settlers. But on the whole the masses of the Near East on the outbreak of the present war were not much further along than at the close of the last war.

Out of the ferment which the present crisis has induced only one idea has thus far emerged, that of Arab or Near Eastern federation—again a political idea. For reasons which need not be elaborated here, the establishment of a voluntary political union is not more likely in the Near East than it is, let us say, among the countries of Latin America, or even among the Scandinavian nations, despite physical proximity, ties of kinship and definite cultural bonds. Parenthetically, the contribution which the principle of regional political federation in general can make to world peace and stability may easily be overrated. It is conceivable that the creation of increasingly large blocs may aggravate rather than cure the world's malady and make for bigger and better wars. Suffice it to recall that at least one "federal union"—namely the German Reich!—was conceived in militarism, was born in a war of aggression and plunged the world into the abyss in 1914 and again in 1939.

But the remoteness of voluntary political union in the Near East need not prevent or even retard economic cooperation and economic regionalism. On the contrary, economic cooperation planned, organized and systematically pursued may pave the way for political union, which may come eventually as the mature fruit of organic growth. No less an authority than Lawrence of Arabia expressed a similar view in the following words: "When people talk of Arab confederations or empires, they talk fantastically. It will be generations, I expect—unless the vital tempo of the East is much accelerated—before any two Arabic states join voluntarily. I agree their only future hope is that they should join but it must be a natural growing-together. Forced unions are pernicious; and politics, in such things, should come after geography and economics."

III.

What are the prospects for economic regionalism in the Near East?

To approach the question realistically we should bear in mind certain negative or limiting factors. The first and most important is the circumstance that the habit and practice of cooperation are not strong in that part of the world. This is illustrated by the fact that the cooperative movement, which has made considerable strides in India and China, has thus far made little headway in the Near East.

Secondly: Such economic development as has been taking place has tended to strengthen commercial relations with overseas countries rather than among the Near Eastern countries themselves.

Thirdly: From time immemorial the lands and peoples bordering on the Mediterranean looked to the West quite as much as to the East. They were part of the Mediterranean world and plied their commerce to the pillars of Hercules and beyond. It will be recalled that Christianity, born in Palestine, spread westward rather than to the East, following well established lines of communication. There is a considerable difference between the countries bordering on the Mediterranean—Egypt, Palestine, Lebanon and Turkey on the one hand and those lying further East and South, on the other. The former have been more continuously exposed to Western influences and the results are evident in their more advanced economy. They are in fact on the periphery of Europe while the others are more definitely Asian.

Fourthly: Whereas in more advanced areas the reduction of tariff barriers and the establishment of a customs union would ordinarily be regarded as the most important and substantial step toward achieving economic regionalism, the same measures need not necessarily produce comparable results in the Near East. In the case of countries with modern and industrialized economies, the removal of tariff barriers may be expected to stimulate and accelerate the exchange of goods and services to a marked degree.

But the economy of the Near East, which is still preponderantly agrarian in character and semi-feudal in form, is not likely to respond so vigorously to such measures. The great money crop of Egypt is cotton; that of Palestine, oranges; of Iraq, dates. The markets for these crops are found not in the Near East but in overseas countries. The same holds true, for that matter, of Iraq oil and Palestine potash. By comparison with these important exports to the outside world, the internal trade of the Near East is light, though war conditions have given it a temporary fillip.

The conclusion to be drawn is not that revision of tariff arrangements on the basis of reciprocal advantage is undesirable or that there is little basis for economic regionalism. The conclusion to be drawn is rather than in the case of the Near East a more fundamental task of a more primary character lies ahead, the task of increasing the production both of agriculture and industry, while providing consciously and deliberately for a greater internal exchange of goods to supplement and balance exports to overseas markets.

So far as agriculture is concerned, a large increase in production is entirely feasible. With the single exception of Egypt where every inch of irrigable and arable soil is irrigated and cultivated, very slight use has been made of the very considerable possibilities for irrigation in many other countries, notably Iraq,. That ancient land was once the home of great empires with populations several times as large as that of modern Iraq. It was the wanton destruction of the complex and highly developed irrigation system, which had been laboriously built up over many centuries, by the Mongol hordes of Genghis Khan that ruined the agriculture and destroyed the civilization of the land and set it on its downward course. But with the aid of modern technology, a far more efficient system of irrigation can replace the old not only in Iraq but in Syria, in Palestine and in other parts of the Near East, with a consequent intensification of agriculture and a steady rise in production and in standards of living.

But the Near East must not be content to depend upon a pastoral and agrarian economy. Its natural resources, its raw materials, the presence of coal in Turkey and oil in Iraq offer inviting opportunities for industrial development. It has been the misfortune of colonial and so-called backward countries—and even parts of the United States—that their wealth has been shipped out in form of raw materials to be processed abroad, leaving the people hardly any better off than they were before. It is only by learning to process their raw materials and to convert them into finished or semi-finished products that the peoples of the Near East may begin to profit substantially from the natural wealth with which their lands have been endowed.

That so-called backward peoples can acquire modern techniques, though with varying degrees of success, has already been proved beyond a doubt. To be sure, the industrialization of the Near East cannot be expected to proceed at an equal pace in all countries. For the reasons I have already mentioned and other reasons, the countries on the Mediterranean littoral are bound to make more rapid strides in that direction than the others. However, even the inland Arabs, though poor in organizing ability, are possessed of a quick intelligence. What is required in their case as a first step towards industrialization is a modern and extensive educational system with particular attention to training in the arts and crafts, the establishment of trade schools and technical colleges. It will take time for them to make the transition from an oriental agrarian and nomadic tradition to the modern outlook and habits of work; but with help from the outside, the process can be accelerated. Already American educational institutions, like the University at Beyrut, have given a considerable impetus in that direction. So has the spectacular success achieved by the Jews in Palestine through the application of modern techniques.

In addition to the intensification of agriculture and the rise of industry, the third great factor in the economic future of the Near East is to be found in the possibilities of trade and commerce. In the ancient world, the countries of the Near East took advantage of their favored geographic position. The great trade routes of antiquity passed through these lands. For the most part it was the Orient that supplied the undeveloped West with industrial products and the refinements of civilization. Silks, spices and precious stones from the East were exchanged for the cruder products of the West. Upon that trade the people of the Levant grew prosperous. They developed shipping. The Phoenicians were as prominent in the carrying trade of antiquity as the Norwgeians are today. There is no reason why a great commercial development should not take place once more. Beyond the Near East is a vast hinterland which includes Persia, Afghanistan and the teeming millions of India and China. Great world markets are spread out to the north and south as well as to the east and west; and the whole of Asia, the greatest potential market of all, is on the threshold of a great awakening. It would be a backward people, indeed, that would neglect the immense opportunities which lie in store.

IV.

But these and other possibilities can be realized only in small part by the peoples and countries of the Near East acting individually and separately rather than by concerted effort. It is only by pooling or combining their natural and technical resources, by making full use of potentialities which are inherent in the region as a region, that the prosperity of each country and of all of them together can be greatly enhanced. Consider for a moment the agricultural sphere and the vital role of artificial irrigation in these semi-arid lands. There are ample water resources in the surface streams alone, not to speak of subterranean waters. But rivers know no political boundaries. The Euphrates flows through Syria as well as Iraq. The watershed of the Jordan is in the Lebanon, as the head waters of the Nile are in the Sudan. The proper control and fullest utilization of these and other streams offer scope for joint planning and joint operation in many instances. Similarly, the agriculture, and animal husbandry of one country may profit by the experimentation and advanced methods developed by its neighbors. Agricultural experiment stations and research laboratories of one may render invaluable service to the others, once the machinery as well as the habit of cooperation is built up.

The possibilities of such fruitful cooperation are, if anything, even greater in the industrial field. The phosphates found in Transjordan may be processed in Palestine and spread upon the fields of Iraq to increase their fertility; while the oil of Iraq may give rise to important chemical industries in the Lebanon or Palestine. The hydro-electric potential of the Quattara depression may be used by Egypt to produce cheap power for an electro-chemical industry, based upon the minerals of the Dead Sea. Or hydro-electric energy produced in Iraq or in Palestine may be transmitted across the border into Syria for industrial purposes, just as Switzerland furnishes power to the cities of southern Germany. Egyptian cotton and Turkish wool offer the possibility of a large textile and clothing industry in Syria and Palestine, while the cottonseed may provide material for important plastics industries. And what cannot be done with the coal and iron of Anatolia? Once a beginning is made in the systematic study of such possibilities, endless vistas of industrial development would be opened up through intelligent cooperation and a steady exchange of goods and services.

The regional approach is equally valid in the field of commerce and shipping. Iraq has the port of Basra. Transjordan has an undeveloped port at Akaba on the Red Sea. Palestine has Haifa and the Lebanon, Beyrut. Egypt has Alexandria and Port Said, with the Suez Canal passing through its territory, while Turkey sits astride the Dardanelles. Taken together, the possibilities of all of them in the direction of international trade are almost unlimited. But common planning and cooperation is an indispensable prerequisite. For one thing, the facilities for internal overland communications and transport must be vastly improved. For many years rail communication from Egypt along the Medit-

erranean coast to Constantinople was incomplete owing to a gap
›etween Haifa in Palestine and Tripoli in Syria. It was only last
·ear, because of the exigencies of war, that this gap was closed.
There is economic justification for the development of Akaba into
.n important port but Transjordan cannot do it alone. Improved
onections between Akaba and Tel Aviv would help. Such in-
·tances can be multiplied without end. Nor is there any reason
vhy with proper organization and cooperation between the com-
nercial interests of several countries a considerable shipping and
·arrying trade should not be developed. Substantial shipments of
·gyptian cotton, Palestine potash and citrus fruits are carried in
·oreign bottoms. A Near Eastern merchant fleet could carry these
.nd other products to Western Europe and return laden with
;oods imported in exchange.

There is yet another highly important form which regional
:ooperation may take. It is in the joint financing of great public
vorks which are regional rather than local in scope and character.
.mportant engineering projects could be undertaken, of great
›otential benefit to several countries. They may be beyond the
inancial resources of one of them acting on its own, but not
›eyond the capacity of two or three if they pooled their
inancial strength in a joint enterprise. This may apply to irriga-
ion projects and reclamation schemes, to the improvement of
·ivers and harbors, to flood control, to hydro-electric projects and
·mproved networks of roads and railways. The combined credit
›f several Near Eastern countries may bring such projects within
he range of financial possibility.

V.

How is a beginning to be made?

I have already cautioned against underestimating social and
historical forces militating against such cooperation. There are
›ther negative factors one might enumerate. But as against cen-
rifugal tendencies there are also powerful centripetal forces

whose operation is no less potent. These forces are more in need of guidance than stimulation. Moral and intellectual energies now being expended and dissipated in unprofitable political discussions in the Near East can be channelized and directed to more productive ends. The excessive preoccupation with "politics" which animates the bazaar and the village cafe is largely the reflex of the rivalries and intrigues of the Great Powers and their endless political maneuverings. If these Powers could moderate their rivalries, if they ceased moving their pawns about on the chessboard of the Near East and applied themselves instead to promoting economic development and cooperation, favorable results would not fail to appear.

At the moment America more than any other country holds the key and may furnish the answer. This is so because there is more confidence in American justice and disinterestedness and also because American statesmen have been conspicuous in evolving new conceptions in international relations. But we, too, must come to the task with clean hands. We should scrupulously avoid the game of geo-politics, which is another name for power politics, and substitute for it the science of geo-economics. Geo-politics is bound up with the pernicious doctrine of *Lebensraum*. Its aims are imperialism and exploitation. The geo-economic approach is based upon free cooperation and mutuality of interest. Little good can come of merely re-drawing the maps, inflating dynastic ambitions, or effecting new political combinations and regroupings which would give nothing of substantial benefit to native masses but would provide new streamlined instruments of power politics. These are old methods and conceptions which run counter to the new democratic strategy we are trying to evolve.

With America taking the initiative I would propose that the United Nations establish an International Commission to aid in the economic development of the Near East. At the same time the peoples of the Near East should be encouraged to establish an Economic Development Council as an instrument of uncoerced cooperation in which all elements, races and faiths and all legitimate economic interests shall be adequately and effectively represented. Such a council should be a non-political body, having no legislative functions and devoting itself exclusively to economic problems. These two organs, the Near East Commission of the United Nations and the Near East Development Council, should cooperate to the following ends:

1. To study continuously and thoroughly all the resources of the Near East, including its human resources and its various potentialities;

2. To stimulate the utilization of the natural resources as well as the adoption of measures for improving the health and education of the masses;

3. To encourage the maximum "internal" exchange of raw materials, finished goods, scientific data and technical assistance;

4. To promote public engineering projects which in their nature must cross boundary lines, linking two or more countries in a common enterprise;

5. To work out the mechanism by which the financial and technical assistance of the more advanced countries may be made available for the benefit of the Near East on a non-imperialist basis.

Such a program will incidentally help to solve some of the thorny political problems of the Near East. If carried out even in part it will generate a new atmosphere even while creating new living space for present and future populations. In Saudi Arabia and Iraq, Syria, Lebanon, Palestine and Transjordan—where some twenty million people now subsist largely in penury and squalor —there will easily be room for forty or fifty million people in years to come. There will be room and to spare for the Arabs and their descendants, for the Christian groups in Lebanon and Iraq, as well as for millions of Jews in Palestine. The Moslem states of Syria, Iraq and Arabia, Christian Lebanon and Jewish Palestine can grow and flourish side by side to the mutual advantage of all and renew the ancient glories of this cradle of civilization. Where there is poverty, ignorance and oppression there are also jealousies and bitter enmity; but suspicion and hostility can be transmuted into friendly cooperation through a common interest in common objectives.

March, 1943

EUROPE

Hannah Arendt

Sholem Asch

Ch. N. Bialik

Leon Blum

B. Z. Dinaburg

Mala Gitlin

Vassili Grossman

H. Leivick

Kadya Molodowska

David Pinski

Charles Reznikoff

Marie Syrkin

The Gentlemen at Bermuda

Editorial

BERMUDA IS a pretty place, especially at Easter time. There are lilies, sunshine, and fine sea bathing. Tire business-men, school-teachers and tourists used to make their reservations at the excellent hotels which the island affords, particularly during Easter week when the Atlantic retreat is at its loveliest. Since the war, things are different. It is not so easy to go to Bermuda these days, unless, of course, you happen to be a government representative going on an official mission. Then you can still go to Bermuda. You can still admire the lilies on Easter Sunday on the way to Church. You also have a chance to get away from it all under the pleasantest surroundings. No one will be able to follow you to Bermuda—no one who may ask embarrassing questions, no one whose voice is too tense with agony, no one whose face may haunt you afterwards.

The gentlemen at Bermuda have had their vacation. They were blessedly undisturbed by any "pressure group." They were guarded from the representatives of Jewish organizations who had worked out concrete plans for the possible salvation of the remaining human beings marked for murder in Hitler's slaughter house. They were protected from representatives of American labor who indicated their desire to participate in the humanitarian enterprise of the Conference. Both Philip Murray of the C. I. O. and William Green of the A. F. L. have made public the refusal of the Government to admit officers of these great American labor organizations to deliberations.

One voice from which the individuals who participated in the Refugee Conference were particularly careful to insulate themselves was that of the hundreds of thousands of helpless men, women and children doomed to be murdered in cold blood by the Nazi executions. While the Bermuda Conference was in session, the secret Polish radio appealed for help in an underground broadcast from Poland. The broadcast pleaded: "The last 35,000 Jews in the ghetto at Warsaw have been condemned to execution. Warsaw again is echoing to musketry volleys. The people are murdered. Women and children defend themselves with their naked arms. Save us . . ." At this point, the station went dead.

"Save us . . ."—that cry did not reach Bermuda. Even before the Conference made its report, consisting of a "number of concrete recommendations," none of which has been made public, it was obvious that no serious rescue program was under consideration. This was plain from the outset. It was plain from the locality selected for the deliberations, from the exclusion of the representatives of those most concerned, and from the secrecy. Above all, it was plain from the funereal croakings which accompanied the deliberations. The delegates chosen for a mission to save lives in the most literal sense went at their task in the spirit of undertakers.

From the first day of the Conference, the meager press releases warned against any high hopes for refugee aid. The United States and British delegations agreed at once that any large scale migration of refugees was out of the question. Mr. Richard K. Law, head of the British delegation, stated that "one must not be betrayed by feelings of humanity and compassion into a course of action which will be likely to postpone the day of liberation." Dr. Harold Willis Dodds, President of Princeton University and head of the American delegation, announced that "The solution to the refugee problem is to win the war." These are impeccable sentiments; unfortunately, their relevance is not clear.

No one disputes the fact that the successful prosecution of the war is the first objective of the United Nations, and that nothing must be done to impede victory. However, none of the detailed rescue programs presented by responsible organizations to the Bermuda Conference could in any way be viewed as conflicting with the primary purpose. Would opening the gates of Palestine beyond the restrictions of the White Paper harm the war effort? Would the granting of havens in neighboring countries hurt any one except the Nazis? Would the adequate utilization of the United States immigration quotas permitted by law "postpone the day of liberation?" Only a small fraction of the 153,000 persons who may be admitted annually into the United States have actually entered. Only 39,389 persons were admitted during 1942. A hundred thousand more human beings could have entered without increasing the total number of immigrants permitted by the present immigration restrictions, if the procedures had been relaxed to permit the application of an unused quota from a given country to that of another where refugees are begging for help. If cargo vessels which now return from their destinations with empty bottoms were to be used for the transportation of human beings each one of whom, depending on age and sex, would be a passionate worker and fighter for democracy, would that be injurious to the cause of the United Nations?

The questions answer themselves. The trouble with the gentlemen at Bermuda was not that they were too martial, but that they were not martial enough. They were afflicted not only with inhumanity, but with timidity and the fatal appeasement blindness for which the world has already paid so dearly. Enough of the proceedings at the Bermuda Conference has leaked out to enable us to gauge the course of events.

At first the Conference apparently discussed the possibility of setting up temporary havens in French North Africa, Cyrenaica and Ethiopia. But at the last minute, even this compromise decision was scrapped. According to the *New York Times* (April 28), "It could not be learned whether the American delegation had refused to allow settlement of refugees in French North Africa or the British had rejected the idea of providing a temporary refuge in Cyrenaica and the Divedawa area of Ethiopia. These were the three regions the delegates were understood to have discussed."

So there we have it. Keep the doomed from the Jewish National Home because Arab fascists might not like it. Don't let them into the United States within the quotas permitted because Hamilton Fish and Father Coughlin might not like it. Scrap even the possibility of sanctuaries in French North Africa because pro-

Vichy anti-Semites, who have been so notable an asset to the battle against Hitler, might not like it. Disregard the protests of the Christian church, of American labor, of every decent, liberal element in the country; disregard the conscience of civilized mankind now on trial, and cower before the howls of notorious pro-fascists. That is the way to win the war, and to make victory worthwhile.

There was one Jew at the Bermuda Conference—Congressman Sol Bloom, Chairman of the House Foreign Affairs Committee. He was a safe, helpful Jew for the gentlemen of Bermuda to have in their midst—a political observer who, it is alleged, has frequently stated that "there is no Jewish Problem." Obviously, a Jew blessed with this astigmatism was the ideal spokesmen of a tortured people. Congressman Bloom cast no discordant note into the sell-out at Bermuda. Referring to the carefully worked out proposals for rescue presented by the Joint Committee on European Affairs, Bloom sagely remarked: "You can't settle such problems in a Madison Square Garden Mass Meeting." Now the gentlemen at Bermuda can claim before the world that a representative of the chief victims of Nazi savagery concurred in their deliberations. Was not Congressman Bloom speaking for the children gassed daily in the lethal chambers and shot down in the narrow ghetto streets? When his voice joined the chorus of undertakers, was not that the sanction of the martyrs themselves? The living, as well as the dead, were buried in Bermuda, and the Jewish Congressman added his spade of earth.

Hitler has won another victory at Bermuda—a moral and political victory in which Nazidom rejoices. Every reactionary who wants the purposes of the United Nations defeated has triumphed in the failure at Bermuda. The so-called Refugee Conference has made a mockery, not only of the agony of millions of helpless human beings, but of the great cause of liberation to which the democratic world is committed, and which alone makes the horror of our time understandable and endurable.   May, 1943

Passover—1944

by Kadya Molodowska

TONIGHT IS PASSOVER; the moon is full.
Twelve plates are on the table, but the chairs
Wait empty.
They did not come. They fell along the way
Fleeing for shelter to some hiding place,
Or else—who knows—the wolves tore them apart.

Enter, Elijah; do not take it ill
Because my chair shakes strangely back and forth.
I am not drunk—I sit upon a chair
Fashioned of grief, charred embers, splintered wood,
And so it shakes without my wish or will.

The door is open; you are in the room.
I know your presence by the ancient sign:
A silver vapor rises from your cup,
And, slowly, low and lower sinks the wine.

But all those other glasses stand untouched.
Full to the brim, they awe and terrify;
Never shone glass with such a dreadful light.
Elijah, lean upon my shaking chair,
And lead the sorrow-seder of this night.

Your garment grows more visible and bright.
Soon I will see you in your majesty.
I am accustomed now for many a month
To welcome shadowy visitors who come
Each evening to my home.

They come whenever I dare close my eyes.
My heart grows hard with pain.
Elijah, lift your hand; appear in power,
And in this hallowed hour
Now prophesy of them.

They are not dry bones lying in a vale.
Their wounds are fresh; their agony is near.
Now prophesy of them who did not come
To sit beside us at the seder here.

"Pour out Thy wrath"—we know the words by heart.
"Avenge Thy people, God"—we pray each year.
Elijah, succor us who grieve.
It is the hour, the eve.
Bring tidings, speak
The promise of the Lord.
Foretell
The plague,
The pestilence,
The sword.

The table lengthens and grows wide.
They have come in. They sit on every side,
Come to demand the keeping of the vow.
All, all are with us now.

Who of us is the living, who the dead—
We, saved by chance, or they?
We sit together now and wait the oath.
Elijah, celebrate
A seder for us both.

Translated from the Yiddish
BY MARIE SYRKIN

The Flag on the Ghetto Wall

by MARIE SYRKIN

ONE OF the first acts of Jewish resistance to the Nazi onslaught occurred in 1933. It was slight, pitiful and hardly to be noticed; it lingers in the memory only because of its helplessness and pathos.

When Hitler came into power and first introduced the anti-Jewish decrees, the world was still sufficiently astonished to bother reading accounts of the earliest discriminatory acts against Jews. No doubt some yet recall the genuine shock occasioned by stories which seem mild and almost benevolent in retrospect. One American correspondent cabled an account of a forced march of Jews with derisive placards on their backs through the streets of Berlin. Such an occurrence seems hardly worth mentioning today, but a decade ago it made an impression, even though the marchers were not being murdered but merely beaten and humiliated. The correspondent described an incident which struck him as particularly poignant: a little Jewish girl kept running alongside her feeble grandfather who was trying to keep up with the march; as she ran, she would hit at the stormtrooper who was prodding her grandfather. The Nazi did not strike the child, and the onlookers for a moment seemed ashamed.

The picture of the child's frail hands trying to beat back the Nazi remains etched in the memory like the face of the weeping Frenchman caught by a news-reel shot of the Nazi's triumphal entry into Paris, or that of the Czech peasant woman lifting one hand in a "Heil" as the Nazis marched past, while pressing a handkerchief to her eyes with the other. The tortured faces of the Czech peasant and the Parisian were snapped by a reporter's camera and have become immortal. They are a part of contemporary history. The little Jewish girl running alongside her grandfather was not photographed, but she too lives in the imagination.

381

There was valor in her small hands as well as helplessness. Above all, there was symbolism. Such has been the spiritual innocence and the physical weakness of the Jewish minority before the barbarians.

In the black decade that has elapsed since the little girl ran along a Berlin street, every aspect of the picture has grown immeasurably grimmer. The Jews that marched in the procession of shame have, most of them, been murdered. If the little girl was not subsequently rescued by a visa, she too has probably been choked in a lethal chamber or thrust into a mass grave by the very storm-trooper who ten years ago could still feel an impulse of compunction. And of valor—the attempt to strike at the enemy with one's weak, bare hands—little has been heard; so little that many in the free world wondered uneasily whether the spirit of resistance had been wholly crushed.

Within the last months, however, reports have come of the grim, foredoomed battle waged by the Jews of the Warsaw ghetto. And in the course of those reports intimations have appeared of a continuous organized attempt to foster the will to resist, of which we have been insufficiently aware. The heroic last stand of the Warsaw ghetto was not a sporadic desperate flare-up. It was the climax of an organized struggle which began when the barbed wires first enclosed the Jews of Warsaw, separating them from the world outside. The stages of that struggle constitute a somber epic for which history has no parallel.

I have before me the map of the Warsaw Ghetto as it was first established. The names of some of the districts are familiar: *Nalewki, Twarda, Gliniana* and others. As teeming centers of East European Jewish life, they have entered into folk-lore and literature. We have read about them; we have fed on them. From those streets have come illumination as well as poverty, wisdom as well as squalor. But on October 16, 1940, brick walls and barbed wire fences shut off the zone of Jewish residence from the rest of the world.

As one reads the elaborate set of regulations and decrees drawn up by the Nazis for the conduct of life in the ghetto, one wonders why they bothered issuing ordinance after ordinance to give a pseudo-legal aspect to their spoliations and killings. The predetermined Nazi program of mass murder was to begin in less than two years; in the light of that knowledge, the stubborn effort of the 500,000 Jews penned within the ghetto to maintain some human standard of existence assumes an even more heroic and tragic character.

October 1940 to May 1943—that was to be the life span of the Warsaw ghetto. Today one reads with awe of that Jewish Council, headed by Adam Czerniakow, which served in the dual role of collective hostage and sole intermediary between the ghetto and the Nazi authorities. It was the members of the Council who had to execute the orders of the enemy; it was they whose lives hung daily in the balance if there were any infractions of a Nazi edict; and it was they who had to organize some kind of an economic, religious and cultural life within the ghetto prison. These men were, in their way, frontline fighters from the beginning and should be honored as such.

We are amply informed as to the physical conditions of life in the ghetto. We know of the systematic starvation—as a prelude to the systematic murder—of the epidemics of typhus without medication, of the unheated hovels in which the population froze and perished, of the incredible misery to which the community had been reduced. The Nazi masters themselves have left complacent accounts of life in the ghetto to which no Jewish journalist need add. But what is less well known is the extraordinary struggle waged in that wretchedness to preserve dignity and hope.

In the *Gazeta Zydowska*, the official paper of the Ghetto published in Polish three times weekly, one can read many German ordinances like the one which specifies that each one-window room must accommodate *no less than three and a half persons*. If one had no other source of information, that would be enough for the least imaginative to get some notion of the congestion in the ghetto. What, however, is less familiar is that outside these one-window rooms, the inhabitants strove to plant window-boxes so that some green blade might spring for the people to see, or perhaps a tomato or a radish for some child to eat. And as late as 1942, hundreds of Jewish boys and girls studied agriculture in classes organized by the *Toporol* (Society for the Promotion of Agriculture among Jews). The sole places where the knowledge of the students could be employed were apartment house courtyards or balconies. The truck-farming diligently taught and studied had no place to flourish save some dingy corner of the narrow ghetto streets, but who will doubt that every leaf that managed to grow on such a plot was a banner of defiance?

The titles of the various courses organized by the Council make strange and bitter reading now. There were classes in engraving and watch-making, leather-work and architectural drafting. There was even a class in "cosmetics"—perhaps the most sadly ironic course of all. What dreams of liberation must have sustained the students, what expectations of new worlds where these laboriously acquired skills could be tried! All this went on in the midst of a shifting population to which fresh thousands of Jews from Germany or other parts of Poland were constantly being added, to replace those who were perishing each hour of disease, starvation and violence.

At the same time, the effort to distribute whatever food and medical care was available continued. Soup kitchens, nurseries, and clinics were established. 120,000 persons received a plate of soup every day. That was their principal meal. The mortality rate kept soaring, of course, according to the Nazi plan, and the medical knowledge of the great Jewish physicians serving in the "clinics" could be of little use in the presence of famine without relief and epidemic disease without medicines. Nevertheless at the same time, be it remembered, there were three Yiddish theaters in the ghetto, and one Polish theater. Occasionally there were even symphonic concerts, though no doubt most of the musical instruments—as everything else of value—had been stolen by the Germans. What means the musicians and artists incarcerated in the ghetto devised to maintain the spirit of the people remains to be told. And in the midst of the horror, a Jewish scholar wrote learned articles on the roots of Jewish optimism in the *Gazeta Zydowska,* while little Jewish children composed poems of faith in the essential goodness of man—poems which can be read today in the bleak pages of the ghetto newspaper.

This greatness irritated the Germans. Despite the infliction of every misery and physical degradation, they had not succeeded in the essential degradation. Those Jews who managed to survive were intent on creating something in the abyss—something which angered and frightened the Nazi thugs. Every precious value of the human spirit—intellect, magnanimity, belief in a moral order —was still rising out of the depths to challenge the zoological world of the Nazi.

Finally, the Germans dropped the shabby mask of ordinances and edicts, of "legal" executions, and the wholesale assassinations began. No need any more for Jewish journalists to pore over the vital statistics released by the Nazis and deplore the astronomic mortality rate and the infinitesimal birth-rate. No need any more to force oneself to read the accounts of little children shot down for sport by Nazi marksmen or thrown down sewer drains. For the Jews of the Warsaw ghetto all this is over, but before they went down, the Jews of the ghetto wrote a page in the history of our time which for agony has no counterpart in this war.

When the "liquidation" of the ghetto through systematic murder began in the summer of 1942, the human beings within its walls believed that the "civilized" world would not let crime on so monstrous a scale go unchallenged. They believed, in their artlessness, that the United Nations, the Church, all humanity above the level of the beast, would find a way to help. This we know from the few who escaped to tell their story. When Adam Czerniakow, the mayor of the ghetto, killed himself rather than fill the daily quota of Jews to be shipped for murder in the "extermination centers," there was the hope that the news of his suicide would in-

form those outside the ghetto walls of the reality of the unbelievable. However, as the knowledge grew that the world would as-
suage its conscience with resolutions of sympathy, that nothing
would be done, the messages that continued to come through the
underground changed in tone. They no longer pleaded primarily
for help; instead they demanded arms. "At least send us arms, so
that we can die fighting."

We know that somehow arms came. We know, through the
underground radio, that the last 35,000 Jews in the ghetto managed to barricade themselves in their homes and give battle to their
murderers. The day came when the Nazi slaughter-squads faced
men and women and children who were able to fight back instead
of letting themselves be herded helplessly into sealed trains or
lethal chambers. The defenders of the ghetto all died. Their
cause was lost at the outset, but hundreds of Nazis were killed and
wounded in the course of the battle.

The details of the struggle cannot be told now. How the arms
came, how the resistance was organized remains for some future
chronicler. We do not know the names of the heroes, and we cannot pin medals on their breasts—even posthumously. But here
and there a figure emerges. We all know the names of Adam
Czerniakow, and of Zygielbojm who killed himself in London in
protest against the indifference of the world. To these names we
can now add that of Zivia Lubetkin, "The Mother."

Zivia, "The Mother," (*die mame*) was not old, nor did she
have children of her own. She lost her life, at the age of 28, as a
leader of the ghetto's final battle. Young as she was, she was the
"mother," by virtue of strength and solicitude, of the crushed,
the abandoned, the helpless.

Before the establishment of the ghetto, Zivia had been known
only as an active and devoted member of Hekhalutz. She had
lived in a Hekhalutz collective. She was a good comrade and a
hard worker. When the incarceration began, this simple young
girl rose to heroic stature. She had the opportunity to escape—an
opportunity of which men, older and better known than she, did

not hesitate to avail themselves—but she chose to share the lot of that great majority who could not flee. She was conscious not of her destiny, but of her task, and her task became her destiny. She knew that one way of preventing the inner disintegration of the ghetto youth was to preserve the form of the collective as far as possible. At first, the Nazis permitted the functioning of the Hekhalutz groups. After these were disbanded, Zivia and her comrades made every effort to maintain the spirit of collective action. When the youth of the ghetto was taken for slave labor, members of the same collective groups would try to go together so as to maintain bonds of unity. When the schools for the children were shut down, Zivia organized secret groups of volunteer teachers, who would go from hovel to hovel to maintain morale even at a foodless table in an unheated room. Those who had read the poems of the ghetto children months earlier knew that there was a Zivia in their midst. Someone was religiously tending the flame of the human spirit in an animal environment. Someone was consciously trying to preserve the young from ultimate corruption by the oppressor.

There was another task that Zivia set herself. There were other ghettos besides that of Warsaw scattered throughout Poland. Contact between these islands of misery had to be established, so that the doomed within should feel less helpless and forsaken. Zivia did not look Jewish. With the assistance of Polish underground groups, she and two other Jewish girls were furnished with Polish passports. It was death to be caught leaving the Ghetto, but Zivia took the risk and travelled secretly from ghetto to ghetto bringing information, directives and hope. An "angel" means merely "messenger"; she was that messenger.

When the mass-deportations for murder began and it became clear that no measure of courage or endurance would suffice, Zivia, just as she had organized for life, began to organize for death. The uprising was carefully planned. We know that Zivia and her comrades, with assistance from the Polish underground, were the leaders. The tactics of guerrilla warfare were employed. Trenches

JEWISH FRONTIER ANTHOLOGY

were dug, and each of the 35,000 fought in cellars and behind barricaded streets. The Nazis had to bring in light tanks, artillery, incendiary bombs and gas, before the last ruin of the ghetto stopped smoldering. We are told that the battle lasted three weeks, beginning in April and ending in May. They are three weeks that will not be forgotten in Jewish history.

There is another circumstance that we must note. The defenders raised a flag to fly from the Ghetto wall. It was the Jewish flag—the Star of Zion.

We know from the poems of the children published in the *Gazeta Zydowska* how much the hope of Palestine, of redemption, had helped to make the horrors of daily living seem a nightmare which would perhaps pass. The same spirit which had fed whatever of grace and dignity could be summoned became the symbol of ultimate resistance. The badge of shame became a banner, and the strength which transformed it, the strength of Zivia and her comrades, came from the most ancient as well as the newest source of Jewish strength—Zion. In their last moment, the Jews of the Warsaw ghetto were not alone. They had lost the present, but they raised the flag which made them one with the past and with the future.

July, 1943

The Last Stand

Editorial

SZMUL ZYGELBOJM, a leader of the Polish-Jewish Socialists and a member of Sikorski's Polish National Council, committed suicide on May 12. According to the *PM* correspondent, Zygelbojm killed himself "out of chagrin." Jaczynski, a Gentile leader of the Polish underground movement, had managed to reach London. He carried a message to Zygelbojm from the remaining Jews in the Warsaw ghetto. Before leaving Warsaw, Jaczynski had been told by the still surviving Jews in the ghetto: "Jewish leaders abroad won't be interested. At eleven in the morning you will begin telling them about the anguish of the Jews in Poland, but at 1 p.m. they will ask you to halt the narrative so they can have lunch. That is a difference which cannot be bridged. They will go on lunching at the regular hour at their favorite restaurant. So they cannot understand what is happening in Poland."

Nevertheless, the Jews of Warsaw had sent a last message. They bade Zygelbojm to urge the Jews of London to go to the American Embassy and the British Foreign Office and stay until driven out. If arrested, they should go on a hunger strike until death.

That was the message. It was not sent with much hope. The Jews still alive in Poland knew beforehand that everybody would keep on lunching, while the massacre went on. Zygelbojm knew it too. No Jews in London were indecorous enough to embarrass the representatives of the great democracies by unseemly demonstrations. No one went on "melodramatic" hunger strikes. The favorite restaurants were not neglected. And the Bermuda Conference washed its hands of blood among the perfume of the Easter lilies. So Zygelbojm took poison, unable to exist further in this well-bred world which could no longer feel horror, or indignation, or sympathy.

Zygelbojm understood that he lived in an unreal world in which he had no part, a world which played an elaborate hocus-pocus game of conferences, and resolutions and declarations while it blocked every avenue of escape, a crazy world which sent ships with helpless human beings to founder rather than let them disembark on any of its vast shores, a barbarous world which could find no room in any of its huge territories for the innocent fleeing from slaughter, an evil world which murdered or silently conspired in murder.

Zygelbojm had to leave the grimacing illusion of a civilized world in which the conventions of humanity prevailed. There was a real world from which he had shortly come and to which he was allied, the grim world of the ghetto where the assassin raged, gassing and choking efficiently, systematically so many thousands per day. Zygelbojm could not divorce himself from that reality; he could not make his peace with the ghostly world of occasional speeches, averted faces and closed doors. He belonged with the dead and those about to die. He belonged with those who knocked at the gate, crying, "Give sanctuary," not with those who, while pretending not to hear, rose and turned the key more securely in the lock.

Adam Czerniakow, the mayor of the Warsaw ghetto, killed himself; Zygelbojm killed himself. And people whose appetites are good, whose nights are calm, protest: "They should have kept on fighting." There are suicide dives with a bomber on the deck of an enemy battleship. The pilot perishes but he is acclaimed a hero. Deaths like Zygelbojm's are suicide dives upon the hardened conscience of the world. Perhaps the steel will be shattered; perhaps the imagination will be stirred.

The Jews in the Warsaw ghetto received no answer to their call; no one was tactless enough to besiege the embassies of the allied nations, as the perishing in their simplicity had begged, nor did any one starve himself to death as a futile gesture. Everyone behaved with admirable reason and restraint. If Zygelbojm had not killed himself, few would so much as have known of the strange request which issued from the thirty thousand Jews who were all that remained of the hundreds of thousands once shut up in the Warsaw ghetto.

But something glorious happened in the Warsaw ghetto which Zygelbojm did not live to witness. The thirty thousand made a last stand. They did not let themselves be led to slaughter. They knew what fate awaited them, and they died fighting. We do not know the details of that fierce and hopeless struggle, foredoomed from the beginning; we only know that the German murderers had to bring up tanks and artillery before they could complete their carnage. The Jews, furnished with arms smuggled to them by the Polish underground, fought fiercely—man, woman and child—barricading themselves in their houses. According to information from the Polish government, nearly a thousand Nazis were killed or wounded before the last of Warsaw Jewry was murdered.

A heroic, somber battle in which the victory is surely not to the thugs who completed their planned assassination! The Warsaw ghetto has been "liquidated." Leaders of Polish Jewry are dead by their own hand. And the world which looks on passively is, in its way, dead too.

June, 1943

Lamnazeakh al Ham'kholot

by CH. N. BIALIK

Bang on the drum! Bang hard and loud!
Fife in your mouth! Screech, curse you, yell!
Saw on your fiddles! Their raucous strings shout,
"Buck up! Play louder! Or go plumb to hell!"
(In the vein of a folk song.)

No meat and no fish and no black bread or white . . .
Why worry? Keep dancing—and hold shoulders tight!

There's a God in the heavens, trust Him, He is strong,
Let us dance in His name, gather strength in a throng.

All our soul's pent up anguish, our heart's deepest burn,
Will be part of our dance and inspire every turn!

Our dance song will mix with the wild lightning's cry,
It will shake up the earth and will anger the sky.

Bang on the drum . . .

No honey, no milk, and of wine not a drop,
But the poisonous cup is filled up to the top.

Let the arm never falter—roar toasts till you're hoarse,
Then drink to the dregs—stamp and leap with full force.

Let your dance gather strength, grow in fury—don't cower.
Let your faces beam brightly, your voices gain power!

Your foe need not know it, your friend need not know it,
Your heart may be raging, but why should you show it?

Bang on the drum . . .

No shirt and no shoe, not a stitch on your back,
What matter? Not bad! . . . They would burden your pack!

We're naked and barefoot as eagles in flight,
We'll lift ourselves upwards and reach for the height.

Let us fly in a tempest and cross in a squall.
And skim over oceans of trouble withal.

With shoes or without them—all one: then be brave,
No matter what way, we shall dance to the grave.

Bang on the drum . . .

No brother, no kinfolk, no rescuing friend,
On whom can you lean? Who will lend you a hand?

Let us join up together, each melt with his brother,
Give spirit, give fury, give strength to each other.

It will be a strange mixture: feet, sandals—forsooth,
The grey-bearded patriarch mingling with youth.

We shall circle around, with no end and no start,
In order, or chaos, or drifting apart.

No homestead, no roof and no shadow of wall,
And why all the flurry, what fear grips you all?

The earth is quite wide, with four corners at best,
So bless Him who brings His folk comfort and rest.

And bless Him who brought forth the sky's starry hood,
He fastened His sun there—a light for our good.

And blessed be He too for His generous grants—
Hallelujah with trumpets! Hallelujah with dance!

Bang on the drum . . .

No pomp and no circumstance, glory or praise,
Are all paths to heaven closed? Not true! What a craze!

Our Watchman won't sleep and will not slight the meek,
He sustains dogs and ravens, our bread He will seek.

We shall scamper before Him and sing Him our song,
And make our amends if we did something wrong.

May our grim dance of death and the song of our terrors,
Be ample atonement for all of our errors.

Bang on the drum . . .

No justice, no mercy, no revenge, and no pay,
Why should you be silent? You have mouths, have your say.

Give voice to your feet to express flame and fury—
Speak your grievance to stones—let them act as your jury.

Let your dance steps be wild, filled with conquering fire,
To burn all around you and blaze like a pyre.

In the storm of your dance and the din of your groans,
Your heads will be shattered on walls built of stones!

Bang on the drum . . .

(Written during the World War in the woods of Malin)
Translation by ESTHER ZWEIG

April, 1938

Exalted and Hallowed

by SHOLEM ASCH

WHEN THE Gestapo in Praga, a suburb of Warsaw, brought Itzig-Meyer to the center where Jews were being rounded up for forced labor, this son of Israel created something of a sensation. One might even venture to say that the Gestapo men, who happened to be present in the large courtyard, surveyed Itzig-Meyer with a feeling akin to pleasure. The troop-leader himself, a young man in his twenties, with a black mustache and small hard eyes, came out of his office to greet him. In all the time that the Gestapo had used the brick building of a former school house, set in the middle of a large yard, as a center for Jews, they had examined various representatives of the race. All sorts of Jews, dragged out of houses or caught on the streets, had been brought before them. They had seen smooth-shaven Jews in European clothes who had pretended to be "Aryans," as well as genuine Jews with full-grown beards and in the traditional long robes. But as yet they had not beheld so authentic a specimen of the tribe. Itzig-Meyer's Jewishness shrieked from him. His long luxuriant beard practically radiated "Jewishness." Long black ear-locks hung down his heavily bearded cheeks; his eyes, large and restless, were dark and shining. He wore a torn old satin coat, pulled together by a belt; best of all, under the folds of his long robe one could see his feet in the white socks worn by orthodox Jews. The men of the Gestapo stood around him, crowing. Even the troop-leader, his hands in his trouser pockets, surveyed Itzig-Meyer with a faint satisfied smile on his generally stern face. All looked gleefully at the victim before them.

"What is your name, Jew?" one of them asked.

"Itzig-Meyer Rosenkranz."

"Itzig-Meyer Rosenkranz? There's a name for you! With Rosenkranz, to boot!" The Gestapo men laughed.

"What is your occupation, Jew?"

"Rabbi."

"A rabbi! A fine occupation! And who are you?"

Itzig-Meyer had made his peace with the world as soon as the Gestapo had caught him, and was prepared for anything. He felt calm and gave no outward sign of nervousness. Even his quick shining eyes looked steadfastly at his examiners. He was puzzled by the question but he answered, "A Jew, naturally."

"A Jew, naturally! This is magnificent!" The men of the Gestapo laughed again.

Only the troop-leader stopped smiling. He grew serious. He wanted to put a finish to the comedy, but the Jew was so choice, so rare a find, that he could not help glancing at him once more. He looked at him carefully, piercingly, as a cat might look at a mouse which it holds caught in its claws. However, the terror in the eyes of the mouse was absent. The Jew showed no fear; his eyes did not flinch; his tall figure did not cower; his lips did not tremble. He stood straight and silent.

The Jew's lack of fear irritated the troop-leader. With a sudden motion, he thrust out his hand and twined his fingers in all the hair on one side of the Jew's face; he caught the ear-lock, a part of the whiskers, and some of the beard. "Repeat, 'I am a Jewish swine—I have no honor,'" the troop-leader commanded.

Itzig-Meyer repeated, "I am a Jewish swine—I have no honor."

"Louder!"

"I am a Jewish swine—I have no honor."

"Still louder!"

"I am a Jewish swine—I have no honor," Itzig-Meyer shouted.

At this point, the troop-leader pulled at the beard he held in his hand. But the hair was so firmly rooted in Itzig-Meyer's flesh that it did not yield. "God damn," the troop-leader cursed and pulled harder. Still the hair did not give way.

"Here's a real Jew for you! A true Jewish beard," the troop-leader said half jestingly to those about him, a bit mortified that the Jewish beard had not given way easily. He thrust his foot into

the Jew's belly and tugged again with all his might. This time he
succeeded and the troop-leader held a piece of ear-lock, a shred of
whiskers, and some thick curls from the Jew's long beard.

"You try it," the troop-leader turned to his men and pointed to
the Jew's beard.

The trial of strength began. Some of the fellows managed to
pull out a handful of the Jew's beard after two or three attempts,
but a short chap won the competition. He pulled out a substantial
handful with only one mighty tug.

While this was going on, Itzig-Meyer kept standing on the
same spot, the white socks showing through his torn slippers.
Gaps appeared in what had been his rich heavy beard; now it consisted only of straggling wisps, stuck together with the blood drip-
ping from the wounds on his face. Itzig-Meyer's beard was no
longer a beard. It was a moist rag attached to a human face. But
the Jew's eyes and bearing remained unchanged. Worst of all, the
Gestapo men suddenly bethought themselves, the Jew had failed
to cry out during the beard plucking. The troop-leader could not
decide whether the Jew's conduct should be viewed as a sign of
courage or of Jewish arrogance. If the first was the explanation of
the Jew's extraordinary behavior, he might even have been ready
to give the Jew credit; but, if this was another instance of Hebraic
insolence, he had to teach the Jew a lesson. So he asked Itzig-
Meyer, "Did it hurt?"

"A little, sir," Itzig-Meyer answered.

The Jew's answer mollified the troop-leader somewhat, but he
wanted to be sure. "And who are you?" he asked.

"I am a Jewish swine—I have no honor," Itzig-Meyer called
out with all his might.

"There's a decent Jew for you," the troop-leader said, satisfied.
"Now we'll see what you can do. Harness him to the wagon."

They led Itzig-Meyer to a wagon which stood in the yard. The
wagon had a harness made of rope and leather straps such as Warsaw porters frequently used. Itzig-Meyer was yoked to the cart,
and several Gestapo men jumped in. One of them seated him-

self on "the coach-box," and began to prod Itzig-Meyer with a whip. "Giddy-ap, Jew, giddy-ap!"

Itzig-Meyer thrust his long neck out of his open shirt and coat. At the smart of the lash, he stretched his neck forward like an ostrich. Because of the plucked beard his head looked disproportionately big and unwieldly on his scrawny neck. Like an ostrich, also, he set down his thin bony feet before him. His slippers stuck in the moist earth; his feet sank into it; sweat poured from his forehead and from his long neck and lean body. With all his might he tried to pull the wagon which kept sinking into the mud because of the weight of the Gestapo men. But the harder Itzig-Meyer pulled the more impossible it became to move the wagon. He tried to change the position of his feet; first he put his right, then his left, foot forward. He tugged with one shoulder, then with the other. Under a rain of lashes he struggled to drag the wagon but he got nothing except mockery for his pains. The wagon did not budge.

"Let another swine help him," called out the troop-leader, who stood watching the scene with his hands in his pockets. The faint gratified smile left his face which again became hard and grave.

A second Jew was dragged forward, a much older man than Itzig-Meyer, with inflamed bleary eyes and a sparse quivering beard. He was harnessed next to Itzig-Meyer. The lashes now fell equally on both Jews. The old Jew tugged at one shaft, Itzig-Meyer at the other.

Itzig-Meyer changed the position of his feet and with all the energy left in his straining breast pulled at the wagon. The old Jew struggled at his side but the wagon did not move. "Let them feel the whip!" the troop-leader ordered.

The lashes fell again, some on Itzig-Meyer, some on the head of the old Jew. Itzig-Meyer, kept silent under the blows and continued tugging but at each lash the old Jew would cry out:

"*Oi,* Father in Heaven! *Oi,* mother mine!"

The Gestapo men mocked him delightedly:

"*Oi, oi,* papa! *Oi, oi,* mamma!"

And suddenly Itzig-Meyer found the needed power. As soon as he heard the derisive cries, "*Oi, oi,* papa," he thrust his neck and shoulders forward, seized the shaft in his bony fingers, planted his feet firmly on the ground, and tugged again with every ounce of strength. The wagon rolled forward. Itzig-Meyer ran, dragging the old Jew with him.

"The Jew did it, the Jew did it!" shouted the men of the Gestapo, stamping on the floor of the moving wagon.

"A decent Jew," called out the troop-leader. "Unharness him."

Itzig-Meyer was unharnessed. The moisture of his body had soaked through his torn satin coat, and the leather strap had left a wide band across his breast.

"A decent willing Jew—Group A. Shave his beard; let him rest today," directed the troop-leader and left the yard to go back to his office.

Itzig-Meyer was led to a corner. A young Jew, who had been assigned the task of cutting beards, came up to him. With a pair of blunt scissors, he sheared off what remained of Itzig-Meyer's beard, ear-locks, and whiskers. He cut the hair of his head in ridges. When this was over, Itzig-Meyer, without a beard as without a soul, like a brute beast, was brought down into a cellar where, lying on straw sacks along the damp well, were other Jews who had been seized on the streets that day and rounded up for forced labor.

It was the twilight of an early autumn day. A large batch of Jews, returning from work, poured into the cellar. Old and young were among them. Some were smooth-shaven and wore suits; others were dressed in long orthodox. Some had had their beards plucked out like Itzig-Meyer; the beards of others had been overlooked. Here and there one could see a face on which the beard had begun to grow again.

The Jews threw themselves down on the ground just as they were, their faces and clothing caked with dirt and sweat. Some lay without speaking, still breathing heavily—the heavy breathing accentuated the silence. Some sat—and remained seated. All kicked off their shoes, boots, or slippers, and clasped their swollen, wounded feet. These looked as though they had marched hundreds of miles, climbed over mountains, or knocked endlessly against rocks. The men, lying or seated, seemed to have become merely —feet. Each man, all his emotions, sensibilities, and interests, was concentrated and absorbed in his swollen, suffering feet.

Suddenly a voice was heard reciting the Hebrew prayer of *Kaddish*:

Yithgaddal v'yithkaddash sheme rabba—"Exalted and hallowed be God's great name."

They turned their heads in the direction of the voice. Their feet were forgotten; the familiar prayer, here sounding so strangely, roused them from their stupor. They could dimly see the figure of a Jew in a tattered satin robe, wearing a hat tied to his head by a colored kerchief as though he had a toothache, swaying back and forth in prayer beside the wall.

The prayer suddenly called them back to a world that seemed to have been lost forever when they had been brought to the cellar. Letting go their feet, a few Jews jumped up and went to the corner where Itzig-Meyer was standing and began to pray with him, swaying back and forth in unison. But the majority remained seated and looked fearfully toward the door. A few voice were heard expostulating:

"Finish your prayers quickly."

"Quicker, quicker, before someone comes in."

They prayed rapidly. Hastily they recited the *Kedushah,* the proclamation of the holiness and kingship of God, and the *Shemoneh Esreh,* the Eighteen Blessings prescribed in the liturgy.

Soon a long whistle sounding through the crowded cellar interrupted the *Hallel,* the psalms of praise. The men grabbed their shoes, bound up the wounds on their feet as best they could, and formed lines. They walked out two by two, each carrying a tin plate. They marched to the pump in the yard, washed their faces and hands, and dried themselves on the corners of their garments. Then they filed into a mess-hall with long benches where Jewish women were preparing a thin potato soup in large kettles. Each person received a plate of soup and a piece of bread, and they sat down to eat.

Like a well-drilled soldier, Itzig-Meyer with his bandaged face had been marching along as though he were a veteran of the labor battalion. The Gestapo man, who kept an eye on him, found no cause for complaint.

Before Itzig-Meyer took a bite, he made the customary benediction on breaking bread. He mumbled the first half but one could hear the concluding words:

"Who bringest forth bread from the earth."

The Jews, who had thrown themselves wolfishly on their meager portions of thin soup for which they had waited all day long, held their spoons still for a moment. Itzig-Meyer's benediction had struck a chord of memory. Some stopped eating and muttered the words after him. Others contented themselves with a brief "Amen." The Gestapo men, stationed at the door of the open kitchen, noticed that something was afoot, but the incident passed so rapidly that none could make out what had happened. When the meal was over, the Jews, Itzig-Meyer among them, cleaned their plates as usual and trooped out.

The next morning, before the dawn had begun to light the cellar windows, the wretched beings lying on the straw sacks were wakened, not by the whistle of the Gestapo guard as usual, but by the voice of Itzig-Meyer reciting the *Kaddish.* A few rose hastily and followed suit; the rest tried to sleep till the blast of the whistle.

When they were all led out into the yard, Itzig-Meyer, the long ends of his robe tucked into his belt, was assigned to work with Group A.

They walked a short stretch outside the city limits to a field through which a road was being cut. There Itzig-Meyer saw other Jews also working under the supervision of Gestapo guards. One group was digging a ditch; another was hauling the excavated earth and throwing it on the road-bed. Many men, naked to the waist, were lifting stones from a great heap and carrying them to the road on their bare breasts. Younger men were harnessed to a great steam roller which they dragged over the stones. Itzig-Meyer was assigned to the group whose task it was to haul stones.

The Gestapo guard ordered him to take off his long robe like the rest. He obeyed. Then he was told to remove his blouse, the small fringed shawl worn by every orthodox Jew under his upper garment, and his shirt. He obeyed promptly except when he had to remove the shawl; then he hesitated for a moment. However, the glance of the guard brought him to. He remained only in his trousers which were held up by suspenders thrown over his bare shoulders. The colored kerchief was still around his face. With one quick tug the guard pulled the kerchief and the hat off his head. Itzig-Meyer's face appeared in its full nakedness. Only yesterday he had created a sensation with his full glistening beard but now he looked like a semi-shaven convict or some other disreputable character. There was no beard left for the guard to pull. Instead, he shoved him in the belly with his booted foot, and sent him to work.

When it came to Itzig-Meyer's work, however, the Gestapo guard could find no cause for complaint. Itzig-Meyer worked peacefully, even eagerly, as though he wished to satisfy some inner standard of his own. He would take as heavy a load of stones as he could possibly carry, and he would go briskly back and forth, allowing himself not a moment's respite.

It was a hot day in early autumn. The sun blazed on Itzig-Meyer's bare head; the sweat running from his brow moistened the dried clots of blood on the torn skin of his face. Drops of blood began to ooze from the clots, mixed with the sweat which dripped from his head and hair, and ran down his perspiring body. But Itzig-Meyer did his job. Occasionally, he would try to wipe his naked body with his bare hands. Most of the time, however, he let the sweat and blood run down and worked away. Even the guard was pleased.

"There's a good willing Jew, a decent Jew. What are you?"

"I am a Jewish swine—I have no honor," Itzig-Meyer shouted.

The half hour of rest which was allotted to the group was spent by Itzig-Meyer like the others: he held his feet in his hands.

Toward nightfall, when the Jews were being led back to their quarters, they came upon a great crowd of people outside the low fence that surrounded the brick building. When they reached the gate, Itzig-Meyer noticed a tall pole rising from the courtyard. Three corpses with long bare feet from which the boots had been stripped were swaying from the top. The crowd outside stood gaping at the bodies which had been left hanging in order to intimidate the population. A few Christian women knelt on the pavement and prayed with eyes closed. Others stood around in a stony silence.

"Isaac has been hanged," a Jew standing next to Itzig-Meyer muttered to himself.

"Blessed be Thy judgments," Itzig-Meyer whispered seemingly to himself.

"He talked back. I told him not to talk back. They call it breach of discipline," the Jew kept muttering.

"We are all in God's hand," Itzig-Meyer whispered.

This time the Jews returning to the cellar were more crushed than usual. Even when they were finally resting on their straw sacks, they did not have the courage to discuss the happening. Death cast its shadow over them. They were even afraid to breathe heavily as on other days. They lay or sat clasping their feet.

"Exalted and hallowed be God's great name." This time Itzig-Meyer's voice sounded louder and stronger.

"Does he want to bring this calamity down on our heads, too?" some began to protest.

"Didn't he see what happened?"

Fewer Jews went to join Itzig-Meyer at the wall. More voices were heard expostulating:

"Quicker, quicker!"

"And thou shalt love the Lord with all thy heart, with all thy soul, and with all thy might," Itzig-Meyer prayed, pronouncing each word clearly.

"Enough, enough," frightened voices urged from every corner. Itzig-Meyer mumbled the rest of the prayer.

The week passed by. Itzig-Meyer distinguished himself by his obedience, good discipline, and industry. He became the favorite of the Gestapo guards. They set him up as a model for the other Jews. "A decent Jew!" Jokingly, they said they would make him the troop-leader of the Jews. And Itzig-Meyer kept doing his work quietly and conscientiously without a moment of protest.

All this went on till Friday. On Friday afternoon, toward sundown, the guard noticed that Itzig-Meyer was restless. Each time he reached the heap of stones to take his load, he would stop and scan the sky to observe the position of the sun. The guard had already roused him several times from his abstraction with a lash of the whip across his head. But Itzig-Meyer continued to be visibly agitated. With large frightened eyes he kept watching the sky.

When the Jews were being led back from work, Itzig-Meyer walked hurriedly as though he would like to get ahead of his group. His partner could hardly keep him in step. Fortunately, they reached their quarters before a star appeared in the heavens. No sooner were they in the cellar than Itzig-Meyer rushed to the wall and began to pray:

"Exalted and hallowed be God's great name."

"Quicker, quicker!"

This time Itzig-Meyer did not let himself be hurried. Reverently he recited the Friday evening prayers. Then from his pocket he took a piece of bread which he had managed to save from his meager ration, and pronounced the *Kiddush*, the hallowing of the Sabbath:

"And the heaven and the earth were finished and all their host . . ."

The solitary service went off quietly without interruption. But the next morning on Saturday, after he had roused every one with his prayers, Itzig-Meyer remained standing beside the wall. When the guard blew his whistle, all rushed to get into line, but Itzig-Meyer did not stop swaying back and forth.

"Itzig-Meyer, come!" one of his fellows called.

He kept on swaying.

"Itzig-Meyer!"

"Drag him from there!"

But Itzig-Meyer would not let himself be pulled away. He kept on praying.

"You're risking your neck, Itzig-Meyer," a final voice was heard pleading.

But Itzig-Meyer remained alone beside the wall.

A few minutes later, he felt the lash of a whip across his head. He heard shrill cries:

"Damn Jew, get going!"

Itzig-Meyer kept on praying. Some one kicked him in the side and punched his face. He nearly fell but regained his balance. A savage voice was shouting at him:

"Get out!"

"Kind gentleman, I can't go today; it is the day of rest," Itzig-Meyer answered meekly, and tried to smile appeasingly in spite of his bloody nose.

"What?"

"Today is our Sabbath, the day of rest. I can't work today."

The guard stopped beating him. He seized him by the arm and led him out of the cellar to the office of the troop-leader. The guard clicked his heels and saluted:

"Heil Hitler!"

"Heil Hitler! What has happened?"

"A breach of discipline."

The troop-leader looked at Itzig-Meyer narrowly. He recognized him. This was the Jew with the long beard about whom he had received a report, "willing." Despite the thorough schooling of the troop-leader, Itzig-Meyer aroused some strain of compassion in him. Whatever the reason, whether it was Itzig-Meyer's exemplary behaviour or the fun of the beard-plucking which the troop-leader still remembered, he wanted, if possible, to save this curious Jew. He rose, walked over to Itzig-Meyer who stood calmly before him with an idiotic smile on his blood-spattered face, and took the whip from the guard. He flashed it over Itzig-Meyer's head.

"What are you?"

"I am a Jewish swine—I have no honor," Itzig-Meyer shouted loudly.

"Well, now go to work, Jew."

"Kind gentleman, I can't work today. It's the Sabbath."

"Take him away," the troop-leader commanded.

"Heil Hitler!"

"Heil Hitler!"

The troop-leader lifted the telephone receiver; then he stopped. Something was bothering him. He called to the guard who was leading Itzig-Meyer away:

"Show him the gallows."

Itzig-Meyer was brought to the scaffold.

"Do you know what this is, Jew?"

"Yes, this is where men are hanged," Itzig-Meyer answered.

"You will hang if you don't go to work."

"Kind gentleman, I have already explained. It's the Sabbath. It would be a sin."

The troop-leader telephoned the authorities for instructions. He received this order: "Hang the Jew, Itzig-Meyer Rosenkranz, for breach of discipline at 6 P.M. today together with two Catholics."

When Itzig-Meyer was led to the gallows, he once more began to scan the sky. He turned to the troop-leader who stood near him:

"Kind gentleman, I want to ask you something; you are good to me."

"What is it, Jew?"

"Please wait until the stars come out. Today is the Sabbath."

"What are you?"

"I am a Jewish swine—I have no honor," Itzig-Meyer called out lustily as he had been taught.

The troop-leader's grim face lit up with a faint smile:

"I'll hang the others before you."

"Exalted and hallowed be God's great name," Itzig-Meyer chanted clearly, and began to sway back and forth.

He was led to the noose in the midst of the *Shemoneh Esreh.* His lips were still whispering:

"Thou art One, and Thy name is One."

When the Jews came back from work that evening, they again found a large crowd outside the fence around the courtyard. Again they saw three bodies hanging. Two of the corpses were still jerking on the ropes, but the long feet of one were already stiff and quiet like the hands of a clock which has stopped. The Jews recognized him.

They walked into the courtyard in silence with heads bowed, trying not to see the three bodies. Nobody made a sound. But no sooner had they reached the cellar than another Jew took Itzig-Meyer's place at the wall where he had prayed each night.

Nobody whispered nervously, "Quicker, quicker!" One after another the Jews arose and stood beside the wall:

Yithgaddal v'yithkaddash sheme rabba. Exalted and hallowed be God's great name. . . .

(*Translated from the Yiddish by* MARIE SYRKIN)

November, 1942

The Children's Odyssey
by Mala Gitlin

ON THE DAY of Rosh Hashana, one month after nine hundred Jewish refugee children reached Teheran from the Soviet Union, the air was pierced by the wailing in the children's camp. It must have started with a small group of children and spread all over the camp. Nine hundred children wept—nine hundred children whose years ranged from a tender age to late adolescence. The young and inexperienced supervisors at first felt lost, but common sence and intuitive wisdom prompted them to let the children have their cry, tears flowing from their own eyes, too. The candy given out to the children in celebration of the holiday failed to tempt a single one of them. Not one touched it and all of it was returned with the request that it be sent to their families left behind in Russia without food. Such was the Day of Mass Weeping, on the threshold of the new life facing the children of Teheran.

Each child came to Teheran after years of wandering, having experienced every conceivable hardship connected with the war. If a child was five year old when he arrived at the children's camp, it meant that he had grown up during the war years. In his eyes the only real world was a world at war, life signified flight, and human beings were to be regarded as enemies. If he reached Teheran at the age of ten or twelve, then his adolescence, lacking those transitional stages so dear to the psychologists, was a sudden maturing which had taken place during the war. It seems to me that it is a tragic error to speak of the "children" from Teheran—the term hardly fits those human minors. The word "child" has a connotation of beauty and of goodness which passes with the passing of childhood years. "Pray, give back my childhood," says the Hebrew poet Tchernikhovsky, with the bitterness of an adult who recalls the bliss and sunniness of his childhood.

It would be best not to let the Teheran children read those lines, at least until the new life in the Land of Israel, and the years have blurred the impress of their own unhappy childhood. Only then, may such a child be able to imagine the meaning of Tchernikhovsky's verse in a spirit of goodness and faith, in the knowledge that there exists a childhood different from his own, a childhood full of sunshine. Then, he may echo, pray, give back his childhood to him who has never had it.

The war has, indeed, yielded us a whole generation of childhoodless children.

And so it came to pass that in the camp at Teheran not even a fleeting smile was seen on the lips of a single one of the nine hundred children there; that quarreling was their daily meed; that they were always on their guard against people, and that every friendly person appeared to them as a wily enemy disguising his sinister designs by honeyed words. And so it came to pass that the camp at Teheran was made up nine hundred old men and women, sorely tried by life, though their ages were nine and ten and fifteen and eighteen years.

How did it all happen?

We still lack information, and we are not as yet certain of the facts that are known to us. But it is very necessary to collate the scattered data that we have. On the basis of what the children themselves have related here and there, and what was recounted by an eye-witness who traveled with children during all the war year and was engaged in responsible work with them at the camp at Teheran, we shall make an attempt to form a picture of the children's Odyssey.

Warsaw, at the end of October, 1939. In a cold night of Polish autumn, the child is taken out of his bed, wrapped in a blanket and taken along in flight. The train is bombed. Everyone is bound for the East, hoping for peace and security on the Russian border. The roads are full of people, some riding in cars or in horse-drawn carts, others making their way on foot. The fugitives are, for the most part, people of means, middle-class and well-to-do. Many are already dead and many children have lost their parents. Already in this first flight the children are used to arouse sympathy. Thus, for example, in the busses, parents push their children forward so that seated passengers may take pity on them and let them have their seats.

After the Russian occupation the children still live with their parents in small towns where the situation is full of hardships but not unbearable. There is still a family, and the child is still a child. But the situation suddenly became much worse when the families were deported to places where they were set at hard labor. The child lived with his family in the family camp (known by the general name *Posidlek*). Nearby there is an encampment, *Lagry,* for adults, and another, *Dietiasli,* for infants up to five years of age. Only mothers who have small children are permitted to remain at home. Those whose children are eight years and older must go to work, and the care of the house devolves on the child. That means not merely cleaning and cooking and taking care of the smaller children, but also providing a livelihood.

The child must find a source of income. He chops wood in the forest and sells it at some profit. Gradually he learns the best ways of making profit. He stands in the queue for bread, salt, and kerosene, the staple needs of the household for which he is the chief provider. Naturally, in everything pertaining to the management of the household the child takes an active part and what he says carries most weight, and in this role, he, the child of twelve, combines the traits of an experienced old person and of a child. When his mother finds the burden of hard work beyond her endurance, he feigns illness, since that is the only way for her to get permission to stay home for a day. But that cannot last more than a single day, for there is wood to be chopped and sold and one must stand in the queue.

With the release of the families in 1941 the wave of migration moved southward towards the Iranian border. By now the migrants are impoverished, miserable, weakened men, women, and children. They reach the South of Asiatic Russia, where there are no longer any camps and every one must shift for himself. Want, misery, squalor and disease are rampant. Children take sick. Parents die. Now begins the terrible stage of orphanhood. By the summer of 1942 about 30 per cent of those who had come were dead. There are many cases of death having taken away the father, the mother, and the brother in a single family, with only a single child surviving. Even where adults have survived the child has become the only provider of the family, and his yoke is much heavier. The adults no longer work on the road. They are ignorant of the local language, so they cannot find light work, and they have no strength for hard labor. The child alone must find the family living.

At night he stands in line to obtain precious foodstuffs, such as sugar. Although distributed by ration cards, such food is very seldom available. When the child does obtain his own and his family's ration, he sells most or all of it on the black market. This is the foundation of the family's subsistence. True, illegal trading is dangerous, but that is why it is the child who is engaged in it, since children are punished more lightly. The little provider is exposed to additional and unsuspected perils even before he has obtained the precious merchandise. In the queue itself, the strongest and the most ruthless who can elbow their way to the front are those who get what they want. Of course, the child cannot match his strength with the adult standing behind him who argues that he, the child, has seized his place. The child must have recourse to lying to convince the adult that he has been standing here for a long time; and if necessary, he will point to someone else, quite innocent, as the one who pushed his way to the front, before his turn. Sometimes, when he cannot manage to gain his point by such lies he feigns sickness to arouse sympathy in his stronger competitor; and when this, too, proves of no avail, the child knows how to burst out crying all of a sudden and to say that he is an orphan. And since there were so many orphans, such a lie would sometimes have the desired effect. In this way the child would "win" and remain in the place he had taken.

The line moves up slowly. If the child is lucky and the distribution is not discontinued just as his turn arrives, as often happens, the little provider obtains his precious sugar late at night or before dawn. He runs home, his brain working feverishly. He has several customers. To which of them will it be most profitable to sell? What price ought he to name this time? How much of the sugar ought he to save for his own household?

He passes near his house but instead of entering he turns back and goes into a side lane. Better to go to his customers immediately and sell all the sugar before he gets home. Better this way. It is so much less dangerous to sell at night; besides, he wants to show his customers how loyal he is to them by supplying them with the best of the merchandise so early; moreover, if he comes home announcing that the sugar has already been sold, there will be no argument about the amount to be sold and the amount to be left for home use, and, what is most important, he will not have to bear that inquiring look in the eyes of his younger brother when tea is served. He knows quite well by now what streets to avoid, so as not to meet a policeman, and what expression to assume when meeting one. And if everything passes safely, he sells the sugar and buys more bread for the family. This, too, has to be bought secretly.

But it happens sometimes that the child is apprehended while transacting his business, or he is denounced, and the police arrest him. Then comes the penalty. The child stands alone, face to face with the law. His parents, if he has any, cannot interfere, because they "know nothing" about the whole matter. Children are subject to less severe penalties than adults, that is the only advantage of his childhood. He submits to the punishment, goes back to his business and tries to be more careful in the future.

This life was but one stage in the child's migrations. It lasted for about six months, until the Polish evacuation. Then came a period which imprinted itself on the child's memory because of his dread of being drafted into the *kolkhoz*. The child knew well what was in store for him if he and his family were deported to a *kolkhoz*. He heard that for leaving one's work at the *kolkhoz* one was liable to several years' imprisonment; that people there ate little and worked extremely hard—and he knew how unfit his parents were for physical labor. But above all was the consciousness that it meant isolation from the mass of migrant Jews, and thus the loss of one's only hope of ever leaving Russian territory.

It was approximately at that time that permission was granted to transfer Polish orphanages to Teheran. That was in the summer of 1942. Then began a horrid chapter which was short enough, but whose effects on the child are likely to last for life. It began with the parting from the child's family. Until then, even amid untold hardships, there was still a family attachment. Now it had to be discontinued. The older generation and the younger were to part, mothers to be separated from their children, the latter to go away to take up a new life, the former to be left to an unknown fate.

In view of their experiences, it is small wonder if many parents were anxious that at least their children should be sent to Teheran. Many a mother seized upon news about the orphans being transferred there as a sign from heaven. Jewish mothers sat late at night, sewing the name and birthplace of their sleeping child and the name of their nearest relative, in America or in Palestine, onto the child's coat so that the good man or woman who might some day adopt their child would know whose child it is. With hearts turned to stone, the mothers sent their children out of a morning into the street: "Remember, for them you are an orphan, a Jewish orphan, don't forget." And the child walks out crying, not because he is alone, but because he knows he has to cry; because by crying he can get himself taken into the orphanage, when the way leads to Teheran. The child cries, repeating the stories he has learned: how his mother died in the epidemic, and how his father was shot; and he keeps on repeat-

ing the stories until the policeman admits him into the gates of
the Orphanage which is to redeem him.

Inside the orphanage there are many hundreds of children
like himself, big and small, Jewish and Christian, orphaned of
both parents, orphaned of one parent, and pseudo-orphans. The
child is careful. It is part of his acquired wisdom that caution
and reticence are paramount qualities. All his comrades in the
institution are silent like himself. Not far from him there is a
child he knows whose parents are also alive, but the two exchange
not a single word, as though they had never known each other.
At the end of the table sits a little Jewish girl with a small crucifix
hanging from her neck; but he pretends not to pay any attention
to her. He and the rest of the Jewish boys always try to manage
not to be sent to the shower bath with the Christian boys. But
among themselves they do not discuss it and do not converse at
all. In the shower bath they do their washing in silence and in
haste, and leave.

Teheran. What will this new and unknown place bring for
them? What is all this talk about another journey to Palestine,
and what is to be their fate over there? Who are all these people
who claim to be concerned about the refugee child and wish, as
they say, to take care of him, people who treat him as if he were
actually a child? The unknown arouses misgivings and suspicion.

Through all this confusion of the days in Teheran, the child
entrenched himself within a thick protective armor of suspicion,
just as lying and tell tales were protective devices in the queue
in the small Russian town, or the trick of weeping and the story
about his dead parents. The constant quarrels among the children
and their thefts from one another, all of them were devices of
self-protection against the insecurity of every day as it came, of
every succeeding moment even. And if the child had a morsel
of bread in his hand at the moment, why should he believe that
he would have enough bread to eat tomorrow as well? Was it
not safer to take the morsel and place it under the pillow, feeling
its hard presence there all night? Did it not hold the promise of

a day of plenty and security and a bracing feeling in the morning
upon getting up? And as for the promises of the supervisor, he
cannot possibly be any better than those grown ups who pushed
him from his place as he stood in line to receive food for his
family.

The family.

Only at Teheran has it become clear to the child what is the
true meaning of his coming there, with all its terrible consequences. Only now has he realized what he could not have realized before entering the orphanage in Russia, when the hope of
reaching Teheran was uppermost in his mind. It has now become
clear to him that he has been entirely severed from his family,
that he has saved his own life and abandoned his family, and that
he may have been left alone in all the world. This confusion of
emotions together with lack of certainty and exaggerated suspicion are psychological and social forces within a child's mind
with potentialities of a particularly destructive nature. Still, a
child remains a child. In spite of everything, the faith persists
within him that there are people who have it in their power to
help him if they so desire. Such a man, for example, is Mr.
Polish Minister. And there began a nervous activity of writing
letters to Mr. Minister.

"To the Minister K——. Dear Mr. Minister," writes a nine-
year-old boy, "I implore you very much to send papers to my
mother so that she may be able to come to me. My daddy is dead
and my sister is dead. My mother is left all alone. She is sick
and she has nothing to eat. I don't know if she even has a place
to live in. Please send her papers so that she should be able to
come to me."

The supervisors sent every letter. The Polish Minister received
hundreds of such letters.

Perhaps now, with the help of this imperfect description, we
may understand the meaning of the nine hundred voices wailing
in the Jewish children's camp at Teheran last Rosh Hashana, a
wailing which no one who has heard it will ever be able to forget.

It has been many months now since the children from Teheran arrived in Palestine. They were welcomed with open arms and with much love, and offered shelter by agricultural settlements and educational institutions all over the country. We are now in receipt of letters and reports from Palestine teachers and youth leaders about the first reaction of the children upon reaching the settlements, and about the slow change in their attitude towards their new life. At first they had to overcome the fear of the "Palestine kolkhoz" as these children called the *kvutza* and the *kibbutz*. The flowers and "lavishly" set tables of our farm settlements overawed the little guests, and filled them with misgivings that perhaps all this was not meant for them, and that perhaps they ought not to partake of it.

Members of various settlements were sent to work for a certain period of time among the children from Teheran. The children could not be made to believe that these people had come of their own free will, that they had left their own children and come to them, because they were more in need of attention than those other children. No such "fairy tales" could be told to them, they kept repeating; these people must have come because they had been ordered to do so on pain of being expelled from the "kolkhoz" by the management and deprived of their share in it. One teacher relates that she made no attempt to convince them that they were wrong, knowing that only experience would prove the truth to them. One day the group went on a visit to the teacher's home village. They observed the happy meeting between herself and her comrades; they saw how everyone laid aside his tools and came running towards her as soon as she was seen approaching with the group of children under her care. She took them to the children's house where they saw how her own baby rejoiced at seeing his mother, and they saw the rest of the children welcome her. Then they saw her take leave of her child and her husband and the rest of her comrades and return with them. They kept silent. That evening a little girl asked her again: "Why did you leave your child and come to work with us?" She answered as she had several weeks earlier: "At this moment my help is more necessary for you than for my child, that is why I have come to work with you." The little girl was quiet. It was a moment of considerable progress. At first she had not believed, now she failed to understand.

Of course, she failed to understand. She could not understand that this meeting between herself and the Palestinian nurse represented a meeting of two different worlds. One, the world of the beaten and the hounded, fighting out of fear; the other, the creative, the producer, the cultivator, who fights out of faith. The little girl's world is the world of blind force suddenly thrust upon her from the outside, without any choice on her part. The world of the nurse is one of her own choosing, which she has shaped into part of herself—and this child of Teheran is part of her world. For without the child of Teheran, her world is incomplete. Her desire to take care of this child or to adopt him does not stem from mere pity or generosity. And the whole *Yishuv* in Palestine has the same attitude. She and her comrades need this child from Teheran, just as the whole Yishuv needs all the children from Teheran, and all those who, to our great sorrow, were unable to come to Teheran.

A woman from one of the agricultural settlements who went to work with the children from Teheran at their camp in Atlit (the last camp they lived in before being sent at last to their permanent homes), writes:

". . . I have observed the children during these days. What is it they need, what do they require of us? . . . Most of these children experienced the shock of being uprooted from their homes, family, and normal life during their very early childhood, before they had time to learn a language properly or to acquire the most elementary knowledge and the primary values of civilized life. The only thing they managed to learn during their protracted migrations is 'geography.' . . . The war years deprived the children of school, of a parental home, of books— giving them instead the burden of earning a livelihood, and hard work. The children are keenly aware of what they have lost and they show a desire—one may well say, a passion—for studies, in order to achieve what they lack. If we could but rid them of their fear, we should be able to call into being within them positive values and a devotion to the land of such an extent that it would become a blessing for the Homeland. . . . A quiet life of work, study, and security is needed to heal their souls and to encourage them." . . .

"To heal their souls." The people of the Homeland know that these children have suffered not alone from physical deterioration; and it is well that they know it. For the Homeland holds the cure for the mental and emotional ailments of the children. Every settlement, especially the rural settlements, opens to the Teheran children numerous opportunities for a new and rich life. The combination of work and study in the rural school is, in my view, the most suitable system for the recuperation of these children.

July, 1944

The Old Teacher

by VASSILI GROSSMAN

T HAT MORNING it was announced that all Jews living in the
city were to report the following day at 6 a.m. in the square
near the flour mill. All were to be sent to the western districts of
occupied Ukraine where a special ghetto was being formed.
Fifteen kilograms of personal belongings were to be brought, but
no food, for the military authorities had arranged to issue dry
rations and hot water.

All day the neighbors flocked to the old teacher to ask his
opinion of this decree. There came the old shoemaker, Borukh, a
wit much given to profanity, and a great master of his trade; there
came Mendel the baker, a quiet philosophical man; there came
Leib the tinsmith, the father of nine children; there came broad-
shouldered, grey-moustached Haim Kulish, a man whose trade
called for the constant use of a heavy hammer. They had all heard
that the Germans had arranged similar evacuations in many other
cities, yet no one had ever seen a single column of Jews along the
distant roads, no one had received tidings of the life in these announced ghettos. They had all heard that the columns of Jews
who left the cities were led not to railway stations nor along broad
highways, but were taken instead to those places behind the towns
where there were gullies and ravines, swamps and old quarries.
They had also heard that, some days after the departure of the
Jews, German soldiers bartered honey, cream and eggs in the
market places for women's blouses, children's undershirts and
shoes, and that upon returning from the market places the local
inhabitants whispered to each other that: "A German traded a wool
jumper which neighbor Sonia wore the morning the Jews were led
out of town"; "A German bartered the shoes worn by the little
boy who had been evacuated from Riga"; "A German wanted

From a novel by the noted Soviet writer.

three kilograms of honey for engineer Kugel's suit." They knew, they guessed what awaited them. But in their hearts they did not believe it. The extermination of an entire people seemed too terrible to believe. Murdering a people! Their spirits could not grasp it.

Old man Borukh said: "How is it possible to murder a man who makes such nice shoes? I wouldn't be ashamed to exhibit them in Paris."

"It's possible, it's possible," said Mendel the baker.

"All right," said Leib the tinsmith, "let's say they don't need my tea kettles, and pans, and chimneys for samovars. But they won't murder nine people, my children, just because of that."

And the old teacher Rosenthal listened to them in silent thought: I did well in not committing suicide. He had passed his entire life with these people and he would be with them in their last bitter hour.

It would be a good idea to take to the forest, said Kulish the laborer, but it can't be done. The police dog our every step. Since morning the block warden has already visited me three times. I sent my little boy to my father-in-law, and the superintendent of my building followed him. He is a good man, but he told me outright: "I was warned by the police, 'If even one little boy fails to report in the square, your life will be at stake, superintendent'."

"Well, it's fate," said Mendel the baker. "A neighbor told my son: 'Yashka, you don't resemble a Jew, flee to a village.' And my Yashka says to her: 'I want to look like a Jew. Wherever they take my father I want to go, too'."

"There is one thing I can say," muttered Kulish, "if it comes to that, I won't die like a sheep."

"You are a good man, Kulish," said the old teacher, "you are a good man; you said a really true word."

*   *   *

In the evening Major Werner received the representative of the Gestapo, Bekker.

If only we can carry out tomorrow's operation systematically, we may sigh with relief, said Bekker. I have exhausted myself with these Jews. Every day there are excesses: five fled, to the partisans it is said; a family committed suicide; three are held for going about without badges; in the market place a Jewish woman was recognized while buying eggs despite the strict rule against their appearing in the market place; two were arrested on Berliner Strasse although they knew very well that they are forbidden to walk on the main street; eight were walking about town after four p.m.; two girls tried to hide in the forest while being marched to work and were shot. All these are small matters. I understand that our troops at the front have to cope with more serious difficulties, but nerves are nerves. Yet all the above occurred in one day, and every day it is the same.

—What will be the order of operations then, asked Werner.

Bekker wiped his *pince nez*. The order had been worked out elsewhere. Naturally, in Poland we had broader opportunities to apply energetic means. And without such means, as a matter of fact, we could not manage, since we are dealing with figures of a considerable magnitude. Here, of course, we have to act under field conditions. The nearness of the front has its influence. Latest instructions permit us to deviate from regulations and to adapt ourselves to local conditions.

—How many soldiers will you want then, asked Werner.

Throughout this conversation Bekker maintained a more than ordinarily dignified manner, so much so that Werner himself, who was commandant, felt an inner timidity while talking to him.

—We arrange things in the following manner, said Bekker. There are two commands, the executing and the security units. The executing unit consists of from fifteen to twenty men, and these must be volunteers. The security unit should be relatively small, on the average one soldier to fifteen Jews.

—Why so? asked the commandant.

—Experience shows that at the moment when the column notices that its route goes beyond the railroad and the highway, panic begins, there are hysterics, many try to flee. Besides, lately we are forbidden to use machine guns in such cases—the percent-age of fatal hits with machine guns is too low—and individual arms are prescribed. This slows down the work tremendously. It should also be added that the executing unit should consist of the smallest possible number—for a thousand Jews a unit of twenty men, no more. While the work goes on, the security unit is quite occupied, too. You will understand yourself, that among the Jews there is a high percentage of men.

—How much time will it take? asked Werner.

—With expert organization, it should take not more than two and a half hours for a thousand people. What is most important is the ability to subdivide the activities, to break up and prepare the groups and to bring them up. The execution itself does not last long.

—How many soldiers will you require, then?

—Not less than one hundred, Bekker answered with finality.

He looked through the window and added: The weather, too, is important. I asked the meteorologist. Tomorrow, calm, sunny weather is expected the first half of the day; toward eve-ning there may be rain, but that does not affect us.

—And so . . . Werner said with indecision.

—The order is as follows: You appoint an officer, naturally a member of the Nazi party. He will choose the executing unit in the following manner: "Fellows, I need several men with strong nerves." This has to be done tonight in the barracks. At least thirty men have to be signed up, since, as experience shows, at least ten percent always drop out. Then there has to be a personal talk with each of the men: "Are you afraid of blood? Can you stand great nervous tension?" No other explanations should be made. At the same time a list of the security unit is to be drawn up. The non-coms are instructed in the evening. Weapons are inspected. The unit forms before headquarters, in helmets, at five o'clock in the morning. The officer discusses the problem in detail, and it is mandatory that the volunteers are again questioned. Then each is issued three hundred rounds of ammunition. At six o'clock they arrive in the square where the Jews are to report. Following is the order: The executing unit marches about thirty meters ahead of the column. In the rear of the column follow two wagons, since there are always a certain number of old women, pregnant women, and hysterical women who lose consciousness on the way.

He spoke slowly so that the Major should not miss any of the details.

—Well, that's about all. Further instructions will be given on the spot by my colleagues.

Major Werner looked at Bekker and suddenly asked: And what about the children?

Bekker hemmed, dissatisfied. This question is outside the scope of practical instructions.

—You see, he said seriously and sternly, looking directly into the commandant's eyes, although it is recommended that they be separated from their mothers and be handled apart, I prefer not to do so. You understand, of course, how difficult it is to tear a child away from its mother at such a sad moment.

When Bekker bid his farewell and departed, the commandant called his adjutant, repeated the instructions in detail and added in a half whisper: Nevertheless I am glad that the old doctor committed suicide before all this, otherwise I would have had a tremendously uneasy conscience about him. After all, he did help me much, and I don't know whether I would have pulled through without his assistance until our own doctor arrived. And lately I really feel fine, I sleep better, my stomach is in order, and two people have already told me that my color has improved a lot. It is possible that this is a result of my daily walks in the park. And the air in this town is excellent. They say that before the war they had sanatoria in this town for lung and heart patients.

And the sky was blue, and the sun shone, and birds sang.

*   *   *

When the column of Jews passed the railroad, and, leaving the highway turned toward the ravine, Haim Kulish inhaled

deeply, and shouting above the tumult of hundreds of voices
cried out in Yiddish: "People, I have lived my life." With his
fist he struck the temple of the soldier marching alongside him
and felled him. He grabbed the automatic from his hands and
having no time to look over the unfamiliar weapon he swung
it heavily, as he used to swing his hammer, and hit a sidewise
blow at the face of the non-com who came running up. In the
ensuing confusion, little Katia Weisman lost both her mother and
grandmother and seized hold of the coat tails of the old teacher
Rosenthal. He lifted her in his arms with difficulty and putting
his lips to her ear he said: "Don't cry, Katia, don't cry."

She had her arm around his neck and said: "I am not crying,
teacher."

The child was heavy in his arms, he felt dizzy, there was a
ringing sound in his ears and his legs trembled from the unaccustomed long walk.

The crowd backed away from the ravine; it would not budge.
Many fell on the ground and crawled. Rosenthal soon found
himself in the front ranks.

Fifteen Jews were led up to the ravine. Rosenthal knew some
of them. There was the silent baker, Mendel; the dental tech-
nician, Meierowitz; the kindly old character, Applefield. His
son had been an instructor in the Kiev conservatory and when he
was a kid Rosenthal had tutored him in mathematics. Breathing
heavily, he held the child in his arms, and concern for her occupied his thoughts. "How can I calm her? How fool her about
what is going on?" he thought, and an endless grief overcame
him. In this last minute there was no one to aid him, no one to
say the word for which he had thirsted all his life more than for
any bookish wisdom or the deep thoughts and great doings
of man.

The little girl turned to him. Her face was calm; it was the
pale face of an adult, full of condescending sympathy. And in
the sudden silence he heard her voice:

"Teacher," she said, "don't look that way, you will be frightened." And with a maternal gesture she covered his eyes with her palms.

*   *   *

But the Gestapo commander had erred. He could not sigh with relief after the Jews had been executed. That evening he received a report that a large armed unit had appeared near the city. At the head of it was the chief engineer of the sugar mill, Shevchenko. One hundred employees of the mill who had missed leaving with their regiment had joined Shevchenko and become partisans. That night there was an explosion in the flour mill which worked for the Germans. Beyond the station the partisans set fire to large supplies of hay that had been gathered by the foragers of a Hungarian cavalry division. All night the town remained awake. The wind was blowing in the direction of the town and the flames could easily spread to the houses and sheds. A heavy, brick-colored flame waved and crawled; black smoke covered the stars and the moon, and the warm, cloudless summer sky was full of storm and flames.

Translated from the Russian by SHLOMO KATZ

December, 1944

The Yellow Badge
by H. LEIVICK

How does the badge of yellow look
With its black or crimson Star of David
Upon a Jew's arm inside Nazi-land,
Against the white face of December snow?
How would that yellow badge
With its black or crimson Star of David
Look on my son's arm, or my wife's,
How on my own—
Against the falling white of New York snow?
Truly,
The question, worm-like, eats into my heart,
And, like a gnat, it burrows in my brain.

But why are words, and words alone, enough?
Why not assume the full, last bond of union
And with one's own hand on one's own arm place
The fated yellow badge with David's Star
Before the eyes of all—New York as in Berlin,
And Paris, London, Moscow, as Vienna.
Truly,
The question, worm-like, eats into my heart
And, like a gnat, it burrows in my brain.

The first snow fell today
And children have gone sleighing in the park.
I, like the children, also love white snow
And most of all I love December days.
    (Somewhere far, far away
    In the snow lies a captive.)

True God of Abraham, of Isaac, and of Jacob,
Punish me not for this old love of mine,
But punish me because I do not shape
A Moses from the scanty New York snow,
Because from snow I do not make Mount Sinai
As once I did in the far years of childhood.
      (Somewhere the snow falls
      Thick on a wanderer.)

Yes, punish me because I do not don
Of my own will the six-towered Star of David
And the round emblem of the yellow badge,
To hearten Israel in the hangman's land,
To praise and to exalt throughout the world
The arm that wears the glory of this crest!
Truly,
The question, worm-like, eats into my heart
And, like a gnat, it burrows in my brain.

                    (*Translated from the Yiddish by* MARIE SYRKIN)
                              January, 1940

Jerusalem in Lithuania

by B. Z. DINABURG

THE CITY of Vilna held an unusual charm not only for its inhabitants but also for everyone who spent some time there. It is set amid beautiful natural surroundings. In its center, the small stream, Vileika, flowing through a deep, narrow valley, empties into the Vilea River. The city itself is surrounded on three sides by sand hills, of which the two highest jut into the heart of the city. The Botanic Gardens lie at their foot. One of these two hills, known as Castle Hill, was the pride of the Jews of Vilna. In that neighborhood are to be found the remnants of the oldest Jewish settlement in the city. The old Jewish cemetery across the river dates from the early seventeenth century and the inscription on its oldest stone is of the year 5396 (1636 A.D.).

The heart of Jewish Vilna was the courtyard of the Great Synagogue. It was like a world of its own, full of contrasting sounds and sights. On entering the courtyard, one would be overwhelmed by the cries of the market women, squatting alongside the houses and crying their wares in terms of monetary units hardly used outside of Vilna—half-kopecks and even quarter-kopecks. The kopeck seemed too large a unit for the standard of living prevailing in Vilna. Porters shouted "Step aside"; "Careful there"; "Young man, keep your eyes on the ground"; and their voices were swallowed up in these of the worshippers, praying continually in the synagogue and the many prayer-houses. There was a prayer-house in memory of the Gaon of Vilna, there was the prayer-house of the Gemilat Hasadim (Free Loan) Society, that of the gravediggers, and the Hassidic center. In the center of the court was the communal well, while farther up, overlooking the women's section of the synagogue, was the communal bath, with its ritual pools.

The strongest charm and attraction of Vilna were to be found, however, in the uniquely exhilarating spiritual atmosphere of the place. At every step one stumbled across so many contrasting things, each detached and different from the other and yet complementing one another and forming one consistent whole. The people themselves seemed to merge into the city's external appearance, its streets, lanes, and houses, forming a unity. One could not help feeling that the city had a soul, and that that soul was in harmony with the body.

*   *   *

Two features marked the history and the social physiognomy of Jewish Vilna: there was the extremely severe struggle for existence of a community in "exile"; and at the same time, the stability of a community profoundly at home. However tense the struggle, one sensed a certainty, a feeling of deep roots, about the Vilna Jews.

The history of Vilna Jewry and the circumstances attending its growth easily explain the tension. There were four periods in that history: the Lithuanian, from the founding of Vilna in 1322 to the Union with Poland in 1659; the Polish, ending with the last partition of Poland, when Vilna became part of Russia (1659-1795); the Russian (1795-1915); and the second Polish period (1922-1939). During the first period there was no organized Jewish community in Vilna. Individual Jews came and went temporarily, and the burghers strenuously fought any attempt by Jews to establish themselves in the city. In 1527 Vilna was given a charter expressly prohibiting the settlement of Jews in the city. It was not until 1573 that Jews were permitted to build the synagogue which marks the beginning of the Jewish community. The synagogue was built on land belonging to a nobleman, and thus was not under the burghers' jurisdiction. But the latter did not give up their opposition to the presence of Jews in the city. For two hundred and twenty years, from the founding of the Great Synagogue until the annexation to Russia, Vilna Jewry was forced to wage a constant struggle for the right of residence in the city. Charters, privileges, decrees, judicial decisions by the score were issued for and against the Jews by monarch and feudal lords; compromises were made and annulled; riots and disturbances, large and small, broke out, coinciding very often with the times when the Jewish status was under discussion.

The unceasing, determined struggle of the Jews, merchant and artisan alike, for their right to remain in the city had its effect on their character, and hardened them for the trials of the Russian period. Then the struggle was not for the right to dwell in Vilna but for the chance to make a living. During the Russian period, the Jewish population of Vilna grew rapidly—from 5,000 or 6,000 at the annexation, to about 24,000 in the middle of the nineteenth century, and 38,000 in the 'eighties. By the close of the century Vilna had 63,000 Jews, forming about 40 percent of the total population. In 1914 there were 72,000.

During the first half of the nineteenth century, Vilna had the largest Jewish community in Russia (outside of Poland); later with the rapid growth of Odessa, it was relegated to second place. By the end of the century, Vilna was fourth in Jewish population in the whole Russian Empire, which then included the Polish cities of Warsaw and Lodz.

*   *   *

From the very beginning, Jewish Vilna was a workers' community. Besides the artisans customarily found among the Jews of Eastern Europe—tailors, furriers, hat-makers, painters, shoemakers, harness-makers, printers, bookbinders—one could find there many laborers of less usual types: porters, drivers, masons, glaziers, roofers, bricklayers, ditch-diggers, woodchoppers, water carriers, chimney sweeps, street cleaners, and general unskilled labor. The Jews in Vilna took up every kind of work which was available. The Vilna Jewish community absorbed various types of Jewish migrants—Jews expelled from villages or fleeing from want in small towns—and provided them with a livelihood of a sort, according to Vilna standards.

Chronic unemployment and restrictions on residence and occupations made qualities of initiative and persistence necessary in order to make a living. The annexation by Russia, opening up new markets, provided an opportunity to utilize these qualities. A distinct Jewish economy, as it were, was formed in Vilna. Variegated products like gloves, socks, and other, similar items were manufactured by home-workers. Tobacco and stationery were produced in factories. The workers, the manufacturers, the merchants, the traveling salesmen, the suppliers of raw materials, and entrepreneurs—all were Jews. Commerce flourished. Vilna was one of Russia's main gateways into Western Europe; it had no Russia population to speak of, except the officials and the garrison, who were in no economic competition with the Jews. Rather were they the customers of Jewish artisans and merchants. Operating on the slimmest possible margin of profit, Jewish trade was successful.

Yet, at the same time, there was appalling poverty in Vilna—poor housing, overcrowding, one-third of the Jewish population dependent on charity. I remember a semi-cellar "apartment" I saw, when a group of us, young people, visited Vilna shortly after the turn of the century. It consisted originally of two rooms and a kitchen, located in a section which was not the poorest part of the city. The rooms had been partitioned into two lodgings apiece, and sixteen people lived there. In 1912 Dr. Makhover made a study of about 200 lodgings in Vilna, which, regrettably, was not published in its entirety. I remember that it was my impression from the newspaper reports that not much had changed since our earlier visit. In the meantime the Jewish population had increased by about ten thousand, and housing construction had fallen behind.

A friend told me this story: His niece, a bright little three year old from one of the Vilna alleys, was brought to his mother's house. At night, on looking out of her window, she clapped her hands and exclaimed in astonishment, "Look, look! What a huge star you have in Bobruisk!" It was the first time she had ever seen the moon.

And yet, there was no sign of degeneration in the Vilna Jewish community. It was sturdy and full of sap, in spite of its frightful poverty. A flourishing Jewish culture protected it.

Vilna was a city with a Jewish quarter, and narrow, segregated, stifling Jewish streets. But an intense Jewish life, pulsating within that ghetto, gave it unusual vigor and vitality. Jewish life there had wholeness, simplicity, and richness.

Let us go into the ghetto between the afternoon and evening prayers. At long tables in the minor synagogues sit Jews just returned from their labor, and study the weeks liturgical Bible reading or a chapter of Mishna, or books of legend and commentary. Or on Sabbath eve, in the little lending-libraries, see the young apprentices and workers, boys and girls, and their alert interest in the literature that opens horizons of fascinating variety before them. Or go and sit at the sermons of itinerant preachers, lecturers, exhorters of all kinds, and watch the thronged audience, its simple, keen, direct remarks and its courteous, attentive manner. Or on Sabbath morn in the courtyard of the Great Synagogue: Everybody has come to hear the guest cantor—thousands, it seems. Only a few are still wrapped in their prayer shawls. The others had long finished their devotions, they had said the sanctification, and tasted the various Sabbath tidbits, and then had gone to hear Sirota, or Rotman, or whatever famous cantor was fortunate enough to officiate in Vilna at the time. Now they stood, or walked, and chatted with discriminating appreciation of the excellencies of the rendition, repeating snatches of liturgical music, and told tales of old-time cantors, and the marvels related about them.

The popular culture of Vilna was also expressed in one hundred and sixty Jewish societies of the traditional type, each one named by some Biblical verse. This is the number that has been counted. I am sure there were far more. I doubt whether this number includes the "Break of Dawn" society, whose members arose at the indicated hour for prayer in common; or the "Tenth in Sanctity" Society, which maintained ten notable and aged scholars in holy studies; or dozens of others of the same type. The most common were charitable and mutual aid organizations. These formed the basis for modern labor organizations which later developed in Vilna   chimney sweeps, tailors, butchers, etc. had long organized their own minor synagogues), as well as for the Hoveve-Zion societies, the forerunners of Zionism.

*   *   *

Vilna was a city of tradition—above all of the tradition of the Torah. Ephraim the blacksmith would say his lesson in Talmud, and Phineas Shokian, one of the devotees of modern Hebrew and secular nationalism, was at the same time a charter member of a Talmud study circle founded by the proto-Zionist Hoveve Zion movement. "Torah," however, was regarded as comprehending secular science and philosophy, and critical judgment from those quarters was welcome as the critical analysis of sages.

Vilna was the largest Jewish printing and publishing center in the world. The famous publishing house of the Widow and Brothers Romm, whose prayer-books, Pentateuch texts—with commentaries—and volumes of the Talmud were known all over the world, was located there. It was the place where the most famous Hebrew books of the beginning of the "Era of Enlightment" were printed: Abraham Mapu's biblical novels; Kalman Schulman's prolific and instructive output; numerous didactic and historical books; the poems of the father and son Lebensohn; the poetry of Judah Leib Gordon; the Yiddish stories of Isaac Meir Dick; and the Hebrew grammars; and the modern revolutionary pamphlets. The first Jewish literary "bohemia" existed in Vilna in the 1870's, with its young writers, women as well as men, careless of convention and fully at ease in Vilna.

Vilna was the residence of the greatest scholar of East European Jewry—the Gaon of Vilna. Other famous men of his type, Rabbi Sabbatai Cohen, Rabbi Moses Rivkes, and many others, flourished there long before; but it was the Gaon Rabbi Elijah who became the symbol and pride of Vilna. His life embodied Vilna's faith in the power of human effort, in the efficacy of individual influence, in the power of reforms made by wise men. The life of the Gaon was that of a saintly recluse devoted wholly to piety and scholarship. The number of his disciples was very small. Few were those who were privileged to be really intimate with him. And yet, through his disciples, his influence was very great. Rabbi Haim of Volozhin founded the famous Yeshiva which revolutionized the study of the Talmud, emphasizing the principles of realistic interpretation, thorough knowledge of the texts, and reliance on early sources. His brother Salman pressed for adequate study of Bible and Mishna, as well as Talmud, in Vilna and insisted on grammatically correct pronunciation of the Hebrew and clear enunciation in prayers and in reading the Torah. Rabbi Menashe of Ilia stimulated communal activity and exercised a strong moral influence. Rabbi Israel of Shklov was the pioneer of the "ascension" of scholars to the Holy Land and established close bonds between Jerusalem and the Diaspora. The Gaon's son, Rabbi Abraham, was among the first to pave the way for historico-literary research in early post-Biblical commentaries. Each of them drew much of his inspiration from the Gaon, as they proudly acknowledged.

The Gaon—literally "the Genius"—symbolized for Vilna the power of human will. It was proverbial in Vilna that only strong will was necessary to reach similar heights. Each section of Vilna Jewry could tell you of its own "genius," and of the powerful will that made his achievements possible. A favorite figure of Vilna Jewry was the famous sculptor Antokolsky, the son of a poor tavern keeper. He drew and moulded in his childhood, spoiling many articles in the house and receiving as many beatings, but was determined to achieve fame as an artist. "By sheer will-power," he did.

There was also the saintly woman of Vilna, Dvoira-Esther Langlefer, a "genius" of alms-giving, about whose patience and determination many tales were spun. She was a poor girl, who in her youth sold cookies in the taverns, setting aside a certain percentage of her earnings for charity. She married a carpenter, and having no children, she became a "genius" in dispensing loans without interest. She never demanded payment, but sat on a low bench in the butchers' lane, waiting for the debtors to make good

their loans. While sitting there she would collect money for various charitable purposes: for curing the poor sick, for providing
poor girls with dowries. The society in her name had a fund of
twenty thousand rubles and a prayer-house of its own. After
Dvoira-Esther's death, women would come to pray at her grave
when their hearts were troubled.

A middle-class Jew in Vilna would tell the story of Israel
Bunimovitch, a self-made banker, who started at the age of thir-
teen as a clerk. And one must remember that Vilna was not
America. Yet, "will-power" made a financial "genius" of him.

The Vilna laborer, member of the "Bund"—the workers' alliance—would tell the story of Hirsh Leckert, who fired at the Russian governor because the latter ordered revolutionary workers
flogged. When asked at the trial why he shot at the governor, he
answered boldly and simply: "I intended to kill him," and for this
he was hanged. Telling this story, the workers would not forget
to add that Leckert was from Vilna—and "he had a strong will."

The same qualities are stressed in the history of that hero of
Jewish Vilna, the proselyte, young Count Valentine Potocki: how
devotedly he studied the Talmud and observed all the commandments, and how firm he was when finally burned at the stake. Any
Vilna Jew pointing to the large bent tree growing over the *Ger-
Tzedek's* grave would stress the will-power and determination of
the saintly proselyte.

*   *   *

This veneration of will-power, determination, and devotion
to principle produced an attitude of tolerance among the various
ideological groupings in Vilna in old and modern times, particularly when one saw these valued qualities in an opponent. In no
Jewish community was the feeling of Jewish unity so strongly developed. One could see it especially in the famous Strashun
Library, crowded with old and young, orthodox and modern, reading rabbinical *responsa* or modern Hebrew novels, and treating
one another with courtesy and respect. There was a tone of good
natured contention in the continual discussions, debates and po-

lemics carried on among Misnagdim and Hassidim, Zionists and Bundists, and other groups. Acrimony was seldom permitted to break bounds since the time when the Hassidim were excommunicated by the Gaon. During the 1905 Revolution, Vilna became the headquarters of every political party in Russian Jewry where they carried on their polemical battles among themselves; always, however, in the distinctive spirit of the city.

Vilna also presented the spectacle of various apparently contrasting cultural and ideological types of Jew borrowing from one another and merging into one another. Ben-Zion Ilfas, a typical orthodox scholar, wrote an ethical tract in the form of a novel which enjoyed unusual success. Gozhansky, one of the pioneers of Bund (Jewish Socialist) propaganda, wrote his first pamphlet in the form of a traditional funeral oration by the city preacher over the death of Tsar Alexander III.

This blending of types and methods had an air of naivete about it. I recall a visit to the Gaon's grave on which lay many written requests by supplicants for the saint's intercession in their behalf. Unable to restrain my curiosity, I picked up a few of them and read. One of them said: "I pray and beg mercy that I succeed in chosing the right books for reading. Shloimo the son of Gittel." For many years I kept in my archives this unique little note written in a large legible handwriting.

This merging of the different currents of Jewish thought and method was not a new thing in Vilna. Its famous Gaon, the most luminous figure of Orthodox Jewry, wrote a book on geometry, stimulated a translation of Euclid into Hebrew, and was anxious to see a translation of Josephus. And yet it was he who ordered that Abba Hlusker, a well-known protagonist of the Enlightenment, be publicly disgraced in the market-place because he was suspected of holding lightly the words of the sages. Rabbi Moshe Maiseles, an employee of the community and an adherent of Hassidism, in his old age quoted Schiller and Goethe by heart to Montefiore's secretary in Hebron. There was, also, Reb Ber, a teacher of religion, who joined the Bund and made his home the hiding-place for illegal literature and weapons.

Vilna was known as "Jerusalem in Lithuania." It did have the characteristics of a national capital where all spiritual influences in the people's life met and crossed. One felt there the fullness of Jewish existence, of the people's will for living and working with their fellow-Jews.

Modern Hebraic movements, such as the Haskalah and Zionism grew out of Vilna's past rather than coming as sudden upheavals. Zionism in Vilna took the form of a natural popular sentiment, which could be opposed only by the unusually obdurate. When Sir Moses Montefiore visited Vilna one hundred years ago, and when Herzl visited it over forty years ago, the Jews in Vilna knew no bounds to their enthusiasm. Montefiore came with the official approval of the Russian authorities and the demonstration was permitted. It reached its peak when the crowd saw the word *Jerusalem* in Hebrew letters on the visitor's carriage. A memorandum was presented to Montefiore, intended for the Russian government. Worded boldly and with dignity, it set forth the grievances of the Jews and their demands. Herzl visited Vilna on his way to St. Petersburg. The public reception was not sanctioned by the authorities; on the contrary, the Jewish leaders of Vilna were warned against it. Cossacks with knouts stood ready to pounce on the participants in the demonstration. And yet it took place. Herzl was presented with a Scroll of the Law and the dean of Vilna's rabbis, Shlomo ha-Cohen, pronounced over him the benediction for princes and rulers. The president of the community, Aryeh Neishul, an embodiment of the Vilna tradition, recited a scroll of "What was in the hearts of the sons of this Jerusalem, which is in Lithuania: Not to us, O Lord, not to us, but to the Jerusalem which is in Judea give honor!"

September, 1944

Kaddish

by CHARLES REZNIKOFF

"Upon Israel and upon the Rabbis, and upon their disciples and upon all the disciples of their disciples, and upon all who engage in the study of the Torah in this place and in every place, unto them and unto you be abundant peace, grace, lovingkindness, mercy, long life, ample sustenance and salvation, from their Father who is in Heaven. And say ye Amen." Kaddish de Rabbanan, translated by R. TRAVERS HERFORD.

Upon Israel and upon the rabbis
and upon the disciples and upon all the disciples of their disciples
and upon all who study the Torah in this place and in every place,
to them and to you
peace;

upon Israel and upon all who meet with unfriendly glances, sticks
     and stones and names—
on posters, in newspapers, or in books to last,
chalked on asphalt or in acid on glass,
shouted from a thousand thousand windows by radio;
who are pushed out of class-rooms and rushing trains,
whom the hundred hands of a mob strike,
and whom jailers strike with bunches of keys, with revolver butts;
to them and to you
in this place and in every place
safety;

upon Israel and upon all who live
as the sparrows of the streets
under the cornices of the houses of others,
and as rabbits
in the field of strangers
on the grace of the seasons
and what the gleaners leave in the corners;

you children of the wind—
birds
that feed on the tree of knowledge
in this place and in every place,
to them and to you
a living;

upon Israel
and upon their children and upon all the children of their children
in this place and in every place,
to them and to you
life.

November, 1942

The Last Visit

by M. G.

WORMS ON the Rhine is the seat of the oldest Jewish community in Germany. The oldest German synagogue was to be found in Worms. The construction of this synagogue, founded by Jacob and his wife Rachel, was completed in 1304. Since then the Synagogue has known good times and bad, but it has always remained true to the purpose to which it had been dedicated. Till the year 1938. On the night of November 9, this synagogue, together with thousands of others in Germany, was consumed by flame. The house of God was burnt down. A part of the ceiling caved in, pulling down with it one of the two high columns. The stone frame of the Holy Ark with the three crowns, surmounted by the fourth larger crown—that of the Good Name,—has remained standing, blackened by fire.

A hole gapes in the wall where the Holy Ark had been. The scrolls of the Torah had withstood the flame but explosives were thrust between the books and they were so destroyed. There had been thirty-six scrolls in the Holy Ark. The famous scroll written on buckskin by Rabbi Meir of Rothenberg (died 1293) during his imprisonment in Ensisheim, was among the scrolls destroyed. Legend says that the scroll came down the Rhine in a boat to Worms where it was brought to land by Jewish seamen.

The Rashi-chapel, built on the west wall, has also burned down. The Rashi chair is missing. There are reports that it was brought to safety.

Above the corridor to the Women's synagogue was a room first used as a community hall, and later as a small Jewish museum. The objects kept there bore a close relationship to the Worms community. There were many valuable documents—the Kaiser's Privileges from 1562 to 1766, letters of safe conduct, letters of protection, a Jewish regulation of the city of Worms dated 1552.

There were also specimens of the art of Worms' silversmiths, magnificent goblets owned by the *Khevrah Kadisha.* The oldest, a superb Renaissance goblet, bore the mark, 1609.

In one case was to be found the *Maase Nissim* book of Juspa Schammes, the "Green Book" in which many important events from 1563 on, had been recorded. In addition there were many *Minhag* books, and finally the two precious prayer-books of Simkha Ben Jehuda of the 13th century. These were inscribed on parchment and were richly illuminated with colored letters and decorations.

Whether these treasures were saved I could not discover on the day when I visited my home city for the last time in order to bid it farewell before emigrating.

Whereas the remains of all burned synagogues in Germany had been thrown down and levelled with the earth, the ruins of our House of Worship still stood. Had they not dared to touch them?

A high wooden fence surrounded the wreckage. Signs announced that admittance was strictly forbidden.

I took the familiar path to the Home for the Aged that stood behind the synagogue in the garden. From there I could reach the synagogue—once a place of devotion—now a scene of horror.

I went up to the spot where formerly the two eternal lights had burned. In contrast to the other places, two eternal lights used to be lit in Worms in memory of the *Schne Orkhim,* the two strangers who, when the Black Death raged in the middle ages, and the Jews of Worms were accused of having poisoned the wells, took the guilt upon themselves, and saved the community of Worms through their death by fire on the stake.

There I said Kaddish for the last time. Then I loosened a few small stones from the ruins of the Holy Ark, pressed them to me and left the sacred place as well as the city on the Rhine where I had been born, and which had been the dwelling place of my family for four hundred years.

July, 1941

The City of Slaughter

by CH. N. BIALIK

ARISE AND go now to the city of slaughter;
Into its courtyard wend thy way;
There with thine own hand touch, and with the eyes of thine head,
Behold on tree, on stone, on fence, on mural clay,
The spattered blood and dried brains of the dead.
Proceed thence to the ruins, the split walls reach,
Where wider grows the hollow, and greater grows the breach;
Pass over the shattered hearth, attain the broken wall
Whose burnt and barren brick, whose charred stones reveal
The open mouths of such wounds, that no mending
Shall ever mend, nor healing ever heal.

There will thy feet in feathers sink, and stumble
On wreckage doubly wrecked, scroll heaped on manuscript,
Fragments again fragmented—

Pause not upon this havoc; go thy way.
The perfumes will be wafted from the acacia bud
And half its blossoms will be feathers,
Whose smell is the smell of blood!

Unto thy nostrils this strange incense they will bring.
Banish thy loathing—all the beauty of the spring,
The thousand golden arrows of the sun
Will bid thy melancholy to be gone;
The seven-fold rays of broken glass
Will bid thy sorrows pass;

For God called up the slaughter and the spring together,—
The slayer slew, the blossom burst, and it was sunny weather!

Then wilt thou flee to a yard, observe its mound.
Upon the mound lie two, and both are headless—
A Jew and his hound.
The self-same axe struck both, and both were flung
Unto the self-same heap where swine seek dung;
Tomorrow the rain will wash their mingled blood
Into the runnels, and it will be lost
In rubbish heap, in stagnant pool, in mud.
Its cry will not be heard.
It will descend into the deep, or water the cockle-burr.
And all things will be as they ever were.

Unto the attic mount, upon thy feet and hands;
Behold the shadow of death among the shadows stands.
There in the dismal corner, there in the shadowy nook,
Multitudinous eyes will look
Upon thee from the sombre silences—
The spirits of the martyrs are these souls,
Gathered together, at long last,
Beneath these rafters and in these ignoble holes.
The hatchet found them here, and hither do they come
To seal with a last look, as with their final breath,
The agony of their lives, the terror of their death.
Tumbling and stumbling wraiths, they come, and cower there.
Their silence whimpers, and it is their eyes which cry
Wherefore, O Lord, and why?
It is a silence only God can bear.

Lift then thine eyes to the roof; there's nothing there,
Save silences that hang from rafters
    And brood upon the air:
Question the spider in his lair!
His eyes beheld these things; and with his web he can
A tale unfold horrific to the ear of man:—
    A tale of cloven-belly, feather-filled;

Of nostrils nailed, of skull-bones bashed and spilled;
Of murdered men who from the beams were hung,
And of a babe beside its mother flung,
Its mother speared, the poor chick finding rest
Upon its mother's cold and milkless breast;
Of how a dagger halved that infant's word,
Its *ma* was heard, its *mama* never heard.

O, even now his eyes from me demand accounting,
For these the tales the spider is recounting,
Tales that do puncture the brain, such tales that sever
Thy body, spirit, soul, from life, forever!
Then wilt thou bid thy spirit—*Hold, enough!*
Stifle the wrath that mounts within thy throat,
Bury these things accursed,
Within the depth of thy heart, before thy heart will burst!
Then wilt thou leave that place, and go thy way—
And lo—
The earth is as it was, the sun still shines:
It is a day like any other day.

D ESCEND THEN, to the cellars of the town,
    There where the virginal daughters of thy folk were fouled,
When seven heathen flung a woman down,
The daughter in the presence of her mother,
The mother in the presence of her daughter,
Before slaughter, during slaughter, and after slaughter!
Touch with thy hand the cushion stained; touch
The pillow incarnadined:
This is the place the wild ones of the wood, the beasts of the field
With bloody axes in their paws compelled thy daughters yield:

Beasted and swined!

Note also, do not fail to note—
In that dark corner, and behind that cask

Crouched husbands, bridegrooms, brothers, peering from the
    cracks,
Watching the sacred bodies struggling underneath
The bestial breath,
Stifled in filth, and swallowing their blood!
Watching—these heroes!—
The ignominious rabble tasting flesh,
Morsels for Neros.
Crushed in their shame, they saw it all;
They did not stir nor move;
They did not pluck their eyes out; they
Beat not their brains against the wall!
Indeed, each wretch then had it in his heart to pray;
A miracle, O Lord,—and spare my skin this day!
Those who survived this foulness, who from their blood awoke,
Beheld their life polluted, the light of their world gone out—
How did their menfolk bear it, how did they bear this yoke?
They crawled forth from their holes, they fled to the house of the
    Lord,
They offered their thanks to Him, the sweet benedictory word.
The Cohanim sallied forth, to the Rabbi's house they flitted:
Tell me, O Rabbi, tell, is my own wife permitted?
The matter ends; and nothing more.
And all is as it was before.

COME, NOW, and I will bring thee to their lairs,
    The privies, jakes and pigpens where the heirs
Of Hasmoneans lay, with trembling knees,
Concealed and cowering,—the sons of the Maccabees!
The seed of saints, the scions of the lions!
Who, crammed by scores in all the sanctuaries of their shame,
So sanctified my name!
It was the flight of mice they fled,
The scurrying of roaches was their flight;
They died like dogs, and they were dead!

And on the next morn, after the terrible night
The son who was not murdered found
The spurned cadaver of his father on the ground . . .

Now wherefore dost thou weep, O son of Man?

Beyond the suburbs go, and reach the burial ground.
Let no man see thy going: attain that place alone,
A place of saintly graves and martyr's stone.
Stand on the fresh-turned soil.
Such silence will take hold of thee, thy heart will fail
With pain and shame, yet I
Will let no tear fall from thine eye.
Though thou wilt long to bellow like the driven ox
That bellows, and before the altar balks,
I will make hard thy heart, yea, I
Will not permit a sigh.

See, see, the slaughtered calves, so smitten and so laid;
Is there a price for their death? How shall that price be paid?

F ORGIVE, ye shamed of the earth, yours is a pauper-Lord!
Poor was he during your life, and poorer still of late.
Hence, if you come to my door to ask for your reward
It shall be opened to you, and you shall see that Lord
Fallen from high estate.

I grieve for you, my children. My heart is sad for you.
Your dead were vainly dead; and neither I nor you
Know why you died or wherefore, nor for whom.
Even as was your life, so reasonless was your doom.

What says the *sh'china?* In the clouds it hides
In shame, in agony alone abides;
I, too, at night, will venture on the tombs

Regard the dead and weigh their secret shame,
But never shed a tear, I swear it in God's name.
For great is the anguish, great the shame on the brow
But which of these is greater, son of man, say thou—
Or liefer keep thy silence, bear witness in my name
To the hour of my sorrow, the moment of my shame.
And when thou dost return
Bring thou the blot of my disgrace upon thy people's head,
And from my suffering do not part,
But set it like a stone within their heart!

T URN, THEN, to leave the cemetery ground,
    And for a moment thy swift eye will pass
Upon the verdant carpet of the grass—
A lovely thing!
Fragrant and moist, as it is always at the coming of the Spring!
The stubble of death, the growth of tombstones!
Take thou a fistful, fling it on the plain
Saying,
The people is plucked grass; can plucked grass grow again?

Turn then, thy gaze from the dead, and I will lead
Thee from the graveyard to thy living brothers,
And thou wilt come, with those of thine own breed,
Into the synagogue, and on a day of fasting,
To hear the cry of their agony,
Their weeping everlasting.
Thy skin will grow cold, the hair on thy skin stand up,
And fear and trembling will take hold of thee:
In such wise does a people cease to be.

Look in their hearts—behold a dreary waste,
Where even vengeance can revive no growth,
And yet upon their lips no mighty malediction
Rises, no blasphemous oath.

Are they not real, their bruises?
Why is their prayer false?
Why, in the day of their trials
Approach me with pious ruses,
Afflict me with denials?

Regard them now, in these their woes:
Ululating, lachrymose,
Crying *I have sinned* from their throes,
Self-flagellative with confession's whips.
Their hearts, however, do not believe their lips.
Is it, then, possible for shattered limbs to sin?
Wherefore their cries imploring, their supplicating din?
Speak to them, bid them rage!
Let them against me raise the outraged hand,—
Let them demand!
Demand the retribution for the shamed
Of all the centuries and every age!
Let fists be flung like stone
Against the heavens and the heavenly Throne!

And thou too, Son of Man, be part of these:
Believe the pangs of their heart, believe not their litanies:
And when the cantor lifts his voice to cry:
Remember the martyrs, Lord,
Bend down from Thy great mansions in the sky
Consider the sucklings, Lord,
And when the pillars of the synagogue shall crack
At this his piteous word
And terror will take and fling thee in its deep,
Then I will harden my heart; I shall not let thee weep!

Should then a cry escape from Thee?
I'll stifle it within thy throat,
Let them assoil their tragedy,—

Not thou,—let it remain unmourned
For distant ages, times remote,
But thy tear, Son of Man, remain unshed!
Build thou about it, with thy deadly hate
Thy fury and thy rage, unuttered,
A wall of copper, the bronze triple plate!
So in thy heart it shall remain confined
A serpent in its nest—O terrible tear!—
Until by thirst and hunger it shall find
A breaking of its bond. Then shall it rear
Its venomous head, its poisoned fangs, and wait
To strike the people of thy love and hate!

Leave now this place at twilight to return
And to behold these creatures who arose
In terror at dawn, at dusk now, drowsing, worn
With weeping, broken in spirit, in darkness shut.
Their lips still move with words unspoken.
Their hearts are broken.

No lustre in the eye, no hoping in the mind,
They grope to seek support they shall not find:
Thus when the tallow's gone,
The wick still sends its smoke;
Thus does the beast of burden,
Broken and old, still bear his yoke.

Would that misfortune had left them some small solace
Sustaining the soul, consoling their gray hairs!
Behold the fast is ended; the final prayers are said.
But why do they tarry now, these mournful congregations?
Shall it be also read,
The Book of Lamentations?

It is a preacher mounts the pulpit now.
He opens his mouth, he stutters, stammers. Hark
The empty verses from his speaking flow.
And not a single mighty word is heard
To kindle in the hearts a single spark.
The old attend his doctrine, and they nod
The young ones harken to his speech; they yawn.
The mark of death is on their brows; their God
Has utterly forsaken every one.

AND THOU too, greet them not, nor touch their wound;
Within their cup no further measure pour.
Wherever thou wilt touch, a bruise is found.
Their flesh is wholly sore.
For since they have met pain with resignation
And have made peace with shame,
What shall avail thy consolation?

They are too wretched to evoke thy scorn.
They are too lost, thy pity to evoke,
So let them go, then, men to sorrow born
Mournful and slinking, crushed beneath their yoke
Go to their homes, and to their hearth depart—
Rot in the bones, corruption in the heart.
And when thou shalt arise upon the morrow
And go upon the highway,
Thou shalt then meet these men destroyed by sorrow
Sighing and groaning, at the doors of the wealthy
Proclaiming their sores, like so much peddler's wares,
The one his battered head, t'other limbs unhealthy
One shows a wounded arm, and one a fracture bares.
And all have eyes that are the eyes of slaves,
Slaves flogged before their masters;
And each one begs, and each one craves:
Reward me, Master, for that my skull is broken

Reward me, for my father who was martyred!
The rich ones, all compassion, for the pleas so bartered
Extend them staff and bandage, say *good riddance*, and
The tale is told:
The paupers are consoled.
Avaunt ye, beggars, to the charnel-house!
The bones of your fathers disinter!
Cram them within your knapsacks, bear
Them on your shoulders, and go forth
To do your business with these precious wares
At all the country fairs!

Stop on the highway, near some populous city,
Your customer, and spread on your filthy rags
Those martyred bones that issue from your bags,
And sing, with raucous voice, your pauper's ditty!
So will you conjure up the pity of the stranger
And so his sympathy implore.
For you are now as you have been of yore
And as you stretched your hand
So will you stretch it,
And as you have been wretched
So are you wretched!
What is thy business here, O Son of Man?
Rise, to the desert flee?
Thy tear upon the barren boulders shed!
Take thou thy soul, rend it in many a shred!
And feed thou thy heart to rage, as to a worm!
Thy tear upon the barren boulders shed!
And send thy bitter cry into the storm!

Translated from the Hebrew by ABRAHAM M. KLEIN

August, 1942

The Austrian Socialists

by CHARLES REZNIKOFF

THE RAIN is falling
    steadily. Two by two,
a column of policemen marches
in the twilight. (Revolution!
Against our boots
strike,
flickering tongues!)
A company of soldiers
with machine-guns,
squad by squad, turns within a square
and marches down a street. (Revolution!
We are the greyhounds—
unleash us!—
to hunt these rabbits
out of the fields. *Listen to me,*
my two wives,
I have killed a man!)
Workingmen troop down the stairs
and out into the rain;
hurrah!
Revolution! (The gentleness of the deer
will never persuade the tiger from his leap.
Strong as a million hands,
what Bastille or Kremlin withstands us
as we march, as we march?)
Who minds the rain now?
How bright the air is;
how warm to be alive!
No children
in the hallways;

the stores closed,
not a motor-car;
except for the rain,
how quiet.
Revolution!
Hurry to the power-house;
let the water out of the
boilers! The wires of the lamps burn dimly,
the lights in the houses
are out. Tie the red flag to the chimney,
but do not go through the streets,
where the steel-helmets have woven nets
of barbed wire;
bring guns and machine-guns
through the sewer
to each beleaguered house;
and send couriers throughout the land,
Arise, arise, you workers!
Revolution!

Put on your helmets;
troopers, tighten the straps
under your chins;
strap on revolvers;
tighten your belts,
and mount your horses; mount!
Send bullets flying
through the panes of glass—
windows, mirrors, pictures;
forward, trot!
I am Fey,
I am Prince Starhemberg;
behind me is the Empire—
the princes of Austria and the captains of Germany,
armored tanks and armored aeroplanes,

fortresses and battleships;
before us only workingmen
unused to arms and glory!

The bones in his neck part as they hang him,
and the neck is elongated;
here is a new animal
for the zoo in which are
mermaid, centaur, sphynx, and Assyrian cherub—
the face human, like their faces,
but sorrowing for a multitude,
hands and feet dangling
out of sleeves and trousers become too short,
and the neck a giraffe's—
as the neck of one who looks away from the
          patch of grass at his feet
and feeds among clouds should be.

Tell of it you who sit in the little cafes,
drinking coffee and eating whipped cream
among the firecrackers of witticisms;
tell of it you who are free to gallop about on horseback
or to ride in automobiles, or walk in gardens,
who say, Do you speak of despondency—
or any ugliness;
"Wie herrlich leuchtet
Mir die Natur!
Wie glaenzt die Sonne,
Wie lacht die Flur!"

Karl Marx Hof, Engels Hof—
Liebknecht Hof, Mateotti Hof—
names cut in stone to ornament a house
as much as carving of leaves or fruit,
as any bust of saint and hero;

names pealing out a holiday among the ticking of clocks!—
speak your winged words, cannon;
shell with lies, radios,
the pleasant homes—
the houses built about courtyards
in which were
the noise of trees and of fountains,
the silence of statues and of flowers;
cry out, you fascists,
Athens must perish!
Long live Sparta!

I Visit a Soviet Kolkhoz

by DAVID PINSKI

THE *kolkhoz* is a step on the road to communism, a step toward the Palestinian *kvutza* which embodies the highest form of communistic life.

The *kolkhoz*, a Soviet community based on a collective economy, operates on the principle of communal ownership of the soil, tools, machines and buildings necessary for cooperative production and the upkeep of everything owned and used cooperatively. But each member of the *kolkhoz* is paid according to the share of labor he contributes.

A daily norm of production is established—qualitatively and quantitatively. An inferior worker who fulfills half the norm is credited with half a day's work; a superior worker who can double or triple it is credited proportionately. This determines his share in the products of field and garden. After the government's share of crops—after the government's own price is delivered and funds for seed and fodder are put aside, the remainder is sold in the open market at prevailing prices. The money thus realized is distributed among the members of the *kolkhoz* according to their labor. Naturally, there are wide discrepancies in income.

Every member has his own little house, and his own bit of land which he can cultivate as he pleases; a cow or two, a goat, a sheep, chickens, and pigs. Any surplus of this little private farm which is not consumed by the family can be sold in the open market. But one may not buy a neighbor's produce in order to sell it. That would be forbidden trading.

Whereas the development of the Palestinian *kvutza* has been the spontaneous realization of a great ideal, the establishment of the *kolkhoz* has been dictated from above and forced upon the peasants. Not without great struggle and bloodshed. But there is no regret among them now. It was this enforced cooperation, and common ownership of the land that made possible the use of tractors and combines. These in turn have given farmers great advantages over weather conditions and assured them of finer crops. Peasants who formerly had to beg for their bread now are credited with hundreds of poods of bread and upward of a thousand rubles annually.

As time goes on and people become rooted in this cooperative life, the Soviet government will more easily be able, at an auspicious moment, to effect the transition from the *kolkhoz* to the communist form of the *kvutza*. The latter will then serve as a valuable model.

(Upon my wife's suggestion that we ought to start communist propaganda toward this end, I assured her that on our imminent visit to the Jewish *kolkhozes*, we would surely tell them all about our Palestinian *kvutzot*.)

We set out for the Crimea and the Jewish Collectives. We visited one after another—five of them—run largely by Jews who not long before had been among the declassed small shopkeepers and merchants.

One *kolkhoz* specialized in grapes, boasting the largest vineyards. The manager welcomed us and while we were enjoying the many varieties of grapes he had to offer, he told us of his experiences. The members of his collective had revolted. What did they know about grapes? Of what practical use were grapes? What, after all, could they make on grapes? And who could wait until the vines actually grew enough to produce grapes? But now they were not sorry. They understood and loved their work and were proud of the results. They had far surpassed the norm assigned by the government.

Another *kolkhoz* specialized in truck-farming—the largest of its kind. Endless fields of cantaloupe, watermelon, eggplant, beans, peas, etc. The superintendent, a husky Jew, good to look at, welcomed us with melons and cantaloupes, and told his story. The work hadn't been easy. It was more than hard to break in, but they did it. There were plenty of Stakhanoffites now, men and women. The old peasants from neighboring Tartar collectives often came over and admired the Jews and learned from them.

In the third *kolkhoz* we found sheep. Planting had been unsuccessful that year. A hailstorm had ruined everything. But the sheep had brought luck—to the amount of about 70,000 rubles.

Each farm had its measure of abundance. Cows, horses, chickens—150 cows, 70 horses, 2000 chickens. Some more, some less. But they were all pretty well off. They took milk and eggs to market. They made good money. And the government got its quota and more.

In addition, every farmer had his little nest-egg—a home, a garden, chickens, a cow and pigs, pigs. . . .

We talked about life in the *kvutza*. All listened attentively. Very fine, indeed. But it was out of the question here. It wouldn't pay. The government still has to maintain its practice of paying according to work done. A group of former Palestinian *khalutzim* had actually tried to organize one of those communist settlements. They had to put up three large buildings to house their communal kitchen, dining-room, nursery, living quarters, and so forth. But the government found it did not pay, and they had to turn it into a *kolkhoz*.

How they all sang the praises of the Soviet Government. What a government! It had loaned large sums of money to every *kolkhoz*, helping to establish them. One had obtained a million rubles, another 600,000. Wasn't it wonderful! Such a large sum! And half of it had already been written off. What was meant by "written off"? Simply cancelled, donated. And what did we think would happen to the other half? The same thing, of course. We'll never be asked for it. Well, what do you think of our government? If only all Jews were so well off!

But—but—why hadn't we seen any young people? Where are your 18- and 20-year-old boys and girls?

Oh, our young people went off to the towns, to study or work in factories. There is no future for them here.

We have nothing against Stalin, a middle-aged woman said to

us, our children are on top of the world, and we'll manage for the rest of our lives.

A seventy-year-old man expressed his happiness because none of his children had remained with him. They were in Kharkov, in Kiev, and Moscow. I'm at the end of the road, he said to my wife, and I don't mind for myself, but our children and grandchildren are better off where they are.

In one *kolkhoz* there was deep satisfaction because 120 of their young people had managed to leave. There now remained 185 under eighteen years who would also scatter when they came of age.

Then what would become of the *kolkhoz?* If the youth left never to return, who would carry on when their time was over?

The less conscientious among them answered: Are we to worry about that?

The more social-minded said: We have done our duty; we worked, built up these collectives, and were useful to our socialist fatherland. When we are gone, our work will be taken over and continued by others—Tartars, Germans, Ukrainians—what matter who? Who cares?

And the work of the Jew on the land?

That was necessary while some of us were declassed. But not any more. Is there a law that Jews must work on the land? We can be useful anywhere now. What do you think will happen to Biro-Bidjan? Jews won't go there. Why should they? Siberia, of all places! Banishment! You've probably met many Jews on your trip. Well, what do they say? Probably the same as we do—

True!

Of course! They'd be fools. Let them send the Jews of Germany and Poland to Biro-Bidjan. I'll be frank with you: To us Biro-Bidjan is a horror. We dread it. If our children went there, we'd feel as if they'd been exiled. . . .

They're not with you anyway.

Nevertheless in the summer they visit or help us. Now you know why the younger generation isn't here. But . . .

Why isn't there a single tree anywhere? Why haven't you

460   JEWISH FRONTIER ANTHOLOGY

any flowers? Don't you long for shade in the summer? Don't you feel the need of the beauty of flowers? Here you have two long rows of bare brick houses cracked and crumbling where the rain has washed down the mortar. They look so neglected and mournful. Why not beautify them with vines and flowers? Is your soil, the soil of the Crimean steppe, not hospitable to tree and shrub?

Oh no! Our soil grows everything that's planted in it. We did at one time plant a little grove of trees, but the cows trampled them. A bit of shade would have been very welcome, but who has time to struggle with the cattle? As for flowers—we've gotten along without them until now. . . .

We told them that in Palestine flowers have become a custom. They plant flowers and sell them. Shopkeepers and workers take them home every Friday evening for the *shabbos*.

And what are your cultural activities here?

We have a club-house. We meet occasionally after work, and spend a little time socially, singing, dancing—we dance all your American dances too—for the children's sake.

Any lectures? Books?

Yes, once in a while, when somebody comes our way, we get a lecture too. Sometimes we read aloud from Sholem Aleichem. But we're beginning to get tired of that.

How about other writers?

What other writers?

The represenatives of the new Soviet Yiddish literature. We know very little about it. How is that? Not interesting. And to tell you the truth: they don't deserve to be read by us. Take David Bergelson. For a whole summer he lived at Yevpatoria and not once did he take the trouble to come over and see a single *kolkhoz* of ours. The same with the others. They come to the Crimea for summer, but they never show themselves here. Only Dobrushin comes once in a while. So, if they're not interested in us, why should we be interested in them? How about the Yiddish language? The answer: they have schools—one school for a few neighboring settlements. Yiddish is taught, but Russian is spoken.

Of course. When the children grow up and go out into the world, Yiddish is put aside anyway. . . .

What will happen to Jewish culture?

We were sitting in the home of an elderly woman who had been introduced to us at a particularly capable person, a Stakhanoffite. She welcomed us with the story of her connections—her cousinship to one of the most splendid personalities in Palestine—and with *gefilte* fish. We had not known it was *shabbos,* and they also told us that in six days it would be *Rosh Hashanah.* How they knew this without a calendar they would not reveal. At the moment when I asked my question about Jewish culture, our hostess' pigs burst into a chorus of grunts. There was general laughter—but I did not need any further answer.

When we returned to Moscow we asked Bergelson and other Jewish writers: Why do you neglect the Jewish collectives?

The answer was a wave of the hand. They know that these collectives will not remain in Jewish hands. There is really no one there worth bothering with. A pity to waste the time. The eyes of Jewish writers are turned to Biro-Bidjan. A home is being built there for Bergelson, and he will settle there.

I was the only one who regretted that these Jewish collectives would disappear. . . .

March, 1937

Racialism in Reverse

by Leon Blum

"NO MORE illusions about Germany!" exclaim extreme nationalists in France. "The framers of the Versailles Treaty deluded themselves into believing that it was possible to found a lasting peace on a subdued Germany. What criminal naïveté! A superficial glance at the history and structure of Germany would have sufficed to indicate that the German people, as soon as it had had a chance to rest and recuperate, would once again turn into a nation of robbers. The phenomenon of Hitlerism is not an historical accident but an essential expression of German evolution. If there were no Hitler, Germany would have found another Fuehrer. It is therefore a mistake to draw a distinction between the German people and its Fuehrer. This is merely a repetition of the error of 1914, when an attempt was made to differentiate between the people of Germany and the militarism of the Kaiser and his Junkers. Efforts were not spared at that time to represent German as possessing a fair side and a foul. Germany has no such fair side. Germany willed Hitler. It called him to power by the vote of a legal majority, which elected him in the full knowledge of his program of vengeance and victory. Germany stands solidly behind him.

"Doubtless," writes their spokesman Kerillis, "Hitler's horrible regime will some day be liquidated. But we would bequeathe to humanity a miserable future if we succumbed to the idea that all that is needed is to change once more the flag and form of government of the Reich. No, what is needed is to break the power of the German Reich. A few French nationalists understood this in 1918; but the peace negotiators, misled by their silly illusions, considered it possible to reconcile Germany with the rest of humanity.

---

*We offer this article written just before the outbreak of war because of its significant bearing on a future peace.—Editors.

But there was no such possibility, and the illusion proved an expensive one; after twenty years, military Germany arose anew, once more threatening a World War. The least we could now do is not to lose sight of this horrible lesson."

Ideas and demands similar to those of Kerillis have repeatedly been voiced in recent weeks: "Should the war start anew, we must not allow ourselves to be taken in again as we did in 1918 . . . Germany is beyond improvement or cure . . . We must sooner or later put an end to it." Against these ideas and demands I wish to formulate in clear and indubitable terms the following idea— one that is shared alike by both French and international Socialism.

Let us consider the aim of the spiritual propaganda presently conducted by France and Britain. Ostensibly, their objective is to convince the German masses that their Nazi leaders are concealing from them the truth about the European situation and about the real attitude of the other nations. Their messages, which are being so strenuously disseminated, say in effect: "Your despots keep you in ignorance, or deceive you through lies. If the truth were known to you, you would free yourselves of them. You would not allow yourselves to be led by them into war in this manner, *because we draw a line of distinction between your tyrants and yourselves;* because toward the German people we entertain no animosity whatever; because we have no desire other than to accord to the German people that place in a peaceful Europe which rightfully belongs to them. . . ."

These motifs, which I have briefly sketched, are the very same ones that were sounded by both Mr. Chamberlain and Lord Halifax. They are also the same as those developed in the Labor Party's noble appeal to the German people. Who cannot see that all this is based on the postulate that the Nazi despots are not the true representatives of the German people, and that between the rulers and the ruled there exists no indissoluble solidarity, but, on the contrary, a manifest division and conflict of opinion? Since Kerillis repudiates this postulate, he deprives this propaganda of the very foundations on which it rests. He thereby allows Dr.

Goebbels and his press effectively to reply: "You can see now quite clearly that we have been telling the truth, and that the enemy propaganda has been lying. You can see quite clearly that the so-called anti-Hitler peace front is nothing else than a military coalition against Germany. You can see quite clearly that to the French the German people are a hated race and the German State a hereditary enemy."

All reliable reports from Germany point to the strong efforts made by the Nazi leaders to propagate the idea of "encirclement," thus hoping to attract to themselves the favorable opinion of a confused and uneasy nation. On every note of the scale they keep repeating: "The very life of Germany is threatened! We may yet be compelled to fight for our very existence." The *Bulletin Quotidien* of the Foreign Ministry has recently published two letters dealing with this situation, addressed to the editor of *The Times* by Norman Angell and Harold Nicolson. Both of these gentlemen, comrade Norman Angell as well as Mr. Nicolson—the latter of whom spoke against the Munich Accord in the House of Commons—emphasized the importance of enlightening the German people on this matter. We must convince Germany, stated the former, that we remain the front-fighters for peace through collective security; that our aim still remains to build a Europe based upon freedom, justice and equality. We must convince Germany, asserted the latter, that no one is thinking of encircling it, and that it depends entirely upon Hitler whether or not Germany will find herself surrounded. These are effective words, all the more effective because they are true. What kind of effect, on the other hand, will Kerillis' message have, especially if it is taken to represent French public opinion and French public policy?

To maintain that there exist no differences between Hitler and the German people can only have the effect of pushing the people closer to Hitler; to maintain that there exists between them a fundamental and indissoluble bond can only have the effect of sealing that bond.

M. de Kerillis does not consider the appearance and success of Nazi racial theories as an historical accident or as the result of the actions of one man or group of men, but as an expression of the peculiar nature of the German people, of its manifest and eternal substance. Because the German people must be what they are, and because they cannot be anything else than what they are, Hitlerist racialism must forever exist. If they had not found a leader in an individual named Hitler, they would of necessity have had to look for him in some other individual. To differentiate between this person and the German people is as absurd as it is illusory, since this individual is nothing else than the symbol and active expression of the nation.

Certainly history recognizes no pure accidents. In his autobiography Hitler strove, with considerable coquettishness, to pose as an absolute originator. If you were to listen to him, you would soon be convinced that he created out of naught. Not only did he erect his structure all by himself; not only did he himself draw up the blue-print, but it was also he who formed the theoretic and political building materials that went into its making. In reality, however, it is definitely established that racialism is a part of Germany's cultural tradition. Now, were it merely a question of connecting Hitler's racism with certain currents that have been active in Germany's culture for over a century, I should certainly side with Kerillis against Hitler. But Kerillis goes infinitely farther. The spiritual currents with which Kerillis links Nazi racialism seem to him, if I may say so, to embrace the whole of the German people, without exception, regardless of class or party affiliation. In his opinion, these concepts, and the political regime which they represent, not only share a universal validity but, more than that, partake of the nature of historic necessity, are predetermined. And this precisely because they represent the German spirit—a spirit which, since the day when it identified itself irrevocably with the Germanic barbarian personality established by Tacitus, has never made an honest attempt to fraternize with Western civilization. The only sane solution, according to Kerillis, is, therefore, to deprive that spirit of the power to inflict injury.

But this is veritable racialism—Hitler's racialism; in practice, naturally, turned against him, but in theory the same as his. When Kerillis insists on the universal individuality of the German people and upon the continuance and indestructibility of their peculiarities, he is applying the very same reasoning process against Germany that Hitler does toward the Jews. Hitler considers the Germans as the *chosen people,* predestined to rule the world. Mr. Kerillis, on the other hand, considers them as the *cursed race,* whose viciousness could be removed only through their complete emasculation. Notwithstanding the two diametrically opposed objectives, the conclusions reached are materially the same. To the two race theories are thus assigned the identical meaning. Such reasoning, however, constitutes a complete negation of all modern culture and human progress; we Socialists must unequivocally reject it. We reject it because science has taught us that nowhere in Europe is there such a thing as a pure race; nor, in the strict sense of the word, anywhere else; that, therefore, no nation has the right to represent itself as a pure race. We reject it also because nowhere in history has a national feeling been produced out of the collective consciousness of an ethnic unity. We reject it further because it is in complete contradiction to actual experience, and because we believe that underneath the superficial mask of a Germany regimented by racialism there lurks a German people of an altogether different character.

The other Germany, which is now in hiding, has long lived and acted in the full light of day. Today it consists of highly respected exiles, thousands of persons in prisons or under suspicion and millions of men and women forced to dumb obedience or blind self-deception. But after the war it unquestionably embraced the overwhelming majority of the people. It held power for 15 years, and on the very eve of the Nazi victory it still controlled half of the votes. We are acquainted with its history, which forms an integral part of modern culture. *No one has the right to doubt the future of this "other Germany."* No matter how great the debasing and degenerating effects of Nazism may be, no matter how strong its influence on the younger generation, which stepped into active life after Hitler's seizure of power, we are still justified in the hope *that the liberation of the German people will witness once again the rise of that "other Germany."* All indications justify the assertion that the Hitlerist disease is not an incurable one, that the Hitlerist stain is not an ineradicable one, and that the "other Germany," once the country is liberated and accepted again into the family of nations, will restore to this people its healthy body.

Hitler's victory over this other Germany, had its causes. No occurrence in history ever took place without its causes; no phenomenon ever appeared that did not have its roots in preceding events. But the causes of Hitler's triumph are of an accidental, and not of an inevitable nature. What I mean to say is that, considering the particular causes that had existed, the result could not have been any different than what it was; but that, on the other hand, it lay within the power of human intelligence and will to prepare such causes as would have had an entirely different effect. To express it more clearly: the proof that Nazism is not the normal, necessary and inevitable expression of the German personality is the fact that it would never have existed, or at least triumphed, if post-war Europe had taken a more clear-sighted and, in the strictest sense of the word, bolder, attitude toward Germany. The more we feel justified in attributing the present unrest and danger of war in Europe to Nazi racialism exclusively, the more also are we justified in placing a large share of the responsibility for the existence of racialism on the shoulders of the victorious Powers.

French Socialism has on numerous occasions called attention to this long chain of errors, has urged that it be acknowledged and combated. Ironically enough, it begins with the Peace Treaty proper. It must be admitted also—and this need cause no surprise —that this treaty has never received a just appraisal. I believe that even while the peace agreements were made the object of some of our sharpest attacks, I personally failed to stigmatize them as "imperialist treaties." Both in chamber councils and at the Hamburg Congress, where the Socialist International was reconstituted, I represented the standpoint that here, for the first time in modern history at the conclusion of a European war, an agreement was reached which excluded the idea of victory, of unjust territorial expansion based on might, prestige or equal balance of power. The guiding principle of the framers of the treaty was in fact the right to self-determination; but they laid themselves open to the reproach that in the application of this principle they were now timid or wavering, now excessively liberal, thus violating certain political and economic realities, which in the course of time and experience became more and more pronounced. It is both interesting and instructive to note that the peace negotiators today recognize in retrospect the claims of Mr. de Kerrilis, who cannot forgive them the fact that they failed to break up Germany and to destroy German might forever. Actually, both Clemenceau and Tardieu opposed with as much energy as did Wilson and Lloyd George the breaking up of Germany. They did not wish to see the "War for Right" end in a peace of conquest. They knew that in the course of time every injustice would be removed; and so refused to condemn Europe to eternal warfare.

By the same token, for the first time in 150 years a peace treaty was signed that did not exact punitive tributes or reparations. All that was demanded of the conquered States was compensation for damages to lives and property caused by their armies, while damages to citizens of the Allies from other sources were assumed by the victorious powers themselves. Against this principle nothing can be said. But its application was even more false and absurd. It was interpreted and executed in such a manner as to create among the German people the feeling that it had been condemned to an impossible life of slavery and payment of tribute, without the hope of ever being able to meet these obligations and be free again. This feeling was reenforced by the Army of Occupation, whose arrival was interpreted by Germany as an act of war against a disarmed people. It was the occupation of the Ruhr that set off the rapid growth of racialism.

The Versailles Treaty rests, to a larger degree than is usually acknowledged, on principles of justice. Despite this, it broke Germany's spirit, even if it did not entirely destroy it. It burdened the Germans with an impossible debt, even if it failed to exhaust their wealth, which consists of their productive powers. The manner in which the reparations and disarmament clauses were applied has immeasurably increased the propaganda value of Hitler and his party, who called for the denunciation of these clauses as the only means of regaining freedom and honor. In addition, the parties of the "other Germany" which signed the treaty, and which waged an ever increasing battle against the rise of Hitlerism, could never obtain from the conquering powers the necessary encouragement and support. The latter failed to display the goodwill and willingness to help them. If after these experiences we could today live over again the history of the past twenty years, all of these mistakes would be avoided, and the other Germany would still be in power. Nazism, therefore, is no preordained expression of the German people; and no one has the right to pronounce as impossible for the future that which was possible in the past.

October, 1939

German Guilt

by HANNAH ARENDT

THE GREATER the military defeats of the Wehrmacht in the field, the greater becomes that victory of Nazi political warfare which is so often incorrectly described as mere propaganda. It is the central thesis of this Nazi political strategy that there is no difference between Nazis and Germans, that the people stand united behind the government, that all Allied hopes of finding part of the people uninfected ideologically and all appeals to a democratic Germany of the future are pure illusion. The implication of this thesis is, of course, that there is no distinction as to responsibility, that German anti-Fascists will suffer from defeat equally with German Fascists, and that the Allies had made such distinctions at the beginning of the war only for propaganda purposes. A further implication is that Allied provisions for punishment of war criminals will turn out to be empty threats because they will find no one to whom the title of war criminal could not be applied.

That such claims are not mere propaganda but are supported by very real and fearful facts, we have all learned in the past seven years. The terror-organizations which were at first strictly separated from the mass of the people, admitting only persons who could show a criminal past or prove their preparedness to become criminals, have since been continually expanded. The ban on party membership for members of the army has been dissolved by the general order which subordinates all soldiers to the party. Whereas those crimes which have always been a part of the daily routine of concentration camps since the beginning of the Nazi regime were at first a jealousy guarded monopoly of the SS and Gestapo, today members of the Wehrmacht are assigned at will to duties of mass murder. These crimes were at first kept secret by every possible means and any publication of such reports was made punishable as atrocity propaganda. Later, however, such reports were spread by Nazi-organized whispering campaigns and today these crimes are openly proclaimed under the title of "measures of liquidation" in order to force "Volksgenossen" whom difficulties of organization made it impossible to induct into the "Volksgemeinschaft" of crime at least to bear the onus of complicity and awareness of what was going on. These tactics resulted in a victory for the Nazis, as the Allied abandoned the distinction between Germans and Nazis. In order to appreciate the decisive change of political conditions in Germany since the lost battle of Britain, one must note that until the war and even until the first military defeats only relatively small groups of active Nazis, among whom not even the Nazi sympathizers were included, and equally small numbers of active anti-Fascists really knew what was going on. All others, whether German or non-German, had the natural inclination to believe the statements of an official, universally recognized government rather than the charges of refugees, which, coming from Jews or Socialists, were suspect in any case. Even of those refugees, only a relatively small proportion knew the full truth and even a smaller fraction was prepared to bear the odium of unpopularity involved in telling the truth.

As long as the Nazis expected victory, their terror organizations were strictly isolated from the people and, in time of war, from the army. The army was not used to commit atrocities and SS troops were increasingly recruited from "qualified" circles of whatever nationality. If the planned New Order of Europe should have succeeded, we would have been witnesses of an inter-European organization of terror under German leadership. The terror would have been exercised by members of all European nationalities with the exception of Jews in an organization graded according to the racial classification of the various countries. The German people, of course, would not have been spared by it. Himmler was always of the opinion that authority in Europe should be in the hands of a racial élite, organized in SS troops without national ties.

It was only their defeats which forced the Nazis to abandon

this concept and pretend to return to old nationalist slogans. The active identification of the whole German people with the Nazis was part of this trend. National Socialism's chances of organizing an underground movement in the future depend on no-one's being able to know any longer who is a Nazi and who is not, on there being no visible signs of distinction any longer, and above all on the victorious powers' being convinced that there really are no differences between Germans. To bring this about, an intensified terror in Germany, which proposed to leave no person alive whose past or reputation proclaimed him an anti-Fascist, was necessary. In the first years of the war the regime was remarkably "magnanimous" to its opponents, provided they remained peaceful. Of late, however, countless persons have been executed even though, by reason of years without freedom of movement, they could not constitute any immediate danger to the regime. On the other hand, prudently foreseeing that in spite of all precautionary measures the Allies might still find a few hundred persons in each city with an irreproachable anti-Fascist record—testified to by former war prisoners or foreign laborers, and supported by records of imprisonment or concentration camp internment—the Nazis have already provided their own trusted cohorts with similar documentation and testimony, making these criteria worthless. Thus in the case of inmates of concentration camps (whose number nobody knows precisely, but which is estimated at several million), the Nazis can safely either liquidate them or let them escape: in the improbable event of their survival (a massacre of the type which already occurred in Buchenwald is not even punishable under the war crimes provisions)—it will not be possible to identify them unmistakably.

Whether any person in Germany is a Nazi or an anti-Nazi can be determined only by the One who knows the secrets of the human heart, which no human eye can penetrate. Those, at any rate, who actively organize an anti-Nazi underground movement in Germany today would meet a speedy death if they failed to act and talk precisely like Nazis. In a country where a person attracts immediate attention by failing either to murder upon command or to be a ready accomplice of murderers, this is no light task. The most extreme slogan which this war has evoked among the Allies, that the only "good German" is a "dead German," has this much basis in fact: the only way in which we can identify an anti-Nazi is when the Nazis have hanged him. There is no other reliable token.

II.

These are the real political conditions which underlie the charge of the collective guilt of the German people. They are the consequences of a policy which, in the deepest sense, is a- and anti-national; which is entirely determined that there shall be a German people only if it is in the power of its present rulers; and which will rejoice as at its greatest victory if the defeat of the Nazis involves with it the physical destruction of the German people. The totalitarian policy, which has completely destroyed the neutral zone in which the daily life of human beings is ordinarily lived, has achieved the result of making the existence of each individual in Germany depend either upon committing crimes or on complicity in crimes. The success of Nazi propaganda in Allied countries, as expressed in the attitude commonly called Vansittartism, is a secondary matter in comparison. It is a product of general war propaganda, and something quite apart from the specific modern political phenomenon described above. All the documents and pseudo-historical demonstrations of this tendency sound like relatively innocent plagiarism of the French literature of the last war—and it makes no essential difference that a few of those writers who twenty-five years ago kept the presses rolling with their attacks on "perfidious Albion" have now placed their experience at the Allies' disposal.

But even the best-intended discussions between the defenders of the "good Germans" and the accusers of the "bad" not only miss the essence of the question—they plainly fail to apprehend the magnitude of the catastrophe. Either they are betrayed into trivial general comments on good and bad people, and into a fantastic over-estimation of the power of education, or they simply adopt an inverted version of Nazi racial theory. There is a certain danger in all this only because, since Churchill's famous statement on the subject, the Allies have refrained from fighting an ideological war and have thus unconsciously given an advantage to the Nazis (who, without regard to Churchill, are organizing their defeat ideologically) and a chance of survival to all racial theories.

The true problem however is not to prove what is self-evident, namely that Germans have not been potential Nazis ever since Tacitus' times, nor what is impossible, that all Germans harbor Nazi views. It is rather to consider how to conduct ourselves and how to bear the trial of confronting a people among whom the boundaries dividing criminals from normal persons, the guilty from the innocent, have been so completely effaced that nobody will be able to tell in Germany whether in any case he is dealing with a secret hero or with a former mass murderer. In this situation we will not be aided either by a definition of those responsible, nor by the punishment of "war criminals." Such definitions by their very nature can apply only to those who not only took responsibility upon themselves, but produced this whole inferno— and yet strangely enough are still not to be found on the lists of war criminals. The number of those who are responsible *and* guilty will be relatively small. There are many who share responsibility without any visible proof of guilt. There are many more who have become guilty without being in the least responsible. Among the responsible in a broader sense must be included all those who continued sympathetic to Hitler as long as it was possible, who aided his rise to power, and who applauded him in Germany and in other European countries. Who would dare to brand all these ladies and gentlemen of high society as war criminals? And as a matter of fact they really do not deserve such a title. Unquestionably they have proved their inability to judge modern political groupings, some of them because they regarded all principles in politics as moralistic nonsense, others because they were affected by a romantic predilection for gangsters whom they confused with "pirates" of an older time. Yet these people, who were co-responsible for Hitler's crimes in a broader sense, did not incur any guilt in a stricter sense. They, who were the Nazis' first accomplices and their best aides, truly did not know what they were doing nor with whom they were dealing.

The extreme horror with which particularly persons of good will react whenever the case of Germany is discussed is not evoked by those irresponsible co-responsibles, nor even by the particular crimes of the Nazis themselves. It is rather the product of that vast machine of administrative mass murder, in whose service not only thousands of persons, not even scores of thousands of selected murderers, but a whole people could be and was employed: In that organization which Himmler has prepared against the defeat, everyone is either an executioner, a victim, or an automaton, marching onward over the corpses of his comrades—chosen at first out of the various storm troop formations and later from any army unit or other mass organization. That everyone, whether or not he is directly active in a murder camp, is forced to take part in one way or another in the workings of this machine of mass murder—that is the horrible thing. For systematic mass murder—the true consequence of all race theories and other modern ideologies which preach that might is right—strains not only the imagination of human beings, but also the framework and categories of our political thought and action. Whatever the future of Germany, it will not be determined by anything more than the inevitable consequences of a lost war—consequences which in the nature of the case are temporary. There is no political method for dealing with German mass crimes, and the destruction of seventy or eighty million Germans, or even their gradual death through starvation (of which, of course, nobody except a few psychotic fanatics dream), would simply mean that the ideology of the Nazis had won, even if power and the rights of might had fallen to other peoples.

Just as there is no political solution within human capacity for the crime of administrative mass murder, so the human need for justice can find no satisfactory reply to the total mobilization of a people for that purpose. Where all are guilty, nobody in the last analysis can be judged.* For that guilt is not accompanied by even the mere appearance, the mere pretense of responsibility. So long as punishment is the right of the criminal—and this paradigm has for more than two thousand years been the basis of the sense of justice and right of Occidental man—guilt implies the consciousness of guilt, and punishment evidence that the criminal is a responsible person. How it is in this matter has been well described by an American correspondent, in a story whose dialogue material is worthy of the imagination and creative power of a great poet.

Q. Did you kill people in the camp? A. Yes.

Q. Did you poison them with gas? A. Yes.

Q. Did you bury them alive? A. It sometimes happened.

Q. Were the victims picked from all over Europe? A. I suppose so.

Q. Did you personally help kill people? A. Absolutely not. I was only paymaster in the camp.

Q. What did you think of what was going on? A. It was bad at first but we got used to it.

Q. Do you know the Russians will hang you? A. (Bursting into tears) Why should they? *What have I done?* (Italics mine. PM, Sunday, Nov. 12, 1944.)

Really he had done nothing. He had only carried out orders and since when has it been a crime to carry out orders? Since when has it been a virtue to rebel? Since when could one only be decent by welcoming death? What then had he done?

In his play, "Last Days of Mankind" about the last war,

---

* That German refugees, who had the good fortune either to be Jews or to have been persecuted by the Gestapo early enough, have been saved from this guilt is of course not their merit. Because they know this and because their horror at which might have been still haunts them, they often introduce into discussions of this kind that insufferable tone of self-righteousness which frequently and particularly among Jews, can turn into the vulgar obverse of Nazi doctrines; and in fact already has.

Karl Kraus rang down the curtain after Wilhelm II had cried, "I did not want this." And the horribly comic part of it was that this was the fact. When the curtain falls this time, we will have to listen to a whole chorus calling out, "We did not do this." And even though we shall no longer be able to appreciate the comic element, the horrible part of it will still be that this is the fact.

III.

In trying to understand what were the real motives which caused people to act as cogs in the mass murder machine, we shall not be aided by speculations about German history and the so-called German national character, of whose potentialities those who knew Germany most intimately had not the slightest idea fifteen years ago. There is more to be learned from the characteristic personality of the man who can boast that he was the organizing spirit of the murder. Heinrich Himmler is not one of those intellectuals stemming from the dim No-Man's Land between the Bohemian and the Pimp, whose significance in the composition cf the Nazi élite has been repeatedly stressed of late. He is neither a Bohemian like Goebbels, nor a sex criminal like Streicher, nor a perverted fanatic like Hitler, nor an adventurer like Goering. He is a "bourgeois" with all the outer aspect of respectability, all the habits of a good *paterfamilias* who does not betray his wife and anxiously seeks to secure a decent future for his children; and he has consciously built up his newest terror organization, covering the whole country, on the assumption that most people are not Bohemians nor fanatics, nor adventurers, nor sex maniacs, nor sadists, but, first and foremost job-holders, and good family-men.

It was Péguy, I believe, who called the family man the "grand aventurier du 20e siecle." He died too soon to learn that he was also the great criminal of the century. We had been so accustomed to admire or gently ridicule the family man's kind concern and earnest concentration on the welfare of his family, his solemn determination to make life easy for his wife and children, that we hardly noticed how the devoted *paterfamilias,* worried about nothing so much as his security, was transformed under the pressure of the chaotic economic conditions of our time into an involuntary adventurer, who for all his industry and care could never be certain what the next day would bring. The docility of this type was already manifest in the very early period of Nazi "gleichschaltung." It became clear that for the sake of his pension, his life insurance, the security of his wife and children, such a man was ready to sacrifice his beliefs, his honor, and his human dignity. It needed only the Satanic genius of Himmler to discover that after such degradation he was entirely prepared to do literally anything when the ante was raised and the bare existence of his family was threatened. The only condition he put was that he should be fully exempted from responsibility for his acts. Thus that very person, the average German, whom the Nazis notwithstanding years of the most furious propaganda could not induce to kill a Jew on his own account (not even when they made it quite clear that such a murder would go unpunished) now serves the machine of destruction without opposition. In contrast to the earlier units of the SS men and Gestapo, Himmler's over-all organization, relies not on fanatics, nor on congenital murderers, nor on sadists; it relies entirely upon the normality of jobholders and family-men.

We need not specially mention the sorry reports about Latvians, Lithuanians, or even Jews who have participated in Himmler's murder organization in order to show that it requires no particular national character in order to supply this new type of functionary. They are not even all natural murderers or traitors out of perversity. It is not even certain that they would do the work if it were only their own lives and future that were at stake. They felt (after they no longer needed to fear God, their conscience cleared through the bureaucratic organization of their acts) only the responsibility toward their own families. The transformation of the family man from a responsible member of society, interested in all public affairs, to a "bourgeois" concerned only with his private existence and knowing no civic virtue, is an international modern phenomenon. The exigencies of our time—"bedenkt den Hunger und die grosse Kaelte in diesem Tale, das von Jammer schallt" (Brecht)—can at any moment transform him into the mob-man and make him the instrument of whatsoever madness and horror. Each time society, through unemployment, frustrates the small man in his normal functioning and normal self-respect, it trains him for that last stage in which he will willingly undertake any function, even that of hangman. A Jew released from Buchenwald once discovered among the SS men who gave him the certificates of release a former schoolmate, whom he did not address but yet stared at. Spontaneously the man stared at remarked: You must understand, I have five years of unemployment behind me. They can do anything they want with me.

a better name we have called the "bourgeois," enjoyed particu-

It is true that the development of this modern type of man who is the exact opposite of the "citoyen" and whom for lack of larly favorable conditions in Germany. Hardly another country of Occidental culture was so little imbued with the classic virtues of civic behavior. In no other country did private life and private calculations play so great a role. This is a fact which the Germans in time of national emergency disguised with great success, but never altered. Behind the facade of proclaimed and propagandized national virtues, such as "love of the Fatherland," "German courage," "German loyalty," etc., there lurked corresponding real national vices. There is hardly another country where on the average there is so little patriotism as Germany; and behind the chauvinistic claims of loyalty and courage, a fatal tendency to disloyalty and betrayal for opportunistic reasons is hidden.

The mob man, however, the end-result of the "bourgeois," is an international phenomenon; and we would do well not to submit him to too many temptations in the blind faith that only the German mob man is capable of such frightful deeds. What we have called the "bourgeois" is the modern man of the masses, not in his exalted moments of collective excitement, but in the security (today one should rather say the insecurity) of his own private domain. He has driven the dichotomy of private and public functions, of family and occupation, so far that he can no longer find in his own person any connection between the two. When his occupation forces him to murder people he does not regard himself as a murderer because he has not done it out of inclination but in his professional capacity. Out of sheer passion he would never do harm to a fly.

If we tell a member of this new occupational class which our time has produced that he is being held to account for what he did, he will feel nothing except that he has been betrayed. But if in the shock of the catastrophe he really becomes conscious that in fact he was not only a functionary but a murderer, then his way out will not be that of rebellion, but suicide—just as so many have already chosen the way of suicide in Germany, where it is plain that there has been one wave of self-destruction after another. And that too would be of little use to us.

IV.

It is many years now that we meet Germans who declare that they are ashamed of being Germans. I have often felt tempted to answer that I am ashamed of being human. This elemental shame, which many people of the most various nationalities share with one another today, is what finally is left of our sense of international solidarity; and it has not yet found an adequate political expression. Our fathers' enchantment with humanity was of a sort which not only light-mindedly ignored the national question; what is far worse, it did not even conceive of the terror of the idea of humanity and of the Judeo-Christian faith in the unitary origin of the human race. It was not very pleasant even when we had to bury our false illusions about "the noble savage," having discovered that men were capable of being cannibals. Since then peoples have learned to know one another better and learned more and more about the evil potentialities in men. The result has been that they have recoiled more and more from the idea of humanity and become more susceptible to the doctrine of race which denies the very possibility of a common humanity. They instinctively felt that the idea of humanity, whether it appears in a religious or humanistic form, implies the obligation of a general responsibility which they do not wish to assume. For the idea of humanity, when purged of all sentimentality, has the very serious consequence that in one form or another men must assume responsibility for all crimes committed by men and that all nations share the onus of evil committed by all others. Shame at being a human being is the purely individual and still non-political expression of this insight.

In political terms, the idea of humanity, excluding no people and assigning a monopoly of guilt to no one, is the only guarantee that one "superior race" after another may not feel obligated to follow the "natural law" of the right of the powerful, and exterminate "inferior races unworthy of survival"; so that at the end of an "imperialistic age" we should find ourselves in a stage which would make the Nazis look like crude precursors of future political methods. To follow a non-imperialistic policy and maintain a non-racist faith becomes daily more difficult because it becomes daily clearer how great a burden mankind is for man.

Perhaps those Jews, to whose forefathers we owe the first conception of the idea of humanity, knew something about that burden when each year they used to say "Our Father and King, we have sinned before you," taking not only the sins of their own community but all human offenses upon themselves. Those who today are ready to follow this road in a modern version do not content themselves with the hypocritical confession, "God be thanked, I am not like that," in horror at the undreamed-of potentialities of the German national character. Rather, in fear and trembling, have they finally realized of what man is capable—and this is indeed the precondition of any modern political thinking. Such persons will not serve very well as functionaries of vengeance. This, however, is certain: upon them and only upon them can there be any reliance when it comes to fighting everywhere against the incalculable evil of which men are capable.

January, 1945

OTHER SUBJECTS

Thomas Mann's "Joseph and His Brothers"

by MAURICE SAMUEL

I.

THERE is assuredly no literary enterprise more daring than the attempt to re-tell a story that has already been told, once and for all, with unique greatness; and among such enterprises there is assuredly none that in difficulty and presumable uselessness approaches the re-telling of the Bible, unique among books. The compulsion behind such an attempt must be either an inspired creative insight or else a most commonplace artlessness; and therefore the result, if it is not to be utterly ridiculous, must be startlingly magnificent: a half way station between these points is inconceivable.

For, to take the initial obstacle, which is a summary of all the obstacles and which (we imagine) it is impossible to hurdle: Where is that uncertainty of outcome which is so necessary to every story if it is to symbolize the uncertainty of our lives and of all life? We already know the final issue, as we know all the intermediary issues which converge on it. We have the framework, the outline, in the fixed tradition. We *know* what happened;— and however the new narrator pauses and dawdles in the re-telling, we can tell him where he has to finish up at last. How, therefore, can he hope to hold our interest? And why should we care about Thomas Mann's way of saying what the Bible has already said about Joseph and his brothers?

But, genius being unpredictable, we find, after we have been held breathless, almost sick, with suspense, in the reading of Thomas Mann's *Joseph and His Brothers*, that what looked like an impossibility was no impossibility at all, and only seemed to be one because we lacked imagination enough to put the question

---

* *Joseph and His Brothers, Young Joseph,* by Thomas Mann. $2.50 each volume. Alfred A. Knopf. New York.

aright. For I said, glibly enough, we *know* what happened in the Bible story. But do we? Yes, we are acquainted with the rapid and exciting outline of incidents, as is every child who has been to *kheder* or Sunday school. But does that mean that we really know *what* happened? Are we possessed of the meaning and true nature of the events, their significant substance, their inwardness and purpose?

By no means. And that is what we discover soon enough. It is as though the narrator (who happens to be a great thinker as well as a great story teller) had begun with: *"Die Sache war eigentlich so;* this and this is what actually came to pass—precisely, in fact, as the Bible tells us, but without explanation and detail." And suddenly we find that we never knew, we never understood. And so, in this re-telling, the events are actually happening anew, that is, they unfold accompanied by their *meaning*. The legend has been familiar to us for centuries; but this illumination fills us with the realization that the familiarity was trivial and superficial.

II.

In the very opening, in the prelude itself, we are shaken out of our complacency by the quiet and subtle preliminary questions of the narrator.

"Very deep is the well of the past," he begins. "Should we not call it bottomless? Bottomless indeed, if—and perhaps only if—the past we mean is the past merely of the life of mankind." Just as, in the opening of Hamlet, the footsteps on the dark rampart and the voices challenging identification prepare us for the deeper challenging of identification which is the theme of the play; and just as in the prelude to *Remembrance of Things Past* the descent into forgotten experience evokes the crystal-gazing mood which is the philosophy and method of Proust; so the first sentences of *Joseph and His Brothers* forecast, and in part contain, the significance which belongs to every scene, person and event in the book, and binds them to each other and the whole.

For at once you ask: "What? Can the past of mankind be considered bottomless as compared with the past of the planet and of the physical universe which is its matrix? Can the writer indeed mean this?" This and nothing else! Dead and delimited things have by their nature a calculable and limited history; but the past of mankind loses itself in unfathomable perspectives of repetition. It is a past which (like space, we are now told) is at least boundless if not infinite, limitless if not eternal. In the mechanical reckoning of years we may reach back before the beginnings of human experience; but in the living sense (giving the word "sense" all its meanings) we recede, with every attempt to evoke the beginning, into twilights of increasing dimness which end with complete darkness. Here are cycles of experience, remotely remembered by the race, and copied from cycle to cycle, in part deliberately, imitatively, and in part because (it would seem) the range of our human faculties and possibilities grows only with imperceptible slowness. When the range is exhausted, mankind begins a new cycle, adding certain variations, no doubt, but (as long as it is mankind, recognizable to us as such with mankind's familiar hopes, fears and delusions) planting the same mileposts along the track of the cycle.

Now this view of our past is no more a philosophy of despair than the recognition of the ineluctable laws of nature is a counsel of resignation. It is rather the key to the meaning of our existence; and to the extent that all understanding is a form of liberation, it frees us while seeming to enslave us. I repeat with emphasis: the meaning of *our* existence. It is to us, here and now, in the turmoil of the twentieth century, and in the immediate vortex of its fourth decade, that this past, or succession of pasts, speaks. *We* shall see this past, in the magical reconstruction by Thomas Mann, otherwise than as our forefathers saw *their* past; we shall see it with our eyes, and through our own twentieth century intellectual terminology. This is, indeed, the variation and the promise of growth. But as our backward- and forward-consciousness grows with our penetration into the experience of our ancestors, we shall also understand that we cannot, with a jump into another form of existence, that is, without ceasing to be human beings, do more than repeat this experience in its larger outlines, only bringing to it (and this is no trifle) the instruments of our particular world of thought.

But if this past of ours has, to all human intent and purpose, no beginning, where shall we stop in our descent? Where shall we start the story? "There may," says the narrator, "exist provisional origins, which practically and in fact form the first beginnings for the particular traditions held by a given community, folk or communion of faith; and memory, though sufficiently instructed that the depths have actually not been plumbed, yet nationally may find reassurance in some primitive point of time and, personally and historically speaking, come to rest there. Young Joseph, for instance, son of Jacob and the lovely, too-soon-departed Rachel; Joseph, living when Kurigalzu the Kassite reigned at Babel. . . ." Young Joseph, then, is chosen as the central figure of one of the countless rehearsals of human destiny; he is chosen more or less at random though we shall see that personal predilection and affinity play a part in the choice. However that may be, Joseph and his brothers and their ancestors, immediate and remote, are the carriers of the story. And it is a story which is, as I have said, filled in Thomas Mann's re-telling of it with the excitement of fateful revelations, even though it does not deviate in one detail of importance from the accepted tradition. As we move from page to page there grows upon us the agitating conviction that the meaning disclosed in this expanded narrative applies to our deepest musings concerning ourselves and our state, and that the narrator is fulfilling with stern honesty the promise implied in the prelude: "I adventure into the past, hence my eagerness, hence my fear and pallor . . . for its theme is the first and last of all our questioning and speaking and all our necessity; the nature of man. That it is which we shall seek out in the underworld and death, as Ishtar there sought Tammuz and Isis Osiris."

III.

The story is of Joseph, his brothers and parents, with throwbacks to the youth and early manhood of Jacob telling of his relations with Isaac, his father, and with Esau, and with Laban in Mesopotamia, and with the sisters he married, the one loved, the other unloved. But the setting is that of all the Bible, with all its civilizations and folklores, its phrases and proverbs passed on from generation to generation, its customs and taboos and myths, as they flowed about for countless generations before they were fastened into a Book and forbidden to wander any more, being finally attached to one place and one meaning. Thus, at the wedding of Jacob they chant verses which we now say belong only to Solomon's Song of Songs; and thus Jacob and his sons celebrate the Passover and propitiate the Avenging Angel and eat the paschal lamb, though these ceremonies we are told to associate only with the Exodus from Egypt; and thus, when Jacob mourns for Joseph, he becomes Job, and his old steward Eliezer becomes a composite of Job's comforters: the same themes recur in the complaint, the rebellion, the reproaches, the very words which are now attributed to Job only. All the Bible is here, a wide sounding board for the *Basses Grundgewalt* of the story.

Now whatever scholars may say concerning these textual displacements, these "anachronisms" and incongruities, the layman will feel that it must have been so, more or less. A *Torah she b'al peh* which was centuries in the making must have wandered freely and loosely and in fragments among the people, and the civilization must have been permeated with these phrases, allusions and myths.

But for other reasons, more profound and more alluring, the reader finds it proper that persons and myths and folk phrases now hardened in the official canon into separate compartments shall be set in flux again, losing this artificial and schematic rigidity. And these reasons have to do with the philosophy of the story, the informing perception of the rhythms of human experience.

Wooed into the dreamy mood of the narrator we understand why he has Joseph stay in the pit into which his brothers have cast him, just three days (three dark days of the moon from death to rebirth). We understand also why the brothers, selling him

to the Ishmaelites, ask at first thirty pieces of silver, though the
official tradition tells us that they finally accepted twenty for him.
We understand further why Reuben who, without the knowledge
of his brothers, has returned to the pit in the hope of rescuing
Joseph, must find the stone rolled away (Joseph having in the
meantime been taken out) and a messenger sitting there. Yes,
"he who had descended into the pit" had risen from it, and Reuben knew not how. We find it proper, too, (having fallen into
this repetitive and evocative mood) that Joseph should not have
died, but that a lamb should have died for him, for Joseph, (who
is also called "he who was mangled") for the son—just as a ram
died for Isaac, the son who was saved. We perceive that all this
happened before, one way or another: brother hatred, the killing
of one and his rising from death, rebellion of son against father
—minglings and echoings of eternal myths which, our wise men
tell you today, have not yet run their course, but are reproduced
in the form proper to our time (*our* talk is of complexes). Abel
and Cain, Isaac and Ishmael, Jacob and Esau, Joseph and his
brothers. These are moulds of life by no means yet broken.

IV.

There are brief cycles and wider cycles, repetitions which
cover succeeding generations (Jacob and Esau paralleled in some
respects by Joseph and his brothers), and repetitions which cover
a span of many generations, recurrent Abrahams and Eliezers stationed dimly at intervals of centuries. Then vaster cycles, each
set in motion by a flood; and still greater vistas, lost Atlantas and
Gondwanas falling backwards into the darkness of the unremem-
berable, from which no echo reaches us even in fable—the past of
mankind which is unfathomable. Of these the narrator makes us
slowly and persuasively aware, dismantling our time-sense of its
too sharp divisions, its over-emphasis of historic epochs.

Those of whom he speaks, Joseph and Jacob and the others,
were not afflicted with our modern eagerness for precision and
tabulation in matters which precision and tabulation essentially
falsify. The narrator tells us that the people were very much like

ourselves "aside from that dreamy indefiniteness in their habits of thought." Yet that is important enough. When Joseph thought of Abraham, his father's grandfather, he was apt to identify him with the original Abraham, the first (if there was exactly a first) moon-wanderer. But this, to us, is inadmissible. Joseph's great-grandfather, Abraham, was not the Abraham who quarreled with Nimrod. Similarly Joseph would, half earnestly and half in play, identify Eliezer, his father's steward (there had always been a chief steward called Eliezer in the household of the clan) with that Eliezer whom the "original" Abraham had sent to Aram Naharaim to bring Isaac's bride—and Eliezer himself indulged and encouraged this fusion or confusion. But it was and was not a confusion; it was, if you like, a play of thought, and yet something more serious than just that. For all of them had that habit. All identified themselves with their prototypes in the recurrent cycles. They were not so concerned as we are with the frightful anxiety to be *einmalig,* non-recurrent phenomena, irrecoverable identities —this being the nature of *our* special egomaniac pride.

They saw themselves only as the bearer of certain themes or significance or destinies; these were what mattered, not they, the persons. It was the idea which pressed for preservation and expression and evolution, not the accidental man. As a single instance, out of many which the narrator treats with infinite skill, we may take Esau. Dimly and powerfully Esau and Jacob and Isaac were aware of what their "mission" was in this world, alike he who stole the blessing, he who was duped and he who was robbed. "Actually," we are told, "nobody was deceived, not even Esau. For if I am venturing here to write about people who did not always know who they were—Esau himself not being of the clearest on the subject, and sometimes taking himself for the original goat of the Seir people and mentioning him in the first person—yet this occasional lack of clarity had to do only with the individual and the time conditioned, and was precisely the consequence of the fact that everybody knew, perfectly well and outside of time, and mythically and typically speaking, who the individual was; and so did Esau, of whom it has not been idly said that he was in his way as pious a man as Jacob. He wept and raved, of course, after the betrayal, and was more murderously inclined toward his brother than Ishmael had been against his. . . . But he did all that because it was the role he had to play; he knew and accepted the fact that all events are a fulfillment, and that what had happened had happened because it must, according to the archetype. That is to say, it was not the first time, it was ceremonially and in conformity to pattern, it had acquired presentness as in a recurrent feast, and come round as feasts do."

And therefore this phrase, "men like ourselves apart from that measure of dreamy indefiniteness in their habits of thought" is perhaps an understatement. Like ourselves they were in one sense, having our egotisms, lusts, dreams and calculations—but these were engaged in the service of another type of fulfillment. And again, what this means is illustrated a dozen times in the narrative, and as well in the case of Jacob and Eliphaz as anywhere else.

Fleeing from the wrath of Esau after the theft of the blessing, Jacob is overtaken by young Eliphaz, son of the wronged brother, a splendid boy seeking vengeance for his father. Unarmed and impotent, Jacob can save himself only by the use of his wits, and that in a manner which much seem ignominious to all of us. He crawls in the dust at the lad's feet, whines, cajoles, flatters, snivels, protests his innocence, blames his mother, the ambitious Rebeccah, and by the utter extravagance of his abasement so dazes the forthright boy that he effects his escape. "What happened then," says the narrator frankly of this slightly sickening incident, "touched Jacob's pride and honor more closely than anything else in all his life; it was calculated to undermine and would have undermined forever the dignity and self-confidence of another man." But Jacob "was obliged—if he wanted to live, and that he did at all costs; not, we must remember, out of common cowardice, but because he was consecrated, because the promise and the blessing handed down from Abraham lay upon him—to try to soften by entreaties the heart of the lad . . ."

V.

More important than life or that "honor" which at bottom is only our proud opinion of ourselves (a folly from which Jacob was not wholly exempt) was the blessing and destiny which Abraham had earned directly from God, to transmit to his posterity and spread about the world. Now what is that blessing, for which the successive generations of brothers fight in imitative sequence? They, the strugglers for it, interpret it each one according to his character. It cannot have meant to Esau the hunter what it meant to Jacob the dreamer, or to the boisterous brothers what it meant to the spiritually adept Joseph. The narrator says bluntly, concerning the other sons of Jacob: "Shepherds and sons of the steppes they were, running almost wild since infancy . . . their concerns were strictly practical, their minds were full of the youthful spirit of defiance which forever looks for insults and seeks out quarrels . . . they were arrogantly proud of their race, knowing nought of the spiritual nobility upon which its true greatness was founded."

This blessing, then, though it carried with it a practical wisdom and grace immensely useful in ordinary affairs, was essentially unworldly. "Disquiet, questioning, hearkening and seeking, wrestling for God, a bitterly skeptical laboring over the true and the just, the whence and the whither, his own name, his own nature, the true meaning of the Highest—all that, bequeathed down the generations from the man of Ur, found expression in Jacob's look. . . ."

On that man of Ur, the original Abraham, who had been unable to countenance the practices of Nimrodi; who had, alone among men, taken offense in the name of the Highest, and withdrawn himself in protest against that which the rest of the world considered proper and respectable—on that Abraham the spirit had descended. And whatever else that spirit is, we are told, it is also "the warning emissary, the principle of contradiction, umbrage and dispersal, which stirs up emotion of disquiet in the breast of one single man among the blithely agreeing and accepting host, drives him forth out of the gates of the past and the known into the uncertain and adventurous, and makes him like unto the stone which, by detaching itself and rolling, is destined to set up an everlasting rolling and sequence of events, of which no man can see the end."

To what extent the original Abraham had by his restlessness and searching merited the friendship of God the narrator advises us in the prelude, and does so in the very spirit of the true tradition, making us understand that the fulfillment of God depended on the existence of such a man, one who by diligent and painful and unremitting self-investigation wins through to a perception of divinity. So successful was the search that "God had kissed His fingertips and cried, to the private resentment of the angels, 'It is unbelievable, what knowledge of me is possessed by this son of earth! Have I not begun to make myself known through his means? Verily, I will anoint him'!"

Here was the beginning of the friendship and covenant, far back somewhere in the experience of the race, the original contact between the godhead and the consciousness of man. Through a hundred hostile generations, amid dangers and bitter humiliations, it was to be carried forward, at all costs, the only significant destiny that can be assigned to man. This was what Jacob had "stolen" from his father, Isaac, (can we say "stolen"? Could Esau have used this particular destiny?) and what Joseph received from his father although he, too, was not the oldest son. The story of Joseph and his brothers is the story of the transmission and cherishing of the blessing and destiny.

VI.

But if this were all, the narrative would still fall short of greatness. Man is more than his past and his history; he is also the present. He is related with mankind in time, on the plane of evolving tradition; he is also related to his contemporaries on the moral and social plane. The story of Joseph and his brothers is also the story of an immense moral experience, a clarification and redemption.

Something less than the genius of Thomas Mann would have made of the protagonists of the story unreal and impalpable projections, ghosts moving through a far off world with strange gestures of mind and body. Such they are not. They are immediate, urgent and contemporaneous with us. They move about us and in us, creating an intimacy which becomes almost painful. That they are symbols, transmitted, meaningful myths made flesh, does not at any moment interfere with the breathlessly living quality of their emotions. The quarrel between Joseph and his older brothers is, indeed, a fulfillment and destiny or predestination; but it has such self-sufficiency and independence and purely human plausibility that we are passionately absorbed by it, often to the exclusion of the larger significance.

Grace, beauty and brilliance were the natural portion of young Joseph, but with these went a childish egotism, ungovernable and immeasurable, rooted ultimately in the strange illusion that all—including his brothers—must love him more than themselves. His prophetic aptitude, his spiritual gifts, his irresistible charm, his learning, induced in him a type of thoughtlessness, of indifference or blindness to the feelings and natural vanities of others which made him appear at times—the narrator uses these words— nothing more than "an unlicked cub." His election and Messianic importance, solemn attributes in themselves, fed—among other things, of course—an absurd and trivial and most incongruous self-satisfaction. He could not forbear to boast of his dreams of aggrandisement; aware of the folly of it, he tattled against his brothers; his delight in himself, and in the privileged position which he occupied in his doting father's heart, overrode his natural faculty for penetrating into the feelings of others.

For this deadly sin of arrogance, which in all great men places their gifts at the service of evil, his father was in part to blame. Jacob had loved Rachel with an exclusiveness and invidiousness which had called down upon him and her the displeasure of the Highest; he was punished first by her barrenness and then by her early death. But he had never learned to curb his emotional weakness. We are told of him: "The perilous thing was that he did not surrender his willfulness, his arbitrary indulgence of feeling, when Rachel died . . . but, as though he would give notice to the Almighty that He might expect to gain nothing by cruelty, he transferred it in all its arrogant luxuriousness to Rachel's first-born, the beautiful nine-year-old lad, Joseph, loving him with a twofold and altogther provocative preference."

The sin itself was twofold. First, it was a trespassing on the prerogative of God (or, rather, of the lingering element of the primitive, jealous, tyrannical desert Yahu-god in God) who himself indulged in these arbitrary preferences. But, more serious, it was injustice, it was egotism, it was discrimination. It confirmed in young Joseph the grave defect of a complacency which even his extraordinary gifts could not rob of its fatuousness. It introduced, further, a principle of discord and hatred into human relations.

Young Joseph was a mixture of the dazzling genius and the spoiled daddy's darling. There was no viciousness or cruelty in his nature; but he could not help showing off; he could not help recounting his strange forevisionings of his future greatness; he could not subdue the mad impulse to disport himself before his brothers in the *k'tonet passim,* which was the symbol of the blessing and the inheritance. It did not occur to him that he was goading his brothers into a madness of resentment. He did not guess at the venomous envy which the mothers of the other sons so thinly veiled behind their gushing admiration when they first beheld him in the shimmering mantle of his election. He was fantastically self-centered.

The purification of Joseph through suffering, that is, his descent into the pit and his emergence in a moral rebirth, is the climax toward which the narrative moves irresistibly. We are given a foretaste of Joseph's transfiguration in the very moment when his brothers, rising in an excess of ungovernable rage, forget their fear of their father, and fling themselves like wild animals on their tormentor. For then suddenly, and with incredulous horror, Joseph realizes what these brothers, whom he actually loves, feel toward him. His amazement is even stronger than his fear: to this pass of hatred and fury, blotting out all prudence, humanity, and filial terror, he had reduced them all by his childish insolence and his blind self-love.

So we learn that there is a type of egoism from which the wisest are not exempt, an egotism so deeprooted that it falls only before the most brutal kind of disillusionment, sheer physical assault. Argument could not have purified Joseph; at argument he was cleverer and more subtle than anyone else; the finer the brain the greater the power of self-deception. Only when his brothers pounced on him like beasts, pummeled him, bashed his eyes in, bellowing and panting their hatred of him, did the raw truth break in on him at last. And then in the pit, where he lay three days and three nights in the shadow of death, there ensued the fearful agony of his moral rebirth—a going down into the bitterness of humiliation, remorse and self-knowledge.

How genius, now purified, cleansed of the irresponsibility of egotism, fared later, what took place in the land into which Joseph was sold, the narrator still has to tell us. But even now the incomplete story has a fulness and greatness which places it among the permanent treasures of mankind.

VII.

How comes it that a stranger, of the seed of the northern races, should have written with such tenderness, clarity and insight of the origins and heroes of our Jewish national myths? To me these books of Thomas Mann have been—as I am certain they will be to many others—the greatest modern illumination of the Jewish past, a *midrash* of incomparable beauty, subtlety and strength. Where did Thomas Mann, the German, acquire, we will not say the scholarly substance which gives weight to the story (such learning, immense but lightly borne, can always be the result of a powerful mind and much application) but the peculiar insight, the gracious intimacy of creative understanding? He tells us that he has always loved these sagas; from early childhood he was fascinated and charmed by the story of Joseph. There is also an instinctive affinity between him and the prototypes of the early Jewish legend. Speaking of Jacob he says: "As for me, I will not conceal my native and comprehensive understanding of the old man's restless unease and dislike of any fixed habitation. . . ." He shares, too, the poignant spiritual inquisitiveness of the first of them, of the dimly seen but heavily felt Abraham. He, Thomas Mann, is authentically of the group, a natural convert, a *ger zedek*, one of those upon whose spirit the words of the first proselytizer would have fallen most fruitfully.

But what awes us most in this spiritual spectacle is the juxtaposition of larger events. At this moment in the current cycle of history, when a psychotic hatred of Jews and the Jewish spirit holds Germany convulsed, it is a German who offers to the world, in contemporaneous language and intellectual terms, the loftiest elucidation of the meaning of the Jewish being. For this is not a commonplace apologia and defense, such as Lessing gave us a century and a half ago, a kindly and rather inane appeal to the surface tolerance: "*Hoert, Kinder;* we are all essentially alike, we don't know who is right and who is wrong; let us therefore behave with forbearance toward one another." That was decent enough on its own plane; but what Thomas Mann does is far profounder. *No, we are not all alike,* he says. We have different myths and cultures. Our manner of reconstructing the universe in symbol and ritual and saga differs from group to group. He does better than ask for uninformed kindness; he reinterprets the symbol and the saga of the Jews, and with such insight that the Jews themselves (whatever the Germans, in whose language the narrative is written, will do) will learn more from it than from anything they themselves have written in modern times. He does not descend to a plea; he rises to the level of supreme understanding.

In the spirit of this work one might say that God has left the German people an anchor to windward: when the time comes for the accounting to be made of their stewardship of power, and they will be asked to explain the frightful evil of their treatment, not of the Jews alone, but of the best there is in Jewish utterance through the centuries (including the Christian tradition), the *melitz yosher* will point to Thomas Mann, saying, "He was of this people." And almost he might add: "In his *zekhut* they are forgiven."

One is invited to this reflection, I said, by the spirit of the narrative. But another reflection follows almost inevitably. In the dreamy mood through which the narrator teaches us to perceive the cycles of historic experience, we ask ourselves what stage of repetition we are now moving through. Are we now in the modern equivalent of the darkest hour of the Egyptian slavery? Have we reached the climax of the agony, the apotheosis of a state hatred and fear of the Jew, and the policy of "Destroy them all"? And if so, is not the next hour the hour of liberation, the marching into the desert, the beginnings of the reconstruction of the promised land? One who reads this work of Thomas Mann in Palestine itself, in the midst of the first evidence of the next stage of Jewish history, cannot help feeling that the book justified itself not only intrinsically, by the merits of its content, but externally and objectively too, as an event in the history and experience of the race.

September-October, 1936

Joseph and His Brothers

by KADYA MOLODOWSKA

This is a tale they tell of ancient Canaan,
Of goats, of bullocks, and a shepherd's fold;
A tale of lusty herdsmen who were brothers,
And how these brothers once their brother sold.

They were fine fellows, each with flock and pasture,
Who lacked for nothing in their father's tent:
For miles around stretched rich and grassy meadows;
Their cattle bellowed everywhere they went.

Old Jacob Israel had some curious notions,
The like of which we still consider queer:
One strange and shining night he caught an angel,
And wrestled with him till the dawn rose clear.

But Jacob Israel of this heavenly struggle,
(For angels jest not), always bore the scars;
And therefore his last-born, from childhood onward,
Saw visions in the dark and gazed at stars.

Yet Jacob Israel with his curious notions,
Upon this youngest let his fancy dote;
And though the other sons railed against Joseph,
He made the lad a many-colored coat.

And every night young Joseph saw some vision,
And every day interpreted its gleam.
All Canaan heard—Is there a fiercer hatred
Than for the one who dares to dream a dream?

So, cheek to jowl, the darkening elder brothers
Whispered and mulled and schemed with all their wit;
And one bright day, just at the hour of noon-time,
They cast their brother Joseph in a pit.

They sold him like a thief to passing strangers,
A caravan that chanced by where they stood.
The lord of dreams was shackled, dragged in bondage—
All Canaan watched the deed and found it good!

Here ends the tale—the rest I have forgotten,
What else befell is from the scroll erased—
Always I hear the clank of chains, the crying,
And see the dreamer trudge into the waste.

Translated from the Yiddish by MARIE SYRKIN
January, 1943

In "Arabia Felix"

by HAYIM GREENBERG

VERY ALARMING reports have reached us recently concerning the Jews in Yemen. A representative of the Yemenite Jews informed a press conference in Tel-Aviv that it had been reliably reported that the Jews of Yemen faced the imminent prospect of extinction: they have been given the alternative of "voluntary" conversion to Mohammedanism or of having to face such conditions as would lead to their "natural death," in a short time, from starvation.

The connections of Yemen with the outside world are very tenuous and the information from there has been far from regular. Thus, we do not know the specific nature of the regulations planned against the Jews if they do not "voluntarily" accept conversion. Yet we have sufficient reason not to doubt that the country's ruler, the Imam Yahya, is capable of ruthlessly carrying out measures of his own for the annihilation of his Jewish subjects. Nor can we expect the people of Yemen to stand up in defense of the Jews, for even if they had any wish to do so they have no political power to oppose their autocratic ruler.

Even in the midst of the current inexorable destruction of the oldest and greatest Jewries in Europe, there are few Jewish communities whose fate evokes such somber reflections as the present situation of the Yemenite Jews. For not even the Italian Jews, the oldest Jewish community in Europe, have so ancient a past in their native land as our community in Yemen. The experiment of Jews and non-Jews living together in the Arabian peninsula has lasted for thousands of years, and now, at its close, Yemenite Jews have been forced to conclude that it was a failure. Today there is no Jew in Yemen who is not eager for the opportunity to escape from his "Fatherland."

When did Jews first settle in Yemen? Neither Jews nor Arabs know with any certainty. The beginnings are hidden in the mists of a distant, legendary past. According to folk-tales recounted in Yemen itself, and reflected in the poetry of our Yemenite brethren, Jews settled there in King Solomon's time, around a thousand years before the Christian era. Tradition has, also, a more conservative account, according to which Jews first came to Yemen about forty years before the destruction of the First Temple in Jerusalem, in the sixth century before the Christian era. Seventy-five thousand Jews, including priests, Levites, military and civil officials, as well as ordinary citizens are said to have crossed the Jordan and the lands of Edom and Seir and come to settle in fertile Yemen, because they believed in the imminent fulfillment of Jeremiah's prophecy of the national disaster. The same tradition has it that they even founded a kingdom, with a fortified town upon the hill of Nakos, and, remaining faithful to the civil laws of the Torah, they established four "cities of refuge."

How close the bond between the Jews and their new home became, may be seen from a legend which is still alive among Yemenite Jews. When Ezra the Scribe returned to Judea he sent word even unto Yemen, calling upon the Jews there to return to their ancient homeland. The Yemenite Jews, however, refused to heed him and did not go back to Judea. (The legend "rationalizes" their refusal, on the grounds that the Yemenites foresaw that the new Jewish state in Judea would not endure for long, for the true time of redemption had not yet arrived.) Because of this attitude Ezra the Scribe cursed the Yemenite Jews and they, in turn, excommunicated him. It was for this reason, many Jews in Yemen believed, that it was not granted to Ezra to die in Judea, and his grave is to be found, "as is well known," in Babylon.

We may leave it for others to determine how much real history is reflected in these legends. It is established, however, that in the second century before the Christian era, several generations before the destruction of the Second Temple, there was already a substantial Jewish community in Yemen. The "Exile in Yemen," sometimes called "The Exile in Hagar," is mentioned in certain quite ancient homilies.

It is not likely that the Yemenite Jews themselves at that time regarded their new home as an "Exile" in the literal and accepted sense of the word. Yemen was a thriving country, known in classical Roman geography as "Arabia Felix." Jewish influence in Yemen was considerable. The Jewish faith which they brought with them established their prestige at a very high level. Large parts of the population, particularly among the urban, commercial and, if one may use the term, "industrial" classes (ancient Yemen had a considerably developed economy and commercial relations with many lands, including India), abandoned their astral idolatry and were converted to Judaism. The spread of Jewish influence among the ruling classes made it quite natural that for a considerable period the kings of Yemen were Jews. "Racially," of course, those kings may have been native Arabs converted to Judaism, but the Yemenite people and the Jews themselves naturally regarded them as Jews in every respect.

From those days to the present, a matter of at least one and twenty centuries, Yemen has never been without its Jewish population. It is probable that even when, as certain evidence indicates, Jews were expelled in Yemen under Abyssinian domination, they merely left the towns and took refuge in the hills together with the Yemenite Bedouins "until the storm should pass." Thereafter, they returned to their former homes in the cities, where for generations they served as an important commercial link between Yemen and Persia, Byzantium, and India.

There would be no point, in a brief comment of this sort, in recounting the various periods in the history of Yemenite Jews. The significant point is that since the country adopted Islam, Jews there have seldom had a happy hour.

The Koran has certain pro-Jewish-sounding verses, and according to Moslem tradition, the "Prophet" once said, "If anyone shall do evil to a Christian or a Jew, I myself shall appear as his accuser before the Heavenly Judge on Judgement Day." One could just as easily cite many philo-Semitic quotations from the early writings and sayings of Martin Luther, but it is well-known that, on the whole, his influence was no little responsible for the hold of anti-Semitism on his people. In Arab countries, Islam was almost always a source of Jew-hatred. It would be pointless to discuss whether Moslem theology is necessarily and essentially hostile to Jews. For many generations Turkey proved that a country can be Moslem, even fanatically and aggressively Moslem, and still be tolerant, even friendly to Jews. In fact, whatever the explanation may be for this, anti-Jewish policies developed in Turkey precisely when it emancipated itself from Islam, and from all religion, and assumed an extreme nationalist and almost "racialist" philosophy. But in the Arab countries, for whatever reasons, Islam was generally hostile to strangers and "infidels," particularly Jews.

Since the beginning of Islam, the Yemenite Jews have been especially exposed to its hostility. The past twelve or thirteen centuries were a continuous nightmare for them, an unending martyr-dom. Who knows how large the Jewish community in Yemen might have been to-day, if not for the slaughters which occurred at various time, and the "conversion" to Islam at the point of the sword. The *"Iggeret Teman,"* the letter of consolation sent by Maimonides to the Yemenite Jews in the twelfth century, vividly reflects to this very day the almost superhuman suffering of that community. Their situation did not improve in the nineteenth and twentieth centuries. On the contrary, it grew worse and worse, and in recent years draws on to a total disaster. If Hitler had known of the legal status of the Yemenite Jews at the begi:.ning of his career, he could have saved himself considerable trouble in the formulation of the "Nuremburg Laws."

A Yemenite Jew may not live together with non-Jews in a forti-fied town. He may not ride a horse or a mule in the street, and even outside town he must dismount when he sees a Mohammedan pass nearby. He is not permitted to build a house more than two stories high, and buildings for Jewish schools or synagogues are generally forbidden. A Jew must not wear white clothes, his cloak must not fall lower than the knees, and instead of a belt (the symbol of "nobility") he must wear a rope. Arms being regarded as an adornment in Arab countries, no Jew may carry weapons, even though Jewish smiths are practically the only ones who know the art, which they have brought to a high development, of making fine swords with intricate encrustation. Jews must pay a special impost over and above the general taxes for the right to appeal to courts if they are robbed. But, in addition, the law requires a Jew who has been robbed to catch the thief and bring him to court, failing which the Jew is jailed for "concealing a thief." Jews are not qualified witnesses in court, and their oaths are not accepted. In such a state of practical outlawry, there is good reason for the Yemenite custom of Jews' getting Moslem "protectors" whom they must serve *gratis*. When a Jew meets a Moslem he must salute him and inquire about his "exalted" health. A Jew may not enter a public bath, except to stoke the fires of Arabs' bath-houses, which is a duty usually imposed on Jews.

That is how "Semites" are treated by other "Semites."

Anyone who has met Yemenite Jews, knows that these and similar persecutions over a period of many generations have not subdued their high intelligence, nor corrupted their virtues, nor called forth among them any morbid bitterness against the world. It is thousands of years that their speech is Arabic, but the Yemenite Jew is rare who cannot make himself understood in Hebrew. They are all literate, and Biblical quotations are always on their lips. In deepest penury, they have preserved to this day their quiet, poised, aristocratic self-respect. They are the most industrious people of the Near East, and the thousands who settled in Palestine after their "rediscovery" by the veteran labor leader, Yavneeli, in the beginning of the present century, have rapidly adapted themselves to the new Jewish life in agriculture, crafts, and industry, in spite of the scant attention which, truth to tell, was given to their care. In Yemen, they have been engaged for generations chiefly in crafts and other manual trades, leaving no possible ground for the charge that they constitute a higher class "exploiting" the mass of the population. Though so long and so far separated from other Jews, socially as well as geographically, they possess a rich Jewish folklore, fascinating folk-music and dance patterns of their own. Centuries of persecution have developed their strain of mysticism, their powerful Messianic longing, their ardor for redemption, and —among their scholars—a keen feeling for Cabbala.

That the Yemenite Jews have not degenerated physically or spiritually is one of the outstanding "miracles" of our history. But they have long known that they cannot continue living in Yemen. The epic tale of those hundreds and thousands of Yemenites who dared undertake the journey to Palestine in recent years, through deserts, amid the daily peril of death, without money or clothing, food or water, and in spite of the strict prohibition against emigrating, must still be written by historians and poets. Though small groups broke through to the United States and Latin America, it was the ideal of every Yemenite to come into his "repose and possession" in Palestine. "Possession" in this case, is a somewhat figurative expression. They require little, and they are ready to do the hardest labor, especially in Palestine, in return for a peaceful and decent life. A few thousand Yemenites are now adrift in Aden without provisions or shelter, waiting for someone to be merciful and allow them to go on to Palestine. And now they hear alarming reports from those who remained in Yemen: new edicts declaring either conversion or starvation.

So ends an experiment of over two thousand years in neighborly relations between one group of "Semites" and another. Over twenty centuries were not enough to strike firm root in that land. Of no avail were the one-time Jewish kings of Yemen, and the Yemenite patriotism because of which the "Zionist" Ezra the Scribe was excommunicated.

To whom shall the Jews of Yemen turn now? To whom shall we appeal in their name? The naive Yemenites know that we have been promised a "home" in Palestine, and, in time of extreme stress, they wish to return home. We are not naive. Shall we now try to interest "high authorities" in a distant Jewish tribe, in Yemen, which is not an occupied country, and over which Hitler had no control? Yemen has no "legitimate" refugees. Yemen is

not a foe of the United Nations, and its Jews are not victims of
Nazism. They are—free game. . . .

July, 1944

For My Child
by GRACE GOLDIN

Then think not overmuch of bitterness
But enter gallantly upon your world;
Turn from the sight of faces in distress,
Note rather with delight, what leaves grow curled,
Or when your back must break beneath one stroke
Murmur aloud, How pleasant is this oak!
For twenty hundred years, my child, so do:
You should have learned by now to be a Jew.

January, 1944

Jewish Indians in Mexico

by Marie Syrkin

THE GODS have not left Mexico. Despite the confiscation of church property, the anti-clericalist edicts, the revolutionary propaganda, Mexico is a land of believers. Anyone who has seen a peon devoutly trudging up a pyramid surmounted by a cross to bring flowers to the Virgin, feels this. Perhaps the children studying in the great modern public school "Revolution," erected by the government, have been emancipated from the grip of the cleric, but no one who has watched an Indian woman, with a child at her breast, praying to the Madonna, can doubt that here is faith at its simplest.

It is piety, pure, uncritical, completely credulous, completely resigned, more impressive in its quiet, motionless grace than the turbulent ecstasy of the Negro. The Gods of miracle and compassion, of kindness and omnipotence, have not been exorcized from the poor Indian's needy heart by rationalist slogans. They are still there—the idols of the Aztec, the saints of the Church; and, unexpectedly enough, Jehovah too may be found in the pantheon.

Tourist guide books make no mention of the Jewish Indians. There are only three thousand of them scattered throughout Mexico. A poor and ignorant lot, with no shrine of gold and alabaster, of silver and obsidian, to attract the average sight-seer. It was only after I had stood before countless rose-bedecked altars hallowed to the Virgin and had marvelled alike at the glory of the church and the beauty of the worshippers, that I learned of my Indian brethren. Their existence has been known for some years, but every Jewish journalist who comes to Mexico discovers them anew. The Mexican Jewish community, itself for the most part only some twenty years in the land, has been taking a protective interest in this strange branch of the tree of Israel, and now a visit to the Indian Jews has become a part of the itinerary of any visitor with specific Jewish interests.

The Jewish Indians are descendants of Marranos who came

to Mexico with the Spaniards at the beginning of the sixteenth century. Most of the Marranos were eventually assimilated (two presidents of the Republic, Porfirio Diaz and Francisco Madero, were of Marrano stock) but some remained Jews. The Jewish Indians date from these Marranos who intermarried with the natives and converted them to Judaism. These Indians, too, led a Marrano existence practicing their Judaism secretly and suffering the persecution of the Inquisition when discovered. The first *auto de fe* in America took place in Mexico in 1574. Not until 1910, the time of the Madero revolution, were the Indians able to avow their Judaism openly.

When they were brought to light, they were found to be observing a curious mixture of pagan, Catholic and Jewish rites. They knew no Hebrew; their children were uncircumcized. During the past few years, the Mexican Jewish community has taken them under its wing. A few volunteer teachers have been instructing them; and now some Hebrew words and prayers have been introduced into their services. They have been taught to unscramble Jewish from Catholic holidays. In short, they are being "enlightened," but, as the gentleman who took me to their synagogue put it, they are no longer as "original" as they were in their pristine state.

The barrenness of the Indian "synagogue," if such it could be called, was startling after the elaborate beauty of the Catholic churches I had been seeing. Nothing but a small, dingy hall on the outskirts of the city, with neither pomp nor grandeur to comfort the believing heart. A plain room with pale blue walls and rough wooden benches. A little table stood in the front of the room instead of a pulpit. No holy scrolls, no velvet curtains, no candelabras—none of the austere ceremonial permitted to Judaism. The sole evidence indicating that we were in a holy place was a large sign inscribed in Hebrew letters: *Shma Israel, adonai elohenu, adonai ekhad,* with a *Magen David* on each end. And then, in the more familiar Spanish, hung a placard: *Silencio en la casas de Dios* (Silence in the house of God).

I looked at the congregation. There were about twenty-five women, fifteen men, and perhaps a dozen children, most of them typical Indians dressed in sarapes and shawls. Here and there one saw a face that looked Spanish, perhaps Semitic. An Indian in overalls entered and carefully unwrapped his Bible from its protective newspaper. An Indian woman courteously handed me a Bible. It was in Spanish, published by the American Bible Society for distribution by missionaries, and consequently contained both the Old and New Testaments.

The "rabbi," a street car conductor on weekdays, wore neither robes nor *talis*. The sole token of the dignity of his office was a purple skull cap. The service began with a Spanish hymn, *Zion bendita seas* (Zion be blessed) sung to a popular Salvation Army tune, and followed by the *Hatikvah* in Hebrew. "Our hope is not lost" chanted my Indian brothers with fervor.

The rabbi's sermon, in Spanish, was obviously addressed to the American visitors as well as to the congregants. The rabbi offered his followers a simple task. European Jews, American Jews, he explained to his listeners, had lost their faith in God. It was the mission of the Indian Jew to give back faith to the world.

The poor handful before him bowed reverently. The mi. on, always the mission, even here amid these worshippers.

Possibly in deference to the presence of strangers, the service was taken over by the most influential member of the congregation, the head of the Marranos, a successful lawyer in Mexico City, obviously a man of consequence and standing. Not knowing Spanish, I could not follow his sermon, but with the aid of my guide I managed to get the drift of his remarks. He covered considerable territory ranging from the Babylonians to "Dr. Theodor Herzl," interspersing his comments with Bible texts. We turned to Jeremiah, Ezekiel, Isaiah and Malachi. The details of the learned exegesis escaped me, but recurrently came the prophetic words all Jews could understand. *Asi dice Jehovah* (Thus spoke the Lord). And there were other words too whose meaning there was no mistaking. *Pueblo Israel*—I knew as well as the shawled

Indian woman that he spoke of the "people of Israel." And "diaspora." Perhaps I understood that better. There were still other old friends running through the discourse: *anti-Semita; anti-Zionista;* "Hitler"; "Ford."

I looked again at the congregation. Simple Indians surely. They could have been bearing roses to the Virgin of Guadalupe; they could have been dancing in the dawn in the religious fiesta at Los Remedios; they could have been kneeling amid lit tapers and the smell of incense in a great vaulted church whose beauty offered the heaven their miserable lives desired; they could have had music and pageantry and the refuge of splendor, denied them otherwise. What strange power kept them here, in a bare room, accepting the Jewish destiny—*anti-Semitisma,* "Hitler," *Dice el Senor Jehovah.*

Splendor was here too, but it was abstract, intangible—*la splendor* of Jerusalem, described in a Spanish hymn superbly sung by a youth whose voice would have been the fortune of any cantor. The service concluded with the same Salvation Army chant with which it had begun.

An old Indian woman came up to me and shook my hand; *Shabat Shalom,* she said.

I saw the Jewish Indians once again in the little village of Venta Prieta, a few hours' ride beyond Mexico City. A group of us had been invited to dinner at one of the Indian homes, thanks to the courtesy of their chief. Venta Prieta had about twelve Jewish families and a number of Catholic Indians, forming a small community. It was a wretched place. A poor and dirty Indian village, though no doubt there are some still poorer and dirtier. The homes were miserable one-room hovels in which the prolific Indian family slept, ate and dwelt. Pigs wallowed in the surrounding mud. The children were dirty, half-naked, many with sore eyes. A few huts had crosses to distinguish the Christian dwellings from those of the Jews. Except for this mark, there was no telling the Catholic and Jewish Indians apart.

Dinner was going to be served in the home of the "rich man" of the community. He actually boasted more than one room, in addition to sleeping quarters; he had a "parlor" furnished with chairs, a table and lace curtains. When we arrived the chairs were all piled in the courtyard while the floor was being freshly scrubbed for the expected company. Great preparations were obviously afoot. The man of the house had gone to the neighboring village to fetch water. The local supply was too filthy even for cooking, let alone drinking. All the women and children were hustling about, preparing the banquet.

We walked around the village to give our hosts an opportunity to finish their preparations. It was hot and dusty. I trudged about in the dirt trying to locate the "Jewishness" I had come to see. A sow and her litter guzzled filth energetically. A squalid and depressing place! Then we were shown the community *shul*. It was naturally even smaller than the one in Mexico City—just a room with a few benches. But it was clean, a clean place amid uncleanliness. Outside the pigs grunted, but inside was sanctuary. There was a Bible on the table, a sign with a *Magen David,* as in the Mexico City synagogue, and a blackboard with a Hebrew prayer. On the wall was the painstaking handiwork of two Indian boys. One had drawn a map of Palestine, neatly coloring and lettering it, so that all could clearly see the holy coast line and the names of the sacred cities. The other boy—the artist—had created an elaborate composition with Moses, the Ten Commandments, and the Lion of Judah helping out. These were the only adornments in the room. The Law had found its way to an Indian village, and the geography of Zion was being studied by a few, semi-literate Indian peasants.

By the time we came back, dinner was ready. It was being served in the courtyard, where a table had been placed. Stone tubs of wash stood about. There were no pigs in this yard, but many dogs, scrawny cats and chickens wandered underfoot. And the flies were legion. I surveyed the feast with terror. I had met flies, God knows, but these were Mexican flies, bearing typhoid and dysentery, as every American tourist has been forewarned. However, to decline the professed hospitality was out of the question. Judaism, I felt, was about to claim another martyr.

It was a real Indian banquet, somewhat tempered for the weak stomachs of the strangers. Our party of five sat down with the men of the household. The only Indian woman at the table was an ancient dame, obviously the matriarch of the tribe. The other women and children were busy serving and baking tortillas, fresh hot batches of which kept appearing. The fare was native; chicken with *molle*, beans with pungent cheese, platters of young fresh corn, and endless heaps of tortillas which were used as spoons by our hosts. All this was washed down by large draughts of *pulke*, the national intoxicant made from the cactus. The bond of *gefilte fish* was absent. This was really alien territory, despite the *Magen David* which our host wore in his lapel.

The children came out to survey the strangers who were being dined in such style. We ate silently and industriously. Conversation came hard even for those of our party who knew Spanish. I marvelled at the generosity of this family which had expended so much time, effort and money on a group of curious tourists. Or were we, so different in every way, more than tourists? Did they feel any kinship? It was hard to tell. We smiled at the women, trying to register gratitude, but communication was difficult.

The old woman who sat with us had a history. Her father had been scalded to death in boiling oil for "Judaizing." This had happened before 1910, when Judaism was still proscribed. We sat together, American Jews, Mexican Jews, the Indian woman whose father had perished for the faith, the Indian men—smiling occasionally at each other and eating tortillas.

It was time to go. Everybody came out to watch our departure. There were children of all sizes—obviously babies came every year without benefit of birth control. We wanted to say something pleasant to the young woman with the smallest baby in her arms— a black-eyed, little Indian boy. We asked through our interpreter as one asks all women: "What is the baby's name?"

And the Indian mother answered: "Israel."   October, 1940

A Psalm of Abraham on Madness

by ABRAHAM M. KLEIN

Lord, for the days allotted me,
Preserve me whole, preserve me hale!
Spare me the scourge of surgery.
Let not my blood nor members fail.
But if Thy will is otherwise,
And I am chosen such an one
For maiming and for maladies—
So be it; and Thy will be done.
Palsy the keepers of the house;
And of the strongmen take Thy toll.
Break down the twigs; break down the boughs.
But touch not, Lord, the golden bowl:
O, I have seen these touched ones—
Their fallow looks, their barren eyes,
For whom have perished all the suns
And vanished all fertilities;
Who, docile, sit within their cells
Like weeds, within a stagnant pool.
I have seen also their fierce hells
Their flight from echo, their flight with ghoul.
Behold him scrabbling on the door!
His spittle falls upon his beard.
He knows his wife and child no more.
He is unclean, and fearsome, weird!
Not these can serve Thee. Lord, if such
The stumbling that awaits my path—
Grant me thy grace, thy mortal touch,
The full death-quiver of Thy wrath!

March, 1942

Saint in Sodom

by HAYIM GREENBERG

TWO YEARS AGO the Japanese police arrested Toyohiko Kagawa for "violating the military code." This formula is used in Japan in arresting citizens accused of espionage, desertion, treason and "moral succor to the enemy." Most likely it was the last named variety of "violating the military code" of which Kagawa was accused. No doubt in an open court Kagawa would readily "plead guilty" to such an accusation.

In April of this year we learned from the Tokyo English-language broadcast that in December of 1941, shortly before the attack at Pearl Harbor, Kagawa had been freed and that he had led several hundred of his followers in fasting and prayer for peace between his country and America. Why the controlled radio in Tokyo found it necessary to inform the outside world of this event is not quite clear: it may have intended to ridicule the fasting and the praying of the Christians which in this case had so little effect on the ways of Providence. Kagawa's friends in America were happy to learn that he was free again and well enough to endure the long fast. But later unconfirmed reports reached us that soon after the outbreak of the war against America he was sent to prison again for "lack of patriotism" and for "sympathies with the enemy."

No one can deny that such charges are well founded. If patriotism means what the ruling military clique in Japan understands by that word, Kagawa is not a patriot, and there is no doubt that he entertains sympathies not merely for America, but for all other "enemies" against whom Japan today wages a war of aggression.

From the very first day of the war between Japan and China, Kagawa has been "helping" the victims of his country's army. He helps them now with a kind word, now with the assurance he gives the Chinese that thousands upon thousands of Japa-

516

nese soldiers go into battle against their will and against their conscience, and that there are still people in Japan who in their hearts condemn the brutal policy of their government. I myself could easily supply any court with material to prove Kagawa's "guilt." Two years age he even composed a prayer for the welfare of China. The prayer was recited in many Japanese Christian churches until the police arrested the ministers and dispersed the worshippers.

Kagawa's life is an open book. He has never had any dealings with secret organizations and he is not involved, nor is he by nature capable of being involved, in any conspiracy. His political career—if it may be so called—began in 1904 when he was stoned by the mobs of Japan's large cities for his pacifist propaganda at the very time of Japan's brilliant victories over Russia. His record was known to the government and it is rather surprising that he had never been arrested until two years ago. Evidently even the Fascist camarilla which rules Japan today could not overcome a certain feeling of awe before the saintly personality of the tubercular old man who possesses an inexhaustible fund of moral energy, who is the friend and benefactor of the poor and oppressed in Japan, who cleared the slums in Japan's ports and who is to millions of his compatriots the conscience of Japan. Similarly Czar Nicholas for many years could not muster the courage to arrest Tolstoy—not as some poorly informed foreign biographers thought because Tolstoy belonged to the nobility of the country (the Czar did not hesitate to exile other counts and princes to Siberia), but because Tolstoy was too much the personification of Russian conscience and exerted too much influence on public opinion.

But there is a limit to the tolerance of the generals and to the respect of the militarists. Japan cannot go on "reorganizing Asia" and permitting Kagawa to undermine the morale of the people by preaching love. Kagawa's articles, sermons and church services were dangerous and contained real dynamite which might in time explode. Once, at the beginning of Japan's "punitive expedition" against China, Kagawa stood still for a long while before a throng of worshippers in a church with his head bent. When he raised his head and spoke quietly, his congregation was amazed to hear the following words: "This is not Kagawa standing before you, but his shadow. The real Kagawa is far, far away in China, with the suffering mothers and children, with the hungry and the wounded and with those made homeless by the war." No military oligarchy could tolerate such "demoralization."

In the eyes of the hundred percenters of Japan, Kagawa is an apostate. He has long since renounced both Buddhism and Shinto-ism. His aristocratic origin did not prevent him from denying the divine origin of the Mikado and the nobles and embracing an alien religion. For over thirty years he has been a Protestant, al-though his theology is not strictly and consistently that of his adopted creed. That all men are created equal and are the chil-dren of God has long seemed to him an obvious and self-evident truth for which he needed neither philosophical nor theological proofs nor the Scriptures of Judaism and Christianity. Since this fundamental tenet of religion is to be found in Buddhism, Lao-Tzeism and all other faiths of the East, one wonders why for the sake of this alone Kagawa found it necessary to join a Chris-tian church. Gandhi, who has a genuine respect for the Bible, both for the Old and the New Testaments, has always felt that there was nothing in Judaism and Christianity to add to what he cherishes in his native faith. It may be that Kagawa found in Chris-tianity a particular emphasis on certain spheres of life or that some early influences made him see in the Christian religion the highest expression of his religious and humanitarian cravings.

Though a pious Christian, Kagawa has long turned his back on formal Christianity and has often condemned the lack of spirit and the hypocrisy of most church institutions. The supporters and directors of the missionary schools in Japan where he studied, who also sent him to study at Princeton University, expected him to become a leading Christian divine in Japan, perhaps a bishop. But Kagawa disappointed them. From America he brought to

Japan an interest in social welfare work, in education, in slum-clearance and in cooperative enterprises rather than in the niceties of Christian theological dogmas. He is too much the prophet to don the garb of the priest and devote himself to priestly duties. The deeper becomes his connection with Christianity as a doctrine of ethical heroism, the more critical he is of Christendom. In one of the last works he published in America* he expressed his attitude in frank and candid terms:

"I have to confess, although I do so with great reluctance, that the Christian Church today is not preaching a gospel which satisfies the whole life of man. That is the reason for the rise of Marxian Communism. If the Church had been fulfilling its mission of love in action in modern times, there would have been no reason for the rise of Marxianism in its present proportions, When the Christian Church went off at a tangent and inclined too much to idolatry, Mohammedanism appeared like a scourge in the hand of God to bring the Church back to the right path. In like manner today revolutionary Communism is scourging us to awaken us again to the Church's true mission. Christians must meet this supreme challenge by putting love into effective action in a world-wide brotherhood movement."

Kagawa's Christianity is carried into practice by the establishment of trade unions and farmer cooperatives, by stevedore strikes free from any physical violence, by teaching the Japanese masses to eat healthy food and to sow soya beans as a change from rice, and by his ardent advocacy of internationalism and absolute pacifism. For many years the poor home in which he lived in Kobe was a welfare center in itself which served as a hospital, an orphanage, a hostel and a church. When asked during his last visit in America what he taught the many tramps, former prostitutes, former criminals and beggars or the tuberculars who came into his house, he replied that he taught them the three R's—reading, writing and . . . respect for human dignity and for themselves. Hundreds, perhaps thousands of poor people learned from Kagawa

---

* *Brotherhood Economics,* Harper and Brothers, N. Y. 1936

that their emaciated ravaged bodies covered by rags carried within them a spark of divinity worthy of respect. "We have in Japan two types of Christians," a Japanese told me in England some time ago, "the so-called 'rice-Christians' who adopt the faith for the sake of the rice packages given out in the missions, and the Kagawa Christians the like of whom is not to be found in England or in America."

Still, rice plays an important part in Kagawa's Christianity. To him the feeding of a hungry man is not a mere act of charity, but a religious sacrament. He likes to quote the account of the Holy Supper at the Sea of Tiberias as told in John, chapter twenty. In that account when Jesus appeared resurrected for the third time before his disciples, he gave them fish and bread, as if for that alone his resurrection in the flesh was worth while. Kagawa likes to recall that for five centuries Christians celebrated this "Supper of Love" and that for many generations a meal consisting of fish and bread has been the third sacrament after baptism and the reminder of the "Lord's Last Supper." In this he sees the "practical" potentialities of the Christian religion for reviving the socialism germane to Christianity which degenerate Christendom suppressed. As patterns of Christians Kagawa often cites in his sermons the "believers" of whom Clement of Alexandria relates that they used to sell themselves into slavery in order to give away their price to the hungry, the sick and the suffering.

Kagawa belongs to the same type as Tolstoy and Gandhi, but he is much less complicated. Perhaps because of that he escaped those pseudo-religious and pseudo-ethical extremes which mark the Russian artist and God-seeker and the Hindu moralist and politician. Unlike Tolstoy and Gandhi, Kagawa is a great admirer of science and technical progress and sees in them a source of liberation rather than of enslavement for humanity. He believes that Asia has not learned enough from Europe and America in the fields of technical development, medicine and social hygiene. While Gandhi sees in the locomotive an evil demon whose smoke drives away the gods from the forests, Kagawa sees in it a blessing. He dreams of such crassly mundane things as bacon on the breakfast table of every Japanese family. He is in his own way a consistent reform socialist and he finds in religion, especially in Christianity, a stimulus for economic progress and social regeneration.

Kagawa has faith in the future of Japan, although he spares no words to condemn the present conditions in his country. The average Japanese, he writes, has now become a robot, and the air is poisoned with servile mechanical discipline. He reminded his countrymen that everything of spiritual and cultural value has come to them from the Chinese whom they were now repaying with bombs. He is deeply grieved by the mad spirit of aggression which enveloped his fatherland, but at the same time he is sensitive to every act which offends the feelings of the Japanese. When the Japanese Exclusion Act was adopted in 1924 by the United States Senate, he wrote:

"The Japanese people are sorry to find out that the spirit of Washington and Lincoln does not abide in the hearts of the United States citizens. America today is only a land of liberty for the White race." And he reminded his American friends that for years the portraits of the two great Americans had hung on the walls of Japan's elementary schools and that Japanese children had been taught that the two great emancipators recognized an equal status for the Japanese. But Kagawa's disillusionment with America did not call forth in him any hatred or bitternesss. He believes that sooner or later Japan and America will cooperate in building a world federation on the foundations of universal social equality.

Kagawa sees two perils facing his country: materialistic Communism with which Russia is likely in a certain situation to inundate Japan, and the crass home grown militarism of her own ruling clique. He has faith in the will of the Japanese people to overcome both menaces. To call such a will into being and to mobilize them, he holds on to life by every thin thread within his reach. He is nearly blind and must dictate his articles and his books, his eyes having been ravaged by a disease he caught from a tramp with whom he shared his own bed during several winter nights; he suffered nine hemorrhages in the course of one year and his tubercular condition is incurable. When asked about his health he invariably replies that it is not good, but that he has no time to die.

The Japanese government made Kagawa "harmless" by isolating him from the public. But Kagawa in prison may sometime prove to be more dangerous to the military oligarchy of Japan than if he were free. Such things have happened in history before . . .

                                                        August, 1942

Lenin—Portrait of a Bolshevik

by Hayim Greenberg

MAXIM GORKI once wrote about Lenin as follows: "In this tough politician one sometimes sees the light of almost feminine tenderness, the dream of future happiness for all. . . . His private life is such that in a more religious age people would accept him as a saint."

On Gorki's part this was not a casual compliment nor would it be correct to say that he had no grounds for this characterization. Many who had known Lenin intimately were overcome by a feeling of inferiority when confronted with his ascetic mode of life and capacity for self abnegation. For *himself*—in the narrow conventional sense of the world—Lenin sought nothing and demanded nothing. One may justly say that of the entire group of old Bolsheviks who in 1917 attained almost unlimited power over a sixth part of the earth's surface, Lenin was almost the only one who did not become dizzy with success and escaped the demoralization that goes with power. He was able to consider himself the tool of the revolution and merely wished that the weapon named Lenin should be properly utilized. The triumph of his party did not even bring him a new suit of clothes. (He did not choose to take it for he had it within his power to take whatever he wanted.) During the weeks that he lived in the Kseshinska palace he walked on the shining tile floors with his old hobnailed boots and wore a pair of old trousers which he had acquired during the poverty stricken days of his exile in Switzerland. The tantalizing luxury of the Kremlin did not arouse within him the slightest temptation for the pleasure of the flesh or even for a measure of elegance in his own mode of life. During the famine years under military communism, when hundreds of subordinate Soviet officials enjoyed plenty and lived in shocking prosperity, Lenin continued to live in the state of need that was at that time the fate of millions of workers. By conviction he was remote from monasticism. He never advocated voluntary asceticism nor sought to force it on others. "Do not make a gospel of torn or patched trousers," he was in the habit of saying. Tolstoy's teachings concerning the noble "simplicity" of peasant needs and the peasant way of life he derided as "the teachings of a crank." For himself, however, he required but little. If he had passions about which he was silent, he must have held them in leash, paralyzed and crushed them for the sake of the one great passion which burned within since his early youth—the passion for the revolution and his role in it. His austerity therefore no doubt rode lightly on him. A true hermit finds it easy to engage in long fasts and self-flagellation. Especially if he is sure that these methods would aid him in bringing about the longed for Messianic end.

But Lenin was not only an ascetic in the common sense of the word. All his life he crushed within himself not only the "carnal" desires but also the passions of the spirit. His vulgar materialism which was not infrequently tinged with spite, he used as a shield to protect himself from intellectual or artistic lusts whenever he feared that these might seduce him from the main task of his life or consume some energy which could best be invested in the attainment of that main goal. When during the period of political stagnation following the revolution of 1905 Bogdanoff, Lunacharski and other philosophically minded Bolsheviks engaged in "God searching" ventures, when Lunacharski spoke of "building up a God"— whatever that might have meant, if it meant anything at all—Lenin even then discerned in such intellectual pastimes nothing short of counter-revolution, heresy, a deadly poison for the revolutionary movement. When he heard Bogdanoff argue that "truth is experience and cannot be objective" or that "sensations are the primary factor in the world" and that "from them (sensations and not matter) physical bodies are formed," Lenin was overcome by a panicky horror. "Who knows," he shouted at Bogdanoff, "where this can lead to? If truth is subjective then even Rome may be right. For there is not the slightest doubt that

even Catholicism is an organized form of human experience."
All his life he was mortally afraid of looking beyond the horizons
prescribed by Marx and losing his faith, of assuming any possibility that our empirical world is irradiated by rays from another,
metaphysical world. One might say that he considered himself a
trustee of the energies at his command who must guard against
wasting them without purpose on idle matters. When Lunacharski
tried to excuse himself by saying: "What harm do we do? We
only search for truth; this is no sin," Lenin answered in the ap-
proved style of an inquisitorial examiner: "Why tell me stories
about seeking after truth? It is not you, it is the bourgeoisie that
is seeking, seeking to ensnare you in its net through philosophy,
art, religion."

One need not be surprised at this answer. Others, greater than
Lunacharski and Bogdanoff, received similar retorts. When Hermann Cohen appealed in the pedagogical press that students of
German high schools should receive a course in higher mathematics to get them used to abstract thinking before entering the
universities, Lenin at once sensed that the philosopher of Marburg
spoke with the voice of the bourgeoisie. Boys and girls about to be
graduated from the high schools are at the dangerous age when
they can become revolutionists; that is why Hermann Cohen demands that their minds be confused with higher mathematics and
they be torn from social reality and dulled to the revolutionary
appeal. Lenin once even allowed himself to offer a vulgar and
crude interpretation of Kant's concept of *das Ding an sich*. In
Kant's words too Lenin heard the voice of the young European
bourgeoisie which sought to poison the proletariat with idealism.
If a worker, Lenin explained, sees his employer eating fresh meat
while he has to be content with foul, hard bologna, the worker
may be moved by anger to revolt. But if the worker becomes a
Kantian and begins to "understand" that both the fresh meat as
well as the foul bologna are mere phenomena and not "things in
themselves," he might conclude that it is not worthwhile to die on

the barricades for the sake of "manifestations," for the sake of something that has no reality in itself.

Basically Lenin's nature was not as unartistic as is generally assumed, or as he tried to make people believe. But he feared art and the enjoyment of art as seducers and wasters of energy. It is true that he was never heard delivering bravely vulgar dictums on artistic values. On the contrary, he frequently found it difficult to hide his great respect for the arts and his capacity for being deeply touched and affected by them. But because art—especially poetry and music—so strongly appealed to him, he ordered himself to come in contact with them as little as possible. It is a well known fact that the so-called proletarian art aroused within him a strong feeling of aversion which he did not always successfully hide. He considered proletarian art to be lacking in genuine feeling, work done to official order; he merely tolerated it on the basis of the Russian peasants' rule that everything comes in handy in a well ordered household. In those rare moments when despite his self-imposed unemotionalism he allowed himself some freedom to "sin" and enjoy art, his favorite poet was Pushkin. But Lenin sinned only rarely, for was he not the hired man of the revolution? If I do not err it was Lenin who coined the characteristic term "professional revolutionist." His professional ethics required—or so he believed they did—the concentration of one's entire being on one point and scorn for everything that could not be used as fuel for the flames of revolution or as bricks for the revolutionary structure. The pious revolutionist faced a long and difficult road and, like a Pharisee of old, believed that one must not for a moment interrupt the study of his revolutionary "Torah" for the sake of enjoying the sight of a beautiful tree or landscape. From time to time the eternally human, the anti-ascetic and the non-professional elements within Lenin attempted to rebel. At such moments he was drawn to Pushkin and to other who "sing as the birds sing." At such a moment tears once welled up in his eyes while listening to a symphony by Beethoven and he said to Clara Zetkin: "What a magnificent world this is and how great are the waves it evokes from the depths." In a similar mood he unburdened himself to Maxim Gorki:

"Often I cannot bear to hear music. It affects my nerves with too much pain. Under its influence one wants to talk nonsense and caress people's heads. . . . But in times like these one may not caress anybody's head for the other may bite your hand. Today one must beat hard and without mercy on these small and miserable heads although ideally we should not have to do anything by force."

Again we see the ascetic, the front line trench soldier, who is weighed down by duties and will not yield to desires and pleasures, who fears the results of gentle or tender emotions. Music becomes dangerous precisely because it makes sense and Lenin feared to admit that the "nonsense" inspired by music was not absurd after all, that the waves of musical sounds bear values of super-historical significance and arouse a sense of the metaphysical. He realized that should one yield to his musical inclinations it would become very difficult to fulfill the duty of "beating hard and without mercy" on human heads. He therefore renounced the pleasure as well as the "too great measure of pain" with which music affected his nerves. For had not the revolution a life long mortgage on the total sum of his psychic energy? In the days of the Apostles the concept of "castration for the attainment of the kingdom of heaven" was very popular. Lenin castrated himself emotionally and spiritually for the sake of the kingdom of the revolution.

There may therefore be no point in asking to what extent Lenin was imbued with a direct and warm love for humanity and with compassion for its fate and suffering. No ardent revolutionist is conceivable without such compassion and sympathy for the hungry, the oppressed and the humiliated in the *background* of his mind. In his very early youth Lenin no doubt deeply experienced moments of rebellion against unmerited human suffering and that compassion which seeks gratification in hatred for those responsible for the pain of millions. Pale undernourished children of city workers in Russia, middle aged people prematurely old in Russia's cities, the inhabitants of entire villages going on a Sunday to the district commander a distance of many miles to be flogged for cutting down trees in a government forest to heat their homes, peasants boasting of the bedbugs in their huts because these insects preferred warm homes—these and similar impressions of his youthful years no doubt evoked within Lenin not only sympathy but also self-identification with the fate of living human beings. But all these emotions Lenin confined in later life to an unfrequented corner of his psyche where they constituted an untouchable fund. Love of humanity and rebellion against its suffering evoked within him the image of a new society, and that as yet non-existent society, which was to come into being with Lenin as one of its chief *accoucheurs,* claimed his entire being. It is true that the dream society whose appearance must be accompanied by great labor pains derived its inspiration from the original springs of sympathy and compassion, but the goal had in the meantime become separated from the causes which engendered it. It became an autonomous entity, independent of those factors which alone could be responsible for the determination to work for its accomplishment. Lenin himself once aptly described this state of mind when he said: "A Bolshevik is a man who once saw a vision of the universe and all the rest of his life remains in love with the creation of his fantasy." Instead of loving humanity Lenin continued to live in a state of infatuation, of almost maniacal fixation on the vision of the universe which he once beheld in a dream. He no longer served *people,* but his dream, the vision as such, and through it he served his own self. The desire to help people transformed him into a daring architect, but the image of the new structure which he undertook to erect so fascinated him that he became capable of immuring in its walls the majority of those same people who had once evoked his love.

With this readiness to apply Pharaonic means to attain Mosaic ends if and when necessary, Lenin entered the Russian revolutionary movement. From the very beginning he claimed for himself the moral right to commit thousands of injustices, to do away with the Ten Commandments for the sake of his own One Commandment—the social revolution and its success. It is impossible to conceive that a man should arrogate to himself such rights for the sake of high humanitarian intentions without at the same time possessing an inner certainty that he had been endowed with a personal historic mission for the accomplishment of which he is alone responsible and to which he must subordinate his entire being, including his conscience and his personal tastes. Such an awareness of mission always lived within Lenin. But he never spoke of it—it would not have fitted into his orthodox Marxist terminology nor would it have been in consonance with the truly democratic traditions of the Russian revolutionary movement. But despite this Lenin possessed no trace of either the theatricality of Mussolini or of the Messianic exhibitionism of Hitler. Lenin's individual mission was his own secret which he no doubt failed to disclose fully even to his own conscience.

But Lenin could never entirely hide his tendency toward personal dictatorship. Even while still in exile he already showed his fist (in the literal sense of the word) to the few members of the central committee of the Social Democratic party. Of that forceful demonstration Trotsky told during the days when he was still adored as a hero. However, even that early demonstration of personal dictatorial tendencies both shocked as well as intrigued Lenin's followers. They were intrigued by his determination, firm "backbone" and undoubting certainty all the time as to what, exactly, had to be done. Of Lenin's youth the Menshevik Martoff wrote as follows: "For a long time Plekhanoff and I propagated our Marxist ideas without success. The adherents whom we gradually acquired, young Social Democrats who came to Europe from Russia and visited us, were always disappointing because of their political helplessness. But when we met Ulianoff (Lenin) we breathed freely. At last, we said to each other, we can be at rest. The cause of the Russian revolution is in good hands. It has found a political leader worthy of it."

In a similar vein were the words of Axelrod, another representative of the Social Democratic intellectuals: "I felt that before me stood a man who would be the leader of the Russian revolution. He was not only a cultured Marxist—we had many of this type—he also knew what to do and how to do it. . . . When I read his first pamphlet I at once became convinced that he had the stuff of leadership in him."

Axelrod was a great Marxist scholar; Martoff had a capable mind and a noble character which Lenin continued to respect even during his most brutal and cynical moments; Plekhanoff was a refined and cultured person as well as the best writer of the group. But all of the above suffered from the typical Russian inferiority complex and from a morbid attitude of disdain toward intellectuals as such and toward themselves as representatives of a type of good-for-nothings. When Lenin accused them on a number of occasions of being Rudins* these Hamletian revolutionists did not know what to say. In the intentionally rude, freckled young man who had the gestures and manner of speech of a Volga merchant and in whose Tartar eyes gleamed the spark of biting irony, they recognized the active revolutionist who was free from moral and esthetic inhibitions, ready to take risks, confront history with accomplished facts and ignore the welfare and even the lives of millions of human beings whom he had set out to serve. The intellectual Social Democrats were shocked at the traits of a Gengis Khan which they sensed in him. At the same time they were deeply impressed by the determination of this revolutionary surgeon who undertook to heal humanity by means of bloody operations, as many as might be required.

If the October revolution in Russia had been a brief one-time act, it could have been accomplished by people lacking Lenin's mentality. But to hold power through a bloody labyrinth of three years of civil war, to create and consolidate a state, to evoke

---

* Rudin was the unheroic hero of one of Turgenieff's novels. The name Rudin later became a synonym in Russia for intellectual indecision and general wishy-washiness.

anarchy, let it rage and then force millions of rebels into channels of slavish obedience, such a revolution required a leader of Lenin's stature and mentality. Only a man who possessed the strange moral courage to consider the population of the entire world as a generation destined to be a burnt offering from whose death agonies a new world would be born could also find the energy to carry out the experiment of the Soviet state as it was during the time of Lenin's rule.

July, 1940

Socialism Re-Examined

by HAYIM GREENBERG

I T IS impossible to predict the shape of the world after the war and what part socialism would play in its reconstruction. In the present conflict there operate dynamic forces and inertias, many of which we can hardly fathom. But it would be altogether impossible to make any kind of prognosis without assuming the following two premises: (1) After a period of armed peace, during which the victorious democracies would exercise broad international police functions, there would be established a stable order of relations based on mutual control and economic cooperation that would eliminate the threat of new wars. (2) Within most countries that control the reserves of natural resources in the world and enjoy a high standard of technological civilization, there would continue to exist (or be reestablished) a liberal political regime guaranteeing unhampered expression and development to all sections of the population and all political ideologies.

These two premises sufficiently prove how minimal are my own "war aims" and how little I expect the world to enjoy a period of complete bliss immediately after the trumpets of victory cease their pealing. But bearing in mind the scope of the destruction that we will be confronted with at the end of the war, even if the democracies should emerge triumphant, the above goals are not as modest as they might appear at first sight. It would be folly to expect a rapid realization of broader socialist aims in a world bled white by the most destructive war in history. But there exists an absolute minimum which must be attained as a result of the war, if there is to be any justification and redemption for the blood that is being shed. This minimum consists of the elimination of further dangers of war through the establishment of a natural equilibrium in international relations, and firmly guaranteeing the basic principles that animated the American and French revolutions. Only these two conditions can create the necessary framework for the free development of socialist thought and the growth of a socialist movement.

Even on the basis of these two premises I do not undertake to draw a detailed portrait of the post-war socialist movement. At best I can try to sketch the outlines of socialism in the coming period, and I am not unaware that I am not free of subjective attitudes and expectations.

The deeper causes underlying the present crisis in socialism are not due so much to strategic errors as to certain "organic deficiencies" from which it suffered. In the future socialism should renounce all pretenses to being a religion. Strange as it may appear at first glance, socialism pretended to be just that, despite the fact that in many European countries it was not only irreligious but even anti-religious. The chief characteristic of a religion are its eschatological predictions and promises. For many years socialist propaganda and education were conducted in such a manner that each new convert was imbued with the consciousness that socialism would not only solve certain economic problems, but would also pave the way to a new earth and a new heaven.

"Happiness" and the establishment of the "Kingdom of Heaven," these were the promises of socialism for many decades. Aware only of "economic man," believing that social class relationships are the only one that count while ignoring transcendental factors, socialism imbued its followers with the belief that as soon as the "lazy bellies" of the world would cease wasting the products of honest toil, humanity would be rid of all tensions, inner contradictions and unstilled desires—humanity would be happy. Thus Fourier promised that under socialism people would be at least "ten feet tall," Karl Kautsky, ordinarily a man of pedestrian ideas, announced that the average citizen of a socialist society would be a superman; Antonio Labriola tried to convince his Italian followers that in the socialist utopia geniuses would grow in bunches on every street corner and Galileos, Platos and Giordano Brunos would run around in herds. Trotzky described the future socialist millennium as one in which "man would become immeasurably stronger, wiser, freer, his body more harmoniously proportioned, his movements more rhythmic, his voice more musical, and the forms of his existence permeated with dramatic dynamism." Nor was that all, "the average man would reach the level of an Aristotle, a Goethe, a Marx." These were all expressions of the naive optimism that characterized socialist movements, of the mystic, redeeming force which was ascribed to the transition from the capitalist curse to the socialist state of bliss. That economic changes for the better possess no such magic powers to transform humanity, that no conceivable social changes can free mankind of conflicts, that suffering is an integral part of man's fate and socialism can at best solve only the problem of "zoological" suffering, these heresies were strictly avoided in socialist education. Bernard Shaw might have been right at that when he compared the world outlook of an average socialist to an Eskimo's idea of paradise—a land of warm waters in which fat fish swim at the surface and do not resist being caught.

This is what I had in mind when I stated that modern socialism sought to wear the mantle of religion to which it had no right. To what extent such a representation of socialism was pure demagogy or a genuine, albeit primitive, conception of world problems, it is hard to determine. But that its consequences were definitely harmful cannot be doubted. A false outlook on life may be absorbed by one's consciousness, but it does not calm the still voice of nagging doubt. Socialism did itself incalculable harm when it starved broad spheres of human spiritual life that do not coincide with economic instincts or the sublimation of those instincts.

Now socialism will have to emerge with a new but legitimate program. It must no longer offer "happiness" (does anyone know definitely what this term means?) nor the elimination of pain and tragedy. Instead it can lay claim to a more modest program, which is nevertheless considerably broader than the formula of Herbert Morrison, the English socialist leader, that "socialism is a good business proposition."

Should one ask the socialist movement today what its goals are, I do not believe that the answer should be—nationalization of the means of production, for we have learned from experience that even within a nationalized economy there can exist class divisions and exploitation. Neither should the answer be that the aim is economic equality. Equality, as an end in itself, is not an ideal state of affairs and can assume the form of a general levelling down such as is practiced in a military barrack. Nor is a high living standard the mark of socialism, and even fascist movements promise it as an inducement to their own peoples. The only thing specific good that socialism can offer is the very thing that it had ignored in the past—the striving after *human dignity* and *social worth* for every individual. (I stress social worth, because those who seek a basis for human worth on a cosmic scale will have to continue searching for it in religious sources for millennia to come, even as they did for thousands of years past.) Fundamentally, socialism, which is much older than any of our socialist movements and theories, never sought anything more than to establish the worth of the individual in society. "Every man under his vine and his fig tree"—a formula based on absolute private ownership—does not differ basically from the modern socialist program of complete collectivization. Both aim at that complete equality of each individual without which one can have no social importance. The collectivization advocated today is merely a practical application of the principle of equality in an epoch that is marked by technological industrialism. In other words, nationalization (or socialization) of wealth, high living standards and economic equality are *not goals* of socialism but *only means* toward attaining, not complete happiness, but merely that measure of social worth to which every person is entitled, and which is impossible to achieve without resorting to certain economic changes.

If I have over-stressed the matter of the importance of the individual in socialism, it is only because we have failed to learn the necessary lesson on this subject from the two revolutions that occurred during the past quarter century. The elan of the October revolution and of the subsequent civil war in Russia derived its inner pathos more from the striving of the forgotten man of our day for social worth than from purely economic interests. The Russian revolution lowered the standard of living of the population for many years, but for millions of people it provided a new feeling of social (in this case proletarian) worth for which they were ready to pay the price of hunger and need. Belonging to the proletariat, the new ruling aristocracy in Russia, provided for many millions a sufficient compensation for their degradation in the past, especially since the one-time ruling classes were deprived of all rights. Reversing the social ladder naturally is not equality. But psychologically it represented a historic reckoning and gave the masses of Russia a new, albeit morally distorted, sense of their importance. The same factor of social worth, although in a different form and feeding on widely diverging sources of energy, figured in the Nazi revolution in Germany. Being part of a "superior ruling race" provided millions of Germans with a new sense of importance which lay not in possessing something, but merely in being something—in being a German—in the belief that a higher grade, "rulers' " blood flowed through their veins. Both the class as well as the race idolatry were only substitutes, *Ersatz*, for the genuine sense of worth of which every individual is capable irrespective of race or class. The very fact, however, that even substitutes like the above could evoke such passionate enthusiasm and blind the masses to real economic interests proves how jealous modern mass man is of his dignity, how uneconomic his approach frequently is, and how important it is for the future of socialism to embody the expression of this striving for universal aristocracy.

I have dealt at considerable length with this phase of the subject. If the above thesis is correct, it becomes of great practical importance for the future program of socialist education. From it we are almost automatically led to other conclusions, that no genuine socialism is conceivable without a certain minimum of *personal freedom,* that establishing economic forms of collectivism on a foundation of political slavery means sanctifying the means while desecrating the ends. Only the false and harmful belief that "the ends justify the means" which modern socialism (even the non-Bolshevist type) always held to some degree could lead to an instance such as that of Hendrik DeMan, who now preaches collaboration with Hitler because Nazism destroys the foundations of classical capitalism and thus, objectively, leads toward a new world order, ergo to socialism. The illusion that it is possible and permissible to achieve human worth for each individual through despotic means that are in crying contradiction to the avowed goal must be uprooted from our minds and hearts before socialism will again be able to start out on a road of healthy development.

It is now no longer necessary to spend much time in proving that political democracy is a higher and more inclusive concept than socialism. For years we had maintained that political democracy is a means toward attaining socialism. This was wrong. The truth is the exact opposite. Democracy is the ultimate goal and socialism is, under modern industrial conditions, the practical means for the attainment of this goal of individual worth and equality. One who believes that democracy is only a means (to be supplanted by other, better, means, should one happen to run across any) must conclude that in a socialist society there would be no room for it. Actually it should be clear to everyone that precisely in a socialist order conditions of true democracy should be established, for no matter how thoroughly socialist economic and social principles are put into effect, life will always be full of tensions, conflicts and contradictions which will have to be solved by citizens enjoying equal rights and equal social standing according to some established democratic procedure.

I now wish to touch upon another aspect which, I hope and trust, will take a prominent place in the consciousness of socialists. This is the idea that *there are no transitional generations in history.* No individual may be considered as a means to advance the interests of another, because each one is an end in himself. Similarly we must not look upon any generation as an instrument to advance the welfare of another, as fertilizer on the fields of future history, because in the endlessness of historical development every generation is also an end in itself. Only one who believes in an ultimate kingdom of heaven, or in some final point in time when all contradictions would be finally solved, can decide that he has a right to sacrifice one generation for the sake of all the future ages so that they should enjoy a state of complete blessedness. But socialism will in the future be more modest and too skeptical to believe in some Canaan for the sake of which it is permissible to sacrifice an entire generation. Socialism must make up its mind that the happiness of no future generation is worth the sacrifice of present day sinners, that we must not show such exalted love for the yet unborn as would justify indifference to current suffering. I realize that this thesis is liable to cause much misunderstanding. Six years ago I developed this idea before labor audiences in Palestine and I was later accused of opposition to *khalutziut* because of the rigors it imposes on its followers. I would be an opponent of pioneering in Palestine if the hardships entailed in the rebuilding of a long neglected country were imposed on Jewish youth from above and against its will, if the pioneers in Palestine were considered as manure on the fields of the country so that a future generation of Jews might enjoy its roses. But pioneering in Palestine is a voluntary task assumed after free deliberation by those inclined to it and finding personal satisfaction in following its call. The same can be said about the group of nuns of the Order of the Sacred Heart who some years ago went to the Molokai Islands and dedicated their lives to the care of the lepers living there. No one compelled them to do so. Out of their own free will they drew the determination to devote themselves to people hopelessly afflicted. They are not "fertilizer" on another's field, nor a means to advance other people's welfare. They are an end in and for themselves, and anyone who is even slightly acquainted with the religious context of their lives will realize that they saw the highest expression of their personal fate in their action.

It is hardly necessary to add that if socialism renounces the conception of a transitional generation and the idea of a "final struggle" after which history would take a jump into a state of permanent bliss, it must also renounce the idea of a social revolution of a catastrophic type that is based on a momentary conjecture of events, such as was popular among socialists for many years. Socialists as well as democrats should visualize only one situation in which it would be justifiable to fan the flames of revolution—when the liberation of society from political despotism, police tyranny and dictatorship are concerned; when revolution can help the establishment, or the reconstitution, of a legal state possessing that minimum of democracy without which no legal state is conceivable. In other words, revolution may be justified if it serves to attain the freedom of the individual to share in his government, but not if it strives after concrete economic changes only. The moment a state is subordinated to the will of the people and the rights of individuals as well as of groups are guaranteed, socialism has no reason to prepare for revolutions and should strengthen the foundations of legality and try to educate the majority of the population toward becoming conscious and responsible participants of the political set-up.

The theses developed above may impress some readers as being primarily negative, in the sense of setting up inhibitions for socialism rather than presenting a positive program. This impression would not be untrue. I did not aim to develop a program for future socialist action, but rather to outline a number of guiding principles without which the socialist movement will always be open to the dangers of political impressionism and the lure of transitory impulses. But if these principles are to be taken seriously, socialism may still meet with defeat, but it could never lose its true stature, its moral force and its chances for influence on the people.

I doubt if I have revealed anything new. Each of the ideas discussed in this article can be found, in one form or another, in earlier writings. Some readers might even associate them with the revisionist trend in socialism. Fundamentally this would be a correct association. But in stressing some particular aspects of the problem I tried to summarize the difficult lessons we have learned on this subject in the last two decades. The main weakness of the socialist revisionists who followed Bernstein's leadership was that their approach lacked the moral pathos without which socialism cannot become a social-educational force.

I would consider it a misfortune if after the present war, in the general atmosphere of tension, bitterness and moral let-down, the socialist movement were again to embark on the path of a superficial revolutionism based on transitory factors. Civil wars that may follow the present planetary bloodletting can only lead to still greater chaos, to new destructive psychoses and endless fictitious "liberations." Uninspiring and unromantic as the words may sound, it must be said at this time: after this war socialism must take upon itself the task of introducing a measure of stability into the world. In a period like the one that will confront us in the near future, stabilization will involve certain compromises. But there are compromises which have a beneficial, healing effect, and facilitate normal changes later, if they are undertaken courageously and responsibly, without obliterating the boundaries between compromise and the basic, unchangeable principle.

November, 1941

The Crisis of Socialism

by WILL HERBERG

For what shall it profit a man, if he shall gain the whole world and lose his own soul?—MARK 8:36

IN THE COURSE of a century and a half, modern socialism has weathered many a storm. At first sight it might appear that the crisis in which socialism finds itself today is merely another of these incidents, though admittedly the worst to date. But such an estimate would, in my opinion, be a grave error. The present crisis is not just a passing phase of a forward-moving cycle of growth. The present crisis is the expression of a profound moral bankruptcy, of an inner collapse, from which there is no way out except by making a new beginning in a new direction.

Until the Bolshevik revolution and the rise of fascist totalitarianism, socialism was regarded by men of good will as a great and noble ideal unfortunately unrealizable in this sinful world. The moral worth of the ideal was freely admitted; what was questioned was the possibility of ever attaining it. Socialists were arraigned by their opponents as well-meaning visionaries who were misleading the ignorant masses with their far-fetched utopian schemes.

Opposition of this kind the socialists could take and thrive upon. Charges of utopianism meant very little to them except as a spur to speed the day of victory and thus refute the skepticism of their opponents. As long as they themselves believed, passionately and unquestioningly, in the moral worth of their goal, as long as they found it generally acknowledged by all decent people, there were no difficulties they could not surmount, no persecutions they could not sustain.

How different is the picture today! No one today will accuse socialists or communists of advocating far-fetched utopian schemes. On the contrary, the trouble with socialism, we are told, is that it is only too practicable, only too real: "Look at Russia if you want to see it in operation. There you have your socialism, but there you have also the most ruthless dictatorship, the most grinding slavery, that mankind has experienced in centuries. That is what socialism leads to."

In other words, what is now being challenged is not the practicability but the *moral* worth of the socialist goal. And it is being questioned not merely by the opponents of socialism but by every honest, thinking socialist.

Here we have the full measure of the depth and gravity of the present crisis of socialism. Socialism, the socialism with which Europe and America have been familiar for decades, is bankrupt: it has lost faith in its own ultimate worth. Party Communists, of course, have no such qualms; they glory in their degradation. But the socialist of integrity stands confused, demoralized, incapable of effective thought or action. How can he be sure that in working for his socialist goal he is not really preparing the way for a Hitler or laying the foundations for a Stalin? If he is at all honest with himself he must confess that the totalitarian collectivism on which the Russian and German regimes are erected bears an uncomfortable affinity to certain aspects of his own socialist faith.

I

Socialism arose in the modern world as a protest against bourgeois society for enslaving man by turning him into a thing, an instrument, a mere depersonalized adjunct of the machine. It held forth the vision of a social order in which "the free development of each will lead to the free development of all." [1] It called for a revolutionary transformation of the economic system, for the replacement of private capitalism by socialism, in order to liberate man and allow him to develop to the full the powers and capacities of his personality. It saw clearly that as long as the workers are kept in economic insecurity and subjection, they cannot be free in any sense. Economic collectivism it regarded as nec-

---

[1] Karl Marx; *The Communist Manifesto.*

essary only in order to provide the basis for freedom and genuine personality under modern industrial conditions. This theme runs through most of Marx's writings, particularly his early works; it is clearly formulated in his draft preamble of the French Socialist program, thus summarized by Engels:[2]

> The worker is free only when he is the owner of his own instruments of labor. This ownership can assume either the individual or the collective form. Since individual ownership is being abolished from day to day through economic development, there remains only the form of collective ownership. . . .

The point is clear. Collectivism has no *intrinsic* value. It is not desirable on its own account. It is desirable only because it helps to assure freedom. Freedom is the aim, the goal, the supreme value. Collectivism is, in the economic sphere, the means whereby that end may best be achieved.

From the very beginning, however, another very different conception has made itself felt in socialist thought, a conception which converted collectivism from a means into an end-in-itself. In this view, collectivism is not merely an economic device to promote freedom. It is a metaphysical principle, a quasi-religious dogma, a kind of higher existence transcending individual isolation and selfishness. The group, the community, the collectivity, is the true person; individual man is merely a poor, miserable fragment, an insignificant cell of the great social organism. In the ideal society of the future man will lose all sense of personality and will be absorbed into the group economically, socially and spiritually. His life will be collective life, his thoughts collective thoughts, his feelings and aspirations the feelings and aspirations of the collectivity. In fact, a distinguished Marxist scholar once wrote that in the future communist society no guarantee of freedom of thought would be necessary since in that blessed state all men would naturally think and feel alike on all questions!

To illustrate this conception of socialism I quote not from a

---

[2] Ed. Bernstein: *Die Briefe von Engels an Bernstein*, p. 34.

German, not from a Russian, but from a Briton. In his work *Socialism and Government*, Ramsay MacDonald wrote:[3]

> In the eyes of the state (MacDonald is here speaking of the socialist state) the individual is not an end in himself but the means to "that far-off divine event to which the whole creation moves" . . . The state represents the political personality of the whole. . . . It thinks and feels for the whole.

This is totalitarianism, of course; we would not be surprised to encounter it in the spoutings of some Nazi demagogue or prophet. Yet this was actually put forward by the spokesman of a democratic socialist movement as a basic principle of modern socialist theory and met with but little opposition from those in socialist ranks. It is true that MacDonald's work was widely criticized, especially on the Continent, for its non-Marxist views on matters economic and political, but its flagrant totalitarianism evoked virtually no comment. Very similar sentiments, though couched in a different terminology, may in fact be found in the quite orthodox writings of Marxists throughout Europe and America. They all argue as if collectivism were of itself sufficient to establish the kingdom of heaven on earth, as if indeed the two were really identical.

These two conceptions of socialism are quite irreconcilable in principle. But in actual socialist thought and feeling the conflict has rarely come to the surface. Socialists have continued to use libertarian language while actually thinking in terms of the totalitarian engulfment of the individual in the community. And when I say socialists I mean socialists of all varieties, socialists of the Right, Center and Left—and with the socialists I would include most liberals and anarchists, although the last-named naturally

---

[3] I have chosen Ramsay MacDonald to cite from because of his unusual directness of expression, but it should be noted that British socialism has been less affected by the totalitarian-collectivist perversion than most other socialist movements, thanks largely to the strong liberal-individualist tradition in British public life and to the religious strain (non-conformist Protestantism) in the British labor movement.

prefer to worship the great Leviathan under the style of Society rather than the State.

* * *

Totalitarian socialism—and I do not hesitate to use this term for the conception that exalts collectivism into an end-in-itself and source of value—finds its inspiration in the Platonic Republic, in Hegelian and neo-Hegelian adoration of the Whole, in the regimented utopias of Fourier and Saint-Simon and in 18th century "organic" sociology. But its ultimate triumph is largely due to the fact that it early fell in with certain underlying trends in modern society as well as with the institutional and political needs of the socialist movement itself.

Very clearly, the totalitarian-collectivist element in socialism has been strengthened through the rapid replacement of small-scale individual enterprise by large-scale "collective" economics. In our epoch, when the economic pattern becomes the paradigm of all social life, the diminishing significance of the individual in economics inevitably tends to rob him of his importance in the entire scheme of things. The individual worker is nothing but a cog in the great industrial mechanism of mass-production; the individual stockholder is little more than an obscure cell in a great corporate organism. What standing then can individual man expect to have in the cosmos? What worth or significance can he lay claim to in comparison with the group, the collectivity? It becomes rather absurd to make the enhancement of his puny personality the goal of our striving. It becomes worse than absurd; it becomes "anti-social" and "individualistic"—a most grievous sin in "socialist" eyes.

The exaltation of the collectivity at the expense of the individual personality has been greatly accelerated by the repercussions of the democratic upsurge of the past century. Modern democracy is a concept pervaded with a radical ambiguity. On the one hand, it means civil and political liberty, protection of the rights of man and the citizen, decisive participation of the "common man" in the selection and control of his rulers. But on the other hand, it may be taken to mean the mass-state, the deification of the masses as the source of all right and authority ("the voice of the people is the voice of God"), the destruction of all barriers to the violence of collective passion and prejudice. According to the former view, the freedom of the individual is the very cornerstone of democracy; according to the latter, it is a blasphemous defiance of the deified People. It is this latter conception that totalitarian rulers have in mind when they speak of their regimes as "true democracies," as "democracies in a higher sense." In fact, the mass-state, rooted as it is in the dread of responsibility so characteristic of the mass mind, is the natural basis of the plebiscitary dictatorships afflicting the modern world.

The cult of the collectivity, which in Plato and Hegel is frankly aristocratic, has thus been brought into accord with the modern democratic temper by making the People (the masses, the folk, the race, society, etc.) the object of its worship. In this form the collectivist *mystique* has become the very core of contemporary "social-mindedness."

The anti-personalist direction of modern socialism is fostered by still another fundamental tendency of our age—the spread of bureaucracy and the bureaucratic spirit to every field of social life. How well calculated the "organic" concept, according to which society is everything and the individual nothing, is to serve as the philosophy of bureaucracy may be seen from the following quotation, again from MacDonald's *Socialism and Government:*

> In the socialist state, all political functions must be specialized . . . and cannot be diffused throughout the whole of the community. What we need is the professional politician. . . . The work of the organic nervous system is paralleled in society by political functions; the function of the nervous system is to coordinate the body to which it belongs and enable it to respond to impressions and experiences received at any point. It may also originate movements itself. Evidently, the individualist cannot admit any such differentiated organ in society. But the socialist, on the other hand, sees its necessity. Some organ must enable other organs and the mass of society to communicate impressions and experiences to a receiving center, must carry from that center impulses leading

to action, must originate on its own initiative organic movements calculated to bring some benefit or pleasure to the organism. This is the socialist view of the political organ on its legislative and administrative sides. It gathers up experience, carries it to a center which decides corresponding movements and then carries back to the parts affected the impulse to action.

The domination of society by permanent officials, professional administrators, "managers," is thus proclaimed to be as inherent in the nature of things, as natural and as desirable as the regulation of the human body by the nervous system!

Corporate industrialism, mass democracy and the trend to bureaucracy all combine to sustain and promote the totalitarian-collectivist bias of modern socialism. And the practical exigencies of socialism as a militant movement work in the same direction. Close organization, discipline and solidarity are certainly indispensable to a movement fighting for power in the world of today, but no less certainly do they tend to curtail individual freedom and exalt the authority of the group and its leaders. Organization makes for bureaucracy; discipline for authoritarianism; solidarity for the submergence of the individual in the mass—in every case the tendency runs counter to the goals that socialism sets out to achieve.

* * *

Here we come to the very heart of the problem. The crisis in socialism is a moral crisis in which everything turns on the relation of means to ends. Socialism is caught in the grip of an ever-present and inescapable dilemma, which in one form or another reappears on every level of socialist thought and action. Perhaps the difficulty can best be formulated along the following lines. Means instituted to achieve a goal, no mattery how effective they may be in serving their intended purpose, have a way of turning around and working in the other direction as well, creating conditions and releasing forces that run counter to the original aim and tend to defeat it. If I were to use a much abused terminology, I would say that the relation between means and ends is dialectical, not only in the important sense that they act and react upon each other but in the still more important sense that their relation is one of tension and conflict so that any balance between them must necessarily be uneasy and precarious.

Thus, to repeat a previous point in another form, economic collectivism possesses not simply a positive libertarian but also a negative totalitarian potential. It harbors within itself two sets of forces, those making for freedom and those making for slavery. Attempt to throw one set into action, and you inevitably release the other as well.

On an even more elementary level, the first step in the realization of any social goal is organization. But organization has this double potential. Without organization nothing can be accomplished. Yet, the very act of organization, as I have already suggested, sets in motion processes that threaten the goal, if that goal is the socialist goal of freedom. For organization, even the simplest, necessarily creates two categories, the leaders and the led, never quite interchangeable and therefore never quite on a par in power and privilege. Here we have in embryo—and how fast the embryo grows!—the authoritarian hierarchy that finds its culmination in the totalitarian leadership principle or in the initiative-killing drill-yard that characterized German social-democracy and contributed so materially to its downfall. You cannot have the advantages of organization without its dangers.

Under modern conditions, social goals are hardly to be achieved without the exertion of political power. It is one of the enduring teachings of Marx that to be effective the socialist movement must be in some sense a political movement, preoccupied with the acquisition and employment of power. But does it need much argument to prove that preoccupation with power tends to vitiate the very ends for which power is sought? The conditions under which power is acquired, the ways in which it is used, the effect it has on the organizations and people who habitually exercise it, are hardly such as to encourage the moral idealism that must animate a new socialist order. Power is a two-edged sword that may maim and destroy its wielder. And yet can socialism abjure the struggle for power?

The struggle for power in the present-day world is a mass struggle, the clash of the massed forces of society. In order to rouse the masses to fighting pitch, socialism is led to cultivate hatred, fanaticism and intolerance as militant virtues; to stir up envy, suspicion and ill will among men. In the interest of the class struggle it is tempted to exploit the dark demonic passions of the human soul. And to what end? In order to gain the power to inaugurate upon earth the kingdom of human solidarity and good will! Was ever a social movement caught in so fatal a contradiction? Hatred has an inexorable logic of its own, a logic of destruction and self-destruction. And yet can the struggle for power be waged in a spirit of humanity and love?

Such are the dilemmas that arise at every turn, at every level of theory and practice, wherever means are used to realize ends. The great defect of traditional socialism, it seems to me, has been its utter failure to grasp this problem in its full amplitude or even to recognize that there is a problem at all. Socialism has never really understood the ambivalent, contradictory relation of means to ends. Socialists have generally tended to take for granted that once appropriate means are set into motion, everything will take care of itself. If such means are applied with vigor, intelligence and determination, under not unfavorable external conditions, the goal will be reached and no untoward by-products need be feared, except accidentally and incidentally. Today we know only too well how dangerously naive this notion is.

But the difficulty exists whether it is recognized or not. How has socialism in fact dealt with it? By systematically sacrificing ends to means whenever the two come into conflict. The dilemma is resolved by the device of suppressing one of its members—the principal one at that—under cover of a few pious phrases and scholastic formulas. Initiated in this way, the process moves inexorably on: ends give way to means, means of a higher order give way to those of a lower—the moral level of the movement sinking uninterruptedly all the while.

Freedom is sacrificed to collectivism. Individual initiative and autonomy to effective organization. Intellectual independence to the regimentation of discipline. Organizational democracy to bureaucracy and efficient leadership. Moral principles to practical necessity. And everything to power politics . . . all with the best of intentions, of course, all in the name of the very highest ideals.

Let me make it quite clear that I am not making this criticism in a spirit of self-righteous perfectionism. I know very well that although collectivism, organization and power gravely imperil the values that give meaning to socialism, socialism cannot do without them if it is to be more than an idle dream. What I am here condemning is not the attempt to adjust principles to practical needs, for without some such attempt, however difficult and unsatisfactory, life itself is impossible. What I am condemning is the irresponsible refusal to face the moral issues involved in such conflict and adjustment. It is the easy, untroubled conscience that I find so disturbing: I cannot help seeing how neatly it plays into the hands of power-mad politicians.

*   *   *

Why has socialism been unable to resist this corruption? I venture to say it is because it has lacked the resources of an adequate ethic. Modern socialism—particularly Marxism—has been rather scornful of ethics and ethical systems, priding itself on its alleged scientific character which presumably enables it to dispense with moral imperatives. It has preferred an extreme moral relativism according to which good and evil are constituted by shifting class interest. Whatever serves the "interest of the proletariat" is good; whatever runs counter to that interest is evil. Everything, literally everything, is permitted if only it promotes the "proletarian class struggle." If we recall how inevitably the interest of the proletariat is identified with the interest of the "party of the proletariat" and the triumph of the party, we can see what the upshot of such an attitude must necessarily be. Party interest—

power for the party and its leaders—becomes the ultimate, indeed the only criterion of right and wrong. Bolshevik amoralism is simply the culmination, brutally frank and consistent, of the ethical relativism that in one way or another is common to all schools of modern socialism.

A genuine ethic is simply the expression, perhaps even the foundation, of one's basic orientation to man and the universe. In attempting to do without an ethic transcending interest, therefore, modern socialism has also attempted to do without religion. Culturally socialism was the heir of bourgeois rationalism and materialism; politically it found itself in desperate conflict with the church, which until quite recently was undeniably a bulwark of reaction. In any case, modern socialism has developed largely outside the orbit of traditional religion. Its attitude has varied from the rancorous hatred of early Bolshevik "militant atheism" to the diplomatic evasion of European social-democracy, but with the significant exception of Great Britain, it has never felt the urge to look to our religious heritage for inspiration and spiritual sustenance.

Is socialism then without a faith? By no means; no great social movement is possible without some faith. Although it has turned its back on Judaism and Christianity, socialism has not dispensed with religion as such. It has simply replaced these historical faiths with a religion of its own. This religion is the neo-Hegelian creed of Dialectical Materialism under a number of variant forms in which God—the "great force not ourselves making for righteousness" (i.e., victory)—appears as the Dialectic, Progress, History, Social Evolution, Economic Necessity, etc. Indeed, it is primarily as a theology that Dialectical Materialism is of interest in the history of ideas. This is hardly the place to attempt to assess its permanent contributions to philosophy, which may turn out to be by no means inconsiderable, but it is clear that it is essentially a type of hylozoistic pantheism: all is matter hierarchically organized, but matter endowed with the principle of activity, with "life"; the All is God. As such, Dialectical Materialism is subject to all the objections to pantheism and hylozoism and to not a few more on its own account. But what is more important in our connection is not its philosophical soundness but its theological function. As a theology it serves to "justify God's ways to man"; to vindicate the aims and to idealize the activities of the movement; above all, to secure its values by guaranteeing the ultimate triumph of its cause.

Dialectical Materialism reveals the hidden god of the socialist religion to whom the true believer may confidently look for ultimate victory despite passing difficulties and defeats. But an invisible god is generally too abstract and remote for the uses of everyday life and so this god has been brought down to earth in a form that modern man can readily understand and worship—the great god Power. The Dialectic prescribes the course of World History and "Weltgeschichte is Weltgericht." Only World History can decide who is right, only ultimate success can vindicate the justice of our cause. Whatever has to be done to assure its triumph will be justified in the outcome. In fact, the only true moral agent is power, for only power can gain a hearing before the court of World History. Ultimate Might makes Ultimate Right. Thus neatly do the ethics and the religion of Power supplement each other.

From the Judaeo-Christian standpoint, of course, the cult of Power is a particularly detestable form of idolatry; it is devil worship in its modern form. How strange that socialism, which drew its original inspiration from the social humanitarianism that is but a secularized version of the Judaeo-Christian ethic of love, should have reached the point where it bows in adoration before the Enemy of God and Man. Surely the most illuminating commentary on the fate that has overtaken socialism is to be found in Dostoevsky's profound parable, The Legend of the Grand Inquisitor, in *The Brothers Karamazov*. It is the Grand Inquisitor, the guardian of the people and the defender of the faith, who feels compelled to send the returning Christ to the stake!

II

If my analysis of what has happened to socialism is at all valid, it must have some bearing on what the socialism of the future can do to avoid the same appalling fate. I think the following remarks on the subject may be ventured.

1. Socialism must be perfectly clear as to its ultimate goal and must never permit its vision of that goal to be obscured for any reason whatsoever. The aim of socialism is to create such economic and social conditions as will secure and enhance the freedom of the individual. The only consistent alternative to this view is the conception according to which the socialist ideal is a sort of super-slave state in which everyone is well-fed, well-housed and well-clad through the ministrations of a benevolent despotism. Between these two conceptions the crucial choice must be made. I will proceed on the assumption that the former is our notion of what socialism is out to achieve.

2. Under present-day conditions, the alternative is not, as it once perhaps was, between "free" capitalism and socialist collectivism. "Free" enterprise in the traditional sense is already a thing of the past. Our economic life is becoming daily more collectivized, daily more subject to social control and state regulation. In certain countries, in certain industries, in certain areas, this process has gone further than in others but everywhere it is obviously under way. And the process is irreversible. There is no more fatuous utopianism than the belief that either America or the world can return to the capitalism of a century ago.

The alternative is not between a "free" capitalism and socialist collectivism; collectivism in some form is here and is here to stay. The alternative that now confronts mankind is between *totalitarian* collectivism and *democratic* collectivism. Is the Russian road the only road collectivism can take? If it is, then mankind is doomed to decades, perhaps centuries, of slavery, corporeal and spiritual. Such *may* be our fate, but it *need* not be. It is true, and we should face the fact in all its implications, that collectivism *in its very nature* operates powerfully to promote totalitarianism. The odds are thus greatly against us, but there is a chance. Democratic collectivism *is* possible. Lewis Corey has rendered a very great service by his attempt to outline with care the economic and political foundations of a democratic collectivist society.[4] A pluralistic economy, avoiding the concentration of economic control in the hands of the state by distributing it among a variety of public and quasi-public institutions and even, as in agriculture and trade, among private enterprisers, is his basic conception. A new system of checks and balances, based on the effective social power of such voluntary non-state associations as trade unions, is another aspect of his program. I certainly do not insist that Corey's ideas are the only practicable ones, but he has at the very least clearly formulated the problem and given some indications as to the direction in which a solution is to be sought.

It is interesting that Nicolas Berdyaev, the distinguished Russian theologian-philosopher, reaches almost the same conclusion in his recent work, *Slavery and Freedom*,[5] although he and Corey are poles apart in general outlook. Berdyaev urges

a pluralistic economy, that is to say, a combination of nationalized economics, socialized economics and personal economics, insofar as it does not admit capitalism and exploitation. . . .

He also calls for

decentralization and federalism and a fight against centralized monstrosities. . . . Only decentralization can ward off the danger of bureaucracy.

Collectivism is *economic,* an economic device to enhance the possibilities of personal freedom for the great mass of the people. It is not a "higher" form of existence valid at all levels of life. "Only economics can be socialized," Berdyaev well says, "the spiritual life cannot, nor can the consciousness and conscience of man. The socialization of economics ought to be accompanied by the individualization of men and women. . . ." The mystical cult of collectivism is the sworn enemy of democratic socialism; it leads straight to totalitarianism. Socialism more than any other social order must preserve a rigid and inviolable distinction between the things that are Caesar's and the things that are God's— between what society may legitimately interfere with and what is

---

[4] Lewis Corey: *The Unfinished Task* (1942).
[5] Nicolas Berdyaev: *Slavery and Freedom* (1944).

inalienably the domain of the individual conscience—for in no other social order is the boundary so easily transgressed.

4. All this adds up to what might be called personalist socialism, socialism rooted in the ethical philosophy of personalism. In this philosophy, personality is the supreme value in the universe and the self-realization of personality the supreme law.[*]

> The entire world (writes Berdyaev) is nothing in comparison with human personality, with the unique person of a man, with his unique fate. . . . Man, human personality, is the supreme value, not the community, not collective realities such as society, nation, state, civilization, church. This is the personalistic scale of values.
> Society is not an organism, it is not a being or a personality. The reality of society consists in the personalities themselves. . . . The enslaving power of society over human personality is the outcome of the illusion of objectivization. Society is presented as though it were a personality of a higher hierarchical degree than the personality of man. But this makes man a slave. . . . Sociologists who affirm the primacy of society over the individual are in fact reactionaries.

The personalist creed is in essence the Judaeo-Christian doctrine of the transcendent worth of the human soul. It is the Kantian precept that every human being is an end in himself and not merely a means to some external purpose. It is the view championed by the young Marx when he protested against the *Verdinglichung* of man in bourgeois society. It is the core of every ethical philosophy that takes man's moral life seriously.

A socialism genuinely rooted in the philosophy of personalism could hardly become the vehicle of totalitarian power politics. Nor could it easily be betrayed into sacrificing its human values for the sake of security, power or expediency. Whatever else might be its fate, it would not lose its soul.

5. The personalist philosophy is at bottom a religious philosophy. And so personalist socialism would naturally not share the anti-religious bias with which modern socialism is still bur-

---

[*] It should hardly be necessary to say that self-realization of personality is utterly different from selfishness. As Berdyaev points out, the highest reach of personal self-realization is sacrificial service to others.

dened. On the contrary, personalist socialism would find itself
profoundly at one with the essential spirit of Judaism and Christianity. In the resources of this faith it would find a deeper understanding of the nature and destiny of man as well as a vantage
point under the aspect of eternity from which to meet the per-
plexing problems, the difficulties and contradictions, that confront an essentially moral crusade such as socialism when it is
compelled to fight its battles in the world with the weapons of
the world.

* * *

Increasing numbers of sensitive people, shocked by the moral
disintegration of the contemporary world, can no longer be content with the glib, hollow phrases, with the once plausible half-
truths that history has turned into dangerous falsehoods. They are
searching for something deeper and more fundamental, and their
searchings seem to take them all in the same general direction.
Ignazio Silone's long, painful pilgrimage from communism to
primitive Christianity is both symptomatic and symbolic of the
new drift. If indeed the seed is there beneath the snow, waiting for
the hard winter to pass in order to spring into life, it is the seed
of a new spirituality in which all that is best in socialist idealism
will be absorbed and transfigured.

                                        September, 1944

Go to Nineveh

by HAYIM GREENBERG

T HE BOOK of Jonah, read in the synagogues every year on the
Day of Atonement, has a lasting moral quality which over-
shadows the scholarly discussions as to when and by whom it was
written. The Cabbalists and early Christians put a mystical interpretation on the book and connected it with their ideas on the immortality of the soul. But anyone approaching the book without
any preconceived ideas can see that there are no mystic elements in
it.

The style is simple, transparent, and not charged with any particular allusions. The story itself is straightforward and its moral
is obvious. Once a man is endowed by God with a prophetic
spirit, then he remains, willy-nilly, a servant of the Lord for the
rest of his life. No rebellion on his part can change this.

Jonah, the son of Amittai, revolted against God. He wished
to place his own will, his own prejudices, and his limited concept
of justice above God's command. Should he "go to Nineveh, that
great city, and proclaim against it," that it should be destroyed by
God's wrath? Why should he? Nineveh was the capital city of
Israel's mightiest enemy, a city rotten with sin and crime, for did
not God Himself say, "their wickedness is come up before me"?
Then let the wicked perish without prophecy, without a warning.
To be sure, God did not send him there merely as a bearer of evil
tidings, to inform the inhabitants that the final sentence from
which there is no appeal had been passed upon them. He suspected God of "weakness" and a desire to act not according to the
strict letter of the law, of seeking to avert a punishment which He
had already decreed upon the people of Nineveh. ". . . for I knew
that Thou are a gracious God, and compassionate, long-suffering,
and abundant in mercy, and repentest Thee of the evil." Jonah
was afraid that perhaps the inhabitants of Nineveh might repent
on hearing his prophecy and God would alter his decision. To use

557

later terms, he considered himself the bearer of "the attribute of justice," and suspected God of being inclined toward the "attribute of mercy." What he forgot was that mercy and forgiveness were in themselves part of a righteous judgment.

Jonah had another motive for refusing to go to Nineveh. Nineveh lay outside of the Land of Palestine, an alien city of pagan, unclean worship. But he was a prophet of Israel and for Israel. He believed that the spirit of prophecy was given to him with the understanding that he pour it out only upon Jewish soil for Jews to hear, that the Gentiles had no part in it. True enough, nearly all the prophets had spoken their word about alien lands and alien peoples. Thus Habbakuk's main theme was the Chaldeans, Obadiah's was Edom, and Nahum's Nineveh itself. But these were prophecies made to the Jews, not directly to the Gentiles. With the possible exception of Elijah whom God once sent to idol-worshipping Sidon, Jonah was the only prophet sent abroad with a direct mission to the uncircumcised. And even Elijah was not sent to the community of Sidon. His mission, as related in the First Book of Kings, seems to have been concerned only with one individual among the non-Jews, the sick child of the Sidonese widow whom he brought back to life. But Jonah was sent not to an individual but to the whole unclean community of Nineveh whom God should have destroyed long before. To bring to them the prophecy of destruction was risky. They might repent their sins: God might hearken to their prayer; and Nineveh might be saved.

"Jonah rose up to flee unto Tarshish from the presence of the Lord," rather than carry out his mission. A later commentary spoke of that flight saying that Jonah would rather have perished in the sea than bring misfortune upon his own people by effecting the salvation of Nineveh. Another commentator, evidently more prosaic, says that Jonah paid a sum as great as the value of the whole ship, for his trip from Jaffa to Tarshish, so strong was his desire to see God's condemnation of Nineveh fulfilled. At any rate, he did not want to help save Nineveh. (Signs of this Jewish "particularism" or "chauvinism" may be seen much later in the New Testament: Jesus himself emphasizes on several occasions that he was sent only to the "lost sheep of Israel" and commands his disciples not to go to the Gentiles with their tidings of gladness.)

Jonah fled, but can one flee from God's command? A week later, legend tells us, the storm affected only that one ship, and all other ships proceeded on their way peacefully. Moreover, the fish which swallowed Jonah had been prepared for that task from the very first day of creation. "And the Lord *prepared* a great fish to swallow up Jonah"; the prophet was not to know of any limitations on the message he was to carry. He must carry it also to the lands of the uncircumcised. And if he wanted to narrow his horizon and narrow his heart, God would show him what narrowness was. He was not to reach Tarshish, and soon God was to hear his prayer "out of the fish's belly."

The rebellious prophet received his punishment by being incarcerated for days and nights in the dark dungeon of the fish's belly. A later commentary says that after the sailors on the ship had seen Jonah spewed out on dry land by the fish, they went to Jerusalem, had themselves circumcised, and devoted themselves and their wives and their children and their belongings to the service of the Lord. This showed that even these uncircumcised, sinful people were not beyond salvation, and what happened to them could also happen to the inhabitants of Nineveh. The God of Abraham, Isaac and Jacob was also their God, and if they did not serve Him today they would be ready to serve Him tomorrow. "Go to Nineveh," He told Jonah.

But the story of Jonah is more than a protest against narrow nationalism. Its moral deals also with the very essence of Jewish prophecy. The prophet is not merely one who predicts events which will or which must occur in the future. If he were no more than that, there would be no difference between a prophet and a pagan oracle. For the oracle there is no "if." It only knows that thus it will be under all circumstances, no matter how man will act

or fail to act. The decree which the pagan oracle knows is categorical and absolute and ultimate. Neither human will nor even
the will of the gods can alter it. It is Fate, unchangeable and immutable. A decree of this sort is independent of punishment and
retribution, of sin and innocence. The catastrophe predicted by
the oracle is not a punishment for transgression, and has very little
relation to morality or immorality. Not only with primitive
peoples but even with such civilized people as the Greeks, Fate is
outside of morality. This is evident in all of Greek mythology as
well as in the highly-developed tragedies of Aeschylus, Sophocles
and Euripides. The essence of classic tragedy is in a large measure
the problem of the "innocently guilty," of the criminal who is so
against his own will and his own intentions, of the helpless individ
ual whom Fate itself leads to sin and crime and misfortune
against all his efforts to avoid them. The best-known example of
this is the legend of King Oedipus. Jewish prophecy, in contrast
to pagan prophecy, knows no fatalism. There is no Fate within
the whole Jewish concept. There is no faith in blind decrees. But
there is Providence watching and listening over the world. Providence may be appealed to, may be prayed to, may be moved to do
man's desire, if that desire is just and pure. Jewish prophecy,
therefore, is by its function and its character conditional rather
than categorical. Jonah wanted to see an immutable decree in
God's decision to destroy Nineveh. Had he been certain that God
interpreted the decision in the same way, he would not have fled
to Tarshish. Therein lay his transgression. Instead of being a
prophet whose prophecy would bring warning and move the sinful
to repent and to purge themselves of their sin, he preferred being
an oracle, a *golem* through whom spoke the blind, brutal, fatal
future. By this he lowered the prophetic calling; he destroyed the
conditional nature of God's decrees. He confused God's hatred of
evil in man with God's hatred of the evil man, as if the evil man
were evil in essence and beyond hope, and condemned forever to
be wicked and with no road of repentance open to him. By his dis-
belief in repentance and in God's "duty" to accept it and to

"rend the evil of His decrees" he became a blasphemer, closer to paganism than to the Jewish God. Still greater was his crime in not wanting to see the uncircumcised of Nineveh begin believing in his God and proclaim a day of fasting, clothing themselves in sackcloth, and the king of Nineveh shed his mantle and cover himself with sackcloth and sit in the ashes on the ground. He was unwilling to rejoice with God at the sight of the drama of human repentance and cleansing. It was for this narrow-minded, unprophetlike inability to rejoice with God that he was severely reprimanded. "Thou hast had pity on the gourd, for which thou hast not labored, neither madest it grow, which came up in a night, and perished in a night; and should not I have pity on Nineveh, that great city, wherein are more than six score thousand persons that cannot discern between their right hand and their left hand, and also much cattle."

That is why the book of Jonah fits so well into the Yom Kippur service. The very sense of the Day of Atonement is faith in Providence and denial of Fate; faith in repentance and in its redeeming power; hatred of the evil in man and hope that man will ultimately overcome that evil. The moral horizon of Yom Kippur is wide and distant, limitlessly universal, in the perspective of which the barrier between one of the Covenant and one of the uncircumcised is obliterated. "And all species may fear Thee, and all creatures may bow to Thee, and may they all become one community to do Thy will with a whole heart." And God is praised for his quality of forgivenness on Yom Kippur: "Thou extendest Thy hand to the sinners and Thy right hand is extended to receive those that return to Thee." For on that day prayers are offered also for the wicked. "For Thou wishest the repentance of the wicked and Thou dost not desire their death, for, as it is said, God said, 'As I live,' says the Lord God, 'I do not desire the death of the wicked, but the return of the wicked from his ways'." On Yom Kippur prayers are offered for Nineveh, for all the Ninevehs of the world.

September, 1942

CONTRIBUTORS TO THE JEWISH FRONTIER ANTHOLOGY

SIR NORMAN ANGELL is a noted British liberal writer, who has received the Nobel Peace Prize.

HANNAH ARENDT, formerly a well-known critic in Germany, has written outstanding articles for *Partisan Review* and other American journals.

SHOLEM ASCH, ranking contemporary Yiddish novelist, has become world-famous through such works as *Three Cities, Salvation, The Nazarene,* and *The Apostle.*

CHARLES A. BEARD is the outstanding American historian, author of *An Economic Interpretation of the Constitution of the United States, The Republic,* and, with Mary R. Beard, of *The Rise of American Civilization.*

DAVID BEN GURION, veteran Palestine labor leader, is the Chairman of the Executive of the Jewish Agency for Palestine.

NORMAN BENTWICH is a prominent British jurist, who was formerly the Attorney General of Palestine.

CHAIM NACHMAN BIALIK was the outstanding Hebrew poet of the twentieth century.

LEON BLUM, famous Socialist leader, and former Premier of France, has been a Nazi prisoner during the war.

KURT BLUMENFELD is a veteran German Zionist leader.

BERNARD DEVOTO, American literary critic, and an acknowledged authority on Mark Twain, teaches at Harvard University.

ABRAHAM DICKENSTEIN is a director of the Workers' Bank in Palestine.

BEN ZION DINABURG is a noted Jewish historian and professor at the Hebrew University in Jerusalem.

URIAH ZVI ENGELMAN is a sociologist, now head of the Bureau of Jewish Education in Buffalo, N. Y.

CARL J. FRIEDRICH is a well-known political scientist, now head of the School for Overseas Administration at Harvard University.

HILLEL GILEADI is a member of the agricultural commune of Deganiah B in Palestine.

MALA GITLIN, now in the United States as a youth leader on behalf of the Palestine Federation of Jewish Workers, is a member of the agricultural commune of Khulda.

GRACE GOLDIN is a poetess, who has also appeared in the pages of the *Menorah Journal* and the *Reconstructionist*.

HAYIM GREENBERG is the editor of *Jewish Frontier*.

VASSILI GROSSMAN is a famous Soviet novelist and war correspondent.

BEN HALPERN is the managing editor of *Jewish Frontier*.

WILL HERBERG, formerly editor of *Workers' Age,* is now research director for the New York Dress Joint Board of the ILGWU.

HON. ROBERT H. JACKSON is an Associate Justice of the United States Supreme Court.

ABBA KHUSHI is the head of the labor organization in the port city of Haifa, with large contingents of both Jewish and Arab workers.

ABRAHAM M. KLEIN is a well-known Canadian Jewish poet, whose most recent published volumes are *The Hitleriad* and *The Psalter of Avram Haktani.*

H. LEIVICK (Leivick Halpern) is the outstanding Yiddish poet in the United States.

JACOB LESTSHINSKY, veteran Jewish scholar and publicist in Russia, Poland, and Germany, is an authoritative writer on Jewish demographic, sociological, and economic topics.

KURT LEWIN, outstanding psychologist in Germany and the United States, has recently founded the Commission on Community Interrelations of the American Jewish Congress.

CLAUDE MCKAY is a well-known Negro writer, author of *Banjo* and other novels.

KADYA MOLODOWSKA is a well-known Yiddish poetess, in Poland and the United States.

EMANUEL NEUMANN, leading Zionist, is the director of the Commission on Palestine Surveys, a research affiliate of the Jewish Agency.

DAVID PINSKI, dean of American Yiddish dramatists, is a leading figure in the Labor Zionist movement.

NATHAN REICH, economist, formerly a teacher at City College of New York and Hunter College, is now director of research for the American Jewish Joint Distribution Committee.

CHARLES REZNIKOFF, poet and novelist, is the author of the novel, *The Lionhearted* and other works of prose and poetry.

MAURICE SAMUEL, by his books and outstanding translations, has become the interpreter of Zionism and Jewish values to the English-reading world.

SULAMITH SCHWARTZ, *Jewish Frontier* correspondent during her stay in Palestine, is now on the staff of the American Zionist Emergency Council.

MOSHE SHERTOK is a leader in the Palestine Labor movement, and head of the Political Department of the Jewish Agency for Palestine.

MARIE SYRKIN is on the Editorial Board of *Jewish Frontier,* and author of the recent book *Your School, Your Children.*

DOROTHY THOMPSON is the famous columist and commentator.

GENERAL SIR ARTHUR WAUCHOPE is a former High Commissioner of Palestine.

JACOB J. WEINSTEIN is on the Editorial Board of *Jewish Frontier* and rabbi of the K. A. M. Temple in Chicago.